The Function and Nature of Imagery

CONTRIBUTORS

JOHN S. ANTROBUS

LEONARD W. DOOB

ROSEMARY GORDON

ROBERT R. HOLT

MARDI J. HOROWITZ

MARTIN S. LINDAUER

PETER McKELLAR

DAVID F. MARKS

ULRIC NEISSER

ALLAN PAIVIO

ALAN RICHARDSON

THEODORE R. SARBIN

SYDNEY JOELSON SEGAL

PETER W. SHEEHAN

JEROME L. SINGER

VLADISLAV ZIKMUND

The Function and Nature of Imagery

Edited by PETER W. SHEEHAN

Department of Psychology
The University of New England
Armidale, N.S.W., Australia

ACADEMIC PRESS   New York and London   1972

ACADEMIC PRESS, INC.
111 Fifth Avenue, New York, New York 10003

United Kingdom Edition published by
ACADEMIC PRESS, INC. (LONDON) LTD.
24/28 Oval Road, London NW1

LIBRARY OF CONGRESS CATALOG CARD NUMBER: 68-8432

PRINTED IN THE UNITED STATES OF AMERICA

CONTENTS

v

Section II   THE FUNCTION OF IMAGERY

Chapter 4   Individual Differences in the Vividness of Visual Imagery and Their Effect on Function

David F. Marks

Chapter 5   Voluntary Control of the Memory Image

Alan Richardson

Chapter 6   The Sensory Attributes and Functions of Imagery and Imagery Evoking Stimuli

Martin S. Lindauer

Chapter 7   A Functional Analysis of the Role of Visual Imagery in Unexpected Recall

Peter W. Sheehan

Chapter 8   Daydreaming, Imaginal Processes, and Personality: A Normative Study

Jerome L. Singer and John S. Antrobus

Chapter 9   Assimilation of a Stimulus in the Construction of an Image: The Perky Effect Revisited

Sydney Joelson Segal

Section III   THE NATURE OF IMAGERY

Chapter 10   Changing Conceptions of Imagery

Ulric Neisser

Chapter 11   A Theoretical Analysis of the Role of Imagery in Learning and Memory

Allan Paivio

LIST OF CONTRIBUTORS

Numbers in parentheses indicate the pages on which the authors' contributions begin.

JOHN S. ANTROBUS, Department of Psychology, City College and the Center for Research in Cognition and Affect of the City University of New York, New York, New York (175)

LEONARD W. DOOB, Department of Psychology, Yale University, New Haven, Connecticut (311)

ROSEMARY GORDON,* Art Department Institute of Education, London, England (63)

ROBERT R. HOLT, Research Center for Mental Health, New York University, New York, New York (3)

MARDI J. HOROWITZ, Mt. Zion Hospital and Medical Research Center, San Francisco, California (281)

MARTIN S. LINDAUER, Department of Psychology, State University of New York, College at Brockport, Brockport, New York (131)

PETER McKELLAR, Department of Psychology, University of Otago, Dunedin, New Zealand (35)

DAVID F. MARKS, Department of Psychology, University of Otago, Dunedin, New Zealand (83)

ULRIC NEISSER, Department of Psychology, Cornell University, Ithaca, New York (233)

ALLAN PAIVIO, Department of Psychology, University of Western Ontario, London, Ontario, Canada (253)

ALAN RICHARDSON, Department of Psychology, University of Western Australia, Perth, W. A., Australia (109)

* Present address: 26 Montagu Square, London, W1 England.

THEODORE R. SARBIN, Adlai E. Stevenson College, University of California, Santa Cruz, California (333)

SYDNEY JOELSON SEGAL,* City College of the City University of New York, New York, New York (203)

PETER W. SHEEHAN, Department of Psychology, The University of New England, Armidale, N.S.W. Australia (149)

JEROME L. SINGER,† Center for Research in Cognition and Affect, City University of New York, New York, New York (175)

VLADISLAV ZIKMUND, Department of Psychophysiology, Institute of Normal and Pathological Physiology, Slovak Academy of Sciences, Bratislava, Czechoslovakia (355)

* Deceased.
† Present address: Clinical Psychology Training Program, 333 Cedar St., New Haven, Connecticut.

PREFACE

In the very early days of psychology the mind occupied the center of the stage and mental imagery was one of our most important concepts for explaining and understanding human behavior. The break between structuralism and functionalism took place, and Watson stepped forward and began modern psychology. Fathering behaviorism, he argued against the mind, and imagery was virtually relegated to the status of the nonexistent. Imagery was translated by Watson into muscular contractions and became suddenly a muted concern of the past. It was not too long, however, before neobehaviorism took hold and Watson's hard line softened. Within the new framework cognitive phenomena were viewed as real and genuine concerns of psychology. The new ideal was to recognize the meaningfulness of concepts like "imagery" but to talk about such terms only after they had been introduced by operational definitions from a physicalistic meaning basis. From the 1930's to the 1950's, when methodological behaviorism came into full force as a framework of thinking, leading behaviorists such as Hull and Spence essentially argued "there is behavior, that is all." Mental phenomena were identified with behavior, and under a new guise of respectability psychologists continued to take great pains to keep the term cognition out of the premises of their arguments. Even though imagery was acknowledged as a real and genuine concern for study, such mentalistic sounding concepts were still relegated comfortably to the world of the poet.

In the 1960's a new style of thinking about imagery began to occupy our attention, and this book tries to capture part of its essence. Imagery no longer just belongs to the world of the aesthetic, it is now in a very real sense also of the world of the scientist who quite definitely acknowledges the value of "imagery" as a term in his premises. What has always been regarded as a "tender minded" area of investigation at last seems to be gaining hard earned respect. There is still caution and discomfort about using the term "imagery" unashamedly, but vast advances have been made in methodological techniques and theoretical sophistication since the early days of introspectionism, and these advances are impossible to ignore. Far too many variables are now being manipulated systematically and related to imagery function for psychology to dismiss imagery as an unimportant construct for the explaining of higher mental functioning. Most recently, scientific psychology has been forced to look searchingly into its legitimate interests by having to account for the stunning effects of imagery as a mnemonic aid. Revitalizing some classical techniques of old, psychologists practicing their science are demonstrating anew that people tutored in the use of imagery skills can perform at remarkable levels in comparison to those common to rote learning situations. Rather unfairly, imagery has had to prove itself worthy of notice by demonstrating more than ordinary effects before it could be rated equally with less exhibitionistic variables.

In 1964 Robert Holt (The return of the ostracized. *American Psychologist,* 1964, **19,** 254–264) heralded the return of the ostracized and called us to "come on in—the water's fine!" In 1970 the ostracized finally returned and many have taken the plunge knowingly. Our avenues of publication prove the acceptance of that change. In 1960 one article on imagery—labeled hesitantly a study of "nonverbal methods"—appeared in the *Journal of Experimental Psychology* (considered our most "rigorous" journal in a recent study of the connotations of psychological journals by L. A. Jakobovits and C. E. Osgood: Connotations of twenty psychological journals to their professional readers. *American Psychologist,* 1967, **22,** 792–800). In that same year only seven references appeared under the rubric "imagery" in *Psychological Abstracts.* Ten years later nine articles titled the word *imagery* (or its derivatives) in the *Journal of Experimental Psychology* and 62 references appeared under "imagery" in *Psychological Abstracts.* To bolster the case just a little further, *Psychological Bulletin* (our most "reputable" and "important" journal) in 1970 devoted unprecedented space to a symposium on imagery in children's learning.

This book does not aim explicitly to capture the trends in imagery research as they are appearing but to simply give them proportionate emphasis. To do so, at least for some of the directions in imagery study now coming strongly to the fore, would unfairly distort the richness of the field. If current emphases were its sole concern, for example, imagery as a mnemonic technique would be discussed in far more detail in the book than it is. The essential aim of the book is rather to sample contemporary research and theory by trying to enlarge methodological and theoretical horizons so that the reader may grasp clearly not just the value of studying imagery and its current relevance to thinking and memory but also the complexities and diversity of the field. Rigid standardization of procedures in research and theory about imagery no longer exist. The contributions here demonstrate a new sophistication and variety in the methodology and theory of mental imagery.

There are 15 chapters in the book each written by a significant worker in the field. Speaking encouragingly, it would take much more than one edited volume at the moment to cover exhaustively all the important research into imagery, or even to state everything of moment psychologists have to say on the topic. This book provides only a relatively small sampling of psychology's current list of productive imagery researchers, but it does, I think, sample a wide range of instructive techniques and theories. Being specialists in the field the contributors more often than not are drawn understandably to cast affectionate and approving glances at the role imagery has to play in our everyday cognition. The book thus suffers from what this or any other editor might call "the inevitability of the positive viewpoint"—in preparing this volume I became increasingly curious as to what committed "nonbelievers" would have to say about the enthusiasm of us all. However, if the authors agree on one thing—that imagery is an enormously worthwhile pursuit—they also admit to many complex issues being far from resolved and recognize both the presence of controversy and the value of differences in viewpoint. There is too much conflict of opinion in the book to argue at this early stage that we have uniformity or agreement on the major issues. I find it sobering, in fact, to think that so much argument goes on over just one modality. The chapters that follow are concerned largely with visual imagery, and I have little doubt that our differences in viewpoint would be compounded in their complexity if other modalities of imagery were tapped as fully.

The book is divided into three main sections. In Section I, Some General Viewpoints on Imagery, Robert Holt, Peter McKellar, and Rosemary Gordon discuss imagery in a general fashion that serves to introduce the reader to the much more specific concerns of the chapters to follow. Somewhat more so than the succeeding chapters, their corporate glance at imagery is historical, introspective, philosophical, and wide ranging in scope. Section II, The Function of Imagery, demonstrates the profitability of manipulating particular variables concerning imagery. David Marks, Alan Richardson, and Martin Lindauer discuss in turn the effect on imagery function of varying *vividness, controllability,* and *sensory reference.* Jerome Singer and John Antrobus, Sydney Segal, and I then take up the study of imaginal and personality processes in daydreaming, assimilation of stimuli in image constructions, and the role of imagery in unexpected recall. Almost all of the contributors to this second section emphasize particular research programs of their own which offer a well-defined look into the analysis of a significant problem in the study of imagery function; chapters here are concerned primarily with the implications of data gathered in an author's specialized area of interest. Section III, The Nature of Imagery, offers a more formal, theoretical glance at imagery. Here, Ulric Neisser, Allan Paivio, Mardi Horowitz, Leonard Doob, Theodore Sarbin, and

Vladislav Zikmund cover a wide range of theoretical viewpoints concerning the nature of imagery. They discuss in turn imaging as a constructive process related to perception, a mediating variable in verbal learning, a process in cognition influenced by psychodynamic factors, a primitive mode of cognition, and an instance of muted role-taking. The final chapter in this section draws comment about the nature of imagery from a review of its physiological correlates.

These three major divisions of the book inevitably blur indistinguishably together at times. It is impossible, for instance, to draw too sharp a distinction between fact and theory, particularly since in all contributions the hand of the researcher is nearly always to be seen. The authors have taken their plunge into the study of imagery in different ways, and chapters cannot but emphasize the special distinctiveness of each author's selected approach.

In conclusion I would like to thank all of the contributors of chapters in this book for their patience and cooperation during its preparation and also the staff of Academic Press for the stimulation of their interest and enthusiasm while the book was being evolved. I am indebted personally to Rita Cuskelly, Jacquelyne Lloyd, Ulric Neisser, and Douglas Tegart for their help at various stages of the book's preparation and to the University of New England for providing funds to facilitate my task. I wish also to thank my wife, Mary, who helped and supported me at all times throughout the project and to whom I dedicate all of my contribution toward this book.

Finally, I would like to pay special tribute to Dr. Sydney Segal who is one of the authors in this book. Her most untimely and tragic death which occurred while the book was in production is a great loss not only to those who knew her personally but to all who eagerly followed her creative work in the field of imagery.

Peter W. Sheehan

Some General Viewpoints on Imagery

1 ROBERT R. HOLT[1]

ON THE NATURE
AND GENERALITY
OF MENTAL IMAGERY

A decade ago, writing about imagery as a long-neglected topic just emerging from ostracism (Holt, 1964), I had no idea that it would so quickly become a vogue. With the notable exception of McKellar (1957), the 1950's had passed without a major book on imagery; now, this book is one of four appearing in about 3 years (Richardson, 1969; Horowitz, 1970; Segal, 1971).[2] The periodical literature has flowered with many experimental and clinical contributions, and the topic has been the subject of numerous symposia and special conferences. It is hardly a coincidence that the term *image* has become a tired cliche in popular writing, even though the intended meaning—something like "conception" or "reputation"—is slightly different from the one used here. Yet there is more similarity than these synonyms suggest; a phrase like "our

[1] Preparation of this chapter was supported by a United States Public Health Service Research Career Award, Grant No. 5-K06-MH-12,455, from the National Institute of Mental Health. I have also been greatly aided in its preparation by the work of my colleagues at the Research Center for Mental Health, but I want to thank particularly Drs. Leo Goldberger, George S. Klein, and Harriet Linton Barr for their extensive help, amounting to collaboration on several of the empirical studies reported here.
[2] The number is even larger if one includes books on specialized topics in the general area of imagery (e.g., Arnheim, 1969; Keup, 1970; Piaget & Inhelder, 1971). The recent reissue (1970) of Jaensch's classic, first published in 1925, is also noteworthy.

nation's image" does carry some pictorial connotations. In a voyeuristic age, the camera—still, movie, or TV—catches and broadcasts through the mass media a concrete picture of every personage, every notable or notorious event, even a great deal of information that was formerly presented in verbal symbolic form. McLuhan (1964), the prophet of the mass media, tells us that the "linear" mode of the written word is passé, that ours is a time of "cool," nonlinear media like television, in which the visual image plays a major role.

It is apparent by now that the resurgence of interest in imagery is part of a larger movement, in science and in popular culture alike: a revival of interest in subjective, conscious phenomena. After a gestation period of many decades, Husserl's phenomenology gave birth to existentialism, and the neonate ultimately grew into a vigorous philosophical and psychotherapeutic school. During the 1960's, psychedelic, "consciousness-expanding," hallucinogenic drugs began as laboratory curiosities, spread with explosive rapidity through many parts of the world, and have become a major social problem as well as a central feature of a new lifestyle. A symptom of the new interest in the subjective world is the fact that words referring to states of mind crop up increasingly in unexpected places. At present, the best-selling nonfiction book is Reich's (1970) analysis of cultural changes, worded in terms of a succession of "consciousnesses." When study groups within the various liberation movements (notably the feminist) meet, it is not for discussion or learning but for "consciousness-raising."

Within psychology and related disciplines, there has been an enormous increase in work on dreams (e.g., Hartmann, 1970), daydreams and fantasies (e.g., Singer, 1966), attention (e.g., Mackworth, 1970), feelings and emotions (e.g., Arnold, 1970), and altered states of consciousness (e.g., Tart, 1969), along with the emergence of cognition as a major preoccupation of intellectual leaders of these fields. Behaviorism and similar hyperobjectivist positions have softened a bit in their strictures against considering such subjective phenomena, but the renewed interest in *mind* and such related concepts as mental imagery has not required the submergence of the old paradigm. Indeed, a good many adherents to the modish cause of cognition have good neobehavioristic credentials, and the research on imagery is not being carried on primarily as part of an antibehavioristic polemic (Palermo, 1970). Just as physiology gave the great boost to research on dreaming by providing a relatively objective technology (the EEG and the EOG), the discovery of such techniques as autoregulation by psychophysiological feedback has helped enormously to stimulate interest in unusual states of consciousness (e.g., Kamiya, 1969).

Yet it seems more than coincidental that this same just-passed decade has seen the wildfire growth of popular quasitherapeutic movements like encounter groups, sensitivity training, and sensory awareness, all of which lay so much stress on inner experience. Indeed, even so-called behavior therapy, for all its objectivist trappings, makes much use of the manipulation of imagery (Lazarus & Abramovitz, 1962; Wolpe & Lazarus, 1966).

How are we to understand the relation between these meaningfully connected trends in psychology and in the larger culture? There is no dearth of sociological hypotheses; indeed, it is rather impressive how social critics as diverse as Roszak (1969), Mumford (1970), Fromm (1955), and Keniston (1960) agree in seeing a great cultural reaction against the dehumanizing, mechanistic trend of what Mumford calls the Megamachine—the hierarchically organized, power-oriented interlock of physical science and technology with the military–industrial complex. In light of the appalling excesses that it is a reaction against (going as far as genocidal war in Indochina, and a trend on both sides of the Cold War to automate the ultimate decision whether to launch thermonuclear ICBM's, creating the possibility that civilization may be destroyed through computer error), it is not surprising that this counterculture tends to go too far. In its indignation, the movement often spills over into a wholesale and self-defeating rejection of *all* science and technology, even of rationality itself.

It is of the utmost importance, since we are dealing with no less awesome issues than the survival of mankind, that we see clearly just who the enemy is: it is surely not the scientific outlook itself or even technology, but the reductionistic and mechanistic tendency in scientists, technologists, and the makers and executors of national policy. The scientific method, our best way of seeking truth, is an indispensable tool in our time of desperate peril. True, it has been perverted by some; but it is the pathological perversion, not the healthy organism of science that must be attacked. In the name of science's requirement of objectivity, those very subjective inner phenomena that are most uniquely human were once proscribed as foci of legitimate scientific concern, so it is no wonder that many young people today and many of their elders on the artistic side of the two-culture gap conclude that objectivity is a false ideal. By giving it up, however, they expose themselves to the danger of "thinking with one's blood," in the Nazi phrase. There must be a place for passion both in the subject matter of science and in the scientist himself (Polanyi, 1958), but never at the expense of rationality. Almost any ideal can be turned into a danger to mankind by exaggeration, even moderation itself. The proper function of objectivity as a scientific ideal is to preserve us from wishful thinking and perceiving, so that we do not delude ourselves nor lose touch with reality. Humanism need not be undisciplined; a warm heart does not preclude a cool head.

Some Philosophical Issues

Here, it is apparent, we are getting into methodology, behind which lie not only epistemological but metaphysical questions. It will be clarifying, in the long run, if we make a temporary detour into philosophy to make explicit some of these issues, which are ubiquitous in the study of imagery though usually not specifically discussed.

To begin with, there is the problem of how to conceptualize the relationship between a subjective, phenomenological concept and two other kinds of entities: the hypothesized events in the brain that accompany it, and the observable public behavior that permits us to infer it. Even the most hardened behaviorist acts in his everyday life as if he distinguishes between conscious phenomena and the external world of things. This common sense distinction may be called *empirical* (as opposed to metaphysical) *dualism;* it is compatible with all of the classical "solutions" to, or positions on, the mind–body problem except the two reductionistic monisms (see Table 1). For us its important form is *empirical parallelism* (Rubinstein, 1965): the recognition that there are parallel sets of events in the mind and in the brain.

Let us put some of these distinctions to work by examining the behavior-

TABLE 1
Classical Positions on the Mind–Body Problem

Monisms: there is only one fundamental realm of reality

    Idealism—only mind is real (reductionistic)
    Materialism—only matter is real (reductionistic)
    Double-aspect or identity theory[a]—phenomena and their neurological substrates are different aspects of a complex total reality

Dualisms: there are two fundamentally different realms of reality

    Metaphysical parallelism—the two worlds are independent but are perfectly correlated and synchronized
    Epiphenomenalism—mental events are caused by physical events, but have no effects themselves
    Interactionism—causal influences go both ways, matter affecting mind and mental events causing physical events

[a] Double-aspect theory and identity theory are closely related positions that are distinguished by some authors. "Psychophysical parallelism" is used to refer sometimes to metaphysical parallelism, sometimes to epiphenomenalism, sometimes merely to empirical parallelism.

ist's epithet, mentalistic. What can it mean to decry something as mentalistic? Do any of these meanings contain valid critique?

Mentalistic may mean simply mental—subjective, phenomenal, belonging to the world of consciousness. Very few psychologists today would take the radical position of the young Watson that mental phenomena do not exist or are negligible if they do. The argument that the subjective world is mere illusion is the position of classical materialism: the only reality is physical. Both reductionistic theories (materialism and idealism) run so contrary to common sense that it is difficult to maintain either for very long outside of purely philosophical discourse.

But the argument that the subjective world of common sense is negligible for science is not so easily disposed of. In terms of the classical solutions this is epiphenomenalism, one of the most widely held positions today (the other being some version of identity theory; Rubinstein, 1965). In terms of this view, we recognize that mental events exist, but we view them as mere curiosities capable of being explained ultimately in terms of the more comprehensive world of physical reality. (Thus, epiphenomenalism contains a reductionistic strain also.) Put in conventional psychological terms, mental phenomena are dependent variables (effects), never independent ones (causes). Therefore they may safely be neglected in the long run, even though in the short run our ignorance of fine neurohistology and neurophysiology may require our studying some problems in purely psychological terms. This "short run" shows no sign of ending, so the distinction between epiphenomenalism and identity theory becomes a difference that makes no difference in practice.

Metaphysical dualism is in general rather out of favor, for there seems to be no need for it, and the contemporary temper dislikes the unnecessary postulation of metaphysical entities. True, no one can fault metaphysical parallelism, the notion of perfect correlation between mind and brain with no causal relation whatever; it accommodates itself perfectly well to any observations, but it is intuitively repugnant to a nonsupernatural view of the universe in which there is no God to account for what otherwise seems an incredible set of coincidences. Granted the facts of empirical parallelism, many people prefer to assume that some causality operates between the physical and the mental (epiphenomenalism or interactionism). Most scientists, however, reject interactionism because it implies the intervention of nonphysical forces or entities into what seems a satisfactorily closed system of physical causality. If they do not consider the mental negligible (epiphenomenalism), they assume a monistic unity that requires neither causal nor coincidental relations between sets of apparently different events that can be looked on as the same totality viewed through the prisms of different disciplines or different methods.

To the extent that mentalism means assigning a separate metaphysical reality to mental events, then, it is an implied metaphysical dualism and as such is subject to the above objections. Such dualism is particularly objectionable in the interactionism implicit in metapsychology, which rejects consciousness as the criterion of "the psychic." Freud believed that only in this way could he retain the necessary hypothesis of unconscious processes like fantasies, with all the properties of conscious daydreams except that they were not in awareness. To be meaningful they had to be mental or psychic. But this implicit metaphysical dualism opened the way to the free postulation of psychic energies and psychic structures, most of which are never in awareness and which do not exist in the material world either—thus, they are forever closed off from any possibility of being directly measurable or observable (Holt, 1967a; Rubinstein, 1967). This status of scientific redundancy remains hidden, however, so that great numbers of psychologists and psychiatrists continue to work over the proliferating excesses of metapsychological statements, unaware that their labors can have no effect on the real world.

Freud considered the possibility that when a conscious wish becomes unconscious, the corresponding brain process continues with only some minor change, but rejected it, believing that the process would then be *merely* physiological and the required continuity of meanings would be lost. Yet he need not have taken the plunge into dualism. There remains an acceptable monistic position that makes it possible to conceptualize the existence and processing of meanings—including iconic meanings like pictures—without the necessity of their being conscious or of postulating an unconscious psychic realm for them to exist in. This stand on the mind–body problem, which I wish to urge as particularly useful for psychologists concerned with imagery, is a version of double-aspect theory: it assumes that organismic processes have a single reality, but that they contain many aspects or levels of emergence, to each of which corresponds a different level of analysis and a different scientific discipline. Thus, molecular processes and structures (chemistry) are emergent with respect to atomic processes and structures (physics), but biological events are emergent above the molecular ones and cannot be wholly reduced to them. Likewise, conscious processes correspond to molar brain processes because they are different ways of looking at a complex unity; both types of process are real and equally dignified as a subject matter of science. In addition, however, this total event is one of information processing; the information, which exists as consciously apprehended meaning under some circumstances, is *encoded* in the biochemical and bioelectric events of the brain process, and as such is not dependent on consciousness for its continued existence. This relationship is perhaps easier to grasp by reference to the electronic computer. We have become accustomed to the fact that verbal, graphic, musical and any other kind of meanings can be encoded into patterns of electrical impulses, processed by the machine, and eventually decoded into an output in the original modality of meaning without any of the loss that Freud feared.

Yet there are many others today who seem caught on the same apparent dilemma. Not seeing how the apparently unrelated and irreconcilable "worlds" of brute and silent physical reality and of human meaningfulness can in fact be brought into the harmonious and efficient collaboration instanced by every operation with a computer, they continue to argue that there is one world (or one culture) of physical science and, across an ontological chasm, a second world (and culture) of meanings, values, lexical and presentational symbols. All too often, this premise is followed by the mischievous corollary that there can be no science in the latter realm, or that if there is some kind of cultural science (*Geisteswissenschaft*) it must have its own, idiographic methodology. Elsewhere (Holt, 1967b) I have tried to demonstrate that there is no such separate methodology and no need to try to develop one. Once we free ourselves from the reductionistic fallacy of nineteenth century mechanism, and put the ideal of objectivity in proper perspective, the scientific method is not only an applicable but an indispensable aid in working with the mental data yielded by introspection.

In the great tradition of science, rigorous method is not procrustean. It does not demand that if a problem cannot be tackled with complete objectivity one should sit with folded hands: the greatest scientists have always addressed important problems with the best tools available, while striving to make them ever more precise and more adequate. The proper implication of objectivity is that one should always measure the errors of one's measurement, and resist the temptation to abandon measurement itself if complete accuracy is not possible.

In that spirit, imagery is a legitimate and feasible as well as a topical subject of scientific inquiry, and a fruitful one. Fortunately, we do not need to rely on theoretical and philosophical arguments against those who would make it taboo. There is no better answer to the charge that a topic is too subjective than a set of stout reliability coefficients. A polemical indictment of introspection as an intrinsically hopeless method cannot stand in face of a demonstration that subjects can give internally consistent data, which can be reliably content analyzed and which are significantly related to independent variables in replicated samples. Indeed, content analysis—that humdrum child of a low-status application of psychology to market research, public opinion polling, and propaganda analysis—has done more to show that subjective meanings and values are a legitimate topic of scientific inquiry than all the books of a pride of philosophers (see Holt, 1961, 1967b).

Some Definitions and Theoretical Propositions

An investigator's stance on the philosophical issues just considered has direct implications for the kinds of definitions that he chooses. A lingering reluctance to define the mental image in frankly phenomenal terms as a kind of subjective conscious experience may be behind the tendency of many investigators to adopt an operational definition of imagery as an intervening variable coordinated to measureable nonverbal behavior. Paivio (1970), for example, seems to take this position, for he accepts "the selection of subjects according to symbolic habits or skills, such as spatial or figural-transformational abilities," adding that "the last of these parallels the earlier definition of imagery in terms of individual differences, but differs from it in that the assessment is based on objective ability measures rather than on subjective reports alone [p. 386]." Meanwhile, others (e.g., Richardson, 1969) adopt a strictly phenomenal definition, while writers from the psychoanalytic tradition (e.g., Horowitz, 1970) tend to accept the implicitly dualistic position that images may be either conscious or unconscious. Here alone is ample basis for confusion. When our definitions differ on this important point, we can easily believe that we are communicating when in fact we are talking past one another.

I propose, therefore, that we base ourselves on the double-aspect-coded-meaning position, tentatively accept the proposition that consciousness may make a considerable difference, and therefore use a different term (a) when we are speaking about a phenomenal content of a sensory or quasisensory nature, and (b) when we are speaking about the same meaning as mediated by (encoded in) a brain process without awareness. Let us reserve the term *image* for (a), the former of these two cases, and *presentation* for the second (b).

It will be apparent that the definition of image given above does not make the usual distinction between percept and mental image. This commonsense distinction is, of course, important, and must be preserved (see below). Nevertheless, we should not lose sight of the fact that the image that is usually called a percept is as much a construct of the nervous system as is a memory image or hallucination. By now we know a great deal about the many extraordinary activities of the visual system that are necessary to create what seems a simple replica of the outer world. It is never simple, and never a mere replica; perception is a highly selective process. Høffding long ago demonstrated logically that memory is involved in almost all perception, for except under highly unusual conditions we do not simply see but recognize what we see. Therefore, in the coming about of the visual image there must be a preliminary stage in which the nascent perceptual presentation is matched with stored memory presentations, which must be scanned until the correct match is found.

There is considerable evidence (see for example Held, 1961; von Holst & Mittelstaedt, 1950) that this interaction of incoming perceptual process and memories does not take place in the memory store proper, but in some kind of staging center where the input is matched with a constructed hypothesis. This last is variously known as *efference copy* (Held, 1961), *search model* (Duncker, 1935), or *perceptual expectancy* (Bruner & Postman, 1949). It may be identified with one form of what Rapaport (1951) called anticipation but should be conceived of as basically a nonphenomenal, neurophysiological entity. These various authors have taken note of the fact that perception is almost never without some preparation; usually, we have more or less well-formed expectations of what we are going to see in an average expectable environment, and there have been numerous demonstrations of the degree to which perception is determined and sometimes distorted by such expectations. They probably exist in some depth— not a single hypothesis, but a small hierarchy covering various aspects of expectable figures and grounds, and of course all sensory modalities. In large part, they serve to mask out the trivial, uninformative and repetitive aspects of the stimulus field and help us focus on what is unusual and adaptively useful. Thus, an efference copy anteceding an eye movement provides a silent corrective that cancels out the swirl of changing retinal information, so that we can scan a visual field that remains steady. Presumably other such constructions cancel out otherwise possibly distracting steady noises, kinesthetic sensations, and visual events like double images, floaters (or muscae volitantes), and other constantly present but rarely noticed entoptic phenomena.

Without other such constructions of coded information from both long-term and short-term memory—let us call them perceptual hypotheses— recognition could hardly be the rapid process it is. When the stimulus itself is impoverished, as in a tachistoscopic study, it is easy to demonstrate how large a role the hypothesis plays in the construction of the final conscious image. For example, in an ascending threshold procedure, correct recognition may be delayed for quite a while if for one reason or another a subject forms an incorrect hypothesis early in the series. This is, of course, merely an instance of the general phenomenon called assimilation by Piaget. This conception fits well many observations about ways in which cognitive style affects perception. Thus, the cognitive control principle of leveling-sharpening concerns the extent to which a person accepts poor matches between hypothesis and input and thus constructs a final perceptual image that may be largely nonveridical. Usually, of course, mismatching sooner or later causes a correction in the perceptual hypothesis and an eventual match (and corresponding percept) that is substantially veridical.

Let us take it as given, then, that all images are the end product of a process of construction, and that the usual dichotomy of percept vs. mental image should be replaced by a continuum on which these opposed notions are ideal cases rarely if ever attained in reality. For, at the imaginal end of the continuous series, Boernstein (1967) has shown how the subjective visual experiences of subjects in the dark (phosphenes and thought images) can be markedly affected by intercurrent stimulation in other modalities. The distinction between hallucination and illusion is extremely difficult to make in clinical practice because the hallucinating patient is always subjected to a highly complex world of stimulation in all modalities, and it is like proving the null hypothesis to demonstrate that *no* external stimuli play a part in the reported experience. Experimental attempts to isolate subjects from all sensory inputs come up against the frustrating fact that the organism is intrinsically self-stimulating—for example, absolute silence is impossible because breathing and the heartbeat generate audible noise, nad even a subject immersed in a tank of tepid water feels skin sensations as his body rises and falls with every breath. In the absence of the usual level of stimulation, these slight remnants become quite focal, as do entoptic and endotic phenomena. Thus, not even the imagery of sensory deprivation can be truly autochthonous or entirely internal in origin, and in much of it the influence of external stimuli (and of internal but peripheral contributions) is easily demonstrable (Goldberger & Holt, 1958; Horowitz, 1970).

At the other end of the continuum, this position implies that a great deal of what usually passes as perception is imaginal. Segal (1971), in a series of studies of the Perky phenomenon, has demonstrated conclusively that there is no intrinsic quality of a percept that distinguishes it from a mental image. Depending on the *S*s' cognitive styles, on how their expectations are manipulated, and on the impoverishment of the stimulus and its setting, an experience that is in fact mostly determined by the sensory input may be experienced as a thought image, and vice versa. Moreover, she shows that a good many of the images subjects report have important constituents from contemporary stimulation, as well as from memory, in an assimilative integration (see Chapter 9, this volume).

I should like to call attention to some implications of the distinction here proposed between mental image and presentation. One is that the functional equivalent of a mental image can be formed and processed extensively with other encoded information without awareness. This assumption makes it possible to clarify a number of apparent paradoxes or puzzling findings. First, the imageless thought controversy: there is no longer any reason to doubt that some people's conscious thinking makes much use of sensory imagery, some people think in largely verbal terms, and others are aware only of abstract meanings. We can understand the apparent paradox of Titchener's triangle: the fact that his usual thought image of a triangle was a curiously twisted fragment that lacked all of the classically defining properties of triangles, yet he did not make mistakes in thinking about geometric problems. (This is a specific instance of a problem many psycholinguistic theorists have worried about: the noncorrespondence or insufficiency of conscious contents to the corresponding meaning; Brown, 1956.) And we can understand how it was possible for such a reliable introspector of inner experience as William James to maintain that he lacked visual imagery, and yet be able to draw an excellent likeness of an absent person—a performance clearly guided by a latent presentation.

In particular, this distinction and the accompanying set of assumptions clarify a persistent problem created by the attempt to assess mental imagery by means of ingenious tasks that seem to require visual imagery to be solved. Thus, Griffitts (1927) attempted to measure "visualizing efficiency" by problems concerning visual orientation; Walter (1953) categorized subjects as visualizers or not by asking them to imagine a painted cube being cut into four smaller cubes, and to say how many faces of each were painted, in what color, etc. But some subjects who say that they experience no visual thought imagery are able to perform quite adequately on such problems. Richardson (1969) summarizes a good deal of such research by concluding: "The part played by visual imagery in tests of spatial or visualizing ability is unclear. It may turn out to be quite irrelevant but it is more probable that visual imagery will be found to have some limited value [p. 53]." There is even evidence that extremely vivid thought imagery may be a handicap in such tests, since it is often not entirely controllable, is of limited flexibility, and may be distracting.

Henceforward, when I use the term *image* without further specification it should be understood to refer to a subjective phenomenon that may have any combination of external and internal influences. When the weight is clearly on the side of sensory input, the common terms *percept* or *perceptual image* will serve interchangeably; and when the weight is on the side of inner, central inputs, I shall speak of *mental images* or of their commonly recognized subtypes like hypnagogic images, drug images, etc.

The elements of a model of image-forming processes are implicit in the above discussion. I would like to be able to report that the experiments that follow were attempts to test out propositions derived from a theory, even if not an explicit one, but I cannot. Actually, my procedure has been more inductive than deductive, and only in thinking about the findings reported in this chapter did I clearly formulate for myself the distinction between the concepts of presentation and image. Nevertheless, I put this much theory first because the argument seemed to develop naturally in that way even if the sequence of the work was different. After presenting some empirical data, therefore, I shall return to the theory and comment on the relevance I see between these two parts of the chapter.

On the Interrelatedness of Various Types of Imagery

One of the greatest contributors to the study of hallucination, Heinrich Klüver, is reported (Scheibel & Scheibel, 1962, p. 16) to have suggested that "the mechanisms underlying hallucinations are the same as, or at least overlapping with, the mechanisms that mediate other imaginal states such as dreams, eidetic images, intense memory images, etc." It is almost inevitable that anyone who delves into the rich literature on the various types of imagery will get the impression that these phenomena form a continuous series, grading insensibly into one another. Surely the simplest and most attractive hypothesis is that the diverse form-varieties differ primarily in their quantitative strength, and that any effective independent variable (drug, state of consciousness, impoverishment of perceptual inputs, etc.) operates primarily as an amplifier (or suppressor) of the preexisting level and kind of imagery.

A hypothesis of this kind was one basis for a large-scale cooperative study of lysergic acid diethylamide (LSD-25) at the Research Center for Mental Health in the late 1950's (Barr, Langs, Holt, Goldberger, & Klein, 1972). From its beginning, the Center's program of research on disordered thinking sought various ways to enhance the emergence of what Freud called the primary process in communicated thought. In various places (Freud, 1921, pp. 77–79; 1923, p. 21), he had intimately connected visual imagery with the primary process; this potent drug, variously characterized as hallucinogenic and psychotomimetic, promised to make every man a poet or madman temporarily by sprouting fanciful imagery in his expanded consciousness.

Briefly, we gave 30 unemployed male actors (psychologically and medically preselected to avoid untoward reactions) 100 μgm of LSD in a glass of lemon-flavored water, and 20 others a similar potion without the drug, intermixed in a double-blind design. All *S*s were continuously monitored throughout the day until the drug effect had worn off, took many tests, were repeatedly asked a list of 74 questions about possible drug effects (Linton & Langs, 1962), and participated in numerous experiments.

Our first disappointment was in the hallucinogenic powers of what was supposed to be a powerful dose of the drug; no placebo *S* reported any particular imagery, but some LSD *S*s reported nothing either, though some did clearly have vivid, startling visual phenomena.[3] The drug did not, therefore, simply make everyone a "visile." We had also read accounts of striking auditory phenomena, including synesthesias, so we included a session of sound-elicited imagery, in which *S*s listened to tape recordings of a number of putatively evocative sounds: a cock crowing, footsteps going down a hall, a baby crying, etc. The results were mainly stereotyped descriptions and drawings of roosters on fences, babies in cradles, and the like, with very little suggestion of any synesthesia.

These initially disappointing results seemed, on second thought, consistent with a well-known fact: the existence of striking individual differences in other types of mental imagery. Moreover, they permitted me to test the generality conception by intercorrelating assessments of drug-induced and various other kinds of imagery. Fortunately, I had measures of several other types of mental imagery on members of the actor sample. The following are the measures to be reported upon.

Isolation Imagery.   Sixteen of the same *S*s served in a study of the cognitive effects of perceptual isolation (Goldberger & Holt, 1961; Holt & Goldberger, 1960). During the 8-hour session, the *S* was confined in a semisoundproof room containing a chemical toilet, an icechest stocked with foods of his own choosing, and a comfortable bed. He wore a flexible leather helmet containing padded earphones, through which came a constant "white" masking noise. He wore pingpong ball cutouts over his eyes, held in place by rubber cement. He was told that it was an experiment in "doing nothing," so he was to recline on the bed and move as little as possible, but to report his thoughts and feelings from time to time. An

---

[3] George Klein and I had hoped that the presumedly facilitating effect of LSD on imagery would make it easier to demonstrate the recovery in such images of a tachistoscopically presented subliminal stimulus, a hope that was dashed by the failure of the drug simply to amplify ordinary thought imagery. In this study (a report of which is in preparation), we did manage to demonstrate a subliminal effect, but the amount of influence of the subliminal input on the *S*'s images was unrelated to his readiness to experience any of the types of imagery we assessed: the highest correlation we obtained (between thought imagery and the amount of subliminal influence) was .11.

E monitored at all times in an adjoining room by means of a two-way intercom system. At the end of the 8 hours, *E* asked *S* to summarize his reactions during the day. Then, after first giving a 90-minute battery of cognitive tests, the *E* went into the isolation room, helped *S* to remove the eyecups and helmet, and interviewed him on his experience. There were questions about imagery and *S*'s feelings about his mental images (all *S*s reported imagery of some type during isolation). Two judges later ranked the transcribed protocols of the entire day and the interview on a number of variables, including imagery; the reliability was satisfactory (rho = .8).

Thought Imagery. In an interview with most of the LSD *S*s the day before they took the drug, I attempted to measure the vividness and controllability of thought imagery, using a technique based on the procedure of Gordon (1949). It was then readministered during the experimental day in a study of the effect of LSD on the control of imagery (see below). The following illustrative protocol was given by a rather colorful *S* under the effects of LSD.

> *E:* Imagine an automobile; when you have a mental image, describe it to me.
> *S:* It looks very much like a porcupine. . . . Wow! Boy, would that stop traffic on the parkway. (Tell me about it.) Boxy square kind of car, cupola on it, gargoyles coming out of the corners; on the radiator cap, on the front of the car, a fountain [he laughs]. Oh lordy, lordy—there are plants growing on the roof and uh, it's quite heavy, an imponderable car. (How do you mean?) What am I talking about—ponderous . . . It's black and gold . . . a remodeled Rolls.
> *E:* OK, now imagine a driver in the car, and it is moving down the street. Can you visualize that?
> *S:* It's driven by a chauffeur. Uh—it's moving down the street. (Do you see it actually move?) Yeah . . . has little houses on it, square like children draw, only better drawn; just a little neat street in a little tidy town, mostly pink and white and coral; great black and gold and green and purple car is lumbering through it [laugh].
> *E:* Now make the car slam on its brakes and get into an accident.
> *S:* Well, I don't know if this is kosher or not—the car didn't stop, kept going about 5 miles an hour and just flattened two Buicks; just slowly crushed those Buicks under it, moving 5 miles an hour. (Did you imagine any sound?) It sort of went [laugh] "Chomp"! A great big bass voice going "Chomp"!— terribly satisfied. This car has just eaten two Buicks.

Three judges independently scored such protocols from the pre-LSD day for the presence or absence of the following characteristics in the reported imagery: movement, color, sound, and other sensory qualities. There was complete unanimity in 77% of these judgments, and an additional 10%

were instances in which one rater was out of step on the question of whether to rate or not (since, as in the example, the E sometimes forgot to inquire specifically about one of the four properties to be scored). The score used was the number of positive reports under these four headings, using the consensus of the judges' ratings. Reliabilities for each judge against the consensus were: .75, .96, .80; a fourth judge, who was able to rate only 29 of the 41 protocols, obtained a reliability of .89; his scores were used to determine consensus on these 29 cases.

Hypnagogic and Hypnopompic Imagery.   In an interview on the predrug day, E also described hypnagogic and hypnopompic imagery to each S and asked him if he had ever experienced them; if so, he was asked to discuss and describe his experiences. This part of the protocol was separately rated on a 4-point scale by three judges, each of whose ratings correlated .93 with the consensus.

LSD Imagery.   There were two independent measures of the degree to which LSD produced vivid, quasihallucinatory images: the Es were instructed to take note of Ss' spontaneous comments and to make a rating on the combined frequency and vividness of imagery several times during the experimental day; and Ss were systematically interviewed at regular intervals by means of the 74-item questionnaire alluded to above. It included a question, "Have you been seeing imaginary things?" answers to which were rated on a three-point scale. These two assessments were highly correlated with each other ($r = .78$), so they were combined to give a measure of maximal differentiation and reliability.

As Table 2 shows, the four measures of imagery have a surprising degree of independence, with one exception: The Ss who were able to form

TABLE 2

Intercorrelations of Various Kinds of Imagery, as Rated on the Same Ss[a]

	Hypnagogic	LSD	Isolation
Thought imagery	.13	.00	.51[b]
Hypnagogic and hypnopompic imagery	—	.00	.29
LSD imagery	—	—	.02
Isolation imagery	—	—	—

[a] $N = 11$–27 male actors.

[b] *Italics* indicate that $p < .05$. In an earlier study (Holt & Goldberger, 1959), a similar rating of thought imagery correlated .64 with imagery in isolation ($N = 9$; $p < .10$).

good thought images of a car tended to report more imagery in the isolation experiment. Surprisingly, our rating of hypnagogic imagery correlates
only .29 with the isolation variable, which is not significant and does not
support the interpretation (suggested by several workers including ourselves) that the phenomena reported by our Ss in isolation were hypnagogic in nature. Examination of the isolation protocols themselves suggests that it is an exaggeration to call what the Ss report anything more
than ordinary thought images. Most of them resemble this: "I thought
about my sister and her husband and I saw their images"; the most vivid
reads: "A lot of things go through my mind . . . why, when I close my
eyes I can see everything as if it was right there before me—Naples,
Venice, Portugal . . . yeah, and the women, laughter, and music." In
only an occasional instance did S seem obviously in a drowsy state.

In another isolation study carried out in our laboratory, using college
women as Ss, imagery was rated in a more differentiated way (Warbassse,
1962). There was enough hypnagogic, hypnopompic, illusory and other
such imagery for her to make separate variables of hallucinationlike
images, on the one hand, and ordinary memory images or imagination
images accompanying fantasy, on the other; these two variables were *not*
correlated significantly with one another.

It seemed desirable to make a more thoroughgoing attempt to explore
the interrelatedness of various forms of mental imagery in a new sample,
to rule out the possibility that the negative findings were a sampling fluke.
It could have been that relations among some of the variables were obscured by errors of measurement, since some of the interviewing about
thought imagery and hypnagogic imagery was done rather casually without
verbatim recording and without adequate probing when answers were brief
and ambiguous.

A New Sample

Taking advantage of an opportunity offered by another experiment on
perceptual isolation by my colleague, Dr. Leo Goldberger, this time using
28 male college students, I constructed an interview assessment of the following types of mental imagery: thought imagery (essentially the same
technique as before), hypnagogic and hypnopompic imagery, eidetic
imagery in childhood, memory image of afterimage (see below), imagery
in daydreams, dream imagery (reported vividness and amount of sensory
qualities in dreams), and miscellaneous types reported too infrequently
to score separately (synesthesia, recurrent images, hallucinations, experienced change in body image, negative hallucinations—making things dis-

appear or merge—, and the *déjà vu* experience). In addition, as a check on the possibility that imagery might be related to awareness of entoptic and dreamlike phenomena, we obtained measures of afterimagery (*S* fixated a black and white design and then viewed a blank white page, describing his experience; later, he was asked to try to recapture the afterimage—see above), phosphenes (reported visual experiences with eyes closed), the frequency of dream recall, and the "falling" experience [defined by McKellar (1957, p. 201) as "The hypnagogic experience of 'falling and waking up with a jerk'."]. In addition, Dr. Goldberger provided a count of the number of images reported during the 8 hours of isolation, and a rating of their vividness.

The interview was administered by a graduate student assistant[4] and was scored by two others[5] with very satisfactory reliability. The two raters agreed completely on over 91% of all scores assigned, and the poorest level of agreement on any single variable was 88% (eidetic imagery).

Table 3 presents the intercorrelations of these 13 variables. Notice that, in general, it is a fairly good replication of Table 2: both are positive matrices and both contain hardly any more significant correlations than would be expected by chance. The one sizeable relationship reported in Table 2, which was a replicated one (see footnote to the table), failed to reach anything like the same level in the present sample: the measure of thought imagery correlated only .2 with either measure of imagery reported in the isolation experiment—still positive, but not significantly different from 0. Disregarding the high correlation between the two related measures of isolation imagery, there are 10 correlations of .32 or larger (significant at the 10% level or better; chance expectation would be 7.8 such correlations). It is noteworthy that six of these involve either the reported frequency of dreaming, or the reported vividness and amount of sensory qualities in dreams: *S*s who report dreaming most often have the richest thought imagery and tend to describe their daydreams as containing visual or auditory images (or both) and to describe their dreams as vivid with sensory imagery. The last two variables are significantly correlated, and it is interesting to see that reports of sensory richness of dream imagery are positively correlated with the incidence of hypnagogic imagery.[6] One variable that was included with few expectations, reports of eidetic or eideticlike imagery in childhood, turned out to have the highest pair of

[4] Dr. Arnold Weiner.

[5] Drs. Darlene Horowitz and Roberta Weiss.

[6] Foulkes, Spear, and Symonds (1966) report only an insignificant correlation of .20 between ratings of "sleep-onset mentation" and "nocturnal mentation" on a scale of dreamlike fantasy, in a study of 32 *S*s who reported their mental content on being awakened in the hypnagogic and REM states in a sleep laboratory.

TABLE 3

Intercorrelations of Various Kinds of Imagery and Subjective Phenomena[a]

	2	3	4	5	6	7	8	9	10	11	12	13
1. Thought imagery (vividness, sensory quality)	.14	.01	.10	-.07	-.04	.18	-.26	-.09	.39	.04	.21	.19
2. Hypnagogic and hypnopompic imagery		-.27	-.06	.19	.39	.32[b]	.02	.12	.03	.29	.16	.01
3. Eidetic imagery as a child			.34[b]	.27	.30	.14	.35[b]	.39	.15	.18	.22	.21
4. Memory image of afterimage				.22	.17	.06	.06	.30	.25	.16	.18	.12
5. Imagery in daydreams					.44	-.22	.20	.07	.35[b]	.01	-.12	-.22
6. Dream imagery (vividness, sensory quality)						.15	.02	.34[b]	.35[b]	.20	-.02	.05
7. Miscellaneous types of mental imagery							.21	.16	.09	.19	-.29	.05
8. Afterimage (convincing description)								.18	-.02	-.25	-.05	.05
9. Phosphenes (familiarity & differentiation)									-.06	-.11	.00	.08
10. Reported frequency of dreaming										.19	.23	.04
11. The "falling" experience (while drowsing)											.08	.26
12. Isolation imagery: frequency												**.74**
13. Isolation imagery: vividness												—

[a] $N = 25$–28 as rated on the same Ss, male college students.

[b] $p = .10$; italics, $p = .05$; **boldface**, $p = .01$.

(nonsignificant) correlations with the measures of isolation imagery, and also tended to be slightly but positively related to most of the other variables investigated except to hypnagogic imagery, especially to two types of essentially retinal phenomena—phosphenes and afterimages, and to the vividness of recall of the afterimage, assessed by a procedure that is rather similar to the way eidetic imagery is often measured.[7]

To the extent that there seems to be evidence of a weak general factor in Table 3, it may well be a kind of introspectiveness or awareness of subjective phenomena in general, including some types of mental imagery but also predominantly peripheral and entoptic experiences like phosphenes and afterimages. There may be a tendency for people to prefer to direct attention inward or outward, which might be expected to introduce a degree of positive correlation into any matrix like those in Tables 2 and 3. Indeed, individual differences in suggestibility or acquiescence would likewise conduce to positive intercorrelations, so the remarkable fact that remains is the demonstrated and replicated independence of the various forms of mental imagery.

Other Relevant Data

Relatively few other investigators seem to have studied this issue. The most apposite data I have found are in a paper by Buck and Geers (1967). These authors distributed a self-administering questionnaire to 91 college students of both sexes, dealing with 10 "varieties of consciousness," which included a few types of mental imagery; they also obtained the number of dreams reported over 30 days (see Table 4). The pattern of relationships strongly resembles that of Table 3, when one takes into account the fact that what is there called "miscellaneous types of mental imagery" includes synesthetic and *déjà vu* experiences. Most of the significant correlations in Table 4 are interrelations among four measures of these "miscellaneous" phenomena, which support my having grouped them together; otherwise, the only significant correlations are those between hypnagogic and hypnopompic imagery and the two types of *déjà vu,* which are of approximately the same order of magnitude as the correlation in Table 3 between hypnagogic and miscellaneous types of imagery. This is on the whole good replication, granted the differences in the two techniques of measuring imagery.[8]

---

[7] Details on the measurement of all variables will be presented in a separate publication.

[8] One reason synesthesias and *déjà vu* experiences were grouped together with the others mentioned above in the text is that they occurred so infrequently: in

TABLE 4
Intercorrelations of Several "States of Consciousness"[a]

	Auditory synesthesia	Hypnagogic experience	Frequency of dreams	Visual déjà vu	Auditory déjà vu
Visual synesthesia	.46[b]	.19	.22	.23	.12
Auditory synesthesia	—	.18	.05	.20	**.28**
Hypnagogic and hypnopompic experiences	—	—	.05	**.35**	**.27**
Frequency of dreams	—	—	—	.19	.17
Visual déjà vu	—	—	—	—	**.39**

[a] Adapted from Buck & Geers, 1967; $N = 91$ college students.
[b] Italics, $p = 0.5$; **boldface**, $p = .01$.

A few other investigators have reported relevant and largely supportive findings. Haber and Haber (1964) reported data indicating that eidetic imagery was distinct from thought (memory) imagery and from afterimages. Seitz and Molholm (1947) found that both schizophrenic and alcoholic patients with auditory hallucinations had slightly *less* auditory imagery than either normal controls or nonhallucinated patients, a finding consistent with the earlier work of Cohen (1938) and Roman and Landis (1945). Thale, Westcott, & Salomon (1950) found that Ss who had poor memory images as assessed under control conditions were prone to develop hallucinations after taking mescaline.

For the most part, however, investigators have pursued their interests in, for example, dreams or hypnagogic images without reference to any other types of mental imagery, or else have simply assumed that similarly described phenomena must be identical. For example, Richardson remarks, after reviewing the variety of images reported by subjects in perceptual isolation and quoting Hebb's description of the typical progression from simpler to more complex forms: "There seems to be little doubt that this description has reference to the same phenomena as those that have been called hypnagogic imagery, photic stimulation imagery, mescalin imagery, sleep deprivation imagery, pulse current imagery, and concentration imagery [1969, p. 102]." The only positive evidence, however, seems to

only 8 and 36% of my 28 Ss (in the new sample), as compared to 73 and 74% (visual and auditory synesthesia), 96 and 84% (visual and auditory *déjà vu*) in the Buck and Geers sample. These frequencies are so much higher than are ordinarily reported as to cast doubt on the validity of the self-report questionnaire as a method of studying such subtle and elusive types of experience.

have come from two studies by Freedman and collaborators: Freedman, Grunebaum, Stare, & Greenblatt (1962) found that among 15 Ss there was an association between reported prior history of hypnagogic imagery (technique of assessment not specified) and reports of imagery in perceptual isolation ($p = .05$; but note that Fisher's exact test for a 2×2 table was used—this is not a test of correlation and its applicability to repeated measurements in a single sample is questionable). Freedman and Marks (1965) exposed 10 male and 10 female college students to photic stimulation (flicker of a homogeneous field), and found that there was a significantly ($p < .05$) greater variety of reported visual forms seen by Ss who gave positive answers to the following item in a self-administering questionnaire: "Many people see quite vivid images when falling asleep or waking up, usually (but not always) with their eyes closed. Has this happened to you?" Again, the frequency of positive answers was high compared to our sample—60% as against 32%; chi square (1 df) = 3.7, $p \doteq .06$.

It is evident, therefore, that there is no *necessary* or intrinsic relation between hypnagogic imaging as a habitual pattern and the experiencing of phenomenologically quite similar images in experimental conditions of various sorts. Since there is no evidence that a history of hypnagogic imagery interferes in any way with having vivid images in experiments on drugs, sensory deprivation, stroboscopic (photic) stimulation, or the like, sampling fluctuations will determine the size of obtained relationships, which vary from the insignificant negative correlation found in our most recent sample to the positive ones reported by Freedman *et al.* What is demonstrated even in the studies with positive correlations, however, is that the experimental phenomena cannot be explained by the simple hypothesis that the manipulated variable merely releases a preexisting tendency to have hypnagogic images. I have such a tendency myself, for example, and fully expected to experience interesting, vivid images when I spent 36 hours in perceptual isolation, but in spite of suggestion, Rosenthal effect, or what have you, the silence, immobility, and homogeneous visual stimulation failed to evoke a single hypnagogic image (Holt, 1965).

Effects of LSD on Voluntary
Control of Imagery

In the research on the cognitive effects of LSD, described above, we tested the hypothesis that the drug enhanced a person's normal powers of imaging by administering the procedure for assessing thought imagery twice: under standard conditions and again under the effects of the drug

TABLE 5

Effects of LSD and Placebo on Controllability of Thought Imagery[a]

Numbers of Ss for whom:

Groups	Standard better than experimental	No difference	Experimental better than standard	Totals
LSD	10	8	0	18
Placebo	1	7	3	11

[a] For the Fisher exact test for 2 × 2 tables, "No difference" and "Experimental better" subgroups were combined and compared with "Standard better"; $p = .0148$.

or placebo. Paired protocols of the two thought-imagery interviews for each S, code numbered and randomly arranged, were given to three clinical judges who were asked to make several relative judgments. In particular the judges indicated for each pair, the one in which S had greater *control* over his imagery, in the sense that he could make it do what was asked.[9]

The findings (Table 5) indicate that LSD tended to make it more difficult for most of the Ss to control their thought imagery, while there was no real difference between standard and experimental performances in the placebo group. There were *no* significant differences with respect to relative vividness and intensity, detail and differentiation, or realism, though the nonsignificant trend was for the LSD protocols to be less realistic. The principal (and unexpected) finding, therefore, was that LSD *interfered* with the summoning up and deliberate manipulation of thought imagery. This fact underlines the finding (Table 2) that Ss who report much spontaneously evoked imagery in the LSD state are not those who are good at producing vivid and detailed thought images under ordinary conditions.

Discussion

Let us consider some further implications of this group of findings. First, the effects of LSD on imagery. Keep in mind, to begin with, that the data

[9] In 71% of the instances, judges agreed. In 34% of the cases there was complete unanimity; when two judges agreed and a third was out of step, it was almost always a disagreement over whether there was any difference or not. Of the 87 instances of possible agreement or disagreement, in only 7 (8%) did one judge say that the standard showed more control while another said that the experimental protocol showed more control. When there was no consensus, the case was automatically assigned to the "no difference" category.

were gathered over a decade ago, before the drug was available through any unofficial channels and just before the great wave of publicity about it that hit the mass media. Our Ss were therefore naive in a way that would be virtually impossible today, and only a couple had had any experience with marijuana or mescaline. It is also well to remember that the 100-μgm dose was small by contemporary standards; with larger doses, no doubt many more of the Ss would have reported LSD imagery.

Our findings on intercorrelation of types of imagery and drug effects on controllability point to the conclusion that the imagery induced by LSD is a different phenomenon from the thought imagery assessed by our interview. These two types differ on the two major dimensions singled out by Richardson (1969): vividness and controllability (see Chapter 5, this volume). LSD images were passively experienced, often fascinatingly intense and compelling; the thought images were less impressive but were actively summoned up and were more subject to voluntary control. (The example of thought imagery produced by an LSD subject is somewhat misleading: his protocol under standard conditions was also witty and unusual, since he was an original and exhibitionistic person.) It seems plausible to assume, therefore, that these two types of mental imagery are produced by different means or mechanisms and have little in common.

A similar conclusion seems to follow from the repeated finding of low and mostly negligible intercorrelations among various varieties of mental images. In the earliest days of work on imagery, such a finding might have been expected, for it was thought that there were discriminable types who had markedly different sorts of mental imagery: the *types visuels,* audiles, etc. Then the work of Betts (1909), Sheehan (1967), and Richardson (1969) demonstrated conclusively that such pure types were rather rare exceptions and that there is a strong general factor of vividness regardless of modality. This fact seems to argue strongly for the generality of imagery; but note that it is only a generality of active thought imagery across sensory modalities. So there is plenty of room for thought imagery itself to be quite uncorrelated with the incidence of other kinds.

Before we accept the data of Tables 2, 3, and 4 at face value, let us consider some other possibilities. One always has to be cautious in drawing any conclusions on the basis of negative findings. The null hypothesis is incapable of proof, and there are plenty of reasons for low correlations besides the possibility that the variates in question are in fact independent and unrelated. Any errors in measurement will attenuate correlations, and our assessment techniques are admittedly crude and not perfectly reliable. If I were planning another replication I should use Sheehan's (1967) revision of the Betts QMI[10] Scale to measure the vividness of thought imagery in various modalities, making a separate assessment of controllability by

[10] QMI = Questionnaire upon Mental Imagery.

the Gordon Test. A much better method of assessing hypnagogic imagery than the kind of inquiry we have used is the technique of Witkin and Lewis (1965) or that of Foulkes, Spear, and Symonds (1966): put the S to bed in a sleep laboratory, monitoring his state by means of a continuous EEG, and arouse him during the drowsy stage just before Stage 1 sleep, inquiring about his mental content. Foulkes *et al.* rated these hypnagogic reports on 7-point scales, which allow for a more differentiated and sensitive analysis, in addition to having better intrinsic validity. When a person says in an interview that he does not believe that he has ever had a hypnagogic image, we cannot know whether he has them but cannot recall them, or does not recognize enough similarity between his own experiences and those described, or in fact has no such imagery.

The satisfactoriness of the usual assessment by interview or by self-administered questionnaire becomes doubtful when we examine another kind of data—the great discrepancies in average frequency of positive reports. McKellar (1957) notes that Müller (1838) had found that only 1–2% of college students acknowledged having had hypnagogic imagery, though his own data agreed with those of Leaning (1925) in that about one-third of a student population reported visual images of this type. When he took auditory and other nonvisual hypnagogic images into account, the percentage rose to 63%. Buck & Geers (1967) got positive reports of hypnagogic images (modality unspecified) from 72%, the highest incidence I have seen. At the least, there should be careful inquiry about hypnagogic images in various modalities in any future research.

The assessment of dream imagery is subject to the same caveats as those just enumerated. There are obvious advantages to using the data from direct awakenings, since everyone has dreams and many people recall little or nothing about them. Yet the laboratory method has its drawbacks, too; to an unknown extent, this unusual situation introduces artifacts at least until the S becomes habituated to the lab and the procedure. We know that the sleep cycle itself tends to be somewhat disturbed initially, and the content of dreams is affected; how far their vividness, sensory content, etc. may be changed is unknown. Moreover, there is a serious problem of sampling—in order to get a substantial and representative body of data from most Ss, they must spend several nights in the laboratory, which is slow, expensive, and laborious. The same point applies, even more strongly, to the assessment of hypnagogic imagery by controlled awakenings, for the most striking instances of this phenomenon occur only sporadically if we may judge by the reports of positive Ss.

An even more herculean labor of gathering data is required of the experimenter on perceptual isolation or sensory deprivation, so that large samples of data are difficult to find. In any small sample of Ss, there may be too few who produce anything resembling hallucinations in the usual sense (vivid and elaborated images in which external stimuli play only an apparently trivial part) to make it possible to measure them separately from various types of active (controlled) and passive (unbidden) images. Goldberger reports (personal communication) that in his recent study, from which the data in Table 3 derive, he classified isolation images in a highly differentiated way, with the result that there were too few of each type to make variables that were satisfactorily distributed for correlational purposes; hence, all kinds were grouped together. That very diversity and heterogeneity may account for the failure of the two measures of isolation imagery to be related to any other variables in Table 3.

Any form of imagery that Richardson calls "uncontrolled," Horowitz calls "unbidden," and I call "passive" is an operant, which may have a small base-rate frequency. The lower the base rate, the more difficult it will be to get a reliable assessment, whether one goes about it by direct sampling or by asking Ss to report retrospectively. Obviously, whether or not such an image will occur at any one time must be a function of many determinants in addition to capacity, so there are many possible sources of noise or errors of measurement. For example, anecdotal reports of the great variability of LSD "trips" suggest that the amount, kind, and vividness of LSD imagery probably vary in response to many unknown parameters. A good deal probably depends on the momentary state of unconscious and ego-alien motive systems, which seem to be much implicated in all these passive forms of imagery (see Horowitz, 1970, and also Chapter 12, this volume). Since impulse-defense configurations vary a good deal from time to time, here is another reason to expect low intercorrelations.

Another reason that correlations may be spuriously low is *restriction of range*. If two variables are to covary, each must vary to begin with. Here we come up against two problems, one already alluded to: something with a very low base rate simply cannot be meaningfully analyzed by means of correlation; the range may be from 0 to 1, with the great majority scoring 0. In our putatively comprehensive assessment interview, for example, we inquired about ghosts, phantasms at times of crisis, and other visions or apparitions; only 3 Ss gave any positive response to this group of questions. Two of these 3 claimed to have hypnagogic imagery also—a finding that could have easily occurred by chance. Clearly, many more Ss would be needed before we could begin to establish a meaningful correlation; but as we have already seen, to do good assessment in this area one must interview carefully and sensitively, using direct sampling of dreams, hypnagogic imagery, imagery under the effect of drugs and of perceptual isolation, etc., all of which requirements sharply limit the size of feasible samples.

The nature of the population sampled obviously affects results, also. Even when the number of Ss is relatively large, if they are all volunteers from college psychology classes who know the topic being investigated, the group may be too homogeneous to provide the necessary range. Unfortunately, the typical sample of Ss in the literature on imagery is restricted in just this way.

Despite all these cautions, I nevertheless believe that the burden of proof is now on anyone who wishes to contend that, in effect, an image is an image and all this attempt at taxonomy and differential assessment is superfluous. There is a real possibility that the many types of imagery usually distinguished have a good deal of intrinsic independence. That is, granted that all persons with normal nervous systems and eyes can form visual perceptual images, can recognize them and otherwise process encoded and stored iconic information, people seem to differ considerably in their abilities and proclivities to construct conscious mental images from this matrix of presentations, whether actively or passively. It may well be that they do so according to a variety of separate "programs" or structures. It may also be, however, that when a number of types of passive imagination images are descriptively quite similar, and typically follow a similar development, one mechanism is involved, but the extent to which the phenomena get the focus of attention and are remembered may depend on so many other determinants that assessments of the various types of imagery turn out to be uncorrelated. Only a good deal more research can provide the answer, and there is little reason to expect that it will come quickly or easily.

Finally, let us consider the implications of the findings, if we take them at face value, for the theoretical beginnings advanced in an earlier section of this chapter. The generally high level of agreement among independent observers who were set the task of rating various forms of imagery on the basis of verbal assessments is a strong argument against old-fashioned behaviorism and any other kind of implicitly materialistic objection to images as legitimate objects of scientific concern. Beyond that elementary point, it is hard to say that the data are relevant to choice among the various positions outlined in Table 1—which merely confirms the well-known fact that metaphysics, by definition, only rarely has any direct intersection with empirical facts. Any of these philosophical points of view could accommodate itself to either generality or independence of the types of imagery.

I believe, however, that the beginnings of a model of image-forming processes presented here can accommodate better than many other such theories the tentative conclusion that there is little if any generality in the realm of mental imagery. According to this model, the raw material for images of any type is neurologically encoded sensory information, which may come from several sources: from memory, from the influence of external stimuli on the sense organs, or from processes internal to the sensory systems (e.g., endotic and entoptic phenomena, the importance of which is suggested by some correlations in Table 3). From this raw material, perceptual presentations and conscious perceptual images are regularly constructed (with more or less influence from cognitive control principles such as leveling-sharpening and field articulation) according to standard, rather universally shared programs. Other phenomenal events, not experienced as perceptual, may arise in much the same way though usually with a much smaller contribution from intercurrent inputs from the sensory organs; according to the present model, they are constructed also, according to other stored, two-stage programs. In general, the independence of the form-varieties of imagery is accounted for by the assumption that there are different programs for each type with separate subprograms that construct the presentation and that achieve phenomenal (conscious) status for it. This last distinction is crucial; it accounts for the low correlations. I assume that any normal person has memory programs that construct sensory presentations even though many persons are unable to experience the corresponding types of sensory imagery. These presentations allow them to recognize sensory inputs, to solve problems and carry out other performances (like drawing pictures) that require the existence and processing of presentations, yet to have a dearth of nonperceptual images in the corresponding modalities.

I am inclined to assume, further, that some of the relevant image-forming programs are under voluntary control while others are not, and that if a person has such control over one image-forming program he is likely to be able to control others. That assumption would account for the generality across sensory modalities of thought imagery, and some of the significant correlations in Tables 2 and 3. Presentation-forming programs, by contrast, would appear to operate without conscious control, though they are controlled by sets some of which may be consciously induced (e.g., the intention to recall a particular face). At all times, presentation-forming programs must be under the control of motive systems of some kind, and there is good reason to suppose that in many if not all people unconscious motive systems over which there is little if any voluntary control are forming and processing sensory presentations a great deal of the time, possibly always. Granted the right set of internal and external conditions, some of these may become conscious images of a passive or unbidden kind.

So far, I have worked with the assumption that it takes a special subprogram to create a mental image from a presentation. When we examine what we know about the conditions favoring various kinds of passive imagery, however, an alternative formulation suggests itself: it may be that the usual consequence of the construction of a sensory presentation is that it should be represented in consciousness *unless* it is barred by defensive or other structural arrangements. There is surely good reason to postulate defenses against awareness of inner, subjective processes, for some persons (notably rigid, authoritarian personalities) are behaviorally characterized by inability to report on such experiences if they do not have "objective," perceptual quality. Moreover, organismic conditions that tend in general to weaken repressions and similar defenses, such as LSD states, febrile illnesses, and certain forms of brain damage, are characterized by vivid, unbidden images. Hypnagogic and hypnopompic images might be similarly conceptualized; the organismic states just before and just after sleep may have the effect of selectively weakening those defenses that are directed against the emergence into awareness of presentations that are controlled by ego-alien motives in certain persons. Since there is no *a priori* reason why these should be the same people whose defenses against imagery are vulnerable to a hallucinogenic drug, there need be no correlation between the two types of imagery, though both are passive and sometimes phenomenologically similar. (Some of the phenomenological distinctiveness of LSD images may well be attributable to the drug's enhancement of entoptic inputs.)

On the defensive hypothesis, why should anyone who can voluntarily form usable sensory presentations of emotionally neutral subject matter be unable to experience these as mental images? The earlier assumption that such persons lack a specific program for making presentations conscious cannot be ruled out, though it smacks of the *ad hoc*. Perhaps a preferable alternative stems from the observation that normally consciousness is a relatively limited field, the unity or coherence of which has obvious biological utility. It is plainly necessary to assume some order-keeping programs, some stored decision-rules to allow thought to have the character of a stream rather than an inundation; and we are familiar with psychopathological conditions in which just such order-keeping structures are impaired (e.g., manic flight of ideas, the pressure of ideation in some early schizophrenic states). Whenever we postulate a kind of program in a general model, we must also as a general principle recognize that it will have many individual variants. In the case of gatekeeping structures, it is an attractive possibility to postulate that they may vary from the relatively lax and unselective, in persons who experience their thoughts in such vividly sensory form as to have difficulty in abstracting, to the normal, where a useful degree and amount of thought imagery is allowed into awareness, to the very highly selective, characteristic of imageless thinkers who may have a certain advantage in abstract thinking while suffering some adaptive disadvantage in other ways.

It is tempting to continue with such speculations, but I shall exert another kind of gatekeeping control over my thoughts until such time as I can present data on the personality correlates of different kinds of mental images, which suggest some further extensions of the model.

References

Arnheim, R. *Visual thinking.* Berkeley: University of California Press, 1969.

Arnold, M. B. (Ed.) *Feelings and emotions: The Loyola symposium.* New York: Academic Press, 1970.

Barr, H. B., Langs, R. J., Holt, R. R., Goldberger, L., & Klein, G. S. *LSD: Personality and experience.* New York: Wiley, 1972.

Betts, G. H. *The distribution and functions of mental imagery.* New York: Teachers' College, Columbia University, 1909.

Boernstein, W. S. Optic perception and optic imageries in man: Their roots and relations studied from the viewpoint of biology. *International Journal of Neurology,* 1967, **6**, 147–181.

Brown, R. W. Language and categories. In J. S. Bruner, J. J. Goodnow, & G. A. Austin (Eds.), *A study of thinking.* New York: Wiley, 1956. Pp. 247–312.

Bruner, J. S., & Postman, L. On the perception of incongruity: A paradigm. *Journal of Personality,* 1949, **18**, 206–223.

Buck, L. A., & Geers, M. B. Varieties of consciousness: I. Intercorrelations. *Journal of Clinical Psychology,* 1967, **23**, 151–152.

Cohen, L. H. Imagery and its relations to schizophrenic symptoms. *Journal of Mental Science,* 1938, **84**, 284–346.

Duncker, K. *Zur Psychologie des produktiven Denkens.* Berlin: Springer, 1935. (Translated by L. S. Lees, On problem-solving. *Psychological Monographs,* 1945, **58**, No. 5, Whole No. 270.)

Foulkes, D., Spear, P. S., & Symonds, J. D. Individual differences in mental activity at sleep onset. *Journal of Abnormal Psychology,* 1966, **71**, 280–286.

Freedman, S. J., Grunebaum, H. V., Stare, F. A., & Greenblatt, M. Imagery in sensory deprivation. In L. J. West (Ed.), *Hallucinations.* New York: Grune & Stratton, 1962. Pp. 108–117.

Freedman, S. J., & Marks, P. A. Visual imagery produced by rhythmic photic stimulation: Personality correlates and phenomenology. *British Journal of Psychology,* 1965, **56**, 95–112.

Freud, S. (1921) *Group psychology and the analysis of the ego.* (Standard ed.) Vol. 18. London: Hogarth Press, 1955. Pp. 69–143.

Freud, S. (1923) *The ego and the id.* (Standard ed.) Vol. 19. London: Hogarth, 1961. Pp. 19–27.

Fromm, E. *The sane society.* New York: Holt, 1955.

Goldberger, L., & Holt, R. R. Experimental interference with reality contact (perceptual isolation): Method and group results. *Journal of Nervous and Mental Disease,* 1958, **127**, 99–112.

Goldberger, L., & Holt, R. R. *Studies on the effects of perceptual alteration.* (USAF ASD Tech. Rep. No. 61–416) Ohio: Wright-Patterson AFB, 1961.

Gordon, R. An investigation into some of the factors that favour the formation of stereotyped images. *British Journal of Psychology,* 1949, **39,** 156–167.

Griffitts, C. H. Individual differences in imagery. *Psychological Monographs,* 1927, **37** (Whole No. 172).

Haber, R. N., & Haber, R. B. Eidetic imagery: I. Frequency. *Perceptual and Motor Skills,* 1964, **19,** 131–138.

Hartmann, E. (Ed.) *Sleep and dreaming.* Boston: Little, Brown, 1970.

Held, R. Exposure-history as a factor in maintaining stability of perception and coordination. *Journal of Nervous and Mental Disease,* 1961, **132,** 26–32.

von Holst, E., & Mittelstaedt, H. Das Reafferenzprincip (Wechselwirkungen zwischen Zentralnervensystem und Peripherie). *Naturwissenschaft,* 1950, **37,** 464–476.

Holt, R. R. Clinical judgment as a disciplined inquiry. *Journal of Nervous and Mental Disease,* 1961, **133,** 369–382.

Holt, R. R. Imagery: The return of the ostracized. *American Psychologist,* 1964, **12,** 254–264.

Holt, R. R. Ego autonomy re-evaluated. *International Journal of Psycho-Analysis,* 1965, **46,** 151–167. (Reprinted with critical evaluations and the author's rejoinder in *International Journal of Psychiatry,* 1967, **3,** 481–536.)

Holt, R. R. Beyond vitalism and mechanism: Freud's concept of psychic energy. In J. H. Masserman (Ed.), *Science and psychoanalysis.* Vol. XI. *Concepts of ego.* New York: Grune & Stratton, 1967. Pp. 1–41.   (a)

Holt, R. R. Individuality and generalization in the psychology of personality. (Rev. version.) In R. S. Lazarus & E. M. Opton (Eds.), *Readings in personality.* Baltimore, Md.: Penguin, 1967. Pp. 38–65.   (b)

Holt, R. R., & Goldberger, L. *Personological correlates of reactions to perceptual isolation.* (USAF WADC Tech. Rep. No. 59–735) Ohio: Wright-Patterson AFB, 1959.

Holt, R. R., & Goldberger, L. *Research on the effects of isolation on cognitive functioning.* (USAF WADC Tech. Rep. No. 60–260) Ohio: Wright-Patterson AFB, 1960.

Horowitz, M. J. *Image formation and cognition.* New York: Appleton, 1970.

Jaensch, E. *Eidetic imagery and typological methods of investigation.* Westport, Conn.: Greenwood Press, 1970.

Kamiya, J. Operant control of the EEG alpha rhythm and some of its reported effects on consciousness. In C. T. Tart (Ed.), *Altered states of consciousness.* New York: Wiley, 1969. Pp. 507–517.

Keniston, K. *The uncommitted: Alienated youth in American society.* New York: Harcourt, 1960.

Keup, W. (Ed.) *Origin and mechanisms of hallucinations.* New York: Plenum, 1970.

Lazarus, A. A., & Abramovitz, A. The use of "emotive imagery" in the treatment of children's phobias. *Journal of Mental Science,* 1962, **108,** 191–195.

Leaning, F. E. An introductory study of hypnagogic phenomena. *Proceedings of the Society for Psychical Research,* 1925, **35,** 289–403.

Linton, H. B., & Langs, R. J. Subjective reactions to lysergic acid diethylamide (LSD-25). *Archives of General Psychiatry,* 1962, **6,** 352–368.

Mackworth, J. F. *Vigilance and attention.* Baltimore, Md.: Penguin, 1970.

McKellar, P. *Imagination and thinking: A psychological analysis.* New York: Basic Books, 1957.

McLuhan, M. *Understanding media.* New York: McGraw-Hill, 1964.

Müller, J. (1838). *The physiology of the senses.* (Translated by W. Baly.) London: Taylor, 1848.

Mumford, L. *The myth of the machine.* Vol. II. *The pentagon of power.* New York: Harcourt, 1970.

Paivio, A. On the functional significance of imagery. *Psychological Bulletin,* 1970, **73**, 385–392.

Palermo, D. S. Imagery in children's learning: Discussion. *Psychological Bulletin,* 1970, **73**, 415–421.

Piaget, J., & Inhelder, B. *Mental imagery in the child.* New York: Basic Books, 1971.

Polanyi, M. (1958). *Personal knowledge: Towards a post-critical philosophy.* (Rev. ed.) New York: Harper Torchbooks, 1964.

Rapaport, D. (Ed.) *Organization and pathology of thought.* New York: Columbia Univ. Press, 1951.

Reich, C. A. *The greening of America.* New York: Random House, 1970.

Richardson, A. *Mental imagery.* New York: Springer, 1969.

Roman, R., & Landis, C. Hallucinations and mental imagery. *Journal of Nervous and Mental Disease,* 1945, **102**, 327–331.

Roszak, T. *The making of a counter culture.* New York: Doubleday, 1969.

Rubinstein, B. B. Psychoanalytic theory and the mind-body problem. In N. S. Greenfield & W. C. Lewis (Eds.), *Psychoanalysis and current biological thought.* Madison: University of Wisconsin Press, 1965. Pp. 35–56.

Rubinstein, B. B. Explanation and mere description: A metascientific examination of certain aspects of the psychoanalytic theory of motivation. In R. R. Holt (Ed.), Motives and thought. *Psychological Issues,* Monograph 18/19. New York: International Univ. Press, 1967.

Scheibel, M. E., & Scheibel, A. B. Hallucinations and the brain stem reticular core. In L. J. West (Ed.), *Hallucinations.* New York: Grune & Stratton, 1962. Pp. 15–35.

Segal, S. J. (Ed.) *The adaptive functions of imagery.* New York: Academic Press, 1971.

Seitz, P. E. D., & Molholm, H. B. Relation of mental imagery to hallucinations. *Archives of Neurology and Psychiatry,* 1947, **57**, 469–480.

Sheehan, P. W. A shortened form of Betts' Questionnaire Upon Mental Imagery. *Journal of Clinical Psychology,* 1967, **23**, 386–389.

Singer, J. L. *Daydreaming.* New York: Random House, 1966.

Tart, C. T. (Ed.) *Altered states of consciousness.* New York: Wiley, 1969.

Thale, T., Westcott, G., & Salomon, K. Hallucinations and imagery induced by mescaline. *American Journal of Psychiatry,* 1950, **106**, 686–691.

Walter, W. G. *The living brain.* New York: Norton, 1953.

Warbasse, A. F. The relationship of self-image variables to reactions to isolation. Unpublished doctoral dissertation, New York University, 1962.

Witkin, H. A., & Lewis, H. B. The relation of experimentally induced presleep experiences to dreams: A report on method and preliminary findings. *Journal of the American Psychoanalytic Association,* 1965, **13**, 819–849.

Wolpe, J., & Lazarus, A. A. *Behavior therapy techniques.* New York: Pergamon, 1966.

2 PETER McKELLAR

IMAGERY FROM THE STANDPOINT OF INTROSPECTION

The tendency to experience and the ability to notice and report mental imagery is certainly very common. Although often underdeveloped, the potential for imagery in man is probably universal. This does not exclude individual variations like those of predominant mode, vividness, and autonomy. Assuming the role of psychologist naturalist interested in describing, classifying and naming, my concern will be to examine the family of natural phenomena we call images. I shall be specially concerned with visual imaging.

It has become traditional to relate the origins of scientific interest in imagery and images to Sir Francis Galton (1880; 1883). Yet incisive thinking on the subject occurred much earlier, and Fechner in 1860 was concerned to differentiate the main phenomena. Attempts to enumerate and list these types of imagery, as Holt (1964) has pointed out, show a direct line of descent from Fechner, through Titchener and Boring, and to Holt himself. Subsequent to Holt, Horowitz (1970) has provided a further classification which has added some new categories. At a very much earlier date the Greeks made their contribution. Even before Plato and Aristotle was the tradition of Simonides of Ceos by which early Greek teachers of oratory and rhetoric achieved increased memory capacity with systematic and disciplined use of visual imagery. To this tradition Aristotle himself makes only passing reference (*De Memoria*, Chapter 2, 452a). The last decade has seen a major historical contribution to our knowledge of visual imagery in this way by Frances Yates (1966). Thus Yates, as an historian has had to remind psychologists of one very important aspect of memory that Ebbinghaus, and too many of his successors, have wholly neglected. Following Simonides we find in Plato (*Theaetetus,* 191) a considerable interest in the differential psychology of memory, and very probably a recognition of imagery differences. Aristotle contributed a great deal on both dream imagery, and memory imagery. He also, in *De Memoria* and several times in *De Anima,* commits himself to the view that thinking cannot occur without imagery. At the turn of this century, in a book which was essentially a sustained introspective study of one kind of imagery, Freud (1900) also contributed a history of ideas about both the imagery of sleep and related waking–sleeping states. Another phenomenon, eidetic imagery, was first reported by Purkinje in 1819, and intensively studied by Jaensch; his major book, published in 1925, received English translation in 1930. The ideas of Jaensch have been developed in relation to imagery more generally by Rosemary Gordon (See Chapter 3, this volume; see also Richardson, 1969). Valuable for its translation of earlier German writings, such as Silberer's brilliant introspective studies of 1909, is Rapaport's volume (Rapaport, 1951). An experimental study within the early tradition of Simonides is reported in another part of this book (Marks, Chapter 4), and a more indepth study is presented by McKellar, Marks, and Barron, (1972, in preparation). The emphasis of the present chapter is phenomenological rather than experimental; it will be to some extent historical and also forward-looking in the light of this historical context.

Three Types of Imagery

I will begin by examining three kinds of imagery: I shall be concerned with their frequency of occurrence, their tendency for incidence to be underestimated, and their possible universality.

Dream Imagery

After a period of sleep some people report regularly, and others more occasionally, visual and other forms of dream imagery. We have introspective, or more strictly, retrospective evidence of this kind. In addition a major scientific breakthrough occurred in the 1950's (Aserinsky & Kleitman, 1953; Dement & Kleitman, 1957). Because of this it now becomes scientifically meaningful, as regards dream imagery, to distinguish recallers from nonrecallers, rather than dreamers from nondreamers. The evidence today suggests that most human dreaming, like most human thinking, is lost through forgetting. If, with Kleitman, we are prepared to accept one rather specific kind of ocular-motor activity, REMs, as evidence of dreaming, then it appears that ordinary introspection underestimates dream incidence. Most people dream, and very probably all people dream. Moreover, by REM criteria there is now also evidence that dreaming occurs lower in the evolutionary system than man. The major discovery of REMs as an externally observable accompaniment of dreaming was, in fact, a rediscovery. This aspect of Ladd's (1892) well-known article was overlooked by many potentially interested psychologists. Eventual rediscovery has helped towards the rehabilitation of "Imagery the Ostracized"; it has resulted in some exciting research developments to be discussed elsewhere in this volume. The present chapter will be largely concerned with introspective evidence. But, as REM studies show, introspective evidence alone appears to substantially underestimate the amount of dream imaging that actually occurs.

Memory Imagery

A second type of experience, memory imagery, presents something of a paradox. In Galton's data we encounter his scientists, many of whom protested that mental imagery was unknown to them: "they had no more notion of its true nature than a blind man who has not discerned his defect has of the nature of colour [Galton 1880, p. 302]." Galton found many good visual and other imagers in the population at large but not in "the great majority of the men of science to whom I first applied [Galton, 1883, p. 58]." Yet, as we have already seen, Aristotle who in many respects established the foundations of these sciences, believed that thinking without imagery was not possible. Galton, whose work did so much to encourage the study of individual differences between people, may well have been investigating processes universal in man. At any rate, numerous investigators since Galton have had far more difficulty in finding nonimagers than imagers. In the case of visual imagery, Carey (1915) with a group of London schoolchildren failed to find any who were totally bereft of such imagery. To cite recent data, my colleague Dr. Marks, working with his *Vividness of Visual Imagery Questionnaire,* the VVIQ, initially studied 190 student subjects. Only one of these gave a rating of "5," this being an indication of "no imagery at all" for all 16 items of the scale. An earlier investigation of my own may also be cited (McKellar, 1965). In a group of 500 nonstudent adults no less than 97% reported visual imagery, 93%

auditory imagery, and 74% motor imagery. Incidence reported for other modes was: tactile 70%, gustatory 67%, olfactory 66%, pain (algesic imagery) 54%, and temperature imagery 43% (McKellar 1965a; 1965b). The amount and range of available imagery for these subjects proved to be extensive. Thus for children, students, and nonstudent adults, the absence of visual imagery seems to be something of a rarity. My own data suggest that the same is true also of auditory, and probably other modes as well. Perhaps through time there has been a change of incidence. Possibly a medium like television has fostered habits of visual recall, though Carey's data of 1915, long before television, clearly indicates that this is not the whole story. The tendency to overlook and to forget imagery experiences is certainly still with us; perhaps this tendency was stronger in Galton's day and age than our own.

Hallucinatory Imagery

Sarbin and Juhasz (1967) trace the first use of the word "hallucination" in English to a 1572 translation of a tract by Lavater, it being used to refer to apparitions. The word has been used for a huge range of different phenomena since: there seems to be little point in these overextended usages of which psychologists themselves have so often been guilty. Even if usage is restricted to manageable proportions, hallucinations are difficult to define as Richardson (1969) shows; they are also, in marginal cases, difficult to differentiate from other imagery phenomena. A distinction is sometimes made between hallucination and pseudohallucination in which awareness is retained of the subjective nature of the apparent percept. Difficulties occur, for example, in the case of the Perky effect when real perceptions are confused with mental images of a kind we would probably not wish to classify as hallucinatory (Perky, 1910; see also Chapter 9, this volume). Even in the case of hallucinatory psychoses we encounter patients (and I have known many) who possess insight into the fact that they are hallucinated. The point about such insight is not its presence or absence, but rather the difficulty of adhering to it consistently at all times.

If psychologists themselves have, on occasion, carelessly misused the term "hallucination" they have probably been more sophisticated than others in resisting the temptation to treat hallucination as a diagnostic symptom of psychiatric illness. A great many seemingly abnormal phenomena prove, on investigation, to be both statistically common and wholly compatible with good mental health. Moreover, many parents and children often need reassurance on this point (McKellar, 1965b). The conditions under which hallucination occurs appear to be numerous and varied. Moreover, by appropriate experimental techniques it is probably possible to produce visual (though less readily auditory) hallucinations in virtually anybody. Experimentally induced hallucinations of touch, taste, and smell were reported by Seashore as early as 1895. Commenting on this, Sarbin and Juhasz (1967) query the tradition by which Esquirol continues to be quoted as the formulator and classic authority on hallucination, while the careful experimental work of Seashore is rarely cited. Apart from experimentally produced phenomena, the spontaneous occurrence of hallucination in normal people is more common than is widely supposed. The classic "census of hallucinations," conducted on many thousands of people, yielded the finding that just under 10% reported at least one such experience (Sidgwick, 1894). Moreover, the census explicitly excluded marginal phenomena. At a later date, Karl Menninger (1949) found the same percentage: 20 cases in a group of 200 students. William James (1902) himself experienced "after getting into bed in my rooms at Cambridge, a vivid tactile hallucination of being grasped by the arm [p. 59]." This was sufficient to make him get up and search the room for the intruder. Yet such an experience as this would certainly have been rejected from the census of hallucinations as a marginal case because of its reference to the state before sleep rather than occurrence in full wakefulness. Writing as a psychiatrist who is prepared to fault the psychiatric textbooks that treat hallucination as diagnostic of mental illness, Medlicott (1958) concludes that hallucinations are common in the sane, as well as in the psychiatric patient. Among hallucinated celebrities, in addition to well-known cases, Medlicott lists: Raphael, Schumann, Goethe, Descartes, Sir Walter Scott, Dr. Johnson, and Guy de Maupassant. The last named experienced autoscopic phenomena. Autoscopic hallucinations of oneself are given interesting treatment by Rawcliffe (1952), and many of his instances are associated with pain, suffering, and accident injuries. Another phenomenon, negative hallucination, seems rarely to occur spontaneously; it is difficult to produce experimentally. Steinberg (1956) encountered some cases in her experiments with nitrous oxide, as when with one subject, the surface of the table disappeared and a pencil and paper remained suspended in mid air. The exception is the state of hypnosis in which negative hallucination can fairly readily be produced in suitable subjects (McKellar & Tonn, 1967). Of interest among the spontaneous phenomena of normal mental life are motoring hallucinations; these seem to be related to tiredness, visual fatigue, and night driving. Preoccupation with hallucinations often of a quite spectacular kind, tempt us to overlook some other dangerous intrusions of imagery. In night or fog driving, cloud flying, or underwater swimming, ordinary visual imagery about where one is, if inaccurate, may be highly dangerous: the motorist at night or in fog may image a turn in the road before he reaches it in reality. Such orientation imagery can give rise to little understood sources of accidents, and more needs to be known about it.

The "Return of the Ostracized" is, as Holt (1964) has argued, long overdue. In the study of memory, Ebbinghaus (1885) did perhaps too much to determine the direction of future research. By ignoring imagery differences, and the substantial literature (compare Yates, 1966) from earliest times on mnemonic systems in which visual imagery played an important part, many subsequent investigators contributed to a dull and rather sterile research literature on verbal learning. Contemporary researches give many indications that, in this field, imagery the ostracized is making a vigorous comeback. Again the gloomy shadow of Watsonian Behaviorism is still with us, and even today for some the admonition "don't introspect" is taken seriously. Too many psychologists never having been taught it have in the past remained and still remain introspectively illiterate. Writing of the lean years of the ostracisim of imagery, Sanford (1965) has argued with some justification that too many psychologists still "do not know what goes on in human beings, and their work shows it [p. 192]." There remain strong barriers to the scientific study, analysis, and recognition of subjective experience. We find this in psychologists and in people in general. In a climate of thought that is antagonistic to scientific introspection much can be overlooked. Galton (1883) himself observed that "the visionary tendency is much more common than is generally supposed" and added that granted favorable social conditions faintly perceived fantasies are "attended to and encouraged, and they gain in definition through being habitually dwelt upon [pp. 127–8]." In this difficult field Horowitz (1970) refers to the dangers of both "false positives," and "false negatives." Despite experimenter effects, and the dangers of suggestion, I would maintain that contemporary psychologists need to be much more vigorously alerted to the phenomena of their own mental life. This applies to dream imagery, memory imagery, and hallucinatory imagery, and to other phenomena next to be discussed.

Hypnagogic Experiences

Some people in the drowsy state before sleep report an anticipatory invasion of consciousness by visual or other dreamlike imagery. The earliest quantitative investigation of hypnagogic imagery appears to have been that of Johannes Müller (1848) conducted on Berlin University students.

Müller concluded that the imagery was a rare form of subjective experience, but later investigators, from Leaning (1925) to Oswald (1962), have arrived at an opposing conclusion. My own investigations of Aberdeen University students yielded an incidence of 76% (McKellar, 1957; McKellar & Simpson, 1954). Owens (1963) placed it at 77% in a female group she studied, and a sex difference favoring women seems to hold. Incidentally, Lorna Simpson and I found auditory hypnagogic imagery more common than visual, while Owens found a higher incidence of visual imagery. Hypnagogic imagery has aroused the interest and curiosity of many, from Aristotle to Kleitman. Maury who in 1848 named the phenomenon experienced it in the "faces in the dark" form. The faces he reported were always of people unknown to him. Earlier, in the Leviathan, Thomas Hobbes in 1651 appears to have included such imagery along with dreams and nightmares as source material for superstition and belief in witchcraft (Hobbes, 1651, Pt. 1, Chapter 2, pp. 15–17). In considering the phenomena themselves, of interest is a letter signed by a correspondent who called himself "An Associate" which appeared in May 1890 in the Journal of the (British) Society for Psychical Research. This described the correspondent's own hypnagogic imagery, and the letter stimulated others to describe theirs. For some the imagery was geometrical: "beautiful decorative patterns, filials, curves, spirals [letter of 1898]." Some referred to architecture, and to landscapes. Faces, unfamiliar faces like those described by Maury, were frequently reported, e.g., "shining and hideous faces grinning at me in the midst of profound darkness." Other correspondents mentioned oddities of color and lighting, e.g., "moon-lighted landscapes." From the data cited in this correspondence, and other sources, we find evidence of two rather different kinds of visual hypnagogic experiences. Elsewhere (McKellar & Simpson 1954), we have suggested that these might be labeled, respectively, the "perseverative" and the "impersonal" types of hypnagogic imagery.

Perseverative Imagery

Perseverative imagery resembles the idealized imagery which Hanawalt (1954) reports, and which both he and his wife experienced after a day spent picking blackberries. A Scottish psychologist, Margaret Sutherland, wrote to me about a very similar perseverative hypnagogic image following strawberry picking (McKellar, 1957; also discussed in Richardson, 1969). Flournoy reported how, after playing chess that day, visions of the board and pieces occurred to him just before sleep. Similarly perseverative forms of motor imagery, experienced hypnagogically, seem commonly to follow such activities as skating, tennis, and golf. In all these instances the imagery while hypnagogic, has resemblance to the phenomena of "immediate memory imagery" to be discussed below. In all cases the reference to previous perception is clear-cut and definite.

Impersonal Imagery

Impersonal imagery is of a different kind. Presumably it also has perceptual origins, but such origins are not obvious. For example, those who experience the faces in the dark kind of imagery are often emphatic that the faces are of people unknown to them. Likewise, many of the landscapes are strangely unfamiliar, as one of my subjects said "like scenes from the kind of travel books I don't read." Some subjects likened their impersonal imagery to surrealist paintings, on the basis of their originality, oddities of lighting, and impossible clarity of detail. The impression that what is occurring is strangely foreign to one's own mental life can be strong. There is clear evidence that writers have, on occasion, drawn on such imagery in their literary productions. Impersonal hypnagogic imagery can give rise to other reactions. Its appearance under such aliases as "omens," "apparition" and "children's night terrors" merits careful investigation in individual cases in which anxiety and terror can prevail (McKellar, 1965b).

From the standpoint of this chapter an interesting feature of hypnagogic imagery is its availability to immediate introspection, as opposed to the purely retrospective study to which dreaming is confined. The classic researches in this field were those of Silberer (1909) who related visual hypnagogic imagery to pictorial concretizations and symbolizations of more abstract forms of thought. During a long period of special interest in hypnagogic imagery I have encountered some remarkable cases of overlooking it. Here, as elsewhere in imagery study, what Horowitz (1970) calls "false negatives" are exceedingly likely to occur: as Horowitz adds "fleeting images are easily forgotten [p. 42]." Moreover, they may also pass unnoticed. In the realm of imagery, vividness has sometimes received rather too exclusive attention. With many visual hypnagogic experiences perceptual-like stability may be more apparent than mere vividness; sometimes the imagery gives the impression, as one of my subjects put it, of being "engraved on the back of my eyeballs." The imagery is as it were "there," but is not always "noticed," and may be "overlooked." A very similar phenomenon occurs with perceptual experiences at the margin of attention which may pass unnoticed until they are made focal. In the case of hypnagogic imagery we encountered good evidence that it can be overlooked for a very long time even by those who subsequently come to realize that they have the experience frequently, or even regularly. On one occasion a subject who was taking part in other experiments assisted me in a preliminary analysis of some completed hypnagogic questionnaires. She expressed herself as interested in, and surprised by, these strange phenomena. Some days later she returned with the information that on the night following she had had a hypnagogic image. Moreover, she then recognized that she had them regularly, often nightly. A psychologist colleague has recently become alerted to hypnagogic imagery, and now experiences them. He told me "I was taken by surprise . . . and then noticed visual faces at the rate of about one every three seconds . . . I was hoping to have them again, and I've looked for them every evening." His strong impression is of previously having had the imagery, and overlooking it. I suspect that in hypnagogic imagery, as in dreaming, we may be dealing with recallers and nonrecallers, rather than imagers and nonimagers. False negatives seem to occur by a process of ignoring what one is not alerted to notice, as well as from emotional blockage. In other cases, including people fully aware of having the imagery, emotion may be strong: the content can be highly disturbing and frightening.

A defining feature of hypnagogic imagery is its marked autonomy, in the sense in which this term is used by Gordon (1949; 1962). It comes of its own accord, can be original and surprising in content, and neither its appearance nor its content is subject to volitional control. In this the imagery resembles the more typical kinds of dreams and hallucinations. When questioned about how the imagery differed from ordinary memory imagery, our own subjects tended to stress this quality of autonomy. Johannes Müller (1848) reports the many conversations he had with an interested Goethe whom he told that he "had no voluntary power over either the production of these images or their changes of form [p. 1395]." In one study Lorna Simpson and I investigated how our subjects knew they were awake and not asleep when having the images. The commonest response was of being able to have other perceptions, e.g., take part in a conversation, while imaging. Others included being able to open the eyes, close them, and continue with the visual imagery. It may be noted that hypnagogic imagery may occur open-eyed in a darkened room, as well as close-eyed.

The perceptual-like quality of these experiences can produce strange behavior even in the sophisticated. The half belief that the imagery is real, and the transient conviction that one is tuned into some mystical and otherworldly "reality" both occur. Confusions of the imagery with reality are also common. The autonomy of the imagery can even create very real problems of adjustment: in visual hypnagogic imagery one feels oneself very much a spectator. To illustrate from a recent experience of my own, hypnagogically I "saw" a group of people, and they were doing nobody any harm; then suddenly a strange man turned up, pulled out a gun, and shot them. Although I was in a sense the "author" of the imagery I felt, and felt very strongly, it was none of my doing: my reaction was one of indignation. Another problem arose on a subsequent, more recent occasion. In reality I have in my office a tank of tropical fish which includes a lively Siamese Fighting Fish (*Betta splendens*). In my hypnagogic image I was "working with" this tank and the fish in question "jumped from the top of the tank and lost itself behind a nearby filing cabinet." In my image a distressed me was just about to "scramble around on the floor and look for it" when I returned to full wakefulness. I was awake and elsewhere, but the fish was "still behind the filing cabinet" and I felt highly responsible with the feeling of obligation that I ought again to drift off towards sleep in order to conduct the imagery "rescue" operation. Fortunately, reality prevailed and I told my wife about it instead. She, for her part, admitted to feeling upset about agreeing to my dream image of me "grovelling around, and ruining my suit behind a dusty filing cabinet, looking for a fish!" In psychosis there are many ways in which autonomous imagery can provide considerable problems of adjustment by its intrusions into perceptual life. Detailed examination of hypnagogic imagery provides opportunity for study of some strikingly similar kinds of intrusion. Perhaps, to paraphrase Jung's remark about psychosis and dreamlife, the schizophrenic resembles in certain respects a hypnagogic imager trying to adjust to a waking world.

As we have seen, hypnagogic imagery is not necessarily visual. The William James "tactile hallucination" discussed earlier could be classified as hypnagogic rather than hallucinatory. My own collection includes hypnagogic tastes, temperature imagery, pains, and electric shocks together with tactile imagery from many subjects. Composite imagery involving two or more sense modes may occur. Confusions with reality are common in these nonvisual other modes. Thus in the case of the auditory imagery, very many subjects reported actions such as getting up to answer the telephone, going downstairs to turn off the radio, or leaving bed to investigate the voices "heard." If lack of insight is to be taken as a criterion for distinguishing hallucination from other imagery phenomena, then—particularly in the case of the nonvisual modes with hypnagogic imagery—this distinction becomes hard to maintain.

Leaning (1925) concludes her scholarly study of hypnagogic imagery by inclining towards a supernatural explanation for it. Others may prefer to interpret the phenomena naturalistically, despite its content. This can, on occasion, be frightening by any standards. One of our subjects reported "I see skeleton figures, firstly very thin, then very fat. They appear alternately . . . I see this very often." Many subjects, sometimes open-eyed and in their darkened bedroom, reported ghostlike apparitions. Hobbes was in advance of his superstitious day and age in maintaining a naturalistic interpretation. Interesting is the fact that contemporary twentieth-century people also report imagery that could well provide subject matter for beliefs in witches, and frightening supernatural beings. We have argued elsewhere (McKellar & Simpson, 1954) that, in accord with Skinner's theory of superstitious behavior, the coincidence of an impressive hypnagogic image with an emotionally important event could well provide potent subject matter for superstition. Psychotic patients sometimes report hypnagogic imagery, and on occasion like nonpsychotics, may interpret them in a matter-of-fact way. Belief systems, whether delusory, naturalistic, or occult-oriented are all important. There is reason to suspect that appropriate imagery can, and does, provide subject matter for psychotic interpretations in terms of delusional systems. Recently a colleague told me about one of his patients whose case notes recorded "hallucinated." Following his investigation the "hallucinations" in question proved to be standard hypnagogic images. Superstition, psychosis, the night terrors of children, and the need to reassure people about the wide range of normal subjective phenomena: all these are areas of importance which justify fuller study of this interesting category of imagery.

Related Imagery Phenomena

The term "hypnopompic imagery" was introduced by F. W. H. Myers to distinguish from hypnagogic imagery the type which occurs "at the moment when slumber is departing." Myers interprets hypnopompic imagery in these terms: "a figure which has formed part of a dream continues to be seen as a hallucination for some moments after waking [F. W. H. Myers 1892, p. 335]." If this distinction is maintained then hypnopompic imagery provides perhaps even more striking confusions between reality and fantasy. Many of our subjects reported imaging sequences like "waking up, washing, dressing, and beginning the events to the day." Elsewhere I have described how a young wife hypnagogically "got up and made breakfast for her husband" who was leaving on a journey early that morning. Subsequently, she in fact woke up and he, having had to make his own breakfast, was kissing her goodbye (McKellar, 1968, p. 106). Because of the circumstances of sleep we might expect reported hypnopompic imagery to be rarer than hypnagogic. Data from two investigations support this. Owens (1963) found an incidence of 51% for hypnopompic, and 77% for hypnagogic. A comparative study of my own yielded 21% for hypnopompic, and 63%, for the same group, for hypnagogic (McKellar, 1957). Both studies refer to incidence in the sense of having experienced at least one such image, and both relate to young adults.

In both the hypnagogic and hypnopompic states body image disturbances can occur. The person concerned has the impression that his body, or one of its members, has grown or shrunk in size, or become in some way distorted. I have no incidence figures to report, but the experience is certainly common, and also one that may give rise to anxiety, fear, and on occasion terror. Forbes (1949) coined the term "dream scintillations" for successions of images which resemble those of the hypnagogic and hypnopompic states but occur at other times. Horowitz (1970) distinguishes them from these two other categories of imagery, associates them with the physical stress which usually precedes them, and suggests that dream scintillations may be more common than the research literature indicates. In investigations of the hypnagogic kinds of imagery I have encountered individuals who report that they have remarkably similar imagery, which occurs to them close-eyed when fully wake. Some of the phenomena mentioned by Galton (1883) appear to be of this kind, and in this area more work of describing, distinguishing and naming is clearly called for.

An additional experience of the hypnopompic state merits mention, and has received attention from such investigators as Mintz (1948), Craik (1966), and Singer (1966). This involves the oddities of speech, or subvocal thought, which may accompany the process of waking up, and which strongly resemble schizophrenic utterances. Mintz examined these resemblances to schizophrenia in some detail. The phenomenon in question—my favorite is the young woman who awoke murmuring "put the pink pajamas in the salad"—may be more related to drowsiness than imagery. Singer, however, inclines to the view that the speech, or subvocal verbalizations, represent a commentary stimulated by previous dream images. Elsewhere, I have discussed these phenomena more fully (McKellar, 1968) and in the absence of established terminology suggested the label "hypnopompic speech."

Synaesthetic Imagery

Sir Francis Galton has sometimes been assessed as responible for the discovery of synaesthesia, though Galton himself refers to numerous earlier studies. Galton (1883) refers to the association of visual imagery for color with sound, chromaesthesia, in the case of the brothers Nussbaumer published in 1873. He also instances a study by Bleuler and Lehmann which tabulated 62 cases. Chromaesthesia, however, represents one special case among the many possibilities of synaesthesia. These other types may be specified by use of a simple convention (Simpson & McKellar, 1955). Using this we may define synaesthesia as imagery of one sense mode closely associated with sensations of another sense mode. Thus, employing two hyphenated words, visual imagery of color and shape accompanying auditory perception would be labeled *visual–auditory synaesthesia*. This is clearly the commonest type: for example, in a study where synaesthesia was reported by 39 individuals, or 21% of a group of Aberdeen university students, all cases were of this type (McKellar, 1968). Similarly, Karwoski and Odbert (1938) studied regular color–music synaesthesia, and reported an incidence of 13% in Dartmouth College students. Visual–auditory synaesthesia was reported by Hofmann when he first discovered by ingestion, the hallucinogenic properties of lysergic acid diethylamide. Passing cars provided auditory experiences which translated themselves into visual images, and kaleidoscopic changes of shape and color.

With the use of the two-word convention as a tool which aids precision, we may examine other possible kinds of synaesthesia. The first of the two words is taken to specify the imagery, and the second the sensation. Thus, the common visual–auditory form differs from the much rarer *auditory—visual synaesthesia* in which auditory imagery accompanies a visual sensation. An interesting case of this involved one man with perfect pitch who used to adjust two moving dials by matching the auditory images he had on observing the movements he visually perceived. This form occurs in the familiar metaphor as when we refer to a "loud tie," or a color combination as "harmonious." Writing of such metaphors M. D. Vernon (1937) suggests the possibility that some linguistic utterances that have become conventionally accepted originated with naturally synaesthetic people describing their own synaesthetic imagery. Among the rarer forms of true synaesthesia, where we have definite evidence of cross-modal imagery-sensory concurrence, *visual–algesic synaesthesia* may be noted. In a very real sense for some people, "pains differ in color." I have encountered cases of children who have resorted to expressing such synaesthesias verbally, and when discouraged have still continued with them as a way of thinking. C. S. Myers (1911) describes a case of *visual–gustatory synaesthesia* in which the subject had color imagery for tastes. It may be noted in passing that the word "orange" refers to both a color and a taste; the same is true of "lemon"; moreover, a raspberry flavored drink colored green would create cognitive dissonance, and few people find blue a drinking or edible color. Luria (1960; 1968) reports many instances of the common visual–auditory synaesthesia in S. V. Shereshevskii, his mnemonist subject, and also of *gustatory–visual* and *gustatory–auditory* types. I have found gustatory–auditory synaesthesia on only one occasion, but in a person who resembled Luria's subject in initially believing that the experience was a universal one.

The interest which Lorna Simpson and I developed in specifying the theoretically possible types of synaesthesia arose during a series of experiments with mescaline and lysergic acid diethylamide. Hallucinogen experiences are often not easily described in words, and some when investigated proved to be the rarer kinds of synaesthesia. It became interesting to examine oddities of mental imagery in terms of their theoretical possibilities. Moreover, equipped with the appropriate set we then proceeded to look for actual instances in our experiments and in the research literature. Figure 1 indicates these theoretical possibilities, and observed instances, as a matrix in which image mode appears on the vertical, and sensory mode on the horizontal (see also McKellar, 1968; Simpson & McKellar, 1955). Some of the cells still remain blank, and would refer to some strange forms of imagery experiences. It will be noted, however, that such oddities as kinaesthetic imagery for smell, and the touch and taste of auditory stimuli, comprise filled cells. Some of the instances are from mescaline or other hallucinogen experiments, and some occurred spontaneously though spon-

Sensory mode

Image mode	V	A	T	G	O	K	Th	Al
V	–	X	X	X	X	X	X	X
A	X	–	X	X	X	X	X	X
T	X	X	–	X	X	X		X
G	X	X	X	–	X	X	X	X
O	X	X	X	X	–	X	X	X
K	X	X	X	X	X	–	X	
Th	X	X		X	X		–	X
Al	X	X	X	X				–

FIG. 1. *Types of synaesthesia. Theoretically possible types of synaesthesia are indicated. Image mode appears on the vertical and sensory mode on the horizontal axis. The* filled *squares comprise the types either observed or reported in the research literature. (V, Visual; A, auditory; T, tactile; G, gustatory; O, olfactory; K, kinaesthetic; Th, thermal; Al, algesic.)*

taneous synaesthesia rarely seems to occur outside the visual–auditory category. Commenting on an earlier, and less complete, version of the accompanying figure, Reese and Lipsitt (1970, p. 248) observe "vision is the only sensory modality that interacts synaesthetically with all other modalities." It would be possible to extend the figure to include interoceptor modes, though I am reluctant to add an additional 16 more cells all waiting, or "shouting" to be filled! Combinations of the auditory and gustatory modes involve complications because of their close sensory interconnections; the same is true of the somatic senses like touch and pain because of perceptual effects resulting from inadequate stimulation of the sense organ.

The previous paragraphs relate to true synaesthesia. From this may be distinguished some interesting uses of language: similes, metaphors, and analogies in which words appropriate to one sense mode are used to refer to another sense mode. Kerr and Pear (1932) suggest that the use of simile and metaphor may perhaps be regarded as the entrance door to synaesthesia. Some synaesthetic metaphors have become conventionalized: colors may be "warm" or "cool" and some color combinations involve "discord"; Simonides was described as "honey tongued"; and some people make "acid remarks." The tasting of wines provides a happy hunting ground for such metaphors. By only a slight effort we can glean some meaning from other synaesthetic utterances as when "Filigree in Sound" is used as the title of a book about Indian music, or when a speaker is assessed as having "a well-manicured voice." Art and literary critics often resort to synaesthetic similes as when one wrote "Rembrandt's paintings seem to roar, and stamp, and pound, while Klee's whisper a soliloquy." Some synaesthetic metaphors represent hostility in the form of wit as when a psychologist colleague once referred to television as "chewing gum for the eyes." Other synaesthetic expressions occur in those interesting utterances that take place in haste or under stress, as when I recently heard someone utter the conventional demand for silence "shsh" meaning "stop doing that"; on another occasion the same individual referred to lukewarm water as "just off white."

Both synaesthetic utterances and true synaesthesia have invited a variety of theoretical explanations which emphasize, respectively, associative learning and regression. I myself suspect that two somewhat different forms of synaesthesia, associative and regressive, occur. Thus a former psychologist colleague experienced a kind of olfactory–auditory synaesthesia, strong olfactory image of the smell of leather when he heard certain waltz tunes. This he explained in terms of associative learning: past experience of these tunes in the atmosphere of a skating rink. By contrast are some of the synaesthesias which occur with hallucinogenic substances. Through a slow process of learning the adult has built up conventions about the sensory information he recognizes as visual, auditory, tactile, etc. At an earlier stage of development the child may not have established these conventions about the various sensory channels, and the regressed adult—in reacting synaesthetically—reveals similar reactions. Yet again quite complex intersensory phenomena may be involved, and of a quite fundamental kind, as is suggested by one of his experiments that Schiller (1935) refers to with tantalizing brevity. Schiller reports that humans respond to musk as having a "bright," and indole as having a "dark" impression. In one experiment he trained fish, *Phoxinus laevis,* to choose a bright and lighted chamber, and a second group to choose a dark chamber. Both groups were then given the opportunity to choose between the two chambers, no longer illuminated, but flavored with the two scents. Their choices were in accord with their previous lighted and unlighted training. Through experiments of this kind we may be able to establish evidence that synaesthetic responses occur lower in the phylogenetic scale than man; perhaps synaesthesia has evolutionary value.

Hallucinogens

Hallucination and imagery have clearly played their part in the magic and witchcraft of earlier times. The association of plants with both folk medicine and the supernatural has often been a close one. Narcotic fumes accompanied the divinations of the oracles of Greece; the mysteries of Elusis began with the taking of a potion; and the witches' brew together with the witches' ointment figure in mediaeval times (Seligman, 1948). In explaining naturalistically many of both the more usual, and the more unusual, features of mediaeval witchcraft Barnett (1965) contends that pharmacology provides a firm basis. Nor should we confine our thinking about witchcraft to the past. There are plenty of areas of culture in the twentieth century where a supernatural view of events, rather than explanations in terms of psychology and pharmacology, is accepted and usual. Writing as a botanist, but one prepared to use the evidence of anthropology, Schultes (1966) estimates that there may be about 800,000 species of plants. During many thousands of years of history, many of these have been consumed by man. Some have been retained as foods, some have proved of medicinal use, and some have been closely associated with supernatural rites. Consider, for example, henbane (*Hyocyamus niger*) used in Greece and Rome to encourage the gift of prophesy; its active principle scopolamine is now isolated and known to be hallucinogenic. Working as a mycologist, Wasson

(1967) has spent some years on the problem of identifying the mysterious plant, Soma, used and deified about 3000 years ago by tribes who inhabited the Indus valley. In 1967 Wasson reached the conclusion that this was probably the fly agaric mushroom (*Amanita muscaria*). Its active principle is the alkaloid, muscarine, though other psychoactive alkaloids are also present. A legend of the Kiowa Indians attributes the discovery of the peyote cactus to a hungry Indian mother who fed it to herself and her child.

The psychological effects of the three most emphasized hallucinogens— mescaline, lysergic acid diethylamide, and psilocybin—appear to be remarkably similar.[1] Synaesthesia and body image disturbances occur in all three. Perhaps more impressive than actual hallucination, are the upsurges of sequences of visual images that have often been likened to the imagery of the hypnagogic state. The resemblances, independently noted by many investigators, have been discussed in detail in an earlier paper (Ardis & McKellar, 1956). From the important investigations of Klüver (e.g., Klüver, 1942) have emerged what he called "form constants," regularities he found in a variety of hallucinatory experiences resulting from different agencies. These included "funnel . . . cone . . . tunnel," "honeycomb designs," "lattices," "spirals," and "tapestry." Klüver instances include such other phenomena of hallucinatory imagery as diplopia, polyopia, micropsia, and macropsia. One very characteristic phenomenon produced by the hallucinogens is hallucinatory distortion of real objects: for example, the faces of the experimenters may seem to pulsate about their real shapes. Auditory hallucinations and images seem to be rare. They are not easy to produce experimentally, though an exception is provided by Steinberg (1956) who, in her work with nitrous oxide, found auditory hallucinations to be more common than visual.

The accuracy of the term "hallucinogen" has been questioned. Some of the phenomena, which can be regular and highly specific, are better described as something other than hallucinations. It is apparent from the research literature, as from experiments I have conducted or have been a subject in, that stress must be placed on the vivid, autonomous imagery

[1] Known to the Aztecs as "peyotl," "teonanacatl," and "ololouqui" these played an important part in Aztec religious ceremonies. Scientific issues around these, and other hallucinogens, are somewhat complex. At least 13 alkaloids have been extracted from the peyote cactus (*Lophophoria williamsii*), and there are other botanical sources of mescaline. The mushroom *Psilocybe mexicana* is one of many hallucinogenic mushrooms, and has yielded both psilocybin and psilocyn. Several botanical sources of lysergic acid diethylamide have been found. A very large number of hallucinogens remain to be discovered for science: the methods of the ethnobotanist, as exemplified by the work of Schultes, involve using folklore and the study of native customs as guides to such discoveries.

which occurs close-eyed. This may be strikingly beautiful, or otherwise absorbing. Such imagery is consistently reported from the earliest experiments with mescaline of Prentiss and Morgan (1895), and Mitchell (1896), through those of Klüver (1928) and Beringer (1927), and up to contemporary research. Beringer, for instance, (cited Lewin, 1924) refers to "endless passages . . . delightfully colored arabesques . . . fantastic architecture . . . luminescent colors [pp. 104–5]." Actual open-eyed hallucinations, perhaps of patches of floating color, or of lattice patterns on the wall may seem relatively insignificant by contrast with this absorbing imagery. Among the actual hallucinations, or hallucinatory distortions, may occur disturbing experiences. Several of our own subjects, during lunch, experienced movement like that of insects, of the crumbs of the bread they were eating. Others encountered what we nicknamed "crawling print" when asked to read from the pages of a book. One, when required to compare the lengths of lines that were presented in pairs was quite unable to do this. Her polyopic reactions made it impossible for her to decide from among the many lines she "saw" which two we meant. Moreover, all these lines were constantly moving, or "marching" as she preferred to call it with a mescaline-enriched vocabulary. There are, of course, many other phenomena not strictly relevant to the study of imagery itself, including oddities of thinking, personality changes, and disturbing persecutory reactions reminiscent of paranoid patients. Moreover, the importance of individual differences and different reactions of the same individual on different occasions cannot be overestimated. Yet the regularities of the imagery phenomena are impressive in their stability, and such upsurges of visual imagery rarely seem to be absent. In laboratory experiments synthetic versions of the hallucinogen are usually employed. Potential investigators should be warned that a history of jaundice and previous liver troubles is a strong counter indication: such a person should never take part as a subject.

It may be noted that in Indian ceremonies with, for instance, the mescal buttons of the peyote cactus, lack of chemical purity may be a factor. Even synthetic mescaline sulfate is itself emetic and nauseating in its effects. William James, it will be remembered, using mescal buttons was violently sick for 24 hours and saw nothing. In the Indian peyote ceremonies of the American southwest, vomiting is a regular and accepted part of the overnight experience, after which the participants settle down to their visions (personal communication, based on Indian informants, reported to me by the anthropologist, Dr. Robin Fox). The importance of situational factors as an influence on hallucinogen experiences merits special emphasis: clearly a scientific experiment in the clinical atmosphere of a medical school, and the taking of raw peyote as part of an Indian ceremony can result both in different experiences, and different interpretations. Of interest is the important contribution of the anthropologist Castaneda (1970) who gives a detailed account of his own experiences with peyote, the psilocybe mushroom, and another hallucinogen—datura—in a context of mystical American Indian teaching.

On occasion during hallucinogen experiences, losses of insight may occur, though for much of the time the subject is in every sense "awake." Loss of insight may be partial in certain interesting ways. In normal states the individual is usually able to maintain a distinction between metaphorical and literal utterances. He is capable of dealing with higher, as well as lower, levels of abstraction. While experiencing ordinary autonomous imagery, he may say that he feels "as if" someone else were putting thoughts into his head. In a time-estimation experiment, he may say that he feels as if there were two kinds of time (felt impressions of time passed may seem to diverge from judgments as to how much time has actually passed). Under the influence of a hallucinogen what has been elsewhere described (McKellar, 1957) as a "loss of the as if" experience is common. He may decide that people are "putting thoughts into" his head; he may experience his reduced coordination as "subjection to new and strange gravitational forces"; or he may talk about "two kinds of time, yours and mine." In addition, he may lose himself in preoccupation with the "reality" of his visual experiences. All these instances taken relate to actual instances observed with mescaline. The ability to retain the sense of the "as if" is an important characteristic of sanity; its loss represents one of the ways in which hallucinogenic model psychoses resemble both the natural psychoses, and dreaming. This "loss of the as if" phenomenon has been discussed in fuller detail, together with other aspects of hallucinogenic phenomena, elsewhere (McKellar, 1957).

Immediate Memory
Imagery

Personally, I should find subjective mental life very different without those transient storages of visual information that follow visual perception. Daily from this imagery I "read" telephone numbers, using the immediate memory image rather than the previous glimpse of the telephone book. Such imagery involves precision and accuracy, and numerous psychologists have distinguished it as in some way different from aftersensations which Neisser (1967) describes as "the senile vestiges of once-useful processes [p. 146]." The experiments of Sperling (1960), Mackworth (1962), and others have recently focused much attention on these phenomena. Neisser (1967) introduced the term "transient iconic memory" for them, and he distinguished such iconic storage from the process of "integration of the snapshots" of long term visual memory. Richardson (1969) discusses them as "memory after images" and refers to Ward's 1883 *Encyclopaedia Brittanica* article for an early account of them. He adds that such imagery may not be as common as Ward implies. Such imagery can prove a nuisance in research involving the tachistoscope. Whatever terminology we use there is abundant introspective evidence, and now (since Sperling's ingenious studies) firm experimental evidence for these phenomena. Research cited by Neisser indicates that the duration of the imagery—originally on Sperling's data thought to last about a second—depends on the lightness or darkness of the exposure field, and can vary from about 1 to 5 seconds. These phenomena do not appear in Holt's (1964) list, and merit differentiation from those we know as aftersensations (or afterimages).

Aftersensations

Aftersensations belong more strictly with eigenlichten, phosphenes and other sensory phenomena. They are but distant relatives of the primary family we know as "Imagery"; they are peripheral both in this sense and in terms of their close association with the after effects of activity of the sense organ. Some early experiments of my own involved exposure of subjects to colored light of known spectral hue followed by darkness. These convinced me of two things: first, that aftersensations do not necessarily follow the text book as regards their hue, and sequences of hues; and second, that dark adaptation increases the duration and intensity of aftersensations (Ferguson & McKellar, 1944). Subsequent research accords with this dark adaptation finding, but suggests an optimal period of about 5 minutes dark adaptation. Aftersensations are covered in an extensive literature which will not be reviewed in detail here; they have recently been discussed in relation to imagery by Richardson (1969). It is well established that they are influenced by such factors as area of the retina stimulated, brightness and distance of the projection field, and the duration and intensity of the previous stimulus. Helmholtz (1909) has much to say about aftersensations. He reports, for example, that both those of the positive and negative kind follow eye movements, and with fixation of a stationary point they remain immobile. They may be viewed as sensory rather than imagery phenomena. Despite their resemblance to percepts I have recently been much interested in observing that aftersensations do not obey the principles of horizontal–vertical constancy that reign in perception. In orientation, as in other respects, the movement and orientation of the sense organ is all important. Determinants of duration and sequences of aftersensations are discussed by Helmholtz, and to his observations may be added the ample evidence available today that chemical agencies, such as the hallucinogens, will affect both vividness and duration. Although the primarily sensory and peripheral nature of the experiences is established, various investigators have suggested that aftersensations and eigenlichten may play some part in dreaming, hallucination, and other kinds of imagery. Klüver (1942), for instance, in his discussion of hallucinatory imagery argues that although various theories have stressed one or other of these, physiological and psychological, peripheral and central, sensory and motor, and cortical and subcortical factors all have their importance.

The previous discussion has dealt with the following phenomena: dreams, memory images, hallucinations, hypnagogic and hypnopompic imagery, synaesthetic imagery, imagery induced by hallucinogen drugs, immediate memory imagery, and aftersensations. There are many unnamed variants of the imaging process not discussed such as the "cinomatographic" imagery of a highly autonomous kind which some people experience on closing their eyes. In a series of letters the late Miss Enid Blyton described to me how she used such imagery in the composition of her books and plays. In one such letter she explained how she would "hear" a character make a joke and while recording this on her typewriter she would laugh and say to herself: "Well, I couldn't have thought of that myself in a hundred years" and then think "Well, who *did* think of it?" Other phenomena include eidetic imagery, body image phenomena, diagram forms (to use T. H. Pear's useful term for number forms, date forms, and their variants). Although I have argued elsewhere (McKellar, 1957) that because of their presumably perceptual origins, all three are in a sense "memory imagery" it may on occasion be helpful to distinguish memory from imagination images, and both from the forms of image used in directed thinking (e.g., the mental blackboards some people use in doing calculations). The possession of vivid and stable memory imagery may be a necessary condition, but it is not itself a sufficient condition for the ability to think and reason visually. As regards these types of imagery, it is interesting to note the development of newer types of tests of imagery which require performance rather than self rating (e.g., Sheehan, 1966). Similarly Juhasz (1969), influenced by the work of Piaget and Inhelder of 1966 has sought to solve the problem of "observing" imagery by using tasks which require the subject not to talk, but to perform. The Juhasz test involves other modes like taste and smell as well as vision and hearing.

A-Thinking and
R-Thinking

Two different forms of the category of "thinking" may be differentiated. This differentiation may be of some value in a concluding examination of the relations of imaging to thinking and to the socially useful products of human thought. Sometimes people think with strict attention to logical inference, and are constrained by considerations of relevance and evidence. Much human thought is of other kinds. Evidence is available daily that prelogical kinds of thinking of the kind which Piaget has studied in childhood can, and do, persist into adult life. In considering daydreams and myths, dreams and superstitions, Eugene Bleuler (e.g., Bleuler, 1912) coined and used the term "autism." Autism is for Bleuler "the unreality function [p. 429]" and shows "disregard (for) reality and logic [p. 436]." It resorts to clang associations, false identifications, and confusions of symbols with reality. Bleuler also repeatedly contrasts autism with the forms of "realistic thinking" which "regulate our relations with the outside world [p. 420]." Autism for Bleuler may be a fleeting episode lasting a few seconds, may last longer in dreams, or may fill a lifetime as in schizophrenia. Following Bleuler, I have found the term autistic thinking, or more briefly A-thinking a convenient one to categorise many of the phenomena discussed. With A-thinking may be contrasted R-thinking which proceeds in terms of logical relations and evidence. Thus we may say that sensory deprivation and hallucinogen experiments increase A-thinking and reduce R-thinking. Hypnagogic imagery involves a transient invasion of partial wakefulness by A-thinking processes; a hallucinatory psychosis is an overwhelming of consciousness by such processes. Freud in his use of the terms primary and secondary processes makes a somewhat parallel distinction, and some investigators (e.g., Singer, 1966) have preferred this formulation.

Elsewhere, I have been concerned with the range of phenomena of A-thinking with which this book deals (McKellar, 1957; 1963; 1968). In particular I have argued that socially useful thought products tend to result from an interaction between A-thinking and R-thinking. The processes of A-thinking have been likened to authorship and its raw materials, while those of R-thinking resemble those of editorship (McKellar, 1963). We have seen that dreaming and hypnagogic imagery can provide raw materials for works of art, and scientific thought products as well. Yet some interplay with R-thinking is also necesary. To instance the well-known occasion when two experiences of hypnagogic imagery provided Kékulé with the clues for his benzene ring theory, two things may be noted. First, the images occurred to a trained scientist well equipped with relevant information; second, Kékulé spent the later part of the night working out the consequences of the hypothesis. In short, although A-thinking occurred it was preceded and followed by R-thinking. Again, on another notable occasion when, while stepping onto a bus, Poincaré had his moment of insight about Fuschian functions. As Arieti (1966) reminds us, Poincaré had worked intensively for the previous 14 days, accumulating relevant information. Some people find A-thinking difficult: they are either not alerted to, or reject too easily their own A-thinking. Receptivity to such processes seems to be a necessary factor in many cases of originality. Thurstone (1952) even goes so far as to suggest that the creatively talented individual may be distinguished by a certain amount of "gullibility." And some people find the R-thinking component the more difficult: the labor by which the raw materials are transmuted into a work of art, or science, or otherwise useful thought product.

The functioning of A-thinking and R-thinking is illustrated by an incident which occurred in one of our mescaline experiments (McKellar, 1957, pp. 100–101). During this the subject was given the proverb "people who live in glass houses . . ." and asked to explain it. After a while she found herself thinking about the "mote and beam" parable, but was reluctant to speak because of her awareness of a typical piece of A-thinking. The intervening processes involved the sequence: the proverb—glass—crystal—palace—castle—moat—mote—mote and beam parable. Realizing the possible illogicality she thought again and now reached the same result by a chain of R-thinking reasoning. The sequence was: the proverb—throwing stones—retaliation—unless unassailable don't throw stones—one rarely is unassailable—don't throw stones—the parable. The subject found herself able to link the proverb and the parable in two separate ways: by A-thinking association, and R-thinking reasoning. When we think and reason we inhibit the irrelevant A-thinking intrusions and R-thinking becomes focal; at other times, as Silberer (1909) when writing of the hypnagogic state, puts it "the third consciousness switches to an easier form of mental functioning [pp. 198–199]."

A-thinking is characteristically associative. But rather than rely too exclusively on the omnibus word "association" we can look at it in another way also. A-thinking accords with what Arieti has called "paleologic" as opposed to "logic." This is influenced by the Von Domarus principle in that the paleologician is prepared to accept identifications merely on the basis of a predicate-in-common. For him "similarity becomes identity [Arieti, 1966]." Since predicates-in-common may be numerous some strange identifications can and do occur in dreams, hypnagogic imagery, and hallucinogen experiences. In human mental life primitive forms of thinking may accompany sophisticated ones. For some of our purposes we may reject irrelevant A-thinking in a purely conscious way, or we may reject it more automatically as the Würzberg psychologists have helped us to understand. In sleep, paleological processes may dominate, and in full wakefulness we may readily overlook them. Education has its requirements, and a teacher or lecturer may demand that the class pay attention and not let their minds wander. During a dull lecture such admonitions may be fruitless and imagination imagery may intervene. As Silberer (1909) says of the drowsy state "such 'picture thinking' requires less effort than the usual kind [p. 198]." Certain cultural, and cultural-temporal conditions likewise may favor either kind of process: one society may accept A-thinking including hallucination, while another is intolerant of even moderate flights of fantasy. Hallucinogen and sensory deprivation experiments foster a flow of imagery, and, perhaps subsequently, those who have taken part are more able to notice and remain alerted to processes that have been there all the time. Writing of thought more generally, Stekel (1924) describes it as "a stream in which only the surface is visible; orchestral music of which only the melody is audible [p. 314]." At all times there is much of our own mental life that we can overlook, and narrowness of the viewpoint and methods of psychology has on occasion fostered such blindness. It is admittedly an oversimplification to refer to the complex interplay of processes that occur purely in terms of A-thinking and R-thinking. Yet, these seem to represent at least two of the important categories, and may thus represent a beginning.

References

Ardis, J. A., & McKellar, P. Hypnagogic imagery and mescaline. *Journal of Mental Science*, 1956, **102**, 22–29.

Arieti, S. Creativity and its cultivation. In S. Arieti (Ed.), *American handbook of psychiatry*. Vol. 3. New York: Basic Books, 1966.

Aristotle. *The works of Aristotle translated into English*. W. D. Ross (Ed.). Oxford: Clarendon Press, 1931.

Aserinsky, E., & Kleitman, N. Regularly occurring periods of eye motility and concomitant phenomena during sleep. *Science*, 1953, **118**, 273–274.

Barnett, B. Witchcraft, psychopathology and hallucinations. *British Journal of Psychiatry*, 1965, **111**, 474.

Beringer, K. *Der Meskalinrauch*. Berlin: Springer, 1927.

Bleuler, E. Autistic thinking. (Orig. publ. 1912.) In D. Rapaport, (Ed.), *Organization and pathology of thought*. New York: Columbia Univ. Press, 1951. Pp. 399–437.

Carey, N. Factors in the mental processes of school children. *British Journal of Psychology*, 1915, **7**, 453–490.

Castaneda, C. *The teachings of Don Juan: A Yaqui way of knowledge*. Harmondsworth: Penguin, 1970.

Craik, K. (Collected writings) In S. L. Sherwood (Ed.), *The nature of psychology: A selection of papers, essays and other writings of the late Kenneth J. W. Craik.* Cambridge Univ. Press, 1966.

Dement, W., & Kleitman, N. The relation of eye movement during sleep to dream activity. *Journal of Experimental Psychology,* 1957, **53,** 339–346.

Ebbinghaus, H. *Memory.* (Orig. Publ. 1885.) (Translated by H. A. Ruger and C. E. Bussenius.) New York: Teachers College, 1913.

Ferguson, H. H., & McKellar, P. The influence of chromatic light stimulation on the subsequent rate of perception under conditions of low illumination. *British Journal of Psychology,* 1944, **34,** 81–88.

Forbes, A. Dream scintillations. *Psychosomatic Medicine,* 1949, **11,** 160–162.

Freud, S. *The interpretation of dreams.* (Orig. publ. 1900.) (Translated by J. Strachey.) Vol. 4–5. *Standard edition complete psychological works of Sigmund Freud.* London: Hogarth, 1953.

Galton, F. Statistics of mental imagery. *Mind,* 1880, **19,** 301–318.

Galton, F. *Inquiries into human faculty.* (Orig. publ. 1883.) London: Macmillan (Everyman), 1907.

Gordon, R. An investigation into some of the factors that favour the formation of stereotyped images. *British Journal of Psychology,* 1949, **39,** 156–167.

Gordon, R. Stereotypy of imagery and belief as an ego defence. *British Journal of Psychology,* 1962. No. 34. Pp. 1–96.

Hanawalt, N. G. Recurrent images. *American Journal of Psychology,* 1954, **67,** 170–174.

Helmholtz, H. *Physiological optics.* Vol. 1. (Translated from 3rd. German ed., 1909.) New York: Dover, 1962.

Hobbes, T. *Leviathan.* (Edition of 1651). London: Oxford Univ. Press (Clarendon), 1909.

Holt, R. R. Imagery: The return of the ostracized. *American Psychologist,* 1964, **19,** 254–264.

Horowitz, M. J. *Image formation and cognition.* New York: Appleton, 1970.

James, W. *Varieties of religious experience.* (Orig. publ. 1902.) London: Longmans, Green, 1928.

Juhasz, J. Imagination and post-mechanical man. *Bennington Review,* 1969, **3,** 24–33.

Karwoski, T. F., & Odbert, H. S. Color music. *Psychological Monographs,* 1938, **50,** (Whole No. 2). Pp. 60–274.

Kerr, M., & Pear, T. H. Synaesthetic factors in judging the voice. *British Journal of Psychology,* 1932, **23,** 167–170.

Klüver, H. *Mescal: The divine plant and its psychological effects.* London: Routledge & Kegan Paul, 1928.

Klüver, H. Mechanisms of hallucinations. In Q. McNemar & M. A. Merrill (Eds.), *Studies in personality in honour of Lewis M. Terman.* New York: McGraw-Hill, 1942. Pp. 175–207.

Ladd, G. T. Contributions to the psychology of visual dreams. *Mind,* 1892, **1,** 299–300.

Leaning, F. E. An introductory study of hypnagogic phenomena. *Proceedings of the Society for Psychical Research,* 1925, **35,** 289–403.

Lewin, L. *Phantastica: Narcotic and stimulating drugs.* (Orig. publ. 1924.) London: Routledge & Kegan Paul, 1964.

Luria, A. R. Memory and the structure of mental processes. *Problems of Psychology,* 1960 (English translation of the journal publ. by Pergamon), **1,** 81–94.

Luria, A. R. *The mind of a mnemonist.* New York: Basic Books, 1968.

McKellar, P. *Imagination and thinking.* New York: Basic Books, 1957.

McKellar, P. Three aspects of the psychology of originality in human thinking. *British Journal of Aesthetics,* 1963, **3,** 129–147.

McKellar, P. The investigation of mental images. *Penguin Science Survey* (Biological Sciences), 1965, 79–94. (a)

McKellar, P. Thinking, remembering and imagining. In J. G. Howells (Ed.). *Modern perspectives in child psychiatry.* Edinburgh: Oliver & Boyd, 1965. Pp. 170–191. (b)

McKellar, P. *Experience and behaviour.* Harmondsworth: Penguin, 1968.

McKellar, P., Marks, D. F., & Barron, B. F. The mnemonic walk and visual imagery differences. In preparation, 1972.

McKellar, P., & Simpson, L. Between wakefulness and sleep: Hypnagogic imagery. *British Journal of Psychology,* 1954, **45,** 266–276.

McKellar, P., & Tonn, H. Negative hallucination, dissociation, and the five stamps experiment. *British Journal of Social Psychiatry,* 1967, **1,** 260–270.

Mackworth, J. F. The visual image and the memory trace. *Canadian Journal of Psychology,* 1962, **16,** 55–59.

Medlicott, R. W. An inquiry into the significance of hallucinations with special reference to their occurrence in the sane. *International Journal of Medicine,* 1958, **171,** 664–677.

Menninger, K. *The human mind.* New York: Knopf, 1949.

Mintz, A. Schizophrenic speech and sleepy speech. *Journal of Abnormal and Social Psychology,* 1948, **43,** 548–549.

Mitchell, S. W. The effects of anhalonium lewinii (the mescal button). *British Medical Journal,* 1896, **2,** 1625–1628.

Müller, J. *The physiology of the senses.* London: Taylor, 1848.

Myers, C. S. A case of synaesthesia. *British Journal of Psychology,* 1911, **4,** 228–238.

Myers, F. W. H. The subliminal consciousness. *Proceedings of the Society for Psychical Research,* 1892, **8,** 333–411.

Neisser, U. *Cognitive psychology.* New York: Appleton, 1967.

Oswald, I. *Sleeping and waking.* Amsterdam: Elesvier, 1962.

Owens, C. A study of mental imagery. Unpublished doctoral thesis, University of Liverpool, 1963.

Perky, C. W. An experimental study of imagination. *American Journal of Psychology,* 1910, **21,** 422–452.

Plato. *The dialogues of Plato.* B. Jowett (Ed.). New York: Random House, 1937.

Prentiss, D. W., & Morgan, F. P. Anhalonium lewinii (mescal buttons). *Therapeutic Gazette.* (3rd ser.), 1895, **11,** 577–585.

Rapaport, D. (Ed.) *Organization and pathology of thought.* New York: Columbia Univ. Press, 1951.

Rawcliffe, D. H. *The psychology of the occult.* London: Ridgeway, 1952.

Reese, H. W., & Lipsitt, L. P. *Experimental child psychology.* New York: Academic Press, 1970.

Richardson, A. *Mental imagery.* London: Routledge & Kegan Paul, 1969.

Sanford, N. Will psychologists study human problems? *American Psychologist,* 1965, **20,** 192–202.

Sarbin, T. R., & Juhasz, J. B. The historical background of the concept of hallucination. *Journal of the History of the Behavioural Sciences,* 1967, **3,** 339–358.

Schiller, P. Interplay of different senses in perception. *British Journal of Psychology,* 1935, **25**, 465–469.

Schultes, R. E. The search for new natural hallucinogens. *Lloydia,* 1966, **29**, 293–308.

Seligman, K. *The history of magic.* New York: Pantheon, 1948.

Sheehan, P. W. Accuracy and vividness of visual images. *Perceptual and Motor Skills,* 1966, **23**, 391–398.

Sidgwick, H. A. Report on the census of hallucinations. *Proceedings of the Society for Psychical Research,* 1894, **26**, 25–422.

Silberer, H. Report on a method of eliciting and observing certain symbolic hallucination-phenomena (Orig. publ., 1909.) In Rapaport (Ed.), *Organization and pathology of thought.* New York: Columbia Univ. Press, 1951. Pp. 195–207.

Simpson, L., & McKellar, P. Types of synaesthesia. *Journal of Mental Science,* 1955, **100**, 143–147.

Singer, J. L. *Daydreaming: An introduction to the experimental study of inner experience.* New York: Random House, 1966.

Sperling, G. The information available in brief visual presentations. *Psychological Monographs,* 1960, 74, (Whole No. 11).

Steinberg, H. Abnormal phenomena induced by nitrous oxide. *British Journal of Psychology,* 1956, **47**, 183–194.

Stekel, W. The polyphony of thought. (Orig. publ., 1924.) In D. Rapaport, (Ed.), *Organization and pathology of thought.* New York: Columbia Univ. Press, 1951. Pp. 311–314.

Thurstone, L. L. Creative talent. In L. L. Thurstone (Ed.), *Applications of Psychology.* New York: Harper, 1952. Pp. 18–37.

Vernon, M. D. *Visual perception.* London: Cambridge University Press, 1937.

Wasson, R. G. Fly agaric and man. In D. H. Efron *et al.* (Eds.), *Ethnopharmacologic search for psychoactive drugs.* Washington D.C.: National Institute of Mental Health, 1967.

Yates, F. A. *The art of memory* (Orig. publ., 1966.) Harmondsworth: Penguin, 1969.

3 ROSEMARY GORDON

A VERY PRIVATE
WORLD

Every man walks around in the world enveloped in a carapace of his own images. Their presence enables him to structure and to organize the multiplicity of the objects and the stimuli which throng upon him; but their presence also distorts, so no one ever perceives exactly what there is in this world or all there is in this world. Yet, man lives in his carapace as naively, innocently, and unwittingly as does the fish in his water, the bird in the air, or the baby in the womb.

This, then is my thesis, my view of the mental life of man. It is what I will examine and argue in this chapter.

When I speak of "an image" I speak of the perception of forms, or colors, or sounds, or smells, or movements, or tastes in the absence of an actual external stimulus which could have caused such perception. This does not mean that such external stimuli did not present themselves in the past nor that the image is independent of such past experience. But it does mean that at the time of the perception of the image no such stimulus is present.

The word "image" usually conjures up the idea of the perception of forms or colors; that is, of visual impressions. But I shall adhere to the definition of an image which is current in psychology, that is, of a perception in the absence of an external stimulus, irrespective of the sensory mode in which this perception occurs. Although the term "image" has been used in this sense for a long time, certainly already by Francis Galton in the nineteenth century, the man-in-the-street and even students from disciplines other than psychology continue to limit the term to visual experience only.

Richardson (1969) has suggested that one of the subjective criteria we use to characterize an image is the "selfconscious awareness" of the presence of such an image. This particular criterion, however, seems to me very questionable. Indeed the principal substance of my paper challenges this very suggestion; for I believe that the carapace of images within which we live and observe the world around us is so very private a world, not only as regards the knowledge other persons can have of it, but also as regards the conscious awareness of the experiencing subject.

The Complexity and
Elusiveness of Imagery

I have recently had a personal experience of how elusive imagery can be while yet creating feelings of great certainty and conviction: England went "decimal" and the English pound sterling ceased to be made up of 20 shillings; instead it became a unit composed of 100 subunits, the pence. I felt most uneasy about this change and thought that I should have much difficulty in adjusting to it. Yet I have traveled a great deal in countries that use the decimal system. As a psychologist and analyst I am, of course, used to introspection and indeed regard it as my professional duty to engage in it, often and efficiently. I also know about form patterns for days of the week, months of the year, and the problem of synaesthesia in general; and I have been aware for many years that I have a distinct form pattern for months of the year. And yet it took quite a bit of time and selfsearching before I suddenly understood the origin of my confusion and difficulty with the decimalized pound sterling. I discovered that besides a months-of-the-year pattern I also have a number pattern and that this number pattern prevents the easy translation of a pound made up of 20 units to a pound made up of 100 units. For while the number 20 is almost due north from my 0, 100 is west–north–west and a long way in a due westerly direction from my 20. Consequently I felt that I had to, as it were, "heave" the pound a long way to the left (westerly) in order to relate it to the new subunits.

But to draw on less directly personal impressions: several times in recent months I have happened to overhear acrimonious discussions between musicians, between visual artists, between painters and their students, between film-makers, designers, etc. In fact these discussions and the heated emotional temperature that they had provoked led me to the thoughts and reflections which prompted this chapter.

Why is it, I asked myself, that these musicians, artists, and film-makers can get so angry with one another? Why is it that each of them is so very certain that the way he perceives and reacts to a particular art form or to a particular work in that art form is the only possible, the only "correct" and reasonable way of reacting to it? Why is it that he becomes so impatient, so intolerant, so uncomprehending of his colleagues if their responses differ from his own? Often so kind and gentle, he reacts in this situation as if the other person was quite particularly obstinate and obstructive or just insensitive and dimwitted. Whence this arrogant certainty?

Examining all this with some care has led me to reevaluate the importance, the privacy and the exclusiveness of the image world in which each one of us has his being.

It is really very natural that our image-worlds should be so different one from the other. For there are indeed a great many variables that characterize images. Quite apart from the incalculable differences of content there are so many other qualities that mark a person's imagery that it is well possible that even now we have only discovered a few of them. Calling some of them to mind may illustrate my point: Of prime importance is the predominant mode, visual or auditory or other, of a person's imagery; this was in fact the first quality of imagery to be investigated systematically because it is the most evident and most easily observed and described. In the modern psychology laboratory Francis Galton's discovery of the different image types, based on predominance of one or other sense modality (Galton, 1907) may seem a well-assimilated piece of knowledge. The ramifications of this knowledge and its practical consequences are really not yet fully understood. This is clear from some of the work McKellar (1963) has done when he investigated several professional groups in terms of the predominant sense-modality of imagery possessed by individuals in these groups and contrasted this with the image type clearly required for skill and efficiency in these different professions. This difficulty in visualizing is undoubtedly a handicap for a student of medicine or architecture; while for the playwright, and certainly for the film-maker or theatre director, both visual and auditory imagery is essential.

But sense modality itself is only a first and crude distinction. The student of architecture may indeed be primarily a visual type; yet if he cannot visualize three-dimensional space, or if he cannot translate a two-dimensional percept—the drawing—into a three-dimensional image he is surely at a disadvantage. But where do teachers in schools of medicine or architecture explore the type of imagery of their students or candidates?

The world must seem to be a very different place to someone whose imagery tends to be fixed and rigid when compared with that of a person living in the same place and at the same time but whose imagery is fluid and flexible. My own research (Gordon, 1962) and those of others have indicated that the world of the former tends to be furnished with objects and experiences that date far back into his past; because they remain relatively uncontaminated by later events they are often essentially oversimplified, stereotyped or even quite out-of-date, so that the world of the latter may seem to belong to quite a different epoch. But if flexibility is extreme there may be a quality of rootlessness and so all in such a world may come to seem insufficiently defined. Hudson (1966) has found a certain correlation between flexible and rigid image types on the one hand, and the tendency toward divergent and convergent thinking on the other. He postulates, very plausibly I think, that extreme flexibility as well as extreme rigidity are the result of ego defensive maneuvers against anxiety, but which themselves create more anxiety by conjuring up a world which appears either as too permanent, so that one feels incapable of affecting it, or else as so effervescent that one thinks that nothing in it is solid and reliable.

There is also likely to be a correlation between rigid imagery and difficulty in controlling imagery, while flexible imagery usually goes with the capacity to control it easily. This in itself must affect the world a person thinks he inhabits and above all his idea of himself as a free and autonomous being. The dimension of activity-passivity, which clearly colors and is colored by both rigid–flexible and autonomous-controlled imagery types, is most likely further affected by whether a person's imagery is predominantly reconstructive or else constructive and inventive. Here, perhaps, lies one of the differences that distinguish an artist from his critic, the appreciator from the performer, the chronicler of history from the maker of history.

Then there is the world of the synaesthetic which is vastly different from the world of the nonsynaesthetic. The nonsynaesthetic may marvel, fear, or envy the sort of world in which lived Shereshevski, a synaesthetic discovered by Professor Luria (1968), where visual images evoked sounds and tastes, and tones were mixed up with colors and touch sensations. An exciting world indeed, but also a very confusing one.

Yet the effectiveness of all these variables depends undoubtedly on the key variable which is, of course, the degree of strength, definiteness, and intensity of the images. This may vary from one sense modality to the other and between rigid and flexible, controlled and autonomous, and constructive and reconstructive imagery. It may also vary for the same individual at different ages, in different situations and contexts and naturally, when drunk or sober, asleep or awake, drugged or straight, conscious or unconscious.

My enumeration and brief description of some of these variables which characterize imagery may already convey an idea of the pervasiveness of imagery and of the enormous and possible differences that mark it.

It is this pervasiveness which makes it that imagery is so secretly ever-present and which makes introspection so exceedingly difficult. Indeed no one can ever be fully aware of all the images that are activated in his mind at any particular time and in any particular situation. The web is closely woven, the strands do not easily tease apart; and so we are rarely aware that our perception of the world filters through to us across this diffracting medium. A look at some of the art forms and the effect they have had on the perception of the general public can serve as amusing demonstrations, using an interpersonal model as a parallel of intrapersonal events. I am thinking, for instance, of those charming sketches of London and Oxford which were drawn by a Chinese painter, Chiang Yee, (1944) before the second world war. Chiang Yee looked at the world through eyes whose vision had clearly been trained by Chinese painters and artists, so that his perception of England transformed it from the England that we "see" into something that, to our eyes, looks very much more like China. Or fingering through a book on the history of opera and glancing at the scenery and costumes designed at different times it strikes one as remarkable how much the costumes bear the mark of the epoch of the creator of the costumes rather than of the period to which the story of the opera assigns it. In his reflections on civilization Kenneth Clark (1969) pointed out how western man was led by the poems and paintings of the artists of the romantic movement, who worshipped nature, to notice and to see the naturalness of the natural world—fields, flowers, trees, animals, cottages. But the "Nature" of the romantics is clearly very different from the "Nature" of, for instance, thirteenth- and fourteenth-century painters who represented plants and trees and animals as witnesses and participants in the sacred drama of life. Or, if one prefers, one can think of the more immediate experience of fashion and how one's own tastes are all too readily shifted and manipulated; what appears attractive one year strikes one as frumpish the next; and the "outrages" become, in no time, "attractive commonplaces."

Thus, though personal and private and difficult to introspect or to communicate, this, our carapace of images, is nevertheless open to influence and change. And so it serves to ensure for imagery both privacy and encounter, cohesiveness and change, concreteness and vivacity. Something of this paradoxical quality of imagery is perhaps best described by the Constructivist, Naum Gabo (1949), when he writes that:

> With indefatigable perseverance man is constructing his life, giving a concrete and neatly-shaped image to that which is supposed to be unknown and which he alone, through his constructions, does constantly let be known. He creates

the images of his world, he corrects them and he changes them in the course of years, of centuries. To that end he utilizes great plants, intricate laboratories, given to him with life; the laboratory of his senses and the laboratory of his mind; and through them he invents, construes and constructs ways and means in the form of images for his orientation in this world of his. (Pp. 72–73)

But as man's lifestyle becomes more complex, as time and space shrink before the advance of technology, and social mobility makes for the constant and frequent meeting of strangers, the development and expansion of consciousness becomes an urgent need. We now must explore this world of images that we, each one of us, inhabits. We each need to know more of the nature and qualities of our images: it will reveal more of ourselves to ourselves. We need to know this better so that we understand the difficulties we can have when we try to speak to one another. We need to know it so that we can stop and think whenever we find that we have become unaccountably puzzled or impatient with someone else's apparent incomprehension of what, to us, seems so clear and obvious. We need to know of it when we come up against unexpected obstacles in various learning situations, be they seen from the position of the teacher or the taught. But, above all, we need to know it in order to enrich our discourse with one another and help us to enjoy rather than resent the exuberance and variety of the image world, which, even if we cannot always convey it, can yet serve as a stimulus to one another. In this then lies the excitement of this search.

Image Modality and
the Artist

As I have mentioned earlier, I personally stumbled into this area of thought, question, and contemplation because my curiosity had been roused by the "arrogant certainty" I had met among so many of my artist friends, for whom I had particular respect and regard. I began to talk to them alone and individually.

One stage designer admitted that he felt anger, impatience, and resentment if the workmen did not find it easy to execute his designs without much verbal elaboration from him, but he had failed to recognize that the reason for his and their difficulties was due to their different image worlds; each of them had taken his own image world absolutely for granted and as selfevident; each of them had looked at the project through the lenses of his own images, ignoring that they were personal, not shared. Naturally, this caused upsets betwen the designer and the men who were to execute his designs. But it created even more difficulty between designer and director. The designer and his men are concerned with one sense-modality only: and the hierarchical structure between them is simple and one-way only. But with the director things are much more complicated: the director's skill depends on several sense modalities; the visual one may not be the most dominant or the most differentiated. The director may, for instance, be deficient in the capacity to transpose on to the larger stage what he sees as a model. In that case he may not be able to imagine away the evident cardboard effect of the model which would in fact be obliterated on the stage. Deficiency in this particular image sense may thus obstruct his capacity to "play," to "make believe," to let the image override the percept, a capacity which he must surely possess in other areas, for without it he could not be a director at all. Probably precisely because he can and does "play" with ease most times while at work he cannot believe that, when certain special sense modalities are involved, he cannot count on it. Similar difficulties may arise when a director can image form and color but not form, color, and movement so that he cannot envisage the joint effect of scenery and costumes. It makes matters worse that the hierarchical order between designer and director is very much more complex and that their interaction has more of a two-way quality.

As another example, I remember observing an artist while he was trying to teach painting to people who had very little experience with it, and some of whom had very little talent. He himself was particularly interested in three-dimensionality, in the rendering of space onto the canvas. The fact that some of the students either failed to "perceive" the spatiality of space or else that, even if they could perceive it, they found it anything but easy and natural to transpose it into a two-dimensional picture left him most puzzled and rather irritated.

A second stage designer described to me how some of his workmen know very quickly exactly what he wants. When this happens it seems to him miraculous and more like a telepathic than a "natural" communication.

While listening to this second designer I thought of my own experience as an analyst, and how often I had recognized, after several sessions with a patient, that the image that had formed itself in my mind while listening to his description of a dream was in fact remarkably accurate in all sorts of minor details, so that my image of his dream seemed identical with his dream.

In the case of the musicians the disputes which were, if anything, more heated seemed to rest on simpler differences. It is possible that as the theatre is essentially a multimedia world those who work in it are, if not explicitly at least implicitly, aware of it and more used to communicating with people possessing different image types. What struck me with musicians was the importance of their early musical background. Those who had much early experience of opera tended to react to music with much visualization; those who had come to it through listening to, or learning, instrumental music were frequently quite outraged by the "visualizers." Perhaps precisely because music is the least representational of the art forms, the most difficult to "verbalize," musicians may be less used to intercommunication, and hence each one is less prepared to allow for the variety of possible individual reactions.

Listening to these artists express so much conviction and certainty reminded me of the famous—or infamous—dispute between psychologists at the turn of the last and the beginning of our own twentieth century concerning the existence of imageless thought. The debate on whether thought could function unaided and unaccompanied by images was fierce and bitter and public. It clearly stirred deep-seated passions and concerns. Even now one can understand why *Freud* should have unleashed such violent reactions in an age that was only slowly emerging from under the long and voluminous Victorian skirts; for his discoveries of pansexuality and the nature of the unconscious challenged man's entire conception of himself. But the ubiquity of imagery seems even today of much less vital or portentous concern. Whence then the enraged nature of this dispute? Is it not likely that if a man is completely enveloped in the mantle of his images, any disagreement with the world as he "sees" it leads him to suspect either tomfoolery or else ill-will?

I am, of course, not the first to suggest that different modes of imaging might be the cause of much intolerance, misunderstanding, and lack of communication. Richardson (1969) does in fact summarize some of the ideas and hypotheses concerning this very question. He himself has carried out much research in which he compared "visualizers" and "verbalizers" for the degree of idiosyncrasy in the connotative meanings attached to words. Most thought and most research done so far in this area has in fact tended to concentrate on these two image types and to hold fast to the differences and possible difficulties of studying them. Yet, we have so far explored only the very tip of this particular iceberg; for the variables involved are infinitely more numerous and subtle, as I have tried to suggest earlier; and my conversations with different artists have confirmed and elaborated this. Clearly, this is an important and also a fascinating field; penetrating further into it may help us discover some of the obstacles to both inter- and intrapersonal communication and so enable us to devise methods to clear them away.

Imagery and
Psychotherapy

Not only the psychologist, but also the psychotherapist has thought much and proposed much concerning the character of images, their function, their possible roots, and their development. Ensconced in the silence of his consulting room, patiently listening, pondering, and responding to another person who gropes to discover and make sense of his own inner world, the therapist has the opportunity to encounter and to observe, as if under a microscope, the world of imagery, both his own and that of his patient. In fact, since the analytic process is but little concerned with discursive thought, the principal medium through which analyst and patient relate to each other is, inevitably, feelings, sensations, and images.

In the context of analysis, images function above all as a means of clothing and giving form to conscious and unconscious experiences: analysts have, therefore, been tempted to consider the psyche as consisting essentially of images which picture all the vital activities, including unconscious and even archaic fantasies. Jung (1923), for instance, believed that any particular image is only indirectly related to the perception of the external object, because it depends so much on unconscious fantasy activity; nevertheless, he also recognized that every image is after all compounded of the "most varied material coming from the most varied sources [p. 554]"; that it is the "concentrated expression of the total psychic situation, not merely, nor even preeminently of unconscious contents pure and simple [p. 555]"; that it is really the "expression equally of the unconscious as of the conscious situation of the moment [p. 555]"; and that it is not "a conglomerate, but an integral product with its own autonomous purpose [p. 555]." He defined an image as a "representation" and postulated that psychic processes can only become consciously apprehended contents if they can be represented in the form of an image. Such a definition seems to me, however, so all-embracing that it fluffs the distinction between the image on the one side and sensation, perception, and emotion on the other.

I am drawing primarily on Jung to represent the thinking of dynamic psychologists concerning the nature of images because, unlike most other analysts, Jung had been involved with experimental psychology. This interest enabled him to concern himself and to discuss concepts like "imagery" in a way that makes sense to the academic psychologist, even if there are disagreements. Jung almost certainly voices correctly how analysts and therapists on the basis of their clinical experience conceive of the nature and role of an image. Thus they would say that, though it draws on perceptions of the external world and on sensations of the internal world, any particular image at any particular point in time expresses the subject's conscious and unconscious preoccupations and attitudes at that point in time. To give an example, a patient described at different times images of his analyst that occurred during weekends, either in wakefulness or when about to fall asleep. Sometimes he saw his analyst surrounded by a vast congregation of relatives and so quite inaccessible to him; sometimes he saw her sitting close by while he was lying on the couch; sometimes he saw her offering him a cup of coffee; sometimes he saw her as taller than in reality; sometimes she looked severe and threatening; sometimes old and frail; and once he imagined her as examining his work, appraising it critically, ridiculing his efforts. Through the recurring image of his analyst this patient revealed his general preoccupations at work and in relationships and his hopes, his fears, his longings and his apprehensions concerning his analyst. Clearly, from the way he described them, his images were primarily visual; only the coffee-drinking episode involved gustatory qualities and in the case of the last-mentioned image, when the analyst turned examiner, he "heard" her comments.

In my experience as an analyst I have never met any patient who did not sooner or later dream and describe his dreams, though many do at first protest that either they have no dreams at all, or that they are quite unable to remember them. A dream is, of course, a sequence of images *par excellence*. I have only once had a patient who insisted that he had no imagery at all. He was a very intelligent and intellectual man who found it difficult to tolerate the open and unstructured situation of analysis. Whenever he arrived at new barracks, so he explained, he would first look at the standing orders. He feared to relate to his own feelings, needs and fantasies, for in that realm lay a great deal of sadness, confusion, and passive longings. He relied on knowledge and intellect in order to seduce and to control the people in his world. He was primarily a verbalizer; his claim that he had no imagery, at least no visual imagery at all, was very soon shown to be a matter of conscious awareness rather than of fact. Even in the first session he recounted several dreams which contained strong and even three-dimensional visual imagery. For instance:

> There is a house door but it is really a wall. Yet it can swivel on a central rod. But if you swing out the wall then it will block the road outside which is worrying. But after a time he realizes that there is in fact a space between the house and the street, so the wall/door could swing out without blocking the road.

Clearly, this dream depends on quite sophisticated visual imagery and is in fact inconceivable without it. Interestingly enough this patient described, soon after starting analysis, that he thought of himself as being just a head and a lower body; he could not really feel that there was something in the middle, that he had a thorax. Although he maintained, with much conviction, that he personally had no imagery, yet I knew that in his professional work he had made it a point to postulate that man perceives the world through a pattern of images and ideas. In other words, intellectually he supported the sort of thesis which I am proposing here. The reason for the absence of a personal experience of imagery began to clarify later as the analysis continued. One day he admitted that he feared that if he imagined an object or a person in a sick or damaged state then he would "freeze" that person or object for ever, as in a photograph, and so prevent any healing or repair. As there had been a good deal of physical illness in his family while he was a child, the image of the sick parent came to be feared as magically "making" this sickness, or at least preventing the unmaking of the sickness. It is obvious that this patient suffered from a considerable split between his personal experience and his intellectual knowledge. What was so surprising, in view of this theoretical thinking, was the strength of his conviction that the absence of imagery was in his case a fact and not a question of awareness. As the analysis progressed this split was reduced, and the patient came gradually to experience and to describe images rich in content, variety, sense modalities, in intensity, in associative links, and in affect and meaningfulness. And he came to experience himself less as a thinking machine and more as a human person. And his life style expanded.

As for the work of the analyst, this would be quite impossible if he could not know and experience his own images. Clearly, his skill and efficacy must in part depend on how extensive and how differentiated is his range of imagery. Where his capacity to image is limited, there he fails to comprehend with ease the experience of his patient; in fact, he may be tempted to disregard, disbelieve or dismiss those experiences of his patient which his own imaginal disposition does not allow him to share. For example, an analyst without any auditory imagery and sensitivity is excluded from a vast part of the experienced world of his musical patient. But if he himself possesses a rich imaginal life then he can help to give impetus to the imaginal development of his patient.

Nearly all psychotherapeutic procedures depend in greater or smaller measure on the presence of imagery. All of them depend on the capacity to recall and to recreate persons and situations, real or fantasied, which are a part, and often a crucial part, of a person's inner world, though they are not concretely present in the therapeutic session. Only through the image can they be actualized and "animated" and so brought into relationship with each other, with the person of the therapist and with the here and now of the patient's actual life circumstances. It may even be argued that the different types of therapy can be distinguished from one another in terms of the extension and the comprehensiveness of the patient's imaginal worlds which they mobilize in order that these worlds shall interact and mutually interpenetrate each other. Behavior therapy, for instance, limits itself on the whole to evoke just that particular situation which handicaps a patient's sense of well-being, having assumed the character of either a phobia or an addiction. Psychotherapy, on the other hand, and even more so analysis seek to develop, to animate, or to reanimate as wide a range of imaginal experience as is possible for any particular individual. To this end the therapist attends to every sign of a potential resource and draws it within the orbit of therapeutic work. Leaving aside here his concern with those forces that actively obstruct the imaginal process—anxious fantasies like those of the patient whom I have just described, conflicts and contradictions between the various intrapsychic structures, and complexes, so that all effort is spent on avoidance, denial, and repression—the therapist draws upon dreams and waking fantasies; he listens carefully to the language of his patient, the metaphors he chooses, the analogies he makes, the elaborations, the vividness or the flatness with which he describes the various facets of his life and the sensitivity or obtuseness with which he perceives and relates to the variety of his experiences. For in many of these will he find the germ of a richer and wider and more intense imaginal development.

Experience with patients in psychotherapy has in fact shown that considerable changes to the image system can and do occur. Rigidities lessen, control increases. If intensity is excessive images become obsessive or else assume hallucinatory qualities. It is then the therapist's job to help limit their impact which he may do by helping the patient toward understanding that these images express a part of himself which he has tried to disown, or by leading him to attend to the wider spectrum of his psychic functioning, which must also include sensation, perception and all the intricacies of interpersonal relationships. Other patients, however, may present an image world which is essentially flat and impoverished. Such patients tend to complain that they feel empty, insubstantial, unreal, a meaningless bundle of discontinuous bits and pieces. When their image world comes to life and when they begin to relate to it, they often have, for the first time, a pleasant sense of possessing a separate and unique identity, and that they are in truth less vulnerable and helpless than they used to feel.

The Function of Imagery

But where and in what, it may be asked, do I see the function and the value of imagery? The first thing that needs to be said is that the capacity to image appears to be a more or less universal phenomenon in man and possibly also in animals. The work of the ethologists and their observations and speculations regarding the "innate releasing mechanism" (IRM) suggests that there is in most animals something in the nature of an image or a potential image whose function it is to trigger off an instinctual response when the appropriate stimulus presents itself. Although the ethologists do not commit themselves as regards the actual nature of the IRM and therefore do not actually speak about an "image," the way the IRM behaves, its apparent role to help select from the environment that perceptual configuration which matches the innate behavior pattern does suggest to me that we are here dealing with what is, or is closely related to, an image: it seems to have qualities which affect the perceptual processes, and which help to select from the multiplicity of objects in the world those that are relevant to species-specific behavior.

This aid to selection is the most basic and most important function of the image: it structures and creates some order that is meaningful and relevant to our physical and our psychological needs out of the terrifying chaos that is the world of sight, sound, smell, taste, touch, and movement. Through the image we sift, select, and render down to a manageable scale both the world of the objects and our own human experience. Furthermore, with the help of images we learn to span time and so relate the objects and experiences from the past to the objects and experiences in the present; this then assists abstraction and classification. Again, by using images of the past as a bridge to the present, man is better able to tolerate discomforts and frustrations in the present for the sake of a future satisfaction. Thus, when an infant manages to survive the mother's temporary absence without panic he is probably enabled to do this because images of the mother's face and body have begun to form themselves and with these he can comfort himself while she is not actually present. The image also "fixes" an experience and so helps to preserve this experience for future use and reference. In the form of an image, experience retains some of the original vivacity and effect.

The Freudian concept of primary and secondary psychic process and the recent reevaluation of the value and functon of these two processes is instructive and relevant. The primary process has been described by Freud as the original and more primitive process, functioning under the aegis of the Pleasure Principle and being the characteristic mode of functioning of the unconscious part of the psyche; its essential mode is "thing-representation," that is, imagery. It stands opposed to the secondary process, which characterizes consciousness, is governed by the Reality Principle and uses verbalization as its mode. It has been thought that the primary process would slowly recede and become obsolete in the course of growth and development, since being unburdened by the demands of reality, time, order, and logical considerations, it seemed to have little place in the world of the grownups. Rycroft (1962), however, has recently argued that the functioning of the primary process is far from redundant in adult life. Since its concern is the expression and communication of feeling it remains truly necessary in order to relate a person realistically to objects that have emotional interest. In fact, only if both primary and secondary processes continue to function and remain associated can fantasy engage creatively with external reality, enrich it and make possible the imaginative elaboration of personal relationships so that they can be understood and appreciated.

In individual development the experiencing of images might be regarded as the first beginning of conscious activity, and of the capacity to abstract. It also aids the process of memory. Above all it delivers the infant from the primary and exclusive dependence on sensation, that is from sole dependence on what is immediately and concretely present. One of the consequences of this expansion of psychic activity is the individual's growing capacity to refrain from the immediate enactment of his reactions; instead he will become progressively more able to delay his responses and to bring them instead into relationship with earlier and perhaps more positive experiences of the same person or situation. In other words, through the development of images and hence memory, emotional reactions can become organized and contained in the pattern of the sentiment, which McDougall already in 1923 had described as the normal developmental sequence.

However, imagery, like every other process, can create difficulties which may obstruct an individual's development. Clearly, if images are overdetailed and overdefined they are liable to hinder abstraction and discursive thought. This seemed to be so in the case of a schizophrenic patient whom Arieti (1955) asked to define words. Thus when asked to define the word "book":

> "Book?" she replied. "it depends what book you are referring to." "Table?" "What kind of table? A wooden table, a porcelain table, a surgical table, or a table you want to have a meal on?" "Life? I have to know what life you happen to be referring to—Life magazine or to the sweetheart who can make another individual happy and gay" [p. 211].

Here imagery had become so concrete and so particular that the patient had lost the capacity to think in terms of connotation and instead responded more and more in terms of denotation. Other difficulties obviously occur if imagery is rigid and uncontrolled, as this burdens a person with a bagfull of antiquated and obsolete views of the world; in which case he must either withdraw and isolate himself in order to protect his out-of-date stock, or else he will fall victim to much conflict and confusion.

Thus, whether images function positively and constructively will depend on the degree of control and the degree of fluidity achieved; it will depend on whether they possess optimum vividness; and finally, on whether a person feels actively related to them rather than a passive bystander or even victim.

Imagery and Art

I believe images are the immediate forerunners of what Winnicott (1953) has designated as the first creative act—the making and the loving of the "transitional object," that object, blanket, vest, teddybear, gollywog, etc.—selected from the array of objects in the external world but invested with a very personal and very important part of one's own self. The image, expressing a coordinated meaning of both the sensuous and the inner mental perceptions, is surely closely linked up with man's creative needs and with his activity in the arts.

When we enter upon a discussion of imagery and art we cannot really do so without digressing to consider the processes of imagination and symbolization.

There is, obviously, a direct etymological link between "image" and "imagination." Many writers do in fact use these two terms interchangeably. But I believe that there is a difference which is worth acknowledging. I think of images as separate and individual representations of sensuous and perceptual experience. I think of them as the raw material of imagination, standing to imagination in the same relationship as the individual still picture stands to a moving film. In other words, I regard imagination as a form of dramatization of images, a collection of images which have been brought together and "produced" in association with other mental processes like thought, past experience, and intention. The special abilities upon which imagination depends are likely to come from the preconscious area, that is, that area or "critical threshold of the conscious–unconscious border" which Rugg (1963) has called the "transliminal state." Clearly imagination is unthinkable in the absence of images, for they are its raw material.

Symbolization also depends on the presence of images. Rugg (1963) believes that it is metaphor which connects concept and symbol; Read (1952) has described the symbol as an image plus its mental associations; and he defines the symbol as a throwing together of tangible, visible objects either with each other or with some immaterial or abstract notion. The philosopher Cassirer (1953) ascribes to the image the function of transforming a sense-image into a metaphor image, while Langer's view (1951), which is pertinent to my point, is that in a metaphor the image of the literal meaning acts as the symbol for the figurative meaning. Thus most modern students of the symbol and the symbolic process regard imagery as the essential material without which the process cannot function or even get under way.

As I have hinted earlier in this chapter there can be no social validation of our images, for there is no way of communicating them directly to one another; discursive thought and language are quite unequal to such a task. Nor can any person ever be completely aware of the whole of his own image world, as the psychotherapist knows only too well.

However, through the forms of art man has found a way of breaking the seal that locks him fast into his inner world. Through the arts he has discovered a language which least distorts the original message and which is as closely as possible analogous to the essential nature of the original message. Thus has man found, after all, a way of transmitting to others at least something of his intimate and personal experience, of gaining for it some social validation and of mediating to himself, to his own conscious self, a part of this elusive inner world. This then, I suggest, is the true and primary function of art. Because the need to know, to communicate and to validate is so strong and urgent, art has been made and art has been appreciated throughout the history of man—as far back as we know it—whatever the vicissitudes or repressions man has happened to encounter.

Yet, though it be the most adequate way of giving substance to images, art can never do it perfectly. Art-makers rarely fail to experience disappointment, which sometimes verges on despair, when a work has been finished and completed. For the work never is and never can be the exact match of the internal image in all its qualities and characteristics. This discrepancy between image and artwork ensures that there will never be a final, a last, a definitive work of art; there can be no end and no conclusion. Through the pain of the artist's travail and despair the continuity of art is assured; being a man, the artist cannot escape the burden and the privilege to imagine, to recollect and to feel in forms.

Summary and Conclusion

I have tried to suggest in this chapter that, on the basis of work and research carried out over the last few decades, particularly in the fields of ethology and psychotherapy, imagery seems to be a universal phenomenon in man and most likely also in many animals.

However, there is much diversity of imagery and this is likely to be even greater than our present understanding of it. Alone, the differences in predominant sense modality, in the degree of control and rigidity, and in the definiteness and strength of the images are likely to account for a great many discrepancies between individuals in the experience of their image world. To this must be added the vast disparity of awareness and consciousness of their images between one person and another, and for the same person between one stage of development and another, one sense modality and another, and one area of concern and another.

Being so very pervasive, happening at all levels of consciousness and unconsciousness and being intimately associated with other mental processes such as perception, thinking, and affect, imagery is not reliably amenable to introspection.

On the other hand, it has become progressively clearer that imagery serves several important biological and psychological functions: primarily it helps the organism to arrange the multiplicity of sensory stimuli into meaningful patterns which then make possible the release of instinctional reactions in appropriate situations. As for man, imagery enables him to classify and to abstract, to relate his present perceptions to past experience—which then aids the process of learning and adaptation—and to tolerate present frustrations for the sake of future satisfactions. Finally, imagery is the raw material of man's capacity to imagine and to symbolize. In this last function imagery reveals itself as the basis and the essential origin and reason for man's need to make art. His apparently inexhaustible and, as far as we know, ever present wish to make art seems to rest on man's need to embody and to bear witness to the existence and to the validity of his inner world. It is, as it were, a defiant assertion that this carapace of images is real and essential, that it is complex and varied and that this is his personal experience of reality. The limitations of thought and speech to express and incarnate an individual's inner world guarantees its privacy; it guarantees also man's continuing quest to break that seal of privacy through the making of art, art which Read (1960) has so aptly defined as "the language of Images."

References

Arieti, S. *Interpretation of schizophrenia.* New York: Brunner, 1955.

Cassirer, E. *An essay on man: An introduction to a philosophy of human culture.* New York: Doubleday, 1953.

Clark, K. *Civilisation.* London: BBC & John Murray, 1969.

Gabo, N. On constructive realism. In K. S. Drier, J. J. Sweeney, and N. Gabo (Eds.), *Three lectures on modern art,* New York: Philosophical Library, 1949. (Quoted by H. Read in *Icon and idea.* London: Faber & Faber, 1955, p. 134.)

Galton, F. *Enquiries into human faculty and its development.* London: Dent, 1907.

Gordon, R. *Stereotypy of images and belief as an ego defence.* London: Cambridge University Press, 1962.

Hudson, L. *Contrary imaginations.* London: Penguin, 1966.

Jung, C. G. *Psychological types.* London: Routledge & Kegan Paul, 1923.

Langer, S. *Philosophy in a new key: A study in the symbolism of reason, rite, and art.* New York: Harvard Univ. Press, 1951.

Luria, A. R. *The mind of a mnemonist.* New York: Basic Books, 1968.

McDougall, W. *An outline of psychology.* Boston: Scribner, 1923.

McKellar, P. Three aspects of the Psychology of originality in human thinking. *British Journal of Aesthetics,* 1963, **3,** 129–147.

Read. H. *The philosophy of modern art.* London: Faber & Faber, 1952.

Read, H. *The forms of things unknown.* London: Faber & Faber, 1960.

Richardson, A. *Mental imagery.* London: Routledge & Kegan Paul, 1969.

Rugg, H. O. *Imagination.* New York: Harper, 1963.

Rycroft, C. An observation on the defensive function of schizophrenic thinking and delusion formation. *International Journal of Psycho-analysis,* 1962, **43,** 32–39.

Winnicott, D. W. Transitional objects and transitional phenomena. *International Journal of Psycho-Analysis,* 1953, **34,** 89–97.

Yee, C. *The silent traveller in Oxford.* London: Methuen, 1944.

The Function of Imagery

4
DAVID F. MARKS

INDIVIDUAL DIFFERENCES
IN THE VIVIDNESS OF
VISUAL IMAGERY AND
THEIR EFFECT ON
FUNCTION[1]

Introduction

The role of imagery in cognitive function is one of the oldest and most difficult problems investigated by psychologists. While many scholars, poets, and mnemonists have thrived on their knowledge in this area for over 2000 years (Yates, 1966), psychologists have floundered. One need only glance at the often referred-to section in Woodworth (1938) on so-called "objective tests" of imagery to gain an impression of psychology's failures in this area. If these were truly objective tests one would be forced to conclude that there was really no such thing as imagery! Yet it is highly improbable that even John Broadus Watson was devoid of a dreamlife. No attempt will be made to describe the long history of research on this topic. This has been dealt with elsewhere (see especially Richardson, 1969).

The purpose of this chapter is to describe a selection of recent studies which were designed to answer one very simple question: in what ways does the behavior of a man who states that he has vivid visual imagery differ from that of another who says that his imagery is vague and dim? By "vividness" we mean a combination of clarity and liveliness. The more vivid an image, therefore, the closer it approximates an actual percept.

[1] The author thanks P. Sheehan, P. McKellar, J. B. Juhasz, B. F. Barron, and W. R. Dexter for their helpful comments on an earlier version of this chapter. Special acknowledgment is given to the assistance of Beverley Barron in collecting and analyzing data.

The validity of verbal reports concerning image vividness constitutes a difficult problem since no individual can directly compare his imagery with that of another. It is obviously important to validate verbal reports of image vividness with behavioral data of a nonverbal kind. From this point of view many of the experiments to be described may be thought of as *validation* studies. Typically, in the studies described, two groups of subjects were chosen according to some criterion measure—score on a questionnaire purporting to assess imaging ability; for example, the Betts Questionnaire Upon Mental Imagery (Betts, 1909). Performance of these criterion groups was then compared on a standard cognitive task. On occasion, subjects have been selected on grounds other than purely a questionnaire score, and quality of performance on a task presumed to involve imagery has been taken into account.[2] Throughout this chapter, experimental groups will be referred to by labels which characterize presumed imagery ability, e.g., "good visualizers," "poor imagers," etc. These labels are intended to serve only as mnemonics and in each case are a shorthand expression for a specific set of operations employed to determine subject allocation to the group concerned.

Emphasis in this chapter is on experiment rather than theory and since many of the reported studies are previously unpublished they will be described in some detail. These are dealt with under the headings of "imagery and memory" and "imagery and perception." This dissection of the data is for organizational convenience, however, and should not be taken to imply a proposed division in the function of imagery process. Indeed, some of the data reported in these two sections relate to dependent variables which were measured simultaneously during performance of a single cognitive task. Both these sets of variables relate to functions, one (accuracy of recall) in the field of memory and the other (eye movements) in the field of perception. Responses to imagery are viewed as outputs from a highly integrated information-processing system.

Imagery and Memory

The main point of interest in studies concerned with the role of images in memory has been the question of whether imagery helps or hinders accurate recall. On the whole, Bartlett (1932) viewed imagery as a hin-

[2] A performance test of imaging ability is currently being developed by Juhasz (1969).

drance. He attributed most of the inventions and importations found in repeated reproductions of prose passages to visual imagery and in discussing results from the *Method of Description* Bartlett (1932) states: "the appearance of a visual image is followed by an increase of confidence entirely out of proportion to any objective accuracy that is thereby secured. 'Seeing is believing' in other realms that the direct percept [p. 60]." He also obtained some evidence that visualization produces inaccurate recall of order information.[3]

We should view Bartlett's conclusions with caution, however, since they were based on differences between subjects classified without any strict criterion as "visualizers" and "vocalizers." In addition, his experiments involved relatively delayed recall, 15 or 30 minutes after presentation, with further reproductions being obtained after several weeks or months. In emphasizing the creative nature of imagery, McKellar (1957, p. 23) has drawn attention to the artificiality of the frequently made distinction between "memory" and "imagination" imagery. If we view all images as reconstructions of past percepts then it is not unlikely that accuracy of the reconstruction will diminish as the delay since perception increases. As time passes, more of the image will involve imaginative components made up from bits and pieces of other memories. So-called "memory" images of sufficiently distant events may eventually become wholly "imagination" images, bearing little or no resemblance to the original stimulus. If these ambiguous terms have any usefulness at all, it would be more accurate to think of them as poles of a continuum and Bartlett's studies seem to have involved imagery relatively close to the "imagination" end of the continuum. The experiments to be described here have been largely concerned with the role of imagery in immediate, or nearly immediate, recall.

Experiments on the function of imagery differences in memory will be dealt with in two groups: those concerned with what will be termed the *literal* function of imagery and those concerned with the *associative* function. It is proposed that imagery functions literally when a subject is asked to remember a stimulus pattern by forming an exact mental image of the pattern. However else the stimulus may be encoded, it is assumed that, during retrieval, the subject obtains at least some of the required information directly from the image, *as if the original stimulus were still present.*

---

[3] There have been many such negative findings, e.g., Aveling (1912); Betts (1909); Bowers (1935); Carey (1915); Fernald (1912); Ruger (1910); Thorndike (1907); and Woodworth (1915). A few notable exceptions, in which vivid imagery has actually been observed to have some cognitive utility, are studies by Davis (1932); Ernest & Paivio (1969); Fracker (1908); C. K. Kuhlman (1960); F. Kuhlmann (1907); Sheehan (1966a, 1966b), and Stewart (1965).

Imagery functions associatively when, during or soon after its presentation, a subject is required to form an association between a stimulus and some previously presented stimulus by use of mental imagery. Storage is mediated, at least partially, perhaps entirely, by the image so-formed and, accordingly, *retrieval occurs by decoding from this image.*

Literal Role of Imagery

A series of studies on the literal function of visual imagery has been conducted by Sheehan (1966a, 1966b, 1967b; Sheehan & Neisser, 1969). In contrast to the many negative results in this area (see footnote 3), Sheehan's experiments provide a definite indication that images are a useful source of information in the performance of certain cognitive tasks. For this reason, and also because they provide a point of departure for the writer's own studies, Sheehan's experiments will be discussed in some detail.

Many of Sheehan's studies have employed a task which shall be referred to as the "pattern construction task." The stimuli were patterns made up of geometric forms—triangles, circles, squares, and diamonds. The patterns contained 9, 12, or 16 elemental forms arranged in a square or rectangular matrix and were exposed from a slide projector onto a screen a few feet in front of the subject. The procedure typically ran as follows. During presentation of the stimulus pattern the subject was required to construct a replica of the display using small, appropriately designed, wooden blocks. When a construction had been completed, the stimulus pattern was removed and the subject was switched for a short period (usually 40 seconds) to an incidental task, involving the solution of problems from the Kohs Block Design Test (Kohs, 1927). The subject was then required to reconstruct the pattern, on this occasion from memory. After completing this second construction the subject (depending on the condition he was in) was asked to rate the vividness of his image of the stimulus. Before the next trial began, the subject again worked at an incidental task. The main dependent variables in the pattern construction task were: (1) the number of original responses, i.e., elements in the memory construction but not present in the original displays; (2) the number of errors of location, i.e., the number of elements in the reconstruction which were not in the correct position; (3) inversions of order, i.e., the number of pairwise inversions needed to transform the subject's ordering of elements in his memory construction to that given in his perception construction; and, for certain instruction conditions, (4) mean vividness rating on Betts' 7-point scale of vividness of imagery (Betts, 1909).

In the studies to be described, subjects were allocated to experimental groups on the basis of their score on a shortened form of Betts' Questionnaire Upon Mental Imagery (Betts, 1909). This brief questionnaire (Sheehan, 1967a; also printed in Richardson, 1969) requires vividness ratings along the 7-point scale for 35 items, 5 items for each of 7 modalities. The Sheehan modification of the Betts 150-item questionnaire (to be called the Betts QMI) takes about 10 minutes to administer and total scores from it were found to correlate highly ($r = .92$) with total scores on the complete scale (Sheehan, 1967a, p. 388).

The first three experiments in the series of five studies are described by Sheehan (1966a). In the first study, the effect of different instructions on accuracy of recall was investigated. These instructions were to "image" the design and then to "construct the pattern of your mental picture and nothing else," and to "recall" the design without trying "to evoke any mental image or picture of the pattern." A control condition involved a second presentation of the stimulus before the memory construction was required. Two conditions of stimulus presentation were employed: "prior-analysis," in which each element of the display was presented in turn for 0.5 second prior to the whole display; and "no prior analysis," in which the whole display was presented from the start of the trial. Experimental groups were matched in terms of imagery scores.

Results showed a tendency, under the prior analysis condition, for "image" instructions to produce fewer original responses, fewer errors of element location, and fewer inversions of order than "recall" instructions. Interestingly, when prior analysis was absent, "recall" instructions tended to give the better performance. The double-exposure condition led to significantly more vivid image-ratings and the more complex stimuli were rated as less vivid. Subjects who reported vivid images tended to have lower and less variable error rates than those who reported images that were vague and dim. As a check that the wording of the "image" and "recall" instructions had not artifactually led to these results due to differences in demand characteristics, Sheehan repeated the study and used two "recall" conditions, one emphasizing accuracy and the other placing no constraint on imaging. The "image" instructions again led to superior recall performance.

In a third study, the effect of increased experience with a stimulus pattern was investigated. On the basis of scores obtained prior to the experiment on the *visual* items of the Betts QMI 10 subjects were characterized as "vivid imagers" and 6 subjects as "poor imagers." Ten trials with the same stimulus pattern were run in each session under the "image" condition. The effect of repeated stimulus exposure on the imagery ratings differed strikingly for the two groups. Poor imagers made no significant adjustment in vividness ratings over trials, while the vivid imagers altered their ratings towards the vivid end of the scale. In addition, a between-subjects accuracy effect was observed: the poor imagers showed more errors of location and more original responses than the good imagers on each of the experimental designs.

In the fourth study Sheehan (1967b) tested the hypothesis that vivid and poor imagers adopt different coding strategies during perception of the to-be-remembered material. He suggested that, because vivid imagers encode pictorial stimuli literally, they are able to code directly and therefore more accurately via their mental imagery, even for relatively complex stimulus patterns. Because of their relative inability to code literally however, poor imagers are forced to attempt some form of symbolic encoding resulting in loss of detail during the necessary transformations of the stimulus. On the basis of his studies of the *Method of Picture Writing,* Bartlett (1932) had previously put forward a similar notion: "There is no doubt that the visualizer tends to deal directly with material that is presented to him. He has a greater proportion of signs that are 'directly' or 'simply' remembered than any other person [p. 110]." To test the literal coding hypothesis, Sheehan employed pairs of stimulus displays which varied in their degree of patterning and complexity. Some evidence was obtained that vivid imagers were less affected by the amount of patterning in the stimulus, although the results were somewhat ambiguous. The results on complexity are shown in Table 1.

A comparison of the low and medium complexity levels gave a significant interaction between complexity and imagery type. The relatively high inversion score for vivid imagers on the *simplest* pattern, however, is inconsistent with the notion that less processing of input was required for these subjects. Further data on the important question of how imagery differences may affect stimulus encoding are clearly needed.

TABLE 1

Mean Inversion Score for Vivid and Poor Imagers for Different Levels of Complexity[a]

Complexity	Vivid imagers	Poor imagers
Low	7.25	4.42
Medium	4.50	8.75
High	7.04	7.05

[a] From Sheehan, 1967b.

TABLE 2

Average Vividness Ratings for Images of the Principal Stimulus
Designs as Functions of Instruction, Order, and Experimenter[a]

Experimenter	Order in which instructions were presented	"Recall" instructions	"Image" instructions
E1	Imagery, recall	5.44	5.50
	Recall, imagery	5.28	4.66
E2	Imagery, recall	3.97	5.09
	Recall, imagery	5.00	4.56
Mean		4.92	4.95

[a] From Sheehan and Neisser, 1969.

In the final study using the pattern construction task, Sheehan and Neisser (1969) investigated procedural variables affecting accuracy and the rated vividness of imagery during performance on the pattern-construction task. To investigate experimenter effects, each experimenter conducted a separate experiment and 8 high Betts QMI scorers and 8 low scorers were run in each. Eight stimulus patterns were presented to each subject, 4 under "recall" instructions and 4 under "image" instructions (with order of instruction varied). An interesting variation in procedure was that, after the first 4 trials, a detailed inquiry was conducted into the subject's imagery of the stimulus designs. After the remaining 4 trials were finished, there followed a second inquiry concerning the principal designs, and the subject was then required to reproduce as many as he could of the incidental Kohs designs that he had previously constructed. He then rated the vividness of his imagery of the incidental designs.

Mean vividness ratings for the stimulus designs for the various experimental conditions are shown in Table 2.

The mean vividness value across subjects was only 4.94 ("vague and dim"). Rated vividness was not affected by instructions but there was a striking interaction between the effect of instructions and the order in which they were administered ($p < .001$). Sheehan and Neisser (1969, p. 78) suggest that this resulted from the imagery inquiry between Trials 4 and 5 either because of increased demand characteristics for vivid imagery ratings or increased "interest" of subjects in their imagery. An experimenter-instruction interaction was also observed ($p < .05$) in which E2 produced rather more vivid ratings in the recall condition than E1. This result points to the possible importance of the experimenter's expectancies and biases in determining the extremity of vividness ratings and such experimenter effects are worth further study.

Accuracy of construction did not differ for the vivid and poor imagers, with a correlation between vividness and accuracy across subjects of only .11. Also in contrast to previous studies (Sheehan, 1966a) "image" instructions did not produce more accurate performance than "recall" instructions. The reasons for these discrepancies in results are unclear. Within subjects, however, there was a relation between reported vividness and recall accuracy: designs receiving the highest accuracy scores were rated more vividly than designs receiving lowest accuracy. A final significant result was the correlation of $-.39$ ($p < .025$) obtained across subjects between vividness ratings (high rating meant "less vivid") and the number of incidental patterns correctly recalled. Further studies of the accuracy–vividness relationship for incidental stimulus material are of considerable theoretical interest (see Chapter 7, this volume).

A further study by Sheehan (1966b) examined the relationship between accuracy and vividness of visual images produced by stimuli in the form of single colored squares. After stimulus exposure for 10 seconds, subjects were asked to "reproduce" the mental image of the stimulus with respect to its size, clarity, and luminance. This was done by adjusting the manual controls of an apparatus which varied the three stimulus attributes. When subjects had "matched" their images of the stimulus display, vividness ratings were given. Image settings were found to be underestimates of the stimulus values, but as in many of the other studies, accuracy of reproductions was significantly correlated with image vividness rating.

Sheehan's series of explorations on the role of imagery differences in recall have yielded important results on the effect of a number of task variables. At some risk of oversimplification, the main findings from these studies may be stated as follows: (1) accuracy of recall is correlated *within* subjects with vivid imagery ratings; (2) accuracy of recall is not consistently associated with differences *between* subjects who differ appreciably in the reported vividness of their imagery; (3) increased stimulus experience leads to more vivid imagery ratings for vivid imagers but not for poor imagers; (4) vividness ratings are susceptible to experimenter effects and possibly to variations in demand characteristics; (5) the effect of instructions to "image" and to "recall" is uncertain; (6) there is some evidence that coding strategies of vivid and poor imagers differ; (7) the relationship between imagery and stimulus complexity does not appear to be a simple one.

One intriguing feature of Sheehan's results was their strong support for a *within* subjects effect, but their varying support for a difference in accuracy *between* poor and vivid imagers. Three reasons for this are suggested. First, in the negative instance (Sheehan & Neisser, 1969) the between-subjects comparisons were based on data from subjects selected on the basis of their total score on an imagery questionnaire (Betts QMI) with items relevant to *seven* sensory modalities. While it is true that imagery scores for different modalities intercorrelate quite highly (Betts, 1909), it would seem more appropriate to select subjects according to their scores in the imagery modality most likely to function in the experimental task to be performed. For Sheehan's pattern-construction task the relevant modality would, of course, have been vision. Second, the material to be recalled in Sheehan's studies comprised geometric patterns. While there is little known about image-vividness for different classes of stimuli, it is not unreasonable to assume that vividness will be related to the interest, affect, meaning, and overall level of arousal evoked by a stimulus. Geometric patterns may have relatively low values on these stimulus variables, and differences between vivid and poor images might consequently be less marked than those observed for other, more vital, stimuli (cf. Pear, 1927, p. 8). Third, in all the studies referred to, vividness ratings on each trial were obtained *after* recall. As any subject will tell you, rating the vividness of a mental image is not easy. The task is highly ambiguous, and offers free rein for the subject's interpretation of what the experimenter wants, that is, for demand characteristics to operate (Orne, 1962). One possible cue, among others, to help the subject perceive the meaning of the imagery-rating task is, on any trial, his apparent success at the main task to be performed—the accuracy of recall. His perception of the purpose of the experiment would presumably be based on the naive (although probably correct) assumption that vivid imagery is expected to accompany high accuracy. If this speculation is correct, and artifact is responsible for the effect, we might expect a reduction in correlation between accuracy and vividness-rating within subjects if the rating on a given trial actually *preceded* recall. Under this procedure, an artifactual basis for a within-subjects accuracy-vividness correlation would be removed.[4]

Some account was made of these notions in two studies conducted by the author. These experiments (reported more fully elsewhere—see Marks, 1972a), employed a specially designed questionnaire, the Vividness of Visual Imagery Questionnaire (VVIQ), and a new task, which shall be referred to as the "picture-memory" task.

The VVIQ. This brief, 16-item questionnaire makes use of items borrowed from Betts and other previous investigators together with some new ones. On the whole, items refer to stimuli which are relatively familiar to most people. Each item is rated along a 5-point scale of vividness (Table 3) which was obtained by dropping two response categories, and modifying slightly in other respects, the 7-point scale of Betts (1909).

---

[4] Oswald (1962, p. 80) raises this same criticism of an earlier experiment of Bowers (1931) who also found a significant correlation between vividness and accuracy using the rating-after-recall paradigm.

TABLE 3
The Modified Betts Rating Scale Used in the VVIQ

	Rating
"Perfectly clear and as vivid as normal vision"	1
"Clear and reasonably vivid"	2
"Moderately clear and vivid"	3
"Vague and dim"	4
"No image at all, you only 'know' that you are thinking of the object"	5

On a sample of 68 introductory psychology students, the VVIQ was found to have a test–retest reliability coefficient of .74. The results to be presented suggest that it is a valid discriminator of subjects with good and poor visualizing ability. The items contained in the VVIQ are presented elsewhere (Marks, 1972a).

The Picture-Memory Task. The stimuli employed were pictorial and colored. Half were photographs of sets of 15 unrelated objects, as illustrated in Fig. 1, and the other half, photographs of complete scenes. Typical examples of the latter stimulus displays were a Venice canal, a New York street scene, a group of bathers, a marketplace, and a Turkish pavement scene.

The stimuli were projected as transparencies on to a screen a few feet in front of subjects. Each trial consisted of three stages: presentation (20 seconds), a delay (40 seconds), and questioning (75 seconds). During the first 30 seconds of the delay a backward-counting procedure was employed. This allowed time for after-images to disappear and backward-counting (in threes) provided an effective technique for preventing rehearsal (cf. Peterson & Peterson, 1959). After the delay the first of five questions was asked. Questions were asked at the rate of one every 15 seconds. To illustrate the type of questions asked, those employed for the stimulus in Fig. 1 were as follows:

1. What color was the woman's hat:
   yellow and red, white and red, or *yellow and white?*
2. Was the very center picture showing a:
   cross, star, or *asterisk?*
3. What was immediately below the letter "M":
   sunglasses, knife, or *cow?*
4. Did the bottom picture show a:
   shoe-brush, tooth-brush, or *hair-brush?*
5. How many pieces were on the chessboard:
   8, 18, or *28?*

FIG. 1.   Typical stimulus display used in the picture-memory task (schematic).

Subjects chose one answer from the three alternatives provided. The main dependent variable for this task was the total number of errors.

In the first study, the VVIQ was administered to 74 introductory psychology students. On the basis of total scores on the VVIQ, the 18 lowest scorers (mean rating = 1.64) and the 18 highest scorers (mean rating = 3.25) were selected to form two experimental groups: "good visualizers" and "poor visualizers," respectively. Nine females and nine males were placed in each group. The experiment was conducted in two large group sessions with subjects sitting an average distance of about 15 feet from the stimulus projection area of 6 × 4 feet. After two practice trials,

subjects performed 14 experimental trials. Mean number of errors for the
four categories of subject are given in Table 4.

Analysis of variance showed that both imagery ($p < .01$) and sex
($p < .05$) were significant effects. The best performances in the picture
memory task were those of the good visualizing female and the worst performances, those of the poor visualizing male.

A second investigation repeated the experiment under slightly different
but more controlled conditions. Viewing conditions, for example, were less
taxing and the number of experimental trials was reduced to 10. In a
10-second interval *prior* to questioning subjects were asked to rate the
vividness of their visual image of the stimulus display along the 5-point scale
of Table 3.

The subjects tested were aged 16–18 years and selected from a total
of 116 young people who had completed the VVIQ. All subjects were
from top streams of local secondary schools and had satisfied New Zealand
University entrance requirements. Eight of the lowest VVIQ scorers in the
sample (mean rating = 1.53) and 8 of the highest scorers (mean rating = 3.15) took part in the study. Results replicated the previous set of
findings at higher levels of significance (for the imagery effect, $p < .005$,
and for the sex effect, $p < .025$). The difference in performance between
the two groups was larger in this study, the poor visualizers making 36%
more errors than the good visualizers. In contrast to the Sheehan and
Neisser (1969) data, accuracy differed significantly *between* groups in
both these studies. Also, the accuracy result in the second study was related
to imagery-vividness differences between groups during the experimental
task. Greater accuracy went with more vivid imagery.

What of the *within* groups correlation between vividness and accuracy?
It will be remembered that Sheehan and Neisser (1969), who obtained
ratings after recall, found this to be significant. To answer this question,
for each subject the rating on the trial with the fewest errors was compared
to that obtained on the trial with the most errors. If more than one trial
gave best or worst recall, the mean vividness rating for such trials was

TABLE 4
*Mean Number of Incorrect Answers per Trial for Good and
Poor Visualizers of Each Sex*

	Female	*Male*	*Means*
Good visualizers ($N = 18$)	1.76	1.89	1.83
Poor visualizers ($N = 18$)	1.98	2.32	2.15
Means	1.87	2.11	1.99

TABLE 5

Mean Vividness Ratings for Each Subject's Highest and Lowest Recall
Scores for Two Orders of Rating and Recall

	Highest recall	Lowest recall	t	p
Rating before recall ($N = 16$)	2.79	2.70	<1.0	n.s.
Rating after recall ($N = 15$)	2.83	3.17	2.34	$< .05$

calculated. Mean ratings for these two categories of performance are given in the first row of Table 5.

The values in the second row of Table 5 were obtained in a pilot study differing in procedure only by its obtaining vividness ratings *after* recall, the order used by Sheehan and Neisser (1969). As indicated in Table 5, when rating came before recall, *no* significant within-subjects relation between accuracy and recall was observed. The absence of such a relationship for the rating-before–recall paradigm may be attributed to the small within-subject variation in the ratings (mean range = 2.0). Subjects had been selected on the basis of their giving either consistently high or consistently low ratings on the VVIQ and such homogeneity in the experimental ratings was therefore to be expected. When the rating followed recall, high accuracy was associated with a low mean rating, representing relative vividness. Hence, these data suggest that image-vividness ratings may be determined, at least partly, by the subject's accuracy of recall. This effect would appear to result from demand characteristics and can be reduced by employing the rating-before-recall paradigm.

In the light of these findings, two of the conclusions arrived at above concerning visual imagery will be reformulated. First, in support of Sheehan's earlier data (Sheehan, 1966a) persons who report vivid visual imagery can produce more accurate recall of pictorial material than those who report poor visual imagery. Second, under the conditions of the picture-memory studies, vividness of imagery and accuracy were related within subjects only if recall preceded the vividness-rating. As suggested by the Sheehan studies, demand characteristics, unless carefully controlled, may play a major role in determining vividness ratings.

Associative Role of Imagery

While the use of association via images as a memory-aid has a long history (Yates, 1966), the scientific study by psychologists of associative mnemonics has occurred only very recently. Paivio (1969, 1970, see also Chapter 11, this volume) and Bugelski (1970) in particular have drawn attention to the important role of imagery in the learning of verbal material.

Hunter's (1956) classification of mnemonic devices includes the category of "visual-symbol" systems in which items to be recalled are associated with an overlearned sequence of stimuli. In one variant of this system items to be recalled are associated, during presentation, with places along some familiar walk which is mentally imaged. During recall the walk is repeated mentally and the items are retrieved from their imaged loci in correct sequence. This was one of the procedures used by Luria's subject Shereshevskii who would distribute the items to be remembered along imaged walks he conducted through Moscow (Luria, 1960, 1968). There have been a number of recent studies of the "mental walk" mnemonic (e.g., Briggs, Hawkins, & Crovitz, 1970; Crovitz, 1969; Ross & Lawrence, 1968) and all have demonstrated how recall of verbal material may be significantly improved by using this technique. Visual imagery in particular has been implicated as the mediator of the place-item associations. If this is so it does not seem unreasonable to predict that subjects who report vivid visual imagery will make more effective use of a mental walk in a memory task than those who report poor imagery. A two-stage experiment was conducted by McKellar, Marks, and Barron (1972) to test this hypothesis.

Stage 1. A mnemonic walk which was circuitous and contained 30 loci was constructed. Two word lists each of 30 items were selected from the list of 925 words presented by Paivio, Yuille, and Madigan (1968). Words were chosen which had middle values in terms of imagery ease, concreteness, meaningfulness, and frequency.

Subjects were 24 undergraduate students, 12 female and 12 male. Six of each sex were "good" and six were "poor" visual imagers as defined by extreme scores on the VVIQ. Three subjects of each category were allocated to a "mental-walk" group and three to a control group. Within the "mental-walk" group each subject was his own control, one list being recalled before, and one list after, the walk had been learned. Items were exposed visually for a single presentation at 10-second intervals. Following presentation and recall of the first list, all subjects were taken for the walk and asked to remember places pointed out to them along the way. Upon return each subject was sent on the walk once more, to ensure complete learning, and the second list was presented. Subjects in the "mental-walk" group were instructed: "This time I want you to imagine that you are going on the same walk, and as you see each word, would you try to form some image or association between it and each place on the walk. You should try in some way to associate the first word on the list with the first place, the second word with the second place, and so on for all the 30 items." The control subjects were not given these instructions but were asked simply to recall as many items as possible.

The datum of primary interest was the change of performance resulting from the mnemonic walk. This was assessed by determining the change in number of items correctly recalled in correct ordinal position. Every subject receiving the "mental-walk" instructions showed increased recall on the second list, the mean increase being 12.8 items. The difference between the "mental-walk" recall and that of the controls was highly significant ($p < .001$). The study replicated the results of other workers (Briggs, Hawkins, & Crovitz, 1970; Crovitz, 1969; Ross & Lawrence, 1968) in demonstrating the effectiveness of the method of loci as a mnemonic device.

The main purpose of the experiment was to investigate individual differences. *Neither imaging ability nor sex was a significant effect.* In the light of the significant results on literal imagery described above, this negative finding was surprising, particularly as many of the subjects had contributed data to both studies. Within-cell variance was large and since there were only 3 subjects per cell, it was decided to "walk" another 12 subjects to increase the size of the experimental group. This was Stage 2 of the study.

Stage 2. As before, extreme scorers on the VVIQ were selected as subjects. Six of the highest scorers and 6 of the lowest scorers from a sample of 116 secondary-school pupils, aged 16–18, were selected. The procedure previously used for the "mental-walk" group was replicated. In addition, after recall of the second list, subjects rated the association formed between each item recalled and its corresponding place as "visual" or "not visual." Scores of Stage 1 and Stage 2 subjects were pooled giving a total of 24 subjects in the "mental-walk" condition. Mean results are presented in Table 6. Once again, neither visualizing ability nor sex was a significant effect.

TABLE 6
Mean Improvement in Recall for Subjects in the "Mental-walk" Group
(Stages 1 and 2)

	Female	Male	Means
Good visualizers ($N = 12$)	14.83	16.33	15.53
Poor visualizers ($N = 12$)	13.50	11.67	12.58
Means	14.16	14.00	14.08

Why did improvement in recall bear so little relation to imaging ability as measured prior to the experiment with the VVIQ? Some light is shed on this mystery by the visual-image reports obtained in Stage 2 of the study following the second recall. The "good" visualizers reported an average of 16 visual images (range = 7–26) and the "poor" visualizers an average of 13 (range = 3–23). *This difference was not significant.* The correlation between recall-improvement and number of visual images actually evoked during the experimental task was +0.67 ($p < .01$). This result strongly supports the notion that visual imagery is the effective mediator of the improved recall.

As Richardson (1969) and McKellar (see Chapter 2) have suggested, while the *ability* to generate and employ mental imagery varies across people, the *potential* to do so is probably universal. Given appropriate and optimal conditions of training and performance it is likely that all persons could utilize imagery-encoded information. The amount of imagery evoked on a given occasion is a more or less complicated interaction between variables of the person concerned and the situation in which he finds himself. Somewhat in contrast to VVIQ items and the picture-memory task, successful use of the mental-walk demands some imagination and creativity. Evidently, in its role as mnemonic device, the mental-walk can evoke a considerable amount of visual imagery even for persons previously reporting poor or nonexisting imaging ability.

Imagery and Perception

Since Perky (1910) demonstrated that low intensity stimuli could be confused with mental images, there has been considerable interest in the possibility that the functional characteristics of perception, both central and peripheral, are identical to those of imagery. The Perky effect has been replicated in a number of elegant studies by Segal and her co-workers (e.g., Segal & Fusella, 1969; Segal & Fusella, 1970; Segal & Gordon, 1969; see also Chapter 9, this volume) in which a reduction of sensitivity in signal-detections occurred during imagery. Of particular significance was the finding that sensitivity was lower when the image was in the same modality as the signal (Segal & Fusella, 1970). This suggested that it was signal confusion rather than distraction which caused the decrease in sensitivity.

Data concerning the effect of visual imagery on peripheral functioning come from studies of eye movements, both during sleep (e.g., Aserinsky & Kleitman, 1955; Dement & Wolpert, 1958; Roffwarg, Dement, Muzio,

& Fisher, 1962) and during wakefulness (e.g., Antrobus, Antrobus, & Singer, 1964; Brown, 1968; Haber & Haber, 1964; Leask, Haber, & Haber, 1967; Lenox, Lange, & Graham, 1970; Reyher & Morishige, 1969; for a detailed discussion and further references, see Chapter 15, this volume). A theoretical outcome of such studies is the hypothesis that eye movements during visual imagery represent "scanning" motions similar to those accompanying visual perception. Neisser (1967), for example, has suggested that imagery vividness is a continuum "loosely correlated with the extent to which scanning eye movements are involved. . . . Visual synthesis of an image without eye motion may be possible, but the better the image the more likely it is to involve some sort of scanning [Neisser, 1967, p. 153]" (for Dr. Neisser's current position, see Chapter 10, this volume). A not dissimilar point of view has been presented by Hebb (1949, 1968).

If the eyes do scan the image in much the same way as they glance at a stimulus object during perception, then more image-scanning should be observed in persons who image vividly than in persons who experience images which, at best, are vague and dim. One of the very few studies to investigate this hypothesis was that of Brown (1968). She compared eye movements of "visualizers" and "nonvisualizers," as assessed by questionnaire, during imaged pursuit (with eyes closed) of a metronome beating at 0.5 cycle per second (cf. Deckert, 1964). The results obtained were somewhat ambiguous. Although visualizers produced more movements than nonvisualizers, "the eye movements were often independent of ongoing visual recall of the motion . . . . The motor activity involved may be recalled in the absence of a conscious visual image of the original movement [Brown, 1968, pp. 305–306]."[5] Successive eye movements accompanying the pursuit of a metronome are not scanning movements—they provide little information other than spatial feedback. Imaged pursuit would seem to involve, therefore, a rather special class of imagery behavior.

Antrobus, Antrobus, and Singer (1964) studied the relative amounts of eye movement which accompanied various classes of imagery and daydreaming. Active images (e.g., a tennis match observed from the net) were associated with more ocular activity than static images (e.g., an illuminated face in a dark empty room). Whether this activity represents scanning of images already available or has some other function (e.g., image generation) is an open and researchable question. The distinction made by Antrobus et al. (1964) between static and active imagery, however, would seem worth preserving and imaged pursuit, whatever other peculiarities

[5] This result lends support to the notion that visual and kinesthetic recall involve modality specific stores (Jones & Connolly, 1970; Posner, 1967).

it may have, is clearly active. In the case of static imagery, there have been no published studies concerning the scanning hypothesis formulated above: *do good visualizers scan their images more than poor visualizers?* Two experiments were conducted to answer this question.

The first study (Marks, 1972b) examined the eye movements of good and poor visualizers, defined in terms of both VVIQ score and accuracy of recall of pictorial material, during the imagery and recall phases of the picture-memory task. These data were collected in the second of the picture-memory studies outlined earlier in this chapter. The subject was seated 40 inches from a screen which gave a stimulus area of $50° \times 36°$. Electrodes were attached to allow bipolar recordings of horizontal and vertical components of the electro-oculogram (EOG) on a Beckman polygraph. Subjects were told the electrodes were for recording "brain-waves." Through questioning at the end of the experimental session, subjects were found to have remained totally naive as to the electrodes' true function. Each subject was told to keep his eyes open at all stages of the experiment and sat with his head in a headrest to prevent head-movement artifacts. Calibration of the EOG record between trials, and the presence of a centrally placed luminous spot, visible between slide presentations, allowed an accurate estimate of "center" on the record.

The first analysis of these data was concerned with eye movement rate (EMR) during the 10-second imaging phase of the task. EMR was obtained by dividing the horizontal EOG record into half-second intervals and determining the percentage of these which contained a movement of greater than $2°$ visual angle. Mean EMRs of good and poor visualizers for the two kinds of stimuli are shown in Table 7.

Within-subjects variability was extremely large and thus for analysis of variance, within-cell variance was estimated by summing scores over subjects for each slide and using within-slides variability to estimate the error term. The difference in EMR between good and poor visualizers was highly

TABLE 7

Mean EMRs of Good and Poor Visualizers for Stimuli Showing Complete Scenes and Unrelated Objects

	Complete scenes	Unrelated objects	Means
Good visualizers ($N = 8$)	23.0	24.5	23.8
Poor visualizers ($N = 8$)	34.8	39.9	37.3
Means	28.9	32.2	30.6

significant ($p < .005$). *More vivid imagery was associated with relatively fewer eye movements.*

The next analysis investigated the eye movement data during recall for evidence of image-scanning. This was achieved by examining chunks of the EOG record which corresponded to questions referring to details in the periphery of the stimulus displays, e.g., Questions 1 and 4 for the stimulus shown in Fig. 1. The visual field was divided into a 3×3 matrix of areas, the central area being defined as a $2° \times 2°$ square. By examining the record of both horizontal and vertical EOG components it was possible to determine where, at any point of time, the subject's eyes were looking relative to center.

To illustrate this scoring method, consider Question 4 for the stimulus in Fig. 1 (*viz.* "Did the bottom picture show a shoebrush, toothbrush, or hairbrush?") This refers, explicitly, to the area of the display directly below center. Hence, if eye movements during imagery are like those accompanying the percept, then in answering this question by "reading-off" from an image of Fig. 1, the vertical EOG component should show a response away from center indicative of downward movement. The horizontal EOG record should not deviate from center however. A subset of 20 questions was selected, each of which had a peripheral reference point. Half of these questions explicitly mentioned the direction from center of the reference point (e.g., Question 4, above) and half did not (e.g., Question 1, above). These two types of question will be referred to as "direction" and "no direction" questions, respectively. Twenty chunks of EOG record were therefore analyzed for each subject, each chunk starting halfway through a question and ending 0.5 second before the subject's answer. For each of these segments, the percentage of noncentral eye-movement path (EMP) on the appropriate reference area was calculated. This score will be referred to as the percentage of EMP "on target." With 8 peripheral or "target" areas altogether, the mean chance rate of response was 12.5. If subjects scanned their visual images, mean percentage EMP "on target" would be significantly greater than this value. Mean scores of the good and poor visualizers for "direction" and "no direction" questions are presented in Table 8.

Analysis of variance gave a nonsignificant imagery effect but a significant effect for type of question ($p < .025$). For "direction" questions, the mean percentage EMP "on target" was significantly greater than the chance level ($p < .01$) but not so for "no direction" questions. These data suggest that if subjects scanned their images at all, they did so only when a directional cue was supplied by the experimenter. Such "scanning" behavior might more cautiously be regarded as an artifactual effect arising from the influence of the demand characteristics present in the situation (Orne, 1962).

TABLE 8

Mean Percentages of EMP "On Target" for Good and Poor
Visualizers, and "Direction" and "No Direction" Questions

	"Direction" questions	"No direction" questions	Means
Good visualizers.($N = 8$)	28.9	13.8	21.4
Poor visualizers ($N = 8$)	22.6	15.3	19.0
Means	25.8	14.6	20.2

For recall episodes uncontaminated by directional cues, the result was clear-cut: *no scanning of visual images was evident.* This result is in complete agreement with the earlier observation that vivid imagery reports were associated with fewer eye movements. Subjects did not move their eyes to scan their images—they kept their eyes still.[6]

A second study examined vividness a little more closely by comparing eye movement rates during a variety of visual imagery tasks (Marks & Barron, 1972). These were characterized as "imagination," "memory," "change," and "eye movement" imagery tasks. For imagination trials, subjects were asked in three separate trials to image "a close-up view of a shark's face," a "racing-car on a bed," and "an elephant made of polished wood." For memory trials, colored transparencies of stimuli referred to in the imagination instructions were displayed for 10 seconds and subjects were told: "After each slide has been removed try to keep a picture in mind of what you have seen." For change trials, subjects were shown a slide for 10 seconds and during presentation were given instructions which involved changing in some way the image of the picture displayed. For example, one slide showed a man and dog at the top of a hill and subjects were told: "After the slide has gone, try to make the dog run down the hill and back to the man several times" (see Richardson's discussion of the controllability of imagery in Chapter 5, this volume). Eye movement trials were presented last to preserve subjects' naivity concerning the purpose of the study and subjects were told: "When I take each one (slide) away, I want you to try and reconstruct the picture by moving your eyes as you try to look at each detail. In other words, try and build-up the picture that was there by moving your eyes from one imaged detail to an-

[6] This result is corroborated by the recent experiments of Hale and Simpson (1970) in which a different method was employed. Instructions either to deliberately make or imagine eye movements were not found to increase the rate of discovery or vividness of visual images.

other." Each trial comprised a 10-second baseline period, 10 seconds of instruction and/or slide presentation, 40 seconds of imaging, and finally, a vividness rating on the earlier mentioned 5-point scale. Subjects for this study were 12 of those taking part in the previous eye movement study. Six were good visualizers, as measured both by low VVIQ score and accurate recall on the picture-memory task, and 6 were poor visualizers with opposite profiles.

EMRs were determined for each type of imagery and its respective baseline. These were obtained by counting the number of half-second intervals containing a movement of more than $2°$ visual angle. Mean percentage EMRs for the horizontal and vertical components of the EOG were then calculated and the difference in mean percentage EMR between each variety of imagery and its respective baseline was obtained. Relative EMRs of good and poor visualizers for the four varieties of visual imagery are shown in Fig. 2.

Analysis of variance yielded the following results: visualizing ability (n.s., $p < .10$); imagery variety ($p < .005$); and visualizing ability $\times$ imagery variety ($p < .01$). Tests of the simple effects of the visualizing-ability factor showed that relative EMRs of good and poor visualizers differed significantly ($p < .005$) for eye-movement imagery, but for none of the other types of imagery. The tendency for EMR to be lower than baseline for imagination imagery was statistically significant ($p < .05$). As observed in the study reported above, and by Antrobus et al. (1964), static imagery was accompanied by ocular quiescence. There was no evi-

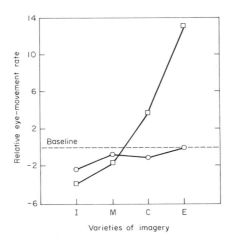

FIG. 2.   Relative eye-movement rate of good and poor visualizers for four varieties of visual imagery: I, imagination; M, memory; C, change; and E, eye movement. (□, Good visualizers; ○, poor visualizers.)

dence of scanning movements. Only if good visualizers were asked to "build-up the picture that was there" by moving their eyes "from one imaged detail to another" did ocular activity exceed baseline levels. Differing sensitivity to demand characteristics may here have been the relevant independent variable. There is no convincing evidence, therefore, that the eye-movement characteristics of visual static imagery are in any way like those of visual perception—this type of imagery is associated with a minimum of ocular activity.

Eye-movement data obtained thus far permit some optimism concerning an operational classification of different imagery experiences (see the chapters in this book by Holt, McKellar and Horowitz; also Horowitz, 1970). It is well-established that dream imagery is associated with characteristic rapid eye movements (Aserinsky & Kleitman, 1955) although the precise function of these movements is unknown (Oswald, 1962). It is established also that afterimages of physical stimuli (e.g., Mack & Bachant, 1969) and of images (Oswald, 1957) move with the eyes. Eidetic images are scanned and remain still (Haber & Haber, 1964). Active "memory" or "imagination" images are accompanied by eye movements (Antrobus *et al.*, 1964; Brown, 1968). Static "memory" or "imagination" images which are perceived to be located internally, as they usually are (e.g., see Weber & Bach, 1969), are not accompanied by scanning movements (Marks, 1972b). Preliminary results suggest that under some conditions *projected* active images, which are perceived as occupying real space, *may be* scanned (Marks & Barron, 1972). Although it is not difficult to predict their characteristics, eye-movement data from the hypnagogic, hypnopompic, and hallucinatory states are urgently needed.[7]

Summary and Conclusions

The experiments reported all tackled a fundamental issue in the study of imagery: does the cognitive behavior of a person who reports vivid visual imagery differ in any observable way from that of another who reports only faint visual imagery? In the field of memory, a simple question-

[7] Of relevance here are two papers by Brady and Levitt (1964, 1966) who used optokinetic nystagmus as an objective criterion for hypnotically induced visual hallucinations of a striped drum in rotation. See also a more recent study by Graham (1970).

and-answer technique was used to test recall of pictorial stimuli. Subjects were scored *prior* to the experiment on the basis of their verbal ratings of image vividness. Good visualizers, so-defined, produced significantly more accurate recall than poor visualizers. The difference in performance was substantial, and, in one study, poor visualizers produced 36% more errors than good visualizers. Evidently, persons who report vivid imagery can utilize a source of information which may not be available to those who report imagery which is vague and dim.

Another memory study looked at the improvement in recall of verbal stimuli effected by a mnemonic device—the "mental walk." Recall improvement was significantly correlated with the amount of visual imagery reported *during* the task but uncorrelated with imagery vividness reported *prior* to the experiment (cf. Ernest & Paivio, 1969). Rather than being fixed, the ability of a person to evoke and utilize imagery is influenced by situational variables—given appropriate conditions, even so-called "poor" visualizers can evoke visual images. The potential for imagery would appear to be universal. Studies of methods by which vividness, and other imagery qualities, can be transiently or permanently altered, should continue to be fruitful.

Studies in the field of perceptual function compared the ocular behavior of good and poor visualizers, doubly defined in terms of both verbal ratings of vividness and accuracy of pictorial recall. Good visualizers made fewer eye movements than poor visualizers while "looking at" static images and no evidence of spontaneous "scanning" movements was obtained from either group. These and other data suggest that, during vivid visual images of static displays, the eyes remain still. Only if an image is *active* (Antrobus *et al.,* 1964; Brown, 1968) or *projected* (Haber & Haber, 1964; Oswald, 1962) may ocular scanning movements occur.

Watson (1928) was naturally highly skeptical of the notion of imagery: "the behaviorist, having made a clean sweep of all the rubbish called consciousness, comes back to you: 'Prove to me' he says, 'that you have auditory images, visual images, or any other kinds of disembodied processes. So far I have only your unverified and unsupported word that you have them.' Science must have objective evidence to base its theories upon [p. 75]." Given the inevitable failure of introspectionism to provide objective measures of imagery, these statements were, at that time, eminently reasonable. Modern experimental and psychophysiological techniques extend quite considerably the subject matter of the science of behavior: the private events of Watson's day are now quite public (cf. Stoyva & Kamiya, 1968). What would have answered Watson's cry for *proof* of imagery remains uncertain, but the data cited in this chapter, and in other chapters, may provide at least some of the objective evidence he asked for.

References

Antrobus, J. S., Antrobus, J. S., & Singer, J. L. Eye movements accompanying daydreaming, visual imagery, and thought suppression. *Journal of Abnormal and Social Psychology*, 1964, **69**, 244–252.

Aserinsky, E., & Kleitman, N. Two types of ocular motility occurring in sleep. *Journal of Applied Physiology*, 1955, **8**, 1–10.

Aveling, F. *The consciousness of the universal and the individual*. London: Macmillan, 1912.

Bartlett, F. C. *Remembering*. London: Cambridge Univ. Press, 1932.

Betts, G. H. *The distribution and functions of mental imagery*. *Columbia University Teachers College Contributions to Education*, 1909, No. 26.

Bowers, H. Memory and mental imagery. *British Journal of Psychology*, 1931, **21**, 271–282.

Bowers, H. The role of visual imagery in reasoning. *British Journal of Psychology*, 1935, **25**, 436–446.

Brady, J. P., & Levitt, E. E. Nystagmus as a criterion of hypnotically induced visual hallucinations. *Science*, 1964, **146**, 85–86.

Brady, J. P. & Levitt, E. E. Hypnotically induced visual hallucinations. *Psychosomatic Medicine*, 1966, **28**, 351–363.

Briggs, G. G., Hawkins, S., & Crovitz, H. F. Bizarre images in artificial memory. *Psychonomic Science*, 1970, **19**, 353–354.

Brown, B. B. Visual recall ability and eye movements. *Psychophysiology*, 1968, **4**, 300–306.

Bugelski, B. R. Words and things and images. *American Psychologist*, 1970, **25**, 1002–1012.

Carey, N. Factors in the mental processes of schoolchildren. *British Journal of Psychology*, 1915, **7**, 452–490.

Crovitz, H. F. Memory loci in artificial memory. *Psychonomic Science*, 1969, **16**, 82–83.

Davis, F. C. The functional significance of imagery experiences. *Journal of Experimental Psychology*, 1932, **15**, 630–661.

Deckert, G. H. Pursuit eye movements in the absence of a moving visual stimulus. *Science*, 1964, **143**, 1192–1193.

Dement, W., & Wolpert, E. A. The relation of eye movements, body motility and external stimuli to dream content. *Journal of Experimental Psychology*, 1958, **55**, 543–553.

Ernest, C. H., & Paivio, A. Imagery ability in paired-associate and incidental learning. *Psychonomic Science*, 1969, **15**, 181–182.

Fernald, M. R. The diagnosis of mental imagery. *Psychological Monographs*, 1912, **14** (Whole No. 58). Pp. 1–169.

Fracker, G. C. On the transference of training in memory. *Psychological Monographs*, 1908, **9** (2, Whole No. 38). Pp. 56–102.

Graham, K. R. Optokinetic nystagmus as a criterion of visual imagery. *Journal of Nervous and Mental Disease*, 1970, **151**, 411–414.

Haber, R. N., & Haber, R. B. Eidetic imagery: I. Frequency. *Perceptual and Motor Skills*, 1964, **19**, 131–138.

Hale, S. M., & Simpson, H. M. Effects of eye movements on the rate of discovery and the vividness of visual images. *Perception and Psychophysics,* 1970, 9, 242–246.

Hebb, D. O. *Organization of behavior.* New York: Wiley, 1949.

Hebb, D. O. Concerning imagery. *Psychological Review,* 1968, **75**, 466–477.

Horowitz, M. J. *Image formation and cognition.* New York: Appleton, 1970.

Hunter, I. M. L. Mnemonic systems and devices. *Science News,* 1956, **39**, 75–97.

Jones, B., & Connolly, K. Memory effects in cross-modality matching. *British Journal of Psychology,* 1970, **61**, 267–270.

Juhasz, J. Imagination, imitation, and role taking. Unpublished doctoral dissertation, University of California, 1969.

Kohs, S. C. *Intelligence measurement.* New York: Macmillan, 1927.

Kuhlman, C. K. Visual imagery in children. Unpublished doctoral dissertation, Radcliffe College, 1960.

Kuhlmann, F. On the analysis of the memory consciousness for pictures of familiar objects. *American Journal of Psychology,* 1907, **18**, 389–420.

Leask, J., Haber, R. N., & Haber, R. B. Eidetic imagery in children: II. Longitudinal and experimental results. *Psychonomic Monograph Supplements,* 1969, **3** (Whole No. 35). Pp. 25–48.

Lenox, J. R., Lange, A. F., & Graham, K. R. Eye movement amplitudes in imagined pursuit of a pendulum with the eyes closed. *Psychophysiology,* 1970, **6**, 773–777.

Luria, A. R. Memory and the structure of mental processes. *Problems of Psychology,* 1960, **4**, 81–94.

Luria, A. R. *The mind of a mnemonist.* New York: Basic Books, 1968.

Mack, A., & Bachant, J. Perceived movement of the after image during eye movements. *Perception and Psychophysics,* 1969, **6**, 379–384.

McKellar, P. *Imagination and thinking.* New York: Basic Books, 1957.

McKellar, P., Marks, D. F., & Barron, B. F. The mnemonic walk and visual imagery differences. In preparation, 1972.

Marks, D. F. Visual imagery differences in the recall of pictures. *British Journal of Psychology.* In press, 1972. (a)

Marks, D. F. Visual imagery differences and eye movements in the recall of pictures. In preparation, 1972. (b)

Marks, D. F., & Barron, B. F. Eye movements during visual imagery. In preparation, 1972.

Neisser, U. *Cognitive psychology.* New York: Appleton, 1967.

Orne, M. T. On the social psychology of the psychological experiment: With particular reference to demand characteristics and their implications. *American Psychologist,* 1962, **17**, 776–783.

Oswald, I. After-images from retina and brain. *Quarterly Journal of Experimental Psychology,* 1957, **9**, 88–100.

Oswald, I. *Sleeping and waking: Physiology and psychology.* Amsterdam: Elsevier, 1962.

Paivio, A. Mental imagery in associative learning and memory. *Psychological Review,* 1969, **76**, 241–263.

Paivio, A. On the functional significance of imagery. *Psychological Bulletin,* 1970, **73**, 385–392.

Paivio, A., Yuille, J. C., & Madigan, S. Concreteness, imagery and meaningfulness value for 925 nouns. *Journal of Experimental Psychology,* 1968, **76**, (1, Pt. 2). Pp. 1–25.

Pear, T. H. The relevance of visual imagery to the process of thinking. *British Journal of Psychology*, 1927, **18**, 1–14.

Perky, C. W. An experimental study of imagination. *American Journal of Psychology*, 1910, **21**, 422–425.

Peterson, L. R., & Peterson, M. J. Short-term retention of individual verbal items. *Journal of Experimental Psychology*, 1959, **58**, 193–198.

Posner, M. I. Characteristics of visual and kinesthetic memory codes. *Journal of Experimental Psychology*, 1967, **75**, 103–107.

Reyher, J., & Morishige, H. Electroencephalogram and rapid eye movements during free imagery and dream recall. *Journal of Abnormal Psychology*, 1969, **74**, 576–582.

Richardson, A. *Mental imagery*. London: Routledge & Kegan Paul, 1969.

Roffwarg, H. P., Dement, W. C., Muzio, J. N., & Fisher, C. Dream imagery: Relation to rapid eye movements of sleep. *Archives of General Psychiatry*, 1962, **7**, 235–258.

Ross, J., & Lawrence, K. A. Some observations on memory artifice. *Psychonomic Science*, 1968, **13**, 107–108.

Ruger, H. A. The psychology of efficiency. *Archives of Psychology*, 1910, No. 15.

Segal, S. J., & Fusella, V. Effects of imaging on signal-to-noise ratio, with varying signal conditions. *British Journal of Psychology*, 1969, **60**, 459–464.

Segal, S. J., & Fusella, V. Influence of imaged pictures and sounds on detection of visual and auditory signals. *Journal of Experimental Psychology*, 1970, **83**, 458–464.

Segal, S. J., & Gordon, P. E. The Perky effect revisited: blocking of visual signals by imagery. *Perceptual and Motor Skills*, 1969, **28**, 791–797.

Sheehan, P. W. Functional similarity of imaging to perceiving: Individual differences in vividness of imagery. *Perceptual and Motor Skills*, 1966, **23** (Monograph Supplement 6-V23). Pp. 1011–1033. (a)

Sheehan, P. W. Accuracy and vividness of visual images. *Perceptual and Motor Skills*, 1966, **23**, 391–398. (b)

Sheehan, P. W. A shortened form of Betts" Questionnaire Upon Mental Imagery. *Journal of Clinical Psychology*, 1967, **23**, 386–389. (a)

Sheehan, P. W. Visual imagery and the organizational properties of perceived stimuli. *British Journal of Psychology*, 1967, **58**, 247–252. (b)

Sheehan, P. W., & Neisser, U. Some variables affecting the vividness of imagery in recall. *British Journal of Psychology*, 1969, **60**, 71–80.

Stewart, J. C. An experimental investigation of imagery. Unpublished doctoral dissertation, University of Toronto, 1965.

Stoyva, J., & Kamiya, J. Electrophysiological studies of dreaming as the prototype of a new strategy in the study of consciousness. *Psychological Review*, 1968, **75**, 192–205.

Thorndike, E. L. On the function of visual images. *Journal of Philosophy, Psychology and Scientific Methods*, 1907, **4**, 324–341.

Watson, J. B. *The ways of behaviorism*. New York: Harper, 1928.

Weber, R. J., & Bach, M. Visual and speech imagery. *British Journal of Psychology*, 1969, **60**, 199–202.

Woodworth, R. S. A revision of imageless thought. *Psychological Review*, 1915, **22**, 1–27.

Woodworth, R. S. *Experimental psychology*. New York: Holt, 1938.

Yates, F. A. *The art of memory*. London: Routledge & Kegan Paul, 1966.

5 ALAN RICHARDSON

VOLUNTARY CONTROL

OF THE MEMORY IMAGE

Memory imagery is the common and relatively familiar imagery of everyday life. It may accompany the recall of events from the past, the ongoing thought processes of the present or the anticipatory actions and events of the future. Though it may occur as a spontaneous accompaniment to much everyday thought of this kind, it is far more amenable to voluntary control than all other forms of imagery.

After describing the phenomenal experiences associated with imagery control, its measurement through self-report will be discussed in relation to all its known correlates. Some preliminary attempts to study the adaptive utility of the imagery control dimension as it interacts with the imagery vividness dimension will then be presented. This chapter concludes with an analysis of the main conceptual and empirical problems involved in studying the voluntary control of memory imagery, and with an outline of some immediate research needs.

The Description, Measurement, and Correlates
of Imagery Control

What does someone do when he voluntarily controls his memory images? To answer this question it will be useful to begin with some descriptions of the controlled and of the uncontrolled or autonomous imager engaged on an imaging task. This leads on to an account of the self-report questionnaire that was developed to help in classifying subjects. At the present time this classificatory procedure is a crude one and is often used in conjunction with information on imagery control obtained from an interview. Nevertheless, a number of associated differences have been found which provide support for the reality of the dimension and for the validity of the procedures by which it is measured.

Description

When Fechner (1860) was studying the qualities which distinguish a memory image from an afterimage his observers were asked to consider the extent to which each could be brought under voluntary control. His results are well-known and can be confirmed by introspection. Under appropriate stimulus and subject conditions the afterimage appears and disappears, is localized in space external to the observer and moves as the eyes move, independently, spontaneously and beyond the abilities of the observer to achieve any degree of voluntary control. The memory image, by contrast, manifests a wide range of individual differences. There are those who find it as difficult to alter as the afterimage, and at the other extreme, those who have no difficulty in changing any aspect of it.

As might be expected Galton (1883) provides an excellent description of the extreme positions on this dimension of voluntary control over the memory image. He begins with an account of the persons whose memory imagery lacks control.

> They find that the first image they have acquired of any scene is apt to hold its place tenaciously in spite of subsequent need of correction. They find a difficulty in shifting their mental view of an object and examining it at pleasure in different postions. If they see an object equally often in many positions the memories combine and confuse one another, forming a "composite" blur which they cannot dissect into its components. They are less able to visualize the features of intimate friends than those of persons of whom they have caught only a single glimpse. Many such persons have expressed to me their grief at finding themselves powerless to recall the looks of dear relations whom they have lost, while they had no difficulty in recollecting faces that were uninteresting to them [p. 75–76].

At the other extreme are those who have "a complete mastery" over their memory images. "They can call up the figure of a friend and make it sit in a chair or stand up at will; they can make it turn round and attitudinize in any way, as by mounting it on a bicycle or compelling it to perform gymnastic feats on a trapeze. They are able to build up elaborate geometric structures bit by bit in their mind's eye and add, subtract or alter at will and at leisure [p. 75–76]."

Measurement

The empirical investigation of imagery control was begun by one of the previous contributors to this book, Gordon (1949), in a study concerned with the relation between imagery control and the simplicity/complexity dimensions of ethnic stereotypes. To aid in the measurement of the imagery control dimension she constructed a set of 11 questions. Each one was read to her subjects with the request that they write down a "Yes" or a "No" in reply. The questions were as follows:

> Can you see a car standing in front of a garden gate?
> What is its color? Try and see it in a different color.
> Can you now see the same car lying upside down?
> Now put the same car back on its four wheels.
> Now can you see the car running along the road?
> Can you see it climb up a very steep hill?
> Can you see it climb across the top?
> Can you see it get out of control and crash through a house?
> Can you now see the same car running along the road with a handsome couple inside?
> Now can you see the car cross a bridge and fall over the side into the stream below?
> Can you now see the car all old and dismantled in a car cemetery?

Because it was thought that this task might require some skill in self-observation it was decided to restrict its use to those subjects who had been exposed to, at least, an elementary course in psychology. The sample consisted of 54 male and 10 female university students plus a further 27 males and 27 females who were attending psychology courses organized by the Workers Education Association. The actual division of subjects into "controlled" and "autonomous" categories was based upon a dual criterion. To be allocated to the "controlled" category, it was necessary for a subject to have answered "Yes" to every one of the 11 questions as well as indicating, at an earlier interview, that they could always control their imagery. All other subjects were placed in the "autonomous" category. The final analysis of results was based upon 74 "controlled" and 40 "autonomous" students. It was found that the possession of "autonomous" (uncontrolled) memory imagery was associated with the evocation of conventional (simple) stereotyped "imagery" to the ethnic stimulus words—Englishman, Chinese, German, and Jew. A second finding was that these highly conventionalized ethnic stereotypes of the "autonomous" students were formed relatively early in life on the basis of characters seen in films or pictures, or read about in books. The less conventionalized ethnic stereotypes of the "controlled" students, on the other hand, were found to have had their origin in the more recent past and to have been affected by personal contact with actual representatives of the ethnic groups concerned. The theoretical implication was accepted that the presence of relatively unchanged and conventionalized ethnic stereotypes was a reflection of the same cognitive rigidity manifest in the inability to maintain voluntary control of the memory image.

Correlates

In a later study, Gordon (1950) argued that because "perceptual and imagery processes are closely interlinked and interdependent [p. 63]" it should be possible to find an association between performance on her measure of imagery control and on an analogous task of perceptual control. Her choice of perceptual task was the Necker Cube and her measure was the voluntary control over reversal rate that a subject could exert when set to increase or decrease the number of reversals occurring in a 1 minute observation period. The subjects were 42 male neurotic patients each of whom was tested individually to obtain data on imagery control and percept control. In classifying subjects as "controlled" or "autonomous" interview data were utilized, once again, in addition to the responses obtained to the 11 questions. Twenty patients were classified as "controlled" and the remaining 22 were classified as "autonomous." It was found that the normal rate of spontaneous reversal for the "controlled" imagers was 10.64 per minute and for the "autonomous" imagers was 10.05 per minute. Group means for the rate of reversal under the fast and slow set conditions were in the predicted direction but were not statistically significant. However, when the difference between each individual's normal and fast rates of fluctuation were calculated, a reliable separation of the "controlled" and the "autonomous" groups was obtained. Similar results were found when the difference between each individual's fast and slow rates were calculated. As predicted, the "autonomous" imagers could exert less voluntary control over fluctuations on this perceptual task than could the "controlled" imagers.

Further support for this finding is provided in data published by Costello (1956). Part of this study involved a direct replication of Gordon's (1950) investigation. Nine males and six females comprised the relevant sample. All the subjects were either psychology students or nurses. On the basis of answers to the 11 questions used by Gordon (1949, 1950) the subjects were classified into a group of 9 "controlled" imagers and 6 "autonomous" imagers. Comparison of these two groups on their Necker Cube performance showed that normal/fast and fast/slow differences in reversal rates were statistically significant and in the direction predicted by the results of Gordon's study.

A further replication was undertaken by Orr (1970) using 30 male army recruits in the sixth week of training at the Wessex Depot, Exeter. On the basis of interview data and scores obtained on the Gordon questionnaire, 9 soldiers were classified as "controlled" imagers and 21 as "autonomous" imagers. The Necker Cube results were as before and in addition it was found that the "autonomous" imagers performed significantly worse on the Stroop test (Jensen & Rohwer, 1966) than did the "controlled" imagers.

The principal finding in another investigation by Costello (1957) was that "autonomous" imagery was more common in a sample of diagnosed neurotics than in a sample of normal subjects. But what was of particular interest was the additional discovery of a qualitative difference between two subsamples of neurotics. Whereas the dysthymics had vivid uncontrolled imagery the hysterics had weak uncontrolled imagery. The imagery of those in the normal group, however, could be either vivid or weak but it was almost always controlled. Among the tentative conclusions drawn from this study was that, "type of imagery indicates more the type of disorder to which the individual may be prone rather than indicating mental disorder itself [p. 848]."

If this were true then it might be expected that an analysis of imaging abilities in relation to Eysenck's (1953) personality dimensions would reveal a similar pattern of results with a sample of normal subjects. Eysenck (1957) defined the dysthymic as an introverted neurotic and the hysteric as an extraverted neurotic. It was predicted, therefore, that a sample of introverted neurotics, extraverted neurotics, and a combined group of extraverted and introverted nonneurotics would have respectively: vivid uncontrolled imagery, weak uncontrolled imagery, and controlled imagery that might be either weak or vivid.

Two studies were conducted to check on these predictions with samples drawn from populations of university students in Western Australia and in the United States of America. Introversion/extraversion and neuroticism were measured on the short form of the MPI (Maudsley Personality Inventory). Vividness of imagery was measured by the short form of the Betts Test (Sheehan, 1967a) and controllability of imagery was measured by the revised version of the Gordon Test (Richardson, 1969). In this the subjects were asked to underline "Yes," "No," or "Unsure," according to their success in visualizing each of 12 scenes. Two marks were allocated for each "Yes" answer, one for each "Unsure" and none for each "No" answer. Thus the range of possible scores extended from a maximum of 24 to a minimum of 0.

One study used a sample of students from the University of Western Australia and the other a sample from the University of Kansas. The results of both studies (Richardson, 1966) supported the prediction derived from the principal finding in Costello's (1957) study. Significantly more of those who scored above the median on the neuroticism scale were unable to control their imagery. But the expected difference in imagery characteristics between the introverted and extraverted "neurotics" was not reliable, though it was in the predicted direction.

This failure to obtain a statistically significant difference could result from several causes of which the difference between a diagnosed neurotic sample and an unselected normal sample may be the most important. It is likely that repression is employed as a more effective mechanism of defence among the hysteric neurotics than among their normal counterparts. If this were so they might be expected to have little awareness of internal events (i.e., weak imagery) which for this reason, would be very difficult to control. With normal subjects who scored high on extraversion and on neuroticism repression should be somewhat less complete and consequently their imagery should be somewhat more vivid.

The Adaptive Utility of Possessing Different Combinations of Imagery Control and Imagery Vividness

In the last study reported in the previous section four subtypes of imagery were distinguished by splitting the samples close to the median on both the vividness dimension and the controllability dimension. This procedure was adopted in most of the investigations reported in the present section and it is thought to reveal much more concerning the adaptive utility of voluntary memory imagery than either dimension when studied in isolation.

Of the four classes of problems discussed some evidence of the adaptive utility of control and vividness combinations is provided in relation to mental practice and hypnotic susceptibility. For the solution of spatial problems and the successful employment of desensitization therapy, combinations of the control and vividness dimensions appear to be relevant individual difference variables, but little work has been carried out so far.

Mental Practice

The first study to be reported concerns the part played by vivid-controlled visual and kinaesthetic imagery in facilitating the mental practice of a perceptual motor skill. Mental practice refers to the symbolic rehearsal of a physical activity in the absence of any gross muscular movements. When a golfer sits in a chair with his eyes closed and in imagination "sees" and "feels" himself going through the motions of putting a golf ball into the hole from the edge of the green he is engaged in mental practice. A review and discussion of the literature on this topic (Richardson, 1967a, 1967b) showed that at least 25 studies had been explicitly concerned with the effectiveness of this procedure. More such studies have appeared since. Though mental practice has been the term used most frequently, the same topic has been investigated under a variety of other names: e.g., symbolic rehearsal (Sackett, 1934), imaginary practice (Perry, 1939), implicit practice (Morrisett, 1956), mental rehearsal (Whiteley, 1962), and conceptualizing practice (Egstrom, 1964).

The part played by imagery in accounting for individual differences in the amount of improvement that occurs under mental practice conditions has been suggested by several research workers. For example, Clark (1960) obtained reports from his subjects on their use of imagery during mental practice of a basketball skill which suggested that both the vividness and controllability of imagery might be important individual difference variables to investigate. That vivid imagery, if it is uncontrolled, might be more of a hindrance than a help is suggested by the observation of one subject who "reported mentally attempting to bounce the ball preparatory to shooting only to imagine that it would not bounce and stuck to the floor. This disturbed him to a point where he could not successfully visualize the shooting technique [p. 567]." At the other extreme it might be expected that vivid-controlled imagery would facilitate the process of mental practice and lead to larger gains in the performance of whatever motor skill might be involved.

In a first attempt to study this problem (Richardson & Start, 1964; Start & Richardson, 1964) an investigation was made into the effect of four imagery subtypes on level of skill attained in performing the gymnastic movement known as the single leg upstart on the Olympic high bar. This movement is regarded as relatively simple and pilot studies had indicated that it would provide a discriminating task on which to assess the effects of mental practice. Predictions were made regarding the effect of each subtype of imagery on the level of physical performance ultimately achieved after equal amounts of mental practice. It was hypothesized that the subjects who possessed vivid-controllable imagery (VCI) would benefit most from mental practice and that those who possessed vivid-uncontrollable imagery (VUI) would benefit least. For the two intermediate groups possessing weak imagery it was reasoned that an inability to control one's weak imagery should result in a less effective utilization of the mental practice periods and therefore, in a lower level of physical performance in the criterion situation.

The subjects in this experiment were 31 men aged between 18 and 20 years and enrolled in the first year at a secondary teachers' college in Western Australia. They were all brought together during a regular class period and the task and method was explained to them. A brief questionnaire was administered to obtain information on age and athletic or sporting interests and activities. Practice periods lasted for 5 minutes on each of 6 days. They were conducted by using standardized instructions based upon an earlier analysis of the sequence of part movements required in the physical performance of this skill. Step by step the subjects were required to "see" and "feel" themselves through each of the movements described. None of the subjects had had any previous experience in the use of the high bar, though all but one had observed a practical demonstration of the skill to be learned. Mental practice sessions took place in a bare lecture room with 5 or 6 subjects practicing at one time.

On the day after the last mental practice session subjects were rated individually on their actual performance in mounting the high bar and the best of three attempts was taken as the final measure of performance. The ratings were made by four independent judges all of whom were familiar with this skill as a result of their experience in judging competitive gymnastics. Intercorrelations between the ratings of the four judges ranged from .92 to .96. In the fortnight following the completion of this part of the investigation the subjects were recalled and given an extensive test battery. To check on alternative hypothesis to the one under examination correlations were calculated between the rank order of the 31 subjects on the gymnastic skill and the rank order of their scores on each of the following tests: Brace Test of motor ability, measure of shoulder and hip strength, height, weight, and intelligence. No significant correlations were obtained.

As earlier work by Jacobson (1932) on the relation of imaging to muscle action currents and by Arnold (1946) on the relation of imaging to body sway, had both implied that a combination of visual and kinaesthetic imagery was more effective than visual alone, vividness scores based upon this combination were used. To test the hypothesis, subjects scoring above and below the median on imagery control were each subdivided at the median again, into a vivid and a weak imagery group. The mean performance scores (T-scores) of the four imagery groups were as predicted:

$$VCI(\overline{X} = 57.10) > WCI(\overline{X} = 51.88)$$
$$> WUI(\overline{X} = 47.89) > VUI(\overline{X} = 47.36)$$

The Mann-Whitney U-Test applied to a comparison of the individual scores in the two extreme groups showed that they were significantly different ($p < .05$; one tailed). Though the results are consistent with the hypothesis, the design does not exclude the possibility of another explanation. A crucial and difficult problem in studies of this kind is to ensure equality of motivation. If motivation differed among the four groups, differences in performance might be due to this factor rather than to the cognitive factor of imagery subtype. An attempt was made to avoid any of the more obvious sources of differential motivation by not selecting groups for analysis until after each subject had completed his actual performance trials. Thus there was no possibility that group differences could be attributed to the growth of competitive attitudes among groups. None of the subjects was ever aware that he had been placed in a particular group and no differences could be found other than the predicted differences in performance levels. Nevertheless, it is still possible that those who were imaging the task successfully during the mental practice periods maintained or increased their interest in performing well on the task, while those who found the mental practice difficult suffered a corresponding drop in motivation to perform well. Other procedures to control for motivational effects should be built into future investigations of mental practice.

Hypnotic Susceptibility

It is known that the vividness of a subject's imagery has a nonlinear association with hypnotic susceptibility. In a study reported by Sutcliffe, Perry, and Sheehan (1970) scores on the short form of the Betts Test were related to scores on the Stanford Hypnotic Susceptibility Scale (Form C) and to another hypnotic susceptibility scale of their own devising. The authors concluded that vividness of imagery is a necessary but not a sufficient condition of hypnotizability. More specifically it was found that hypnotizable subjects invariably had vivid imagery and that unsusceptible subjects had weak imagery but, not all subjects with vivid imagery were hypnotizable. Other studies supporting a positive relationship between vividness of imagery and hypnotic susceptibility are reviewed elsewhere (Sheehan, Chapter 7, this volume).

The possibility that controllability might be an important additional dimension of imagery to incorporate in future studies of hypnotic susceptibility is suggested by some findings from a study of body sway. One of the best measures of hypnotic susceptibility is the extent to which a subject sways when instructed by the experimenter to "fall forward." It was reasoned that the subject who has weak but controlled imagery may more easily dismiss, if he wants to, the "falling" imagery suggested by the experimenter. The ideomotor connection should be slight because the subject's imagery is weak and whatever connection exists should be easy to control and break altogether if desired. At the other extreme the subject who has vivid uncontrolled imagery would be more likely to find himself possessed of a vivid image of himself falling forward but with little ability to dismiss it from his consciousness. Because of these differences in imagery subtype the mean amount of body sway to be found in the former should be significantly less than in the latter. Between these extremes the vivid controlled imagers might be expected to sway less than the weak uncontrolled imagers. In summary the prediction was made that the order of body sway from maximum to minimum would be as follows:

$$VUI > WUI > VCI > WCI$$

The relevant data to test this prediction were collected while the writer was a visitor at the University of Kansas. A total of 42 student subjects completed the tests of imagery vividness and control. Some days later a 90 second test of body sway was administered using a tape recorded set of "falling" instructions. Scores on vividness and controllability were rank ordered and split at the median to establish the four imagery subtypes. All falls and body movements of 10 inches or more were arbitrarily scored as 10 inches and the mean amount of body sway calculated for each of the four groups. The results showed that the mean number of inches moved by the four groups was in the order predicted though the difference between the terminal groups failed to achieve a satisfactory level of statistical significance:

$$VUI(\overline{X} = 4.30) > WUI(\overline{X} = 4.00)$$
$$> VCI(\overline{X} = 3.33) > WCI(\overline{X} = 3.00)$$

In studies of this kind it is of course necessary to check the extent to which subjects attempt to resist the suggestions made to them.

Solving Spatial Problems

Most writers on the subject have believed that memory imagery plays at least some part in aiding a subject to solve at least some types of spatial problem. (See the discussion by Richardson, 1969, pp. 53–56). No simple linear relationship exists however, and in a factor analytic study carried out by Downey (1966) it was found that scores on vividness and controllability of imagery did not load on any of the factors loaded by a selection of spatial and visualizing tests. The main evidence of some connection existing between imagery and a spatial type of task comes from work on imagery vividness and the reproduction of simple stimulus patterns (Sheehan, 1966, 1967b). When imagery vividness scores are plotted against accuracy of reproduction the relationship is found to be nonlinear. Though weak imagers might be accurate or inaccurate, those with vivid imagery were almost always more accurate. Similar results have been obtained by the writer using a series of simple memory for designs stimuli.

The temptation to assume that vivid-visual imagery is necessary to successful performance on spatial tasks has led a number of researchers (e.g., McBain, 1954; Rimm & Bottrell, 1969; Whiteley, 1962) to use performance on selected spatial tasks as measures of visual-imagery vividness. At the present time there would appear to be insufficient justification for this practice, though future research may show that some relatively simple spatial tasks can be scored in such a way as to produce linear correlations with scores obtained by trained self observers employing the short form of the Betts Test of imagery vividness.

It might be expected that the absence of linear relationships between vividness of imagery and scores obtained from spatial tasks would result, in part, from a failure to test for the effect of controllability. Spatial manipulation, for example, involves the notion of controllability, yet no studies have examined performance on a spatial manipulation task in relation to the four imagery subtypes obtained by combining high and low scorers on the two imagery dimensions of vividness and controllability. The only study that has touched upon the problem of imagery control is the one discussed earlier in which Costello (1956) compared 9 controlled and 6 autonomous subjects from his normal groups on a spatial test known as NIIP Group Test 80A. He found that those with controlled imagery performed at a significantly superior level. No significant differences were found between the controlled and autonomous imagers on the Raven's Progressive Matrices or on the Mill Hill vocabulary scale.

Desensitization Therapy

In discussing the crucial factors in desensitization therapy Lazarus (1964) wrote: "An essential prerequisite for successful desensitization is the patient's ability to picture the imagined scenes sufficiently clearly,

vividly, and realistically for them to evoke anxiety at the outset [p. 66]."
However, it might be expected that the possession of vivid imagery without
a corresponding ability to control it could result in a complete failure to
benefit from this form of treatment. No adequate test of this expectation
has been attempted though three studies have examined the association
between imagery vividness and a variety of outcome variables. Grossberg
and Wilson (1968) found that self-ratings of visual-imagery vividness had
a significant correlation with changes in heart rate accompanying a request
to visualize scenes which were personally frightening. Similar results were
obtained by Rimm and Bottrell (1969) using self-ratings and a Picture-
Memory Test as two independent measures of imagery vividness. Their
one outcome variable was based upon changes in respiration rate accompanying the request to imagine two frightening scenes. In another study
by Davis, McLemore, and London (1970) it was found that among a sample of subjects suffering from snake phobia a nonsignificant but positive
partial correlation existed between vividness of visual imagery and improvement scores based upon tolerance for physical proximity to an actual
snake.

Immediate Research Needs

. Research is needed to replicate and extend the kind of results reported
in the last section. Until this is undertaken it will not be certain that there
is anything to explain. Once the results are well established, however, there
can be little advance in understanding the adaptive utility of memory
imagery until two fundamental problems have been solved. The first of
these is the conceptual problem of determining beyond reasonable doubt
that the voluntary control of vivid imagery is necessary to these behavioral
achievements. The second problem is an empirical one and involves the
construction of more reliable and valid measures of the vividness and controllability of voluntarily produced memory imagery. As these problems
impinge upon all aspects of imagery research no more will be attempted
here than to stress their importance and suggest a few lines of inquiry.

The Conceptual Problem

The assumption that we become aware of task relevant quasiperceptual
events (memory images) which serve the same purpose as their genuine

perceptual counterparts has not yet been demonstrated. Two objections must be answered before its apparent plausibility can be given any serious consideration. The first asserts that even vivid and controlled-memory images do not have the qualities necessary for the tasks that they are supposed to facilitate, while the second asserts that even if the necessary qualities were present there are alternative explanations that have not yet been eliminated. Each of these objections will be discussed in turn.

Inadequacy of the Memory Image. It has been assumed that to benefit most from, for example, the mental practice of a perceptual motor skill, a vivid-controllable sequence of imaged movements must occur like those required in the physical performance of the skill. When an imaged tennis ball is thrown at an imaged target covered in imaged chalk a subject may report an imaged puff of white at the point where the imaged ball has struck the imaged target (Whiteley, 1962). This information is then said to be used by the subject to make a correction to his next imaged throw and so on throughout the period of mental practice. But how much detail is available in a memory image, and can it be regarded as adequate for the purpose of making a correction? It is known (Woodworth, 1938) that even a vivid imager is unable to observe a 6×6 letter square for 60 seconds and then, when it is removed, to read off letters from the memory image of the square in any order requested (e.g., to name the letters in the six diagonal cells beginning at the bottom right and ending at the top left). Accuracy of recalled detail comparable with the accuracy of perception is extremely rare, even among those few people who possess eidetic imagery (Stromeyer & Psotka, 1970) and most of these latter are unable to cope with tasks of the letter square variety (Leask, Haber & Haber, 1969).

The voluntary act of vividly imaging an object or event not only fails to provide clearly observable details but typically results in only part of a total object or event being present in awareness at any given moment. Just as perception has a motor component (e.g., eye movements in visual perception) which build up its object from a series of quick successive fixations, so it is likely that an image of the same object is reconstructed from a similar series of partial images mediated by a minimal amount of motor activity associated with the appropriate eye movements (Deckert, 1964; Singer & Antrobus, 1965; Zikmund, 1966; see also Chapter 15 this volume). Certain it is that memory images are often fragmentary and we cannot observe all parts of an imaged object with equal clarity at the same time.

Accepting that the amount of concrete detail available in the memory image of part of an object or event is relatively slight, what evidence can be found which might suggest that it is, nevertheless, sufficient? The first line of work that has produced results of relevance to this question has been opened up by Sheehan (1966, 1967b). He has been able to show that a group of subjects who have been required to *image* an object and to use this image in reconstructing the object from memory are more accurate than a comparable group who have been required to observe the object and *recall* it later. When those who imaged the stimulus patterns (objects) were asked to rate their vividness it was found that the simple patterns were rated as more vivid than the complex patterns. These studies seem to show that the process of imaging cannot make available very much vivid detail but that it still provides the basis from which more accurate memories can be reconstructed. The second line of work helps us to understand why even a very little information conveyed by a memory image may still be sufficient to trigger significantly more of the memory than would occur otherwise. Work on memory processes, as well as everyday experience, demonstrates quite clearly that if a complete memory is to be evoked it may require no more than a very slight sensory cue from the context in which the original event was experienced. Perhaps the ability to obtain vivid controlled images gains its adaptive utility by providing a relevant series of quasisensory prompts.

Inadequacy of the Explanation.   Even if one accepts that the imaging process is adequate for the job that it is supposed to do, might there not be other equally plausible explanations? It is to this problem that we must now turn and it is with some of the known correlates of imagery that our search can most profitably begin. For example, reports by Bartlett (1932), Jenkin (1935) and Doob (1966) all indicate that the availability and use of imagery is associated with a greater sense of confidence in the user, even when it is not associated with a greater degree of accuracy in what is recalled. Is it confidence in one's ability to improve physical performance by way of mental practice that is the main determinant of the actual improvement found by Start and Richardson (1964)?

Again, differences in task performance between vivid and weak memory imagers might be due to one or more of those personality characteristics that have been found to differentiate those who report frequent and vivid imagination images from those who report few and weak imagination images (Foulkes, Spear, & Symonds, 1966; Goldberger & Holt, 1961; Holt & Goldberger, 1959). For example, Freedman and Marks (1965) concluded, "that an artistic, sensitive, and creative self concept is related to a syndrome that includes imagery [p. 110]." An obvious task of future research is to examine the relation between the short form of the Betts Test of imagery vividness and such measures as the "enjoyment of daydreaming" factor reported by Singer and Antrobus (1963; and Chapter 8, this volume) or the subscales from the questionnaire of subjective experiences devised by As (1962). Is the assumed efficacy of vivid- and controlled-memory imagery due to the correlation of these dimensions with other measures of access and attention to internal events; and is it to some process associated with these other measures that we must look for an explanation?

The Empirical Problem

Improvement in the reliability of the Gordon Test and in its other psychometric characteristics need not wait upon the results of studies designed to clarify the conceptual problem. Three types of investigation are required immediately. First of all, it is necessary to construct a longer test which will include items from all sense modalities and not leave it limited to the visual modality only. Second, it is necessary to include the test in a carefully selected battery of other rigidity–flexibility tests with the object of clarifying the nature of the general ability of which it may be a special example. Third, it is necessary to conduct base line studies in an attempt to establish its independence of the vividness dimension. At the moment, substantial correlations can be expected between scores on the controllability dimensions and scores on the vividness dimension (Downey, 1966).

Improving the Reliability of the Gordon Test.   Nothing is known about the test-retest characteristics of this test or its susceptibility to such response sets as social desirability or acquiescence. But before checks of this kind are applied it will be necessary to start from the beginning and revise the visual items in addition to constructing new items in relation to other modalities. Experience has shown that some subjects who have been involved in car accidents or feel anxious about the possibility of such accidents are unable to visualize the unpleasant scenes like that of the car getting out of control and crashing into a house. The choice of some more neutral object would seem advisable.

As with imagery vividness the investigator of imagery control would like to know whether there is a general factor of imagery control which extends across all modalities or whether control may show itself in one set of modalities but not in another. Sheehan's (1967a) test of imagery vividness was constructed on the basis of a large pool of items available from the original test constructed by Betts (1909). His final test comprises 35 items; 5 each for the measurement of 7 modalities. Though more difficult to construct suitable items for a test of imagery control the following examples provide an idea of what is required.

Visual	Can you see a man standing at the base line of a tennis court about to make his first serve?
	Can you see the same man in the same place but now dressed in red bathing trunks?
Auditory	Can you hear a brass band playing God save the Queen?
	Can you now hear it played by a single violin?
Tactile	Can you feel the texture of an ordinary bristle nailbrush rubbed across the tips of your fingers?
	Can you feel what it is like if the brush suddenly changes to a wire one?
Kinaesthetic	Can you feel the movement of your muscles as you attempt to throw a tennis ball just as far as you can?
	Now, can you feel the same muscles as you throw the ball, very gently, to a small child?
Taste	Can you taste the strong, sour taste of raw lemon?
	Can you now add the flavor of white granulated sugar to that of the lemon?
Smell	You come into a freshly painted room. Can you smell the paint—it's strong and rather overpowering?
	Can you now smell the same room filled with the scent of lavender?
Bodily sensations	Can you feel yourself very sleepy, beginning to yawn and unable to keep your eyes open?
	Can you now feel yourself tingling with vitality, alert and ready for anything?

Apart from the problem of constructing items which have the appropriate form, there is the problem of constructing items which have the appropriate content. All items must have a content that is of nearly equal familiarity to all of the subjects likely to receive the test.

One last consideration in the measurement of imagery control by subjective report procedures is the desirability of individual testing. The subject must understand the nature of the task upon which he is engaged and for this reason, it is useful to conduct a preliminary interview in which the nature of the subject's own imagery can be probed and discussed in relation to the nature of imagery in general. The standardization of an interview guide for this purpose would be of great value to research in this area.

In the writer's experience the administration of imagery tests in a group situation should be avoided if at all possible. More needs to be known about the effects of group administration. Above what size of group does the reliability and validity of measurement begin to fall off sharply or is the decline a simple linear one? Is it better for the experimenter to read out the questions or for the subject to read the questions to himself? Studies of this kind were very common in the past, particularly in relation to intelligence testing, but they must be repeated for imagery testing because the task is a very different one. For some people, attention to internal events is not a familiar activity so that training in their recognition, examination, and report may be required before formal testing of imagery vividness and control can be started. Even the afterimage is not familiar to everyone. As Woodworth (1938) observed: "Many students require some practice before seeing the after image, because it is one of those subjective phenomena which our whole practical life leads us to disregard [p. 557]."

Improving the Validity of the Gordon Test. The way in which we conceive of this test or of the improved and more reliable version proposed, and the knowledge already available concerning its sensory–perceptual correlates, both imply the measurement of some kind of rigidity–flexibility dimension. As all the evidence indicates that no unitary general trait can embrace the wide variety of phenomena that have been described as manifestations of rigidity–flexibility, it is necessary to investigate the special properties of those abilities associated with imagery control. Some guidance is provided by Frick, Guilford, Christensen, and Merrifield (1959) who undertook a large scale factor analysis of most tests that have been proposed as measures within this domain. The factor of interest in this discussion is one which was loaded by tests which required the ability to change one's set to meet the shifting requirements of the situation. Not only the description but also one of the tests (hidden figures) have a close resemblance to the conceptual properties of imagery control and its correlates. It is known, for example, that scores on the hidden figures test have a significant correlation with scores on the Stroop Test. Frick *et al.* (1959) called this dimension *adaptive flexibility* and distinguished it from *spontaneous flexibility* which was loaded by tests which measured the diversity of ideas that a subject could produce. It is of interest that the Luchins Water Jar Test was unrelated to either factor but had is largest loadings on two factors named *logical evaluation* and *general reasoning*. A new battery of tests needs to be selected based upon marker tests from the main factors just discussed and including the Necker Cube Test, Stroop Test, the yet to be constructed test of imagery control and any other tests that have some initial face validity as measures of adaptive flexibility (see Chown, 1959).

Whereas the Gordon Test, the Necker Cube Test and the Stroop Test may all be regarded as expressions of the same underlying cognitive ability, perhaps the ethnic stereotype finding of Gordon (1949) and the neuroticism findings of Costello (1957) and Richardson (1966) should be considered as independent individual difference conditions which influence the behavioral manifestations of this ability. The conventionalized ethnic stereotypes that Gordon (1949) found to be associated with "autonomous" imagery may imply the presence of other relatively simple cognitive structures. As simplicity of cognitive structures, if generalized across several content areas is likely to be more common among persons of relatively low general intelligence, studies are required which aim to establish a direct correlational link between general intelligence and controllability of imagery.

Neuroticism, as it has been conceptualized and measured in the studies reported earlier in this chapter, is Eysenckian neuroticism. However, though Eysenck views neuroticism, conceptually, as a genetically based predisposition, associated with the functions of the autonomic nervous system and manifest in a tendency to respond to stimuli with either more or less emotionality (activation level), he recognizes that his self-report measures of this construct have been contaminated by acquired neurotic traits which include the tendency towards inflexibility of response. Experiments are required to examine the effects of stress (inducing high activation levels) on the voluntary control of the memory image.

When the effects of intelligence and of motivation on adaptive flexibility are understood a better basis will exist for deciding whether or not they need to be controlled in particular investigations concerned with the controllability of memory images. These comments raise another aspect of the general need for base line studies and it is with this that I want to conclude.

The Need for Baseline Studies.   It has been suggested already that the measurement of imagery control cannot be made without reference to imagery vividness. If someone claims a total absence of visual imagery then with no imagery to control a theoretical score of 0 is inevitable on any measure of imagery control. If someone claims that he possesses visual imagery that is especially hazy, incomplete, and fleeting, it is at the same time weak and lacking in controllability. However, this lack of imagery control appears phenomenally to result from the extreme intangibility of the "object" to be controlled. Where the memory image of the "object" is somewhat more definite, complete and enduring, the meaning of controllability is different. Whether or not this more vivid imagery can be altered or replaced is a question that the self-observer is able to answer more readily.

These comments suggest that for any measure of imagery control base line studies are required to examine test-retest reliabilities for controllability at each of, for example, four levels (quartiles) of imagery vividness. It might be predicted that reliability coefficients for control should increase in magnitude for each increase in the level of imagery vividness and that the correlation between the dimensions, within any particular quartile, should approximate 0.

Whatever the actual results turn out to be, a better empirical basis will exist for the conduct of future studies involving both these dimensions of imagery. Only by conducting base line studies of this kind is it possible to select subjects with a reasonable assurance that imagery vividness and imagery control are not confounded but can be measured independently of each other.

Concluding Comment

The measurement, correlates, and adaptive utility of the control dimension of memory imagery constitute a relatively unknown domain within the recently rediscovered territory of mental imagery. What will be confirmed concerning these early reports and what remains to be discovered will be established in future investigations. It has been the main purpose of this chapter to provide some orientation to the more accessible and important areas to be explored.

References

Arnold, M. B. On the mechanism of suggestion and hypnosis. *Journal of Abnormal and Social Psychology,* 1946, **41**, 107–128.

As, A. A factor analytic study of some subjective personal experiences and their bearing on theories of hypnosis. *Acta Psychologica,* 1962, **20**, 196–209.

Betts, G. H. *The distribution and functions of mental imagery.* New York: Teacher's College, Columbia University, 1909.

Bartlett, F. C. *Remembering.* Cambridge: Cambridge Univ. Press, 1932.

Chown, S. M. Rigidity—A flexible concept. *Psychological Bulletin,* 1959, **56**, 195–223.

Clark, L. V. Effect of mental practice on the development of a certain motor skill. *Research Quarterly,* 1960, **31,** 560–569.

Costello, C. G. The effects of prefrontal leucotomy upon visual imagery and the ability to perform complex operations. *Journal of Mental Science,* 1956, **102,** 507–516.

Costello, C. G. The control of visual imagery in mental disorder. *Journal of Mental Science,* 1957, **103,** 840–849.

Davis, D., McLemore, C. W., & London, P. The role of visual imagery in desensitization. *Behaviour Research and Therapy,* 1970, **8,** 11–13.

Deckert, G. H. Pursuit eye movements in the absence of a moving visual stimulus. *Science,* 1964, **143,** 1192–1193.

Doob, L. W. Eidetic imagery: A cross cultural Will-o'-the-Wisp? *Journal of Psychology,* 1966, **63,** 13–34.

Downey, R. *Mental imagery and spatial abilities.* Unpublished masters thesis, Univ of Western Australia, 1966.

Egstrom, G. H. Effect of an emphasis on conceptualizing techniques during early learning of a gross motor skill. *Research Quarterly,* 1964, **35,** 472–481.

Eysenck, H. J. *The structure of human personaliy.* London: Methuen, 1953.

Eysenck, H. J. *The dynamics of anxiety and hysteria.* London: Routledge & Kegan Paul, 1957.

Fechner, G. T. (Orig. publ. 1860.) *Elements of psychophysics.* New York: Holt, 1966.

Foulkes, D., Spear, P. S., & Symonds, I. D Individual differences in mental activity at sleep onset. *Journal of Abnormal Psychology,* 1966, **71,** 280–286.

Freedman, S. J., & Marks, P. A. Visual imagery produced by rhythmic photic stimulation: Personality correlates and phenomenology. *British Journal of Psychology,* 1965, **56,** 95–112.

Frick, J. W., Guilford, J. P., Christensen, P. R., & Merrifield, P. R. A factor analytic study of flexibility in thinking. *Educational and Psychological Measurement,* 1959, **19,** 469–496.

Galton, F. (orig. publ. 1883.) *Inquiries into human faculty.* London: Dent, 1905.

Goldberger, L., & Holt, R. R. *A comparison of isolation effects and their personality correlates in two divergent samples.* (ASD Tech. Rep. No. 61–417) Wright-Patterson A.F.B., Ohio, 1961.

Gordon, R. An investigation into some of the factors that favour the formation of stereotyped images. *British Journal of Psychology,* 1949, **39,** 156–167.

Gordon, R. An experiment correlating the nature of imagery with performance on a test of reversal of perspective. *British Journal of Psychology,* 1950, **41,** 63–67.

Grossberg, J. M., & Wilson, H. K. Physiological changes accompanying the visualization of fearful and neutral situations. *Journal of Personality and Social Psychology,* 1968, **10,** 124–133.

Holt, R. R., & Goldberger, L. *Personological correlates of reactions to perceptual isolation.* (WADC Tech. Rep. No. 59-753) Wright-Patterson A.F.B., Ohio, 1959.

Jacobson, E. Electrophysiology of mental activities. *American Journal of Psychology,* 1932, **44,** 677–694.

Jenkin, A. M. Imagery and learning. *British Journal of Psychology,* 1935, **26,** 149–164.

Jensen, A. R., & Rohwer, W. D. The Stroop colour-word test: A review. *Acta Psychologica,* 1966, **25,** 36–93.

Lazarus, A. A. Crucial procedural factors in desensitization therapy. *Behaviour Research and Therapy*, 1964, **2**, 65–70.

Leask, J., Haber, R. N., & Haber, R. B. Eidetic imagery in children. II. *Psychonomic Monographs* 1969, **3** (Whole No. 35), 25–48.

McBain, W. M. Imagery and suggestibility: A test of the Arnold hypothesis. *Journal of Abnormal and Social Psychology*, 1954, **49**, 36–44.

Morrisett, L. H., Jr. *The role of implicit practice in learning*. Unpublished doctoral dissertation, Yale University, 1956.

Orr, A. C. *A further test of the Gordon hypothesis*. Unpublished undergraduate honours project, University of Exeter, 1970.

Perry, H. M. The relative efficiency of actual and imaginary practice in five selected tasks. *Archives of Psychology*, 1939, **34**, 5–75.

Richardson, A. Unpublished data, 1966.

Richardson, A. Mental practice: A review and discussion. (1) *Research Quarterly*, 1967, **38**, 95–107. (a)

Richardson, A. Mental practice: A review and discussion. (2) *Research Quarterly*, 1967, **38**, 263–273. (b)

Richardson, A. *Mental imagery*. London: Routledge & Kegan Paul, 1969.

Richardson, A., & Start, K. B. Imagery and mental practice. *Proceedings of the XVII International Congress of Psychology* (Washington, 1963). Amsterdam: North-Holland Publ., 1964.

Rimm, D. C., & Bottrell, J. Four measures of visual imagination. *Behaviour Research and Therapy*, 1969, **7**, 63–69.

Sackett, R. S. The influence of symbolic rehearsal upon the retention of a maze habit. *Journal of General Psychology*, 1934, **10**, 376–395.

Sheehan, P. W. Functional similarity of imaging to perceiving: Individual differences in vividness of imagery. *Perceptual and Motor Skills*, 1966, **23** (Monograph Supplement, 6-V23) 1011–1033.

Sheehan, P. W. A shortened form of Betts' questionnaire upon mental imagery. *Journal of Clinical Psychology*, 1967, **23**, 386–389. (a)

Sheehan, P. W. Visual imagery and the organizational properties of perceived stimuli. *British Journal of Psychology*, 1967, **58**, 247–252. (b)

Singer, J. L., & Antrobus, J. S. A factor-analytic study of daydreaming and conceptually-related cognitive and personality variables. *Perceptual and Motor Skills*, 1963, **17** (Monograph Supplement, 3-V17) 187–209.

Singer, J. L., & Antrobus, J. S. Eye movements during fantasies. *Archives of General Psychiatry*, 1965, **12**, 71–76.

Start, K. B., & Richardson, A. Imagery and mental practice. *British Journal of Educational Psychology*, 1964, **34**, 280–284.

Stromeyer, C. F., & Psotka, J. The detailed texture of eidetic images. *Nature (London)*, 1970, **225**, 346–349.

Sutcliffe, J. P, Perry, C. W., & Sheehan, P. W. Relation of some aspects of imagery and fantasy to hypnotic susceptibility. *Journal of Abnormal Psychology*, 1970, **76**, 279–287.

Whiteley, G. *The effect of mental rehearsal on the acquisition of motor skill*. Unpublished diploma in education thesis, University of Manchester, 1962.

Woodworth, R. S. *Experimental psychology*. New York: Macmillan, 1938.

Zikmund, V. Oculomotor activity during visual imagery of a moving stimulus pattern. *Studia Psychologica*, 1966, **8**, 254–274.

6 MARTIN S. LINDAUER

THE SENSORY ATTRIBUTES
AND FUNCTIONS OF
IMAGERY AND IMAGERY
EVOKING STIMULI[1]

Images are commonly referred to as "pictures in the mind's eye," but they could just as well be "sounds in the mind's ear," or taste, smell, and tactile mental representations (among others) of the various sensations (Woodworth, 1938, pp. 39–45). Sensory referents are an obvious feature of imagery, appearing as a common characteristic of many of the 13 principal types listed by Holt (1964, p. 255), presumably because an image's sources are largely dependent upon sensation and perception. McDougall noted that "we seem to experience in a faint, thin, ghostlike fashion the sensory qualities on which we rely in perception [McKellar, 1968, p. 111]." Psychological dictionaries also affirm this sensory dimension, defining imagery as "a revived sense experience, in the absence of the sensory stimulation [Drever, 1963]" ". . . which reproduces or copies in part, and with some degree of sensory realism, a previous perceptual experience [Warren, 1934]."

In light of the resurgence of interest in imagery, a topic which Neisser (1970, p. 159) emphatically asserts "stands at the very center of psychology," this chapter attempts to direct renewed attention to its sensory di-

[1] Some of the research reported in this chapter was supported by several Faculty Fellowships and Grants-in-Aid from the Research Foundation of State University of New York. Wilma Gottlieb and Lynn C. Reukauf assisted at various stages of the research. The contribution of John Jamele is also gratefully acknowledged, and Dr. Peter W. Sheehan's comments on an earlier version of this chapter were very helpful.

mension. This reaffirmation of what should be elementary is important since sensory imagery has been neglected in much of contemporary research, including, but not limited to, the study of learning. In this chapter it will be argued that sensory imagery, a phenomenological attribute of imagery which refers to the sights, sounds, and the like aroused by imaged stimuli, has been insufficiently explored or understood, if indeed, it has been considered at all. Empirical investigations and theoretical discussions of the general role and function of imagery require a clarification of the essential component of sensory imagery. In order to exemplify this argument, sensory aspects of imagery in a general context, including its role in language and aesthetics, will first be discussed. This will be followed by a review of imagery research which has included the sensory dimension, referring to the study of individual differences in types of imagery and their relationship to performance variables. In addition, attention will be paid to the neglect of the sensory dimension in studies of imagery's role in learning, an area considered fundamental to an understanding of the imaging process. Finally, some recent unpublished research, which stems from this thesis of the importance of the nature and contribution of sensory aspects of imagery, will be summarized. In terms of the comprehensiveness of this review, it should be understood that given the variety of interests which currently characterize the imagery area, topics other than those chosen for discussion could very well have been selected as demonstrating the inadequacy of the treatment accorded to sensory imagery.

General Aspects of Sensory Imagery: Language and Aesthetics

The psychological study of the metaphor indirectly refers to the sensory dimension of imagery. In Asch's (1955) analysis of the common psychological properties jointly shared by persons, objects, and events, he states that "our language draws upon nearly the entire range of visual, auditory, tactual, kinesthetic, thermal, and olfactory experiences for a description of psychological properties [p. 29–30]." Thus, both people and objects are deep–shallow, hard–soft, warm–cold, bright–dull, smooth–slippery, straight–crooked, etc. This shared duality of meaning was found to be true for adjectives compared across historically unrelated languages (Asch, 1958). Similarly, Osgood, Suci, and Tannenbaum (1967, pp. 170–176) also found that the connotative meaning of concepts, as measured by such evidently sensory scales as "hot–cold," "sharp–dull," etc., were consistent across cultures. Knapp (1960) has used metaphors, many of which are rich in their sensory illusions to imagery, to investigate differences in people's relatively unconscious attitudes and concepts towards such categories as the self ("a burning candle," "a splashing fountain"), time ("a dashing waterfall," "wind-driven sand"), conscience ("a vexing itch," "a probing searchlight," "a buried splinter"), death ("a chilling frost," "a misty abyss"), love ("a bitter-sweet drink," "the melting of winter snows," "a feverish madness"), and success ("a shining sword," "a triumphant song," "a greased pig"). This brief discussion of the expressive meanings and emotions attributed to language as well as perceived objects is related to the broader phenomenon of physiognomy (Werner, 1955, pp. 11–18; 1956). Thus, some physiognomic effects, e.g., "threatening clouds," "awesome mountains," etc., may be facilitated by the sensory richness of the images evoked. Another phenomenon closely related to sensory imagery is that of synesthesia (McKellar, 1957, Chapter 4; see also Chapter 2, this volume), in which a stimulus evokes an image in a sensory mode other than the one in which the initiating stimulus was presented, e.g., a musical note calls forth the image of a color. Thus, early work in aesthetics (Chandler & Barnhart, 1930, p. 176) refers to the presence and role of auditory imagery in musicians and in the response to music. Recent studies in synesthesia also parallel some of the major interests of imagery research, concentrating on individual differences (Simpson & McKellar, 1955), and placing a major emphasis on visual–auditory combinations (Osgood, 1953, pp. 642–646). However, work in synesthesia also tends to focus on relatively more specialized areas than generally found in imagery research. Thus, unlike many of the interests found in imagery, a good deal of the research in synesthesia is tied to color perception, and the arousal of emotions. This discrepancy between the concerns of these two topics may be due to synesthesia's less frequent occurrence in the population than is the case for imagery, and synesthesia's effect may be more a matter of associations and memory than of the images evoked.

Turning to another discipline whose analyses may also bear on psychology's concerns (although usually ignored), literary critics have also examined the sensory component of imagery for its crucial role in the comprehension and enjoyment of literature (Friedman, 1953). An author's use of metaphors and similes in describing likenesses, e.g., "the ship plows the sea," "cheeks like roses," depends very much on the use of sensory imagery. An example of a poem which relies on various modes of imagery for effect is Wordsworth's sonnet "To Sleep" (quoted in McKellar, 1968, p. 111).

> A flock of sheep that leisurely pass by,
> One after one; the sound of rain, and bees
> Murmuring; the fall of rivers, winds and seas,
> Smooth fields, white sheets of water and pure sky . . . .

Although most analyses of imagery in literary materials have been thematic or subjective, a few quantitative studies of interest to psychology have been accomplished. Spurgeon (1952) relied on a frequency count of the images in the works of Shakespeare, many categories of which were sensory (e.g., "pain"), in order to compare his works, to test his authorship with that of Marlowe and Bacon, and to examine the playwright's personality. As a means of studying literature systematically, Dudley (1928) devised a classification of imagery as the basis for its analysis, largely derived from Titchener, among others: "The simplest classification [is a] division according to the kinds of sensation [in images] [p. 32]." Questions regarding aesthetic enjoyment may also be relevant to imagery, i.e., the kinds of images aroused by poetry, to which readers may be differentially sensitive. Although little empirical work has been done on this question, Friedman (1953) refers to discussions by Coleridge and Meredith on the sensory content of imagery in poetry. While somewhat critical about frequency counts of imagery, Friedman indicates that such analyses have shown that Browning's imagery was mostly tactile, and that Shelley and Keats differed on tactile, motoric, and organic imagery but not on a variety of others (p. 27). Although Richards (1925) accepts the argument that sensory quality, vivacity, clearness, and the fullness of detail of the images evoked by a poem are important to its experience, he concludes that the exact relationship between pleasure and the presence of imagery is not an obvious or simple one.

Sensory Imagery and Individual Differences

The first systematic research of imagery was conducted in the late nineteenth century by Galton. Using a questionnaire rich in its ability to arouse sensory images (Galton, 1907, pp. 255–256), interest was directed toward the study of individual differences, with particular attention paid to a person's capacity to evoke different kinds of sensory images. Thus, Ss were requested to recollect their breakfast table, and to note the clarity of the resulting images. In addition, they were asked to image such events as "the beat of rain against the window panes," "an oil-lamp blown out," "a crisp dead leaf," "the taste of lemon juice," and a host of other sensations, e.g., heat, hunger, cold, thirst, fatigue, fever, drowsiness, and a bad cold. This interest in types of imagery remains dominant today (Richardson, 1969), particularly manifesting itself in tests of imagery. An example of perhaps the briefest sort of test is Brower's (1947) investigation of the relative predominance of several modalities, in which Ss were asked if they could see, hear, smell, taste, feel, etc. a pan of onions frying on a stove. Sheehan's (1967) work is more representative of a long line of test development. In response to sets of phrases pertaining to seven modalities, e.g., "the sun sinking below the horizon," Ss rated the vividness of the imagery which was aroused. Sheehan found individual differences in a general imaging ability across the entire range of sensory modes, rather than a specialization of imagery in one particular sense. On this point, however, there appears to be some disagreement, although this may be due to whether or not the imagery obtained in different studies was requested (voluntary) or spontaneous. McKellar (1957, p. 19) found that "mental imagery appears to vary . . . in the domain of one or other of the sense modes . . . ," specifying elsewhere (McKellar, 1965) that visual and auditory modes are most predominant. He suggests in another context (McKellar, 1968; Chapter 4) that various types of imagery may characterize workers in different occupations, as well as refer to unrelated psychological functions. Although McKellar rejects any crude typology based on such differences (McKellar, 1968, pp. 114–116), he does affirm an important distinction. On the one hand, there is the availability of sensory images, which McKellar, among others (Brower, 1947; Raju, 1946), found to be fairly equally distributed among the senses. On the other hand, availability is not the same as the predominance (or frequency of use) of imagery, which Bowers (1929) established, for visual and auditory words at least, as remaining relatively constant over time. In other words, Ss who display imagery can call forth a variety of modalities, but are likely to use one or another mode more than others. This differentiation between availability and predominance, and their relationship to voluntary and spontaneous imagery, remains unclear. However, these undefined features of imagery may help account for the ambiguity and contradictions of many of the findings in this area. Investigations have not sufficiently distinguished the components of availability and predominance of imagery, as well as degree of spontaneity, in their procedures or analyses. To illustrate one consequence of these possible sources of confusion, there is the wide range of imagery reported in different studies, varying in its presence from just a few to many Ss (Lindauer, 1969, pp. 213–214). In addition, there is the general inconclusiveness of the attempt to link individual differences in sensory imagery to various psychological dimensions. This is exemplified by the failure to find a correlation between self-reports of types of imagery and tasks involving different kinds of imagery (Chowdhury & Vernon, 1964), or between the vividness of imagery reported in any one of seven modalities and the performance of a physical skill (Start & Richardson, 1964). Yet Davis (1932) found that although several modes of imagery were reported during tasks dealing with vision, audition, and kinesthesis, the dominant images noted were appropriate to the relevant modality. In Neisser's (1970) evaluation of the contrary results in this area, he accepts both the striking individual differences found and their noncorrelation with performance variability. He concludes that despite the reality of the image to the person "it does not endow him with any special capacities [p. 176]."

Among other lines of research related to imagery typing, less of a distinction has been made between sensory modalities than between visualizers and verbalizers (Roe, 1951, 1953; Short, 1953), perhaps because this sort of difference, unlike that between sensory modes, appears to refer to a more reliable typology (Richardson, 1969, p. 62). Further, the characteristic emphasis has usually been on the visual mode and its various attributes (e.g., high or low imagery, concrete or abstract reference, etc.), and to a lesser degree, audition. For example, visual imagery has been related to personality (cf. Steward, 1965) and to physiological indices such as the pupillary and galvanic skin response (cf. Colman & Paivio, 1969); visual imagery for pictures versus words representing those pictures have been compared (Paivio & Yarmey, 1965), as have visual and auditory presentations (Patel & Shastri, 1961). An exception to this narrow preoccupation with one or two senses is the work of Sarbin and Juhasz (1970), who refer to the different roles played by various imagery modalities in imagination. This interest in only a few modes results in the priority and dominance of the visual and auditory modalities in imagery research. This possibly narrow preoccupation with two senses may be due to the high frequency of such words in language and therefore their overuse as materials, the limited techniques available for stimulus presentation, and the importance of seeing and hearing in evolution and their adaptive role in everyday affairs. The apparent importance of the visual mode [but see Duran (1969) on its relative unimportance in the blind] might in addition be due to Es' familiarity with a host of other well-known phenomena related to imagery which are primarily visual, e.g., hallucinations, eidetic imagery, mnemonic devices, etc. As a consequence of these factors, the reliance on visual and auditory modes and materials to the exclusion of other senses may be excessive, and the engrossment with their role in imagery perhaps an unfortunate restriction of the problem. Possibly more critical, research which focuses on individual differences in sensory imagery relies mainly on correlations between factors already existing in Ss rather than directly manipulating those variables thought to be responsible for imagery (Cronbach, 1957). Thus, generalizations refer more to differences between Ss' sensory imagery and the consequences thereof than to the processes involved in sensory imagery. On the other hand, the following review of learning research in which imagery variables have been directly manipulated, has remained indifferent to the role of individual differences.

Sensory Imagery
and Learning

Together with the study of individual differences, the topic of learning has received major attention from researchers in the field of imagery (see, for example, Chapters 7 and 11, this volume). The latter line of inquiry may be of special value if it be granted that acquisition and retention processes are basic to an understanding of the origins and functions of imagery in all its various manifestations. Furthermore, research strategies in this area tend to rely more on the experimental rather than the correlational approach to imagery, the search being directed more toward generalizations about processes than to individual differences. Early research (Bowers, 1931) used verbal materials selected on the basis of their face validity reference to three modalities. The results indicated that immediate and delayed recall of visual and kinesthetic words, but not auditory, were positively related to their rated imagery. In another study (Bowers, 1932), it was found that recall for visual words did not vary as a function of Ss' reported degree of imagery. The inconsistency of these results, also characteristic of the investigations which dealt with individual differences from which this early work in learning stemmed, may have been due to the basis upon which the materials were chosen. Words were selected apparently on an intuitive level, rather than by specified and controlled procedures. The obvious consequence for Bowers' and similar research which chose their materials on an *a priori* basis, was most likely the confounding of modality differences with familiarity. For example, high recall for visual rather than kinesthetic words may be due to the greater exposure and use of the former type of material in reading.

During the hiatus into which imagery research fell for 20–30 years until the present (Holt, 1964), virtually nothing was done to relate learning to sensory imagery. However, even when careful and rigorous techniques were developed as part of the most recent extensive investigations of the parameters of imagery (Paivio, 1969), sensory aspects of imagery have generally been ignored. Contemporary research has concentrated for the most part on traditional concerns of rote learning, neglecting much of the aspects of imagery already reviewed in the context of individual differences. For example, learning studies have been concerned with whether imagery (irrespective of type), evoked by paired-associate material (irrespective of S characteristics), acts as a kind of "peg" upon which to "hang" associations (Paivio, 1969), reduces intralist interference by differentiating the material (Dominowski & Gadlin, 1968; Raser & Bartz, 1968), or is a form of conditioned sensory response (Staats, 1968, pp. 141–150). Also illustrating the neglect of the intrinsic features of imagery is the exclusion of sensory qualities among the many stimulus attributes which have been used to manipulate imagery. Included among the stimulus characteristics studied, of particular note is the concrete–abstract dimension, as well as the materials' association value, generality–specificity, and emotionality, and the traditional variables of meaningfulness and frequency (Paivio, Yuille, & Madigan, 1968). With the exception of the study by Yuille and Barnsley (1969), who used paired-associates composed of items which simultaneously aroused different degrees of imagery in three modalities (visual, auditory, and kinesthetic), the sensory aspects of the materials to be learned have not seriously been taken into account. Instead, the focus remains fixed on the visual component of imagery (Bower & Winzenz, 1970; Bugelski, Kidd, & Segmen, 1968). The neglect of other sensory modes of imagery also typifies normative studies which have established the imagery values of words in relation to familiarity and other verbal dimensions (Haagen, 1949), or as a basis for the analysis of serial learning (Tulving, McNulty, & Ozier, 1965).

These divers investigations have not been altogether unaware of imagery's sensory features. Its importance is referred to in discussions of the problem, as well as in instructions to Ss, in which the "picture in the head" analogy is frequently used (cf. Paivio, 1969, p. 243; Walker, 1970, p. 165). Interestingly, sensory associations to verbal materials have been categorized in studies of concept formation, e.g., as round, cold, sharp, rough, etc. (Underwood & Richardson, 1956a,b), but have ignored imagery referents. This somewhat paradoxical omission is particularly surprising since recent work in this area parallels many of the interests of researchers in imagery, e.g., the effect of mode of presentation (Otto & Britton, 1965), and a concern with the scaling of stimulus attributes (Roberts, 1968).

A Program
of Research

Summarizing the research reviewed, interest in the sensory aspect of imagery is high in the study of individual differences, although its role appears unclear; in contrast, the sensory dimension is relatively ignored in the area relating imagery to learning. One might be patient with an inability to understand the phenomenon of sensory imagery whose existence is at least recognized, but it is difficult to acknowledge the failure to consider its possible function. The situation is exacerbated by the absence of systematic research which specifically focuses on the sensory attribute of imagery. Holt (1964, p. 261) has asserted that there is ". . . a striking dearth of phenomenological and taxonomic studies . . . to examine the contents of consciousness attentively and [to] laboriously classify the types of imagery." Chowdhury and Vernon (1964, p. 363) also express their dissatisfaction with the current state of knowledge about imagery in similar terms. "There is certainly room for further work in reaching a more adequate classification and assessment of introspection about imagery." Thus, it would seem that an important priority can be made for the establishment of norms for the sensory and imagery content of verbal material, and then to use such standardized items in further investigations along any one of the lines of inquiry reviewed thus far. It may be quite possible that some of the difficulties already noted in the field, such as relating individual differences in imagery to skills and abilities, and the specific function of imagery in learning, might be clarified to the extent that the sensory attributes of the materials used could be more adequately taken into account.

Sensory Attributes of Imagery Evoking Materials

As a means to these ends, sensory and imagery norms for 228 words were established by Lindauer (1969). The sensory dimension of these materials, taken from an original pool of 1115 items selected from a book of synonyms (Fernald, 1947), were judged by several groups heterogenous in background (total $N = 28$). The 228 words finally selected were those which Ss indicated showed a high degree of reference to one of five sensory modalities. E.g., "Does the word refer to vision [etc.] or no sense, and to what degree [on a three-point scale]?" The assignment of stimuli into five sensory modes resulted in the predominance of words referring to vision and sound (equally accounting for about half of the total number), taste and touch words were intermediate in the relative frequency of their occurrence, and words that dealt with smell lowest (accounting for only 19 of 228 words). The distribution of these highly sensory words paralleled the frequency of occurrence with which the five modality references were found in the original population of over 1000 words. Having established a consistently high sensory referent for 228 words, two groups ($N = 21$ each) composed of Ss who reported having at least good imagery, then rated the ease or vividness of the imagery of these sensory words. E.g., "If the word arouses an image, indicate [on a three-point scale] the ease with which the word does this [or] the vividness of the evoked image." The ease and vividness attributes of imagery were used, although a variety of other terms have been used to describe and measure imagery (e.g., strength, importance, clarity, and frequency). The two types of ratings for each word, which were more similar than different, were combined. This index provided the best over-all estimate of the imagery arousal capacity or potency of the sensory stimuli. The results indicated that the highest imagery was aroused by words which referred to the taste and touch modalities, visual words were about equally distributed among high, moderate, and low levels of imagery, and smell and sound words were assigned to the lowest degree of imagery potency.

While the relatively small and unequal number of words used in several modalities may limit generalizations somewhat, the results suggest that the high priority given to visual and auditory modes and materials in most studies of imagery may be misplaced. In the above study, imagery for visual materials, the mode most frequently studied, was not as high as that found for taste and touch. The latter two stimulus modes, despite their capacity to evoke the highest degree of imagery, are rarely studied in imagery research. Further, auditory imagery, the mode next in order of appearance in imagery investigations, had one of the lowest imagery evoking capacities in relation to the other senses. The neglect of the sensory value of imagery is further affirmed when comparisons of this list of imagery materials were made with other compilations which did not systematically attempt to include the sensory dimension. Such juxtapositions revealed that the exclusion of sensory considerations in the derivation of imagery lists has resulted in very little correspondence with the present list. For example, only 81 items in the Paivio et al. (1968) list of almost 1000 nouns, the largest compilation of imagery words, were found in the originally used pool of over 1000 sensory words (which included all verbal forms of expression). One might therefore speculate that part of the inconclusiveness of the research which correlates performance with individual differences in imagery (cf. Neisser, 1970), as well as some of the disagreement on the role of imagery in learning (cf. Dominowski & Gadlin, 1968), may be due to the uncontrolled and limited effectiveness of the stimulus materials' capacity to arouse imagery. That is, the potency of the imagery evoking stimuli used in different studies varied, was low, or divergent because of the neglect of their sensory attributes. Another consequence of the differences found in the degree of imagery evoked by materials with different sensory referents is to support a view of the senses as differentiated and distinct, rather than as relatively unitary and interrelated (Bartley, 1958, pp. 57–66; Borenstein, 1955–56; v. Hornbostel, 1955). This point would be entirely in keeping with Holt's (1964, p. 261; see also Chapter 1, this volume) contention that ". . . all kinds of imagery do not fall on a simple continuum, but may call for separate mechanisms."

Sensory Imagery and Learning

As part of a continuing program for using these established sensory imagery materials in the area of learning, two unpublished studies have been carried out by John Jamele. The first study presented 35 Ss, in a free recall paradigm, the previously established sensory materials of high and low imagery. Subjects were given three immediate recall trials followed by a one week delayed test trial. The list to be learned was composed of 60 sensory words (12 from each of the 5 modalities, equated for frequency), which were selected so as to be equally divided into words high and low in their imagery potency. Examples of the words in each sense modality (with high and low imagery indicated, respectively) were as follows: smell (pine, camphor), taste (salt, spicy), touch (velvet, prickly), vision (glaring, beautiful), and sound (percussion, voice). Each word, arranged into one of three different orders in the list, was projected before small groups of Ss for 5 seconds, with a 1 second interstimulus interval, and a 5 minute period at the end of the list presentation for the recall of the items in any order. The results with respect to recall differences between modalities indicated that, in general (statistical significance was found for Trials 1 and 2 only), words referring to smell were recalled more frequently than the four other modalities, taste words were poorest in recall, and the other modes were intermediate. Unexpectedly, low imagery words were better recalled than high imagery items (a difference not statistically maintained on the last two test trials).

Results from this study tend to affirm the point made earlier about the overdependence upon the visual and auditory modes in imagery investigations. When the number and degree of sensory referents were controlled, as in this study, recall for materials in the visual and auditory modes were not particularly distinguished, and were in fact superseded by other modes. The most startling finding, however, was the relatively poor recall for sensory stimuli of high imagery potency. Although the unanticipated finding of better recall for low imagery arousing sensory materials would be a sufficient impetus for replication, this result was even more ambiguous in the light of a significant interaction between imagery and modality at every test trial; this indicated that the imagery effect depended upon the particular stimulus modality that was learned. For example, low imagery was superior to high imagery potency for vision and touch stimuli but not for other modes (although this varied somewhat with trials). Additional examination of the data suggested that this interaction effect, and possibly the effectiveness of the low imagery items as well, were due to Ss' organization of the materials into clusters, a variable discussed by Shuell (1969).

In effect, Ss may have integrated the materials along lines which cut across the experimentally manipulated distinctions of degree of imagery and type of modality, perhaps by linking associations "that have to do with the senses" irrespective of the particular sense and the imagery involved. This interpretation implies that the specific learning paradigm used, and its contribution to Ss' set, need to be evaluated in investigations of the role of sensory imagery in learning (as they have been in studies in which sensory components of imagery were not included).

At this point in the sequence of investigations under way, it was felt that the effect of imagery potency and the sensory value of imaged stimuli in learning should be experimentally disentangled from one another and from other variables, such as organizational factors. The study reported above was confounded to some extent by organizational processes, these being presumably augmented by the use of a repeated measures design. That is, the previous procedure allowed each S to receive all treatments, i.e., the list of stimuli contained items both high and low in imagery potency, and simultaneously represented five modalities, a combination which may have facilitated the organization of the materials along lines supplementary to those intended by E. Hence, in the next experiment in the program, an attempt was made to unravel high and low imagery potency from the sensory characteristics of the stimuli. This was accomplished by using a design in which different groups each received a different combination of conditions. In a factorial design (composed of 20 groups with 12 Ss each, equally divided by sex), each group received stimuli from but one sensory mode and each was either high or low in imagery potency. In addition, half of the 12 items in the list presented to Ss also included concrete or abstract materials taken from the Paivio et al. (1968) lists, which was another means of representing high and low stimulus imagery, respectively, in the various groups. Thus, each condition included stimuli from one sensory mode, and one level of imagery which included both the imagery potency of sensory words and the concrete–abstract dimension of nouns. One immediate free recall trial was obtained, with the other procedures essentially the same as those used previously.

The results for this experiment, possibly more reliable than the earlier one because of its improved design and larger N, clarifies some of the earlier findings, as well as raises additional questions. Modality differences in retention revealed the relatively low recall of taste references, as before, but now included visual materials as well. The smell mode again, along with touch and sound items, were learned best. These findings support the earlier contention that the visual modality has been overemphasized in research relevant to both individual differences and learning. Also supporting imagery's noncorrelation with performance, reviewed earlier, it was also found that recall was not consistently related to degree of imagery. Taste and vision words, for example, shown by Lindauer (1969) to evoke high and moderate imagery, respectively, yielded the poorest recall; the other modes, with varying degrees of imagery, had the best recall.

The effect of imagery on learning contrasted somewhat with the results of the earlier study. Not only was there no interaction between imagery and modality, but the expected superiority of the recall of high over low imagery items was now found. However, this was not due to the high imagery potency of the sensory stimuli, but to the contribution of the concreteness dimension of the materials. That is, a significant interaction between imagery and list type (i.e., sensory vs. concrete–abstract) revealed that the recall for low imagery abstract items was not only worse than high imagery concrete nouns, but also poorer than both high and low imagery sensory words; the last three classes of words did not differ among themselves. The ineffectiveness of high in comparison to low imagery potency for sensory materials tends to corroborate, at least partially, the earlier finding of high imagery's inferiority to low imagery when manipulated by sensory materials. It would therefore seem that relative degrees of imagery for strongly sensory materials may be functionally irrelevant. Emphatically sensory items with relatively low imagery potency, by virtue of their sensory implications alone, may in absolute terms be sufficiently high on imagery to be equivalent in their effect on recall. Thus, despite different relative degrees of imagery potency, apparent imagery differences which are based on a high sensory reference nevertheless act similarly to facilitate learning. In addition to this interaction between imagery and types of materials, which suggests several directions for further research, the results were shown to be even more complicated by the finding of a sex difference which indicated that females recalled more than males. However, this effect also interacted with modality and imagery, e.g., males did better on the visual mode than females, but this was true for high and not low imagery. This result regarding sex differences is a strong argument for including in the next stages of research the individual differences variable in the attempt to relate learning processes to the role played by the sensory value of imaged stimuli. In this manner, it may be said that research on sensory imagery and learning has come around full circle to those efforts which began with the work by Galton.

Summary

The sensory aspects of imagery, which refer to the sights and sounds and other modality references with which images are often imbued, are an essential phenomenological feature of imaging. Despite the resurgence of interest in the topic of imagery and its various manifestations, sensory imagery in studies of individual differences has been insufficiently understood, and has hardly been considered in investigations of imagery's role in learning. An evaluation of these fields as neglectful of the role of sensory imagery, and unsystematic in its treatment when this variable has been included, may account for some of the inconclusiveness, ambiguity, and controversy which appear to characterize some of the topics reviewed. On this basis, these two major areas of interest in imagery were critically examined, together with a survey of the role of sensory imagery in psychological aspects of language and aesthetics.

With respect to individual differences in sensory imagery, several issues were discussed. These refer to the existence, type, degree, and manifestation of sensory imagery, its correlation with various skills and performance, and the overpreoccupation with one or two modes. While many of these issues appear unresolved, they should at least be recognized. In the case of learning research, whether investigations are normative, correlative, or experimental, the sensory component of imagery is largely neglected or casually treated, although it is usually presumed, implicit, or indirectly referred to.

As a consequence of these considerations, a program of research was outlined. Initially, materials were standardized for their sensory reference and their imagery evoking potency. These materials were then used in several studies of free recall learning. Among the various conclusions which emerged from the program of research, the following were most salient. First, the modes most often studied, vision and audition, were neither highest in imagery or best in recall in comparison to taste, touch, and smell modality references. This supports the contention that there has been an overreliance on limited modes of imagery and materials in most research on individual differences and learning. Second, high imagery for a particular mode, e.g., taste, did not necessarily lead to better recall. This parallels a frequently found failure to find correlations between imagery and various performance variables. Third, differences between sensory modes in the imagery they arouse and their recall suggest qualitative distinctions between the senses which go beyond merely quantitative variations in the general nature of their functioning. Fourth, different degrees of imagery for sensory materials may be nonetheless functionally equivalent. Materials with a high degree of sensory reference, whether relatively high or low in their imagery arousal capacity, may equally facilitate learning. This implies that differences hitherto found between stimuli high and low in imagery may disappear to the extent their sensory content is controlled for. Fifth, in addition to accounting for the imagery and modality characteristics of the materials to be learned, other important variables to be considered in future research include the type of learning paradigm used, organizational factors, the concrete–abstract attribute of meaning, and sex differences. This last point, the consideration of sex differences, emphasizes the need to recognize the role of individual differences in the study of learning and imagery.

References

Asch, S. E. On the use of metaphor in the description of persons. In H. Werner (Ed.), *On expressive language.* Worcester, Massachusetts: Clark Univ., 1955. Pp. 29–38.

Asch, S. E. The metaphor: A psychological inquiry. In R. Taguiri and L. Petrullo (Eds.), *Person perception and interpersonal behavior.* Stanford: Stanford Univ., 1958. Pp. 86–94.

Bartley, S. H. *Principles of perception.* New York: Harper, 1958.

Boernstein, W. S. Classification of the human senses. *Yale Journal of Biology and Medicine,* 1955–1956, **28,** 208–215.

Bower, G. H., & Winzenz, D. Comparison of associative learning strategies. *Psychonomic Science,* 1970, **20,** 119–120.

Bowers, H. The constancy of imaginal content. *Journal of Educational Psychology,* 1929, **20,** 295–298.

Bowers, H. Memory and mental imagery. *British Journal of Psychology,* 1931, **21,** 271–282.

Bowers, H. Visual imagery and retention. *British Journal of Psychology,* 1932, **23,** 180–195.

Brower, D. The experimental study of imagery: II. The relative predominance of various imagery modalities. *Journal of General Psychology,* 1947, **37,** 199–200.

Bugelski, B. R., Kidd, E., & Segmen, J. Image as a mediator in one-trial paired-associate learning. *Journal of Experimental Psychology,* 1968, **76,** 69–73.

Chandler, A. R., & Barnhart, E. N. *A bibliography of psychological and experimental aesthetics 1864–1937.* Berkeley, California: Univ. of California, 1930.

Chowdhury, K. R., & Vernon, P. E. An experimental study of imagery and its relation to abilities and interests. *British Journal of Psychology,* 1964, **55,** 355–364.

Colman, F. D., & Paivio, A. Pupillary response and galvanic skin response during an imagery task. *Psychonomic Science,* 1969, **16,** 296–297.

Cronbach, L. J. The two disciplines of scientific psychology. *American Psychologist,* 1957, **12,** 671–684.

Davis, F. C. The functional significance of imagery differences. *Journal of Experimental Psychology,* 1932, **15,** 630–661.

Dominowski, R. L., & Gadlin, H. Imagery and paired-associate learning. *Canadian Journal of Psychology,* 1968, **22,** 336–348.

Drever, J. *A dictionary of psychology.* Baltimore, Maryland: Penguin, 1963.

Dudley, L. *The study of literature*. Cambridge, Massachusetts: Riverside, 1928.

Duran, P. Jr. Imagery and blindness: A personal report. *Journal of Humanistic Psychology*, 1969, **9**, 155–166.

Fernald, J. C. *Standard handbook of synonyms, antonyms, and prepositions*. New York: Funk & Wagnall, 1947.

Friedman, N. Imagery: From sensation to symbol. *Journal of Aesthetics and Art Criticism*, 1953, **12**, 25–37.

Galton, F. *Inquiries into human faculty and its development*. (2nd ed.) New York: Dutton, 1907.

Haagen, C. H. Synonymity, vividness, familiarity, and association value ratings of 400 pairs of common adjectives. *Journal of Psychology*, 1949, **27**, 453–463.

Holt, R. R. Imagery: The return of the ostracized. *American Psychologist*, 1964, **19**, 254–264.

v. Hornbostel, E. M. (Orig. publ. 1938.) The unity of the senses. In W. D. Ellis (Ed.), *A source book of Gestalt psychology*. New York: Humanities, 1955. Pp. 210–216.

Knapp, R. H. A study of the metaphor. *Journal of Projective Techniques*, 1960, **24**, 389–395.

Lindauer, M. S. Imagery and sensory modality. *Perceptual and Motor Skills*, 1969, **29**, 203–215.

McKellar, P. *Imagination and thinking*. New York: Basic Books, 1957.

McKellar, P. The variety of human experience. In R. S. Daniel (Ed.), *Contemporary readings in general psychology*, 2nd ed. Boston, Massachusetts: Houghton, 1965. Pp. 122–126.

McKellar, P. *Experience and behavior*. Baltimore, Maryland: Penguin, 1968.

Neisser, U. Visual imagery as process and as experience. In J. S. Antrobus (Ed.), *Cognition and affect*. Boston, Massachusetts: Little, Brown, 1970. Pp. 159–178.

Osgood, C. E. *Method and theory in experimental psychology*. New York: Oxford Univ. Press, 1953. Pp. 642–646.

Osgood, C. E., Suci, G. J., & Tannenbaum, P. H. *The measurement of meaning*. Urbana, Illinois: Univ. of Illinois, 1967.

Otto, W., & Britton, G. Sense-impression responses to verbal and pictorial stimuli. *International Review of Applied Linguistics in Language Teaching*, 1965, **31**, 51–56.

Paivio, A. Mental imagery in associative learning and memory. *Psychological Review*, 1969, **76**, 241–263.

Paivio, A., & Yarmey, A. D. Pictures versus words as stimuli and responses in paired-associate learning. *Psychonomic Science*, 1965, **5**, 235–236.

Paivio, A., Yuille, J. C., & Madigan, S. A. Concreteness, imagery, and meaningfulness values for 925 nouns. *Journal of Experimental Psychology*, 1968, **76** (1, Pt. 2).

Patel, A. S., & Shastri, A. L. Efficiency in serial rote learning as a function of visual vs. aural presentation of learning material. *Psychological Studies, Mysore*, 1961, **6**, 1–11.

Raju, P. T. A note on imagery types. *Indian Journal of Psychology*, 1946, **21**, 86–88.

Raser, G. A., & Bartz, W. H. Imagery and paired-associate recognition. *Psychonomic Science*, 1968, **12**, 385–386.

Richards, I. A. *Principles of literary criticism*. New York: Harcourt, 1925.

Richardson, A. *Mental imagery*. New York: Springer Publ., 1969.

Roberts, D. M. Meaningfulness of Underwood and Richardson's (1965a) sense impression descriptive adjectives. *Psychonomic Science*, 1968, **13**, 121–122.

Roe, A. A study of imagery in research scientists. *Journal of Personality*, 1951, **19**, 459–470.

Roe, A. *The making of a scientist*. New York: Dodd, Mead, 1953.

Sarbin, T. R., & Juhasz, J. B. Toward a theory of imagination. *Journal of Personality*, 1970, **38**, 52–76.

Sheehan, P. W. A shortened form of Betts' questionnaire upon mental imagery. *Journal of Clinical Psychology*, 1967, **23**, 386–389.

Short, P. L. The objective study of mental imagery. *British Journal of Psychology*, 1953, **44**, 38–51.

Shuell, T. J. Clustering and organization in free recall. *Psychological Bulletin*, 1969, **72**, 353–374.

Simpson, L., & McKellar, P. Types of synesthesia. *Journal of Mental Science*, 1955, **10**, 141–147.

Spurgeon, C. F. E. (Orig. publ. 1935.) *Shakespeare's imagery and what it tells us*. London: Cambridge Univ. Press, 1952.

Staats, A. W. *Learning, lanugage, and cognition*. New York: Holt, 1968.

Start, K. B., & Richardson, A. Imagery and mental practice. *British Journal of Educational Psychology*, 1964, **34**, 280–284.

Stewart, H. Sensory deprivation, personality, and visual imagery. *Journal of General Psychology*, 1965, **72**, 145–150.

Tulving, E., McNulty, J. A., & Ozier, M. Vividness of words and learning to learn in free-recall learning. *Canadian Journal of Psychology*, 1965, **19**, 242–252.

Underwood, B. J., & Richardson, J. Some verbal materials for the study of concept formation. *Psychological Bulletin*, 1956, **53**, 84–95.   (a)

Underwood, B. J., & Richardson, J. Verbal concept learning as a function of instructions and dominance levels. *Journal of Experimental Psychology*, 1956, **51**, 229–238.   (b)

Walker, H. J. Imagery ratings for 338 nouns. *Behavior Research Methods and Instrumentation*, 1970, **2**, 165–167.

Warren, H. C. *Dictionary of psychology*. New York: Houghton, 1934.

Werner, H. (Ed.) *On expressive behavior*. Worcester, Massachusetts: Clark, 1955.

Werner, H. On physiognomic perception. In G. Kepes (Ed.), *The new landscape in art and science*. Chicago, Illinois: Paul Theobald, 1956. Pp. 280–282.

Woodworth, R. S. *Experimental psychology*. New York: Holt, 1938.

Yuille, J. C., & Barnsley, R. H. Visual, auditory and tactual imagery. Paper presented at the 19th International Congress of Psychology, London, England, 1969.

7
PETER W. SHEEHAN

A FUNCTIONAL ANALYSIS
OF THE ROLE OF VISUAL
IMAGERY IN UNEXPECTED
RECALL[1]

Some Historical Antecedents

The question of the adaptive significance of mental imagery has long plagued psychology. Historical reviews debate fervently, for instance, the relationship of imagery to general accuracy of recall with results persisting in being both positive (e.g., Kuhlman, 1960) and negative (e.g., Leask, Haber, & Haber, 1969). It is hard indeed not to be forcibly impressed by the "adaptive luxury" of Galton's (1911) view of imagery where imagery is an inventive, highly useful mechanism allowing actions of any kind to be easily and effortlessly recalled. Yet, Jenkin (1935) found no such evidence for the impressive nature of imagery; to her, visual imagery was vastly inferior to other aids to memory. We are to be caught, it seems, somewhere between the conception of images "as an army of helpers rushing to the mind's assistance [Betts, 1909, p. 53]" and more sobering notions of imagery such as the view that it goes farther to individualize situations than is at all biologically useful (Bartlett, 1927).

Amid the chaos the early literature on imagery reveals a surprising degree of uniformity on one particular aspect of the adaptiveness of mental imagery. Some order may be introduced into the introspectionists' data by drawing distinctions both among the kinds of imagery evoked and the

[1] The program of research reported in this chapter was financed in part by research funds from the University of New England, and in part by a grant from the Australian Research Grants Committee. Special thanks are due to Jacqueline Lloyd for her help throughout the work.

types of recall situations in which the imagery is aroused. There seems to be quite a clear consensus, for example, about the role spontaneous (as opposed to voluntary) imagery plays in situations where a subject is baffled or puzzled in his thinking. Betts (1909) found that when one is confused in the direction of his thinking a flood of imagery typically appears and that the greatest function of imagery is to be found where the meaning sought best lies in the percept rather than in its relations: "In all places where we would welcome the percept but cannot have it, the image may serve as a very acceptable substitute [1909, p. 93]." When one is confused in the direction of thinking, or finds it hard to understand the difficulty of a proposition it does not always follow that a "percept" would, in fact, be of service. But Betts here appears to argue that the introspecting subject faced with perplexity experiences the need for a percept and it is in the obviousness of its absence that imagery may serve a useful function.

Fox's pioneering research (Fox, 1914) on the conditions which arouse mental images in thought was essentially in agreement with the conclusion that imagery has a definite function to serve where percepts might be of service in the solution of a problem. He found that subjects' attempts to overcome difficulty in understanding a proposition produced abundant mental images and that any conflict in consciousness was a most favorable condition for arousing relevant mental images which then functioned adaptively to help towards the cessation of the conflict. Comstock (1921) later replicated Fox's experiment with positive results. Overall, the weight of the historical evidence is heavily in agreement with the now much-ignored contention that a primary function of imagery manifests itself wherever a reaction is hesitant. Essentially the same position was expressed by Finkenbinder (1914) who argued that problems which present novel features to the observer are recalled most predominantly in visual imagery, and Woods (1915) who found that imagery was richest when stimuli had only a slight degree of familiarity to the observer.

Introspectively speaking, the situation where there is confusion in direction or there is a struggle in consciousness seems at least partially analogous to the case where a subject is asked to recall material he does not expect at all that he will be required to remember. Shepard's oftcited example (Shepard, 1966) of trying to remember the number of windows in his house serves to illustrate my point. We are forever observing the house we live in, but we never actually commit to memory the number of windows in the building. Verbal aids seem to help very little in a situation of this kind, where as Betts might argue, a percept would be enormously helpful. Here, we have a problem of recall—one that is paradoxically novel and where our reaction, initially, may well be one of bafflement and hesitancy. The usefulness of imagery is exemplified introspectively by Shepard who maintains that to answer the question and recall accurately he must *picture* his house as viewed from different sides or from within different rooms and then count the windows represented in his various mental images. His experience touches the main concern of this chapter and recalls the relevance of the early data pointing to the particular role imagery has to play in a situation where we are hesitant, there is a delay in consciousness, or there is a problem to be solved. Viewed in one way the window problem raises the issue of "incidental learning" and its suitability to imagery evocation. To Shepard, information about the number of windows in his house might well have been learned incidentally and it is for this reason that his answer was not easily forthcoming on the test of his recall and so his imagery was aroused. When a nonvisual account of originally visual information is required (as in the answer "ten windows") two possibilities exist: either the information is coded appropriately at the time of original presentation, or it is not. Where the information has been verbally coded (say) at inspection we may speak of "intentional learning." Here, no confusion is present; the subject has no real problem in recalling the information (provided he has not forgotten it) and with no bafflement or confusion present imagery is not obviously needed. If, however, the information was not coded adequately at inspection the situation may be essentially an incidental learning one. Here, bafflement will be present, and imagery required.

Whatever the reasons for Shepard's imagery it is perhaps a measure of the importance of his predicament that most of our learning seems to be of the variety where the demand for memory is unexpected (Berlyne, 1960), and it is disconcerting indeed that so little attention has been paid to the role imagery plays in this context. In this chapter I am concerned with trying to make up for this deficiency and to offer a close, contemporary look at the role imagery plays in unexpected recall. The following section, preparatory to discussion of my own program of research, reviews briefly the evidence to date which directly or indirectly bears on the hypothesis that imagery has a particular role to play in the recall of material learned incidentally. Attention has already been given to the relevance of introspective data to the effect in question. We have just seen for example, how unexpected recall may involve a situation where the subject doesn't initially know the answer and where bafflement or confusion exist leading to the arousal of imagery. The review which follows looks aside from such evidence and examines the relatively sparse number of experimental studies in the literature pertinent to the notion being examined.

Relevant Experimental
Evidence

Kurtz and Hovland (1953) indirectly furnished evidence bearing on the function of imagery in incidental learning. In their study, children were exposed to a series of objects where half of the subjects circled the name of each object while saying the name aloud and the remaining subjects circled a picture of each object in a photograph depicting all of the test stimuli. The study is relevant to our purposes because no subject was led to expect that he would later be recalling the objects. In a test of recognition half the stimulus material appeared as pictures and half as nouns. Results showed that the object-naming group recognized insignificantly fewer items on the picture portion of the recognition test than the picture-control group. The unexpected lack of superiority for the verbal mode lends itself to the hypothesis that the high potential of pictures for arousing images (Paivio, 1969) was at least part determinant of subjects' recognition of stimuli in the incidental learning situation. In another study comparing the retention of visually and verbally presented material under conditions of unexpected recall Farrimond (1968) found a significant advantage in retention for visual information. In explanation of his data, he argued that visual stimuli provide ready coverage in the subject's storage system by offering the degree of redundancy necessary for recall. In a third experiment Bower (1972) investigated whether the superior learning displayed under imaginal elaboration was dependent upon subjects' "intention-to-learn." Groups of subjects were given intentional (INT) or incidental (INC) learning instruction under an imagery orienting set at inspection. The subjects in the INC condition were given the cover story that norms were being collected for the English department on the vividness of mental pictures to particular word pairs. The outcome of the study was a comparable degree of recall for both INC and INT subjects. Although the imagery value of stimuli to be recalled was not varied systematically, Bower's experiment demonstrated that imagery instructions to INC subjects were quite sufficient to break down the typically reported inferiority of INC as compared to INT learning.

Some very recent experiments bear closely on the issue under study. Butter (1970) exposed concrete and abstract noun-digit pairs to subjects who were not instructed to learn the pairs but merely to name them. Over a short period of time recall was superior for the concrete pairs suggesting that imagery (as related to stimulus concreteness) was an influential factor in INC learning. Yuille (1971) subsequently replicated this aspect of Butter's data. Yarmey and Ure (1971) also adopting the verbal learning paradigm produced evidence that imagery effects are undiminished in INC as compared to INT learning and Bugelski (1970) found that subjects instructed to image, but not to learn were actually unable to prevent learning.

Additional studies lend considerable weight to the notion that subjects' imagery habits are relevant to the incidental learning situation. In the first of two studies Ernest and Paivio (1969) found that subject differences in ability to image as defined by variation in performance on spatial ability and other tests were positively related to memory for the irrelevant components of color-word compounds. High imagery subjects were superior in their recall to low imagery subjects. In the second study, Ernest and Paivio (1971) extended their "imagery ability" notion to demonstrate the importance of sex differences. They found better incidental memory on an item-recognition task for females (but not males) with high imagery scores.

The notion of imagery "ability" aside, the hypothesis that imagery response has a *special* contribution to make to unexpected recall arose most immediately for me from an experiment by myself and Ulric Neisser (Sheehan & Neisser, 1969). This study (discussed elsewhere in other contexts—see Chapters 4 and 10, this volume) will be related in some detail since in a sense it is the direct precursor to the program of research reported in the remainder of this chapter.

In the experiment, subjects worked with two types of block designs. The main stimulus patterns were complex geometrical designs; subjects were asked either to evoke visual images of them and to reproduce these images as closely as they could (imagery instructions) or else to recall the patterns with the aid of whatever strategies of memory they could muster (recall instructions). High and low imagers, preselected by scores on an imagery questionnaire, worked with sets of small blocks to construct these geometrical designs as they remembered them. The typical procedure was as follows. Each subject was shown the inspection stimulus on the screen and asked to construct a copy of it while it remained there. As soon as the "perception" construction was completed the stimulus was removed and the subject asked to construct a second set of (simpler) designs—this time, two *Kohs Block Design* patterns. The Kohs task controlled for subjects' activity between each instance of perceiving and recalling of the experimental stimuli. After this intervening task was finished the subject was given either the imagery or the recall set of instructions and asked to reproduce the pattern he had seen earlier on the screen by means of the blocks provided him. The experimental display patterns provided test of intentional learning and the Kohs designs provided test of incidental learning. Subjects typically expected only to be asked to recall the principal stimuli and were unprepared to be asked at the end of the study to remember the intervening task material. After subjects had complied with the experimenter's surprise request to reproduce the incidental Kohs designs, they were asked whether they had employed imagery in their unexpected recall and to rate the quality of their imagery on a 7-point rating scale (Betts, 1909) measuring vividness of imagery.

Although the experiment was primarily concerned with intentional recall of the experimental displays, analysis of the Kohs data presented evidence strongly suggesting that imagery functioned adaptively in the unexpected recall situation, more so in some respects than in the intentional context. Although within subjects better recalled designs were described as being accompanied by more vivid imagery, results showed that good and poor imagers preselected on the questionnaire did not differ in the accuracy of their recall of the intentionally learned stimuli. In contrast, the incidental data showed a significant correlation between accuracy of recall and rated vividness of imagery. Also, the images reported in the unexpected recall situation were much more vivid than those reported in the intentional context. In the incidental situation 81% of the ratings referred to images that were at least "moderately clear and vivid" but only 20% of the ratings reached this level of vividness for the principal designs. Twenty-one subjects gave a higher rating to their imagery in the incidental situation than they had ever given in the rest of the study and, in addition, most subjects reported that their imagery was deeply involved in the recall process. The implication of the data was that subjects may have been forced to rely on imagery in their unexpected recall since they had not verbalized the INC designs at presentation.

Although relevant to the hypothesis under study, this experiment of ours afforded no firm test of the role and function of imagery in unexpected recall. Our design answered, much more adequately, questions about the adaptive utility of imagery in the intentional context. There are too many possible explanations of the difference in results found between the two kinds of material in the experiment for us to be very clear about what was happening in unexpected recall. Tasks, for example, were different for INC and INT recall, the time between presentation and test of retention varied as did also the number of presentations for the two kinds of material. Results, though, seemed to me to be too suggestive of a positive relationship between imagery and incidental learning for the evidence to be ignored. Consequently, the nature of this hypothesized relationship was tested systematically in a program of research involving three experiments which aimed specifically to follow up the phenomenon. The series of studies involved three quite separate experiments which are integrated into a single unit of research for the purposes of this chapter.

Investigation of imagery function is possible within many methodological cal frameworks. This book well demonstrates the variety of those which are available. The verbal learning paradigm as used by Bower (1972), Bugelski (1970), Paivio (1969; see also Chapter 11, this volume) and others affords one of the most objective ways of analyzing imagery functioning. Although in many ways restrictive, such a paradigm makes possible a considerable degree of control over subjects' imagery behavior within the experimental setting and accordingly, it is this framework that was adopted to test systematically the notion hereto proposed that imagery plays a special role in unexpected recall. In the sections to follow I will focus on one particular verbal learning research methodology, outline the specific hypothesis that pertains to it, and discuss the program of research that follows from test of that prediction. Finally, a brief, but tentative explanation of the phenomenon under scrutiny will be attempted and some conclusions drawn.

Formulation of a Hypothesis

It is well known (McLaughlin, 1965) that instructions to learn leading to clear expectation of recall produce appropriate "representational responses" (Deese, 1964) or "differential responses" [as Postman (1964) prefers to term them] during inspection of the material to be learned. This is the case to a much lesser degree in incidental learning defined as a situation where test of memory is unexpected. Preexperimental habits which a subject may bring to a learning situation are many; they include associative responses to the inspection items, habits of classifying and grouping, imagery evocation and various selective reactions to significant features of the stimulus materials. The amount of intentional (INT) or incidental (INC) learning may be said to rely greatly on the representational responses that the subject brings to his task at inspection and those aroused by the procedures of the experiment. When recall is tested (expected, or unexpected) it is these responses which largely must serve to facilitate memory. Intentional learners are motivated to respond to items at the outset and will evoke greater representational responses to items, although the difference between the two types of learners may be a matter of degree, not kind. Analogous to the discussion of "association value" of test stimuli by Postman, Adams, and Phillips (1955) this framework of thinking implies that the difference in amount recalled by intentional and incidental learners will be a function of the imagery arousing properties of items on an inspection list. The imagery value of an item is here defined as an index of the readiness with which it will elicit nonverbal representational responses appropriate to recall.

Some stimuli do lend themselves more readily than others to the evocation of imagery. Evidence has shown clearly that concrete and abstract nouns differ greatly in their image-arousing properties, concrete nouns being much more the effective stimuli for evoking vivid imagery. Concrete as opposed to abstract nouns should therefore be recalled relatively well by both groups of learners (INC and INT subjects alike) since stimuli which easily evoke images will evoke strong mediating responses for all subjects at inspection. As stimuli decrease in their capacity to evoke imagery, however, INT learners motivated by the knowledge that they will be later asked to recall will evoke more effective representational responses at inspection than INC subjects. Imagery is not a readily available mediating response for the abstract stimuli and at inspection, other responses will be elicited more freely. In summary: the higher the imagery value of stimuli, the less difference there will be between INC and INT learners; the poorer the imagery value of stimuli, the more important will be the presence of a learning set for accurate recall.

Referring, then, to a concrete stimulus as a high imagery-arousing item for recall, and an abstract stimulus as a poor imagery-arousing item for recall, the following hypothesis may be stated formally: the pattern of abstract–concrete response in incidental learning will differ from the pattern of response subjects will show in intentional learning. It is predicted specifically that there will be a greater number of concrete as compared to abstract stimuli recalled in INC than in INT learning. The greater difference score in the incidental condition denotes that concrete as distinct from abstract stimuli arouse mental images which play a more specific function in incidental learning than they do in expected recall.

This hypothesis makes a number of assumptions that do not appear to be too demanding. The prediction as formulated assumes that the kind of activity a subject is engaged in at inspection is highly relevant to understanding the nature of his recall; also, that imagery as a response is more readily aroused by some stimuli than by others; and that the imagery arousing properties of stimuli such as concrete and abstract nouns are related unequivocally to ease of learning. Data available appear to support all three assumptions. The nature of a subject's activity at inspection has been shown conclusively to be critical to the efficiency of unexpected recall (Bobrow & Bower, 1969; Whimbey, Mechanic, & Ryan, 1968). There is much evidence to support the contention that imagery is aroused more quickly and easily by some stimuli than by others (Paivio, 1969). And where arousal occurs, imagery has been shown to be a potent correlate of recall (Paivio, Smythe, & Yuille, 1968; see also Chapter 11, this volume). Accordingly, the above stated hypothesis was deemed feasible and tested in a program of research involving three studies. Study I (Sheehan, 1971a) aimed to establish the phenomenon under test. Study II (Sheehan, 1972) essentially aimed to replicate the confirming conditions of Study I, and Study III (Sheehan, 1971b) investigated the basic hypothesis in relation to established individual differences among subjects in the vividness of their mental imagery. In the course of discussion of these experiments previously unpublished data will be examined on the vividness of imagery reported by subjects at time of recall and inspection of the material-to-be-learned. It is this program of research with which the rest of this chapter will be primarily concerned.

A Program
of Research

Study I

In this experiment (Sheehan, 1971a) independent sets of 18 subjects were given either incidental or intentional learning instruction and inspected the material-to-be-remembered under one of two orienting tasks requiring response to 18 concrete (high imagery-arousing) nouns such as "nail" and "tomb" and 18 abstract (low imagery-arousing) nouns such as "justice" and "theory." Stimuli were equated for meaningfulness (m) and frequency of word usage (f) and were selected from the list of stimuli whose values for concreteness are reported by Paivio, Yuille, and Madigan (1968). Concrete and abstract noun stimuli were indexed by mean values of 6.25 and 3.08, respectively, on the 7-point rating scale used by Paivio *et al.* (1968) to index ease of imagery evocation. All subjects were told initially when they entered the experimental room that the study was concerned with individual differences in rating scores on a number of different variables; such instruction served to justify to INC subjects the "nonlearning" nature of their task. Subjects at inspection either judged the familiarity of words on a 7-point scale of frequency of word usage in everyday speech (subsequently to be termed FAM set) or the vividness of imagery voluntarily requested in association with each stimulus item and rated on a 7-point scale of vividness of imagery (to be termed subsequently, IMG set). Intentional learning subjects were treated identically to INC subjects except that just before inspection of stimuli INT subjects were told additionally that their task was also a learning one and that the experimenter would be later testing for recall. Concrete and abstract stimuli were randomly interspersed and each individual item on the list of 36 noun stimuli presented tachistoscopically for four seconds. Time between stimulus onset and rating judgment was recorded for each item and subjects tested for both free recall and recognition of experimental stimuli. Free recall was tested in the standard fashion and a postexperimental inquiry was then conducted to investigate subjects' expectations about test of memory as well as the vividness of any imagery they might have had at recall and at initial inspection of the correctly remembered items. Following this inquiry a recognition test was administered in which subjects were presented with a list of 100 nouns (balanced for imagery value) which included the experimental stimuli. Subjects circled those nouns which they recognized as having been seen earlier.

Following the logic of the basic hypothesis it was predicted that if imagery plays a special role in INC learning then the difference in retention of the concrete and abstract words would be greater in INC than in INT learning. Table 1 sets out the number of concrete and abstract nouns correctly remembered under each orienting task and set of instruction for both types of memory tests. Results supported the hypothesis for the test of recognition only and under familiarity rather than imagery orienting set. As reported in Table 1 the mean difference in correct recognition scores between concrete and abstract stimuli under FAM set was 3.50 for INC subjects and 2.00 for INT subjects. This difference between learning groups was significant supporting the prediction under test ($t = 1.74$, $df = 34$, $p < .05$). Results for "false alarm" responses indicated that the predicted effect was relevant to correct rather than to incorrect recognition responses. The mean difference in "false alarm" recognition scores between concrete and abstract stimuli under FAM set was $-.61$ for INC subjects and $-.50$ for INT subjects. Frequency analysis of these difference scores for the two learning groups showed no appreciable difference: ($\chi^2 = .48$, $df = 1$, $p > .40$).

It is not entirely surprising that the predicted phenomenon was apparent under a *familiarity* orienting task since data elsewhere have shown that high imagery-arousing words are better recalled even when subjects are instructed to use verbal mediators at inspection (Paivio & Yuille, 1969). It is somewhat more difficult to account, though, for the fact that the predicted effect failed to emerge when subjects under IMG set were asked specifically to image at inspection. Two explanations of the finding are possible. Under explicit instructions to image subjects may have made effective use of imagery for the abstract words, thus reducing the differentiation of concrete and abstract stimuli which is critical for the hypothesis to be confirmed. Data of McDonald (reported by Paivio, 1969) supports

TABLE 1

Mean Number of Concrete and Abstract Stimuli Correctly Remembered
by Each Experimental Group in Tests of Free Recall and Recognition[a]

| Test | Orienting task | Instruction | Type of stimulus | | Difference score |
			Concrete	Abstract	
Free recall	IMG	INC	5.61	5.56	− .05
		INT	6.89	6.61	.28
	FAM	INC	6.94	5.00[c]	1.94
		INT	7.00	5.44[b]	1.56
Recognition	IMG	INC	17.22	14.33[d]	2.89
		INT	17.00	14.33[d]	2.67
	FAM	INC	16.50	13.00[d]	3.50
		INT	16.17	14.17[d]	2.00

[a] A modified version of this table appears in Sheehan, (1971a).

[b] $p < .05$ for the difference between number of concrete and abstract stimuli recalled, or recognized for each of eight experimental comparisons.

[c] $p < .01$.

[d] $p < .001$.

this interpretation. McDonald found that subjects asked to evoke imagery often stated that concrete imagery was aroused by one or both members of abstract pairs. Analysis of subjects' reaction times at inspection in Study I, however, revealed a second hypothesis which plausibly accounts for the data. Subjects typically spent a longer time inspecting abstract than concrete stimuli. Under the imagery set, subjects had more time to employ representational responses to aid the recall of the abstract stimuli. This hypothesis is consistent with introspective data obtained from subjects. Subjects in the INC condition under IMG set (but not FAM set) reported that they repeated abstract stimuli to themselves at inspection because they found these stimuli particularly difficult to associate with mental images.

Although Study I confirmed the prediction under test it can be criticized on three grounds. First, the obtained differences were significant (at the .05 acceptance level) in only one out of four possible test comparisons thus suggesting that the outcome was chance, not real. Second, the effect found in the test of recognition could have been an artifact of the procedures adopted for measuring retention (all subjects it will be remembered, were tested for recognition *after* they had been tested for free recall). Third, the study did not adopt the most sensitive procedure available for

investigating subjects' expectations about recall. A truly perceptive procedure demands that the postexperimental inquiry be conducted "blind." The
experimenter who is inquiring should be unaware both as to the identity
of the person he is investigating (whether he is an INC or an INT subject)
and the nature of the subject's performance on the actual memory task.
Study II, to be reported below, attempted to replicate the confirming conditions of Study I and to meet the above-named objections. Using the same
research methodology as before, it provided a much more exact test than
Study I of the hypothesis under investigation.

Study II

This study (Sheehan, 1972) aimed specifically to replicate those conditions associated with confirmation of the prediction in Study I. Accordingly, all subjects rated the familiarity of words at inspection and received
either INC or INT instructions which were identical to those given subjects
in the earlier experiment. Subjects, however, were tested for recognition
alone (the same concrete and abstract stimuli as used before were im-
bedded among stimuli in a 100-item recognition list balanced for concreteness) and an independent, "blind" experimenter who had no knowledge
of each subject's identity or of his memory performance investigated expectations about recall. Results replicated the previously found effect: more
concrete than abstract stimuli were recognized in the INC as compared
to the INT condition ($p = .06$).

The postexperimental inquiry revealed that subjects in the INT condition (who were led to believe initially that the study they were enlisting
for was a rating experiment) actually made little effort to learn the material. Their introductory perception of the study as a rating experiment was
not sufficiently altered by subsequent indications that their experimental
task was really a learning one. Consequently, a third group was added
to this second study to highlight more distinctly the "learning" nature of
the INT subjects' task. Twenty additional subjects inspected stimuli in the
same way as the other two groups except that they were instructed emphatically, just prior to inspection of stimuli, that the test they were about
to do was primarily a learning one and that the experimenter expected
them to make an effort to learn the words. When the results for this group
were compared with the INC group the predicted effect was much stronger
($p < .01$).

Figure 1 sets out the mean number of concrete and abstract stimuli for
FAM set-recognition conditions in both Studies I and II. The symbols,
"INC" and "INT," refer to groups treated identically except that INT sub-

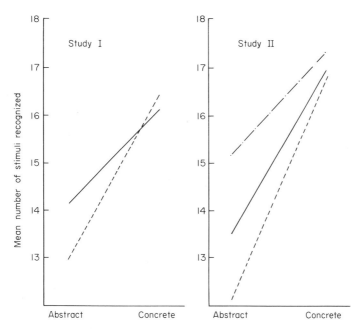

FIG. 1. *Mean number of high imagery-arousing (concrete) and low imagery-arousing (abstract) stimuli recognized by incidental and intentional learning subjects under FAM set in Study I (original) and Study II (replication). (———INT; - - -INC; ·———·INT-Motivated.)*

jects were told before inspection that their task was a learning one. The symbol, "INT-Motivated," refers to the additional group of subjects in Study II to whom the learning nature of their task was emphasized.

Figure 1 graphically demonstrates the phenomenon under test. In both studies the pattern of concrete and abstract response for INC learning was the same. While concrete stimuli were maintained under INC and INT conditions, abstract stimuli were much more poorly recognized under the former set of instructions. The effect was stronger in Study II than in Study I where subjects in the intentional group were made clearly aware of the learning nature of their task. Results are consistent with the rationale outlined earlier in this chapter. Items of high imagery-arousing value were recognized just as well by INC subjects as by INT subjects. Strong nonverbal representational responses evoked by concrete items functioned in memory independently of instructions to learn. Imagery responses were not so readily evoked, though, by abstract nouns and consequently, results for the low imagery stimuli demonstrated a learning inferiority in subjects not expecting recall. For the most discrepant groups in Fig. 1 (the "INC" and "INT-Motivated" groups in Study II) concrete stimulus recognition was maintained under both expected and unexpected recall ($t = 1.24$, $df = 38$, $p > .10$) while abstract stimuli were much more poorly recognized under INC than under INT instruction ($t = 3.33$, $df = 38$, $p < .01$). Analysis indicated that it was the number of correct stimuli recognized that again was related to the predicted effect. Frequency analysis of differences in "false alarm" recognition scores between concrete and abstract stimuli showed no appreciable variation between the two instructional groups ($\chi^2 = 2.60$, $df = 1$, $p > .10$). The special contribution of imagery to INC learning may be inferred from the fact that imagery functioned so adaptively (for the imageable stimuli) in the unexpected recall situation that there was no loss in efficiency of learning relative to a situation where subjects were motivated to remember.

Some visual images are especially vivid while others are not. It seems reasonable to argue that if imagery is adaptive in INC learning, then vivid imagery will characterize those aspects of the learning situation which make for most efficient recall. Intuitively speaking, it must be the vivid, memorable imagery rather than the weak, diffuse imagery which makes it particularly worthwhile for us to replace verbal with nonverbal modes of representation—we know through experience that verbal modes can be so extremely efficient. Although, if recall is to be aided by imagery, the imagery flowing into consciousness must be relevant and not irrelevant—one cannot but be cautioned by Binet's assertion (quoted by Pear, 1927, p. 7) that "with the thought of a hundred thousand francs one has images of four sous."

The variable of vividness is both difficult to measure and conceptually elusive and is a variable virtually ignored by most verbal learning paradigms. As Bower (1972) points out, vivid imagery is stable while faint imagery is difficult to fix. It may be that weak imagery is associated with low performance level, not because the imagery as such lacks vividness, but because poor imagery might be rapidly replaced by alternative imagery responses so reducing effective "inspection time" for any particular word item which is later to be recalled. The following section considers especially "vividness of imagery" in relation to the phenomenon analyzed in this chapter (For more general discussion of the variable, however, see Chapter 4, this volume). It reports unpublished data on subjects' introspections about the vividness of their imagery in INC learning which were collected during the course of Studies I and II discussed above.

Close analysis of introspective data collected in Studies I and II allows us to examine two important questions about the role imagery plays in unexpected recall. First, to what extent do INC subjects experience vivid imagery at inspection irrespective of the nature of the activity subjects are engaged in when stimuli are first presented? Second, to what extent do INC subjects arouse vivid imagery at the moment of recall relative to the quality of imagery aroused by subjects who definitely expect a test of memory? Answer to the first question clarifies the nature of "representational responses" and response habits which the INC subject brings to the learning task. Answer to the second question offers some insight into the nature of subjects' mentation at the "moment of struggle in consciousness" when they are faced with the somewhat novel problem of trying to recall material they did not think they would ever be asked to remember.

Questions related to the vividness of imagery at inspection when stimuli are presented under a nonimagery set (FAM set) may at first seem meaningless. Research has shown, however, that imagery may still be a potent correlate of recall even when subjects are asked to operate under verbal sets (Bower, 1972; Paivio & Yuille, 1969), and it has been often noted that subjects are quite capable of giving responses to inspection stimuli other than the ones the experimenter requests (e.g., Craig & Raser, 1969). It seems pertinent, then, to raise the issue of vividness of imagery for both the IMG and FAM sets at inspection.

Imagery at Inspection. The problem analyzed here is whether, or not, the presence of imagery and its vividness when stimuli are first perceived are relevant to the role imagery plays in unexpected recall. In Study I, previously discussed, ratings of vividness of imagery were obtained directly at inspection for subjects oriented to perceive the noun stimuli under IMG set. For those subjects in Studies I and II who were asked to rate word frequency at inspection (FAM set), however, the experimenter had to wait until after subjects had tried to recall the stimuli before he could legitimately inquire into subjects' imagery at inspection. If the subjects under FAM set said they did evoke imagery initially, they were then asked to indicate how vivid it was. Both groups of subjects were given the same detailed inquiry into the vividness of their imagery at the moment of recall. For every stimulus correctly remembered subjects were asked whether they had evoked an image and if so to rate its vividness on Betts' 7-point rating scale (Betts, 1909). The scale ranged from "1" ("Perfectly clear and vivid") through "3" ("Moderately clear and vivid") down to "7" ("No image present at all").

In summary, then, all subjects reported under identical procedures on their imagery at recall, but subjects oriented under IMG and FAM sets reported on their inspection imagery at different times—IMG subjects reported at the actual time of inspection and FAM subjects did so later, after recall. Interpretation of inspection imagery ratings given by the subjects under the FAM set must of necessity be equivocal, since these ratings were open to contamination by subjects' judgments about their recall imagery made previously.

Analysis of inspection ratings in Studies I and II showed that imagery was as vivid for INC subjects as it was for INT subjects. Table 2 reports the mean vividness ratings at inspection reported by all groups of subjects in Studies I and II for both concrete and abstract stimuli. There were no significant differences between the two learning conditions in the vividness of imagery reported by subjects in Study I and this absence of imagery differences among learning groups was replicated in Study II. In fact, the trend for concrete stimuli in both experiments was for the INC condition to yield slightly *more* vivid imagery at inspection than the INT condition; this effect was regardless of the nature of subjects' orienting activity at inspection. Table 2 also shows that concrete stimuli were imaged more vividly than abstract stimuli by all groups independent of orienting set and type of learning instruction (F for main stimulus effect $= 220.58$, $df = 1,68$, $p < .001$). Results overall suggest that the vividness of imagery elicited at inspection was independent of subjects' intent to learn. Nonverbal representational responses in the incidental learning situation were clearly present for the imageable stimuli and not at all lacking in vividness regardless of what the subject was doing when he first perceived the stimuli.

Imagery at Recall.   Analysis of vividness ratings at recall tended to confirm the findings of Sheehan and Neisser (1969) and support indirectly the early introspectionist evidence for "rich" imagery flowing into consciousness whenever there is a struggle or a novel problem requiring solu-

TABLE 2

Mean Vividness Ratings Given at Inspection *in Studies I and II*
for Learning Conditions, Orienting Tasks, and Types of Stimuli

	Learning condition	Orienting task	Type of stimulus	
			Concrete	Abstract
Study I	INC	IMG	1.66	4.26
		FAM	3.57	5.77
	INT	IMG	1.76	4.21
		FAM	3.73	5.38
Study II	INC	FAM	2.74	5.02
	INT	FAM	3.46	4.62
	INT-motivated	FAM	2.99	4.59

TABLE 3
Mean Vividness Ratings Given at Recall in Studies I and II for
Learning Conditions, Orienting Tasks, and Types of Stimuli

Learning condition	Orienting task	Type of stimulus	
		Concrete	Abstract
Study I			
INC	IMG	2.33	4.99
	FAM	3.22	5.43
INT	IMG	2.79	4.54
	FAM	4.01	5.22
Study II			
INC	FAM	2.67	4.61
INT	FAM	2.97	4.38
INT-motivated	FAM	2.89	4.27

tion. Ratings reported by subjects indicated that vividness of imagery definitely characterized subjects' mentation at the moment of recall. Table 3 sets out the mean vividness ratings at recall reported by subjects in Studies I and II on the 7-point scale of vividness (as before) for each of the orienting tasks and type of stimuli. In Study I, INC subjects reported significantly more vivid imagery at recall than INT subjects for the concrete as compared to the abstract stimuli ($F = 7.15$, $df = 1.68$, $p < .01$). This trend (though not significant) was maintained in Study II. In both studies the greatest vividness of imagery was reported by subjects in the INC condition for the imageable stimuli. Vividness of imagery at recall, then, was positively associated with the maintaining of concrete stimulus recognition in the unexpected recall condition. The effects reported here for vividness of imagery associated with the noun stimuli cannot be explained simply in terms of preexisting group differences in subjects' abilities to image. In the course of the two studies all subjects were given a self-report questionnaire (Sheehan, 1967a) which assessed each subject's general ability to image (in a variety of sensory modalities) independent of his particular experimental rating performance. All experimental groups were comparable on the questionnaire in their average capacity to image vividly.

Studies I and II both presented data suggesting that vividness of imagery inside the experimental setting is positively related to the predicted effect. This finding directly led to the third and final study in this program of research. The next study aimed to examine specifically the relevance of interindividual variation in imaging habits to the occurrence of the predicted effect. Emphasis here was on subject variation in imagery aptitude brought from outside to the experimental setting rather than quality of imagery aroused within the setting itself.

Study III

Extreme groups of good and poor imagers were screened by administering to a large group of subjects outside the experimental setting a reliable self-report questionnaire (Sheehan, 1967a; 1967b) measuring vividness of mental imagery in a variety of sensory modalities. Subjects typically imaging very vividly or very poorly were selected out and tested on the "FAM set-recognition" conditions which had established the predicted INC effect in Studies I and II. These conditions were replicated for both extreme groups of imagers. On the prediction that imagery aptitude will be relevant to the INC predicted effect it was hypothesized that more concrete than abstract stimuli will be recognized in INC than in INT learning by vivid imagers, but the predicted effect will not occur obviously for subjects who characteristically do not image vividly. Arguing from the earlier mentioned findings of Ernest and Paivio (1971), who found INC effects for high scoring females, it was further hypothesized that the predicted effect will be more obvious for strongly imaging females than for strongly imaging males.

Three-hundred and sixty-three students from the University of New England were administered the questionnaire on imagery (to be termed the Betts QMI). An imager was classified as good if he rated items on the visual section of the questionnaire indicating that his imagery was at least "very clear and vivid," and in addition obtained a comparable rating across all seven modalities tapped by the test. A subject was rated "poor" who indicated his imagery on the test was less than "moderately clear and vivid." Forty good and forty poor imagers were selected who were sharply differentiated ($p < .001$) in the vividness of their visual and general mental imagery as assessed by items on the Betts QMI. Stimuli were as presented in the previous two studies: all subjects judged the familiarity of the concrete and abstract stimuli at inspection and were tested for recognition memory only. Instructions for incidental and intentional learning were identical to the "INC" and "INT-Motivated" conditions in Study II. In summary, 4 groups of 20 subjects ($N = 80$) were tested in a 2×2 factorial design. Independent sets of 20 "vivid" (good) and 20 "nonvivid" (poor) imagers were assigned to each of the two learning conditions (INC and INT). As before, two experimenters conducted the study. One experimenter tested the learning performance of subjects and the second experimenter who was "blind" examined subjects' expectations about recall.

Table 4 sets out the mean number of concrete and abstract stimuli recognized by the 10 best and 10 poorest Betts QMI (visual) imagers in each of the two instructional groups. This sample of 40 subjects represented the most extreme scoring group in the total sample of 363 subjects

TABLE 4

Mean Number of Concrete and Abstract Stimuli Correctly Recognized
by Good and Poor Imagers Given INC or INT Instruction
in Study III

| Imagery category | Instructional group | Type of stimulus | | Difference score |
		Concrete	Abstract	
Vivid imagers	INC ($N = 10$)	16.3	11.5[a]	4.8
	INT ($N = 10$)	17.0	14.9[a]	2.1
Nonvivid imagers	INC ($N = 10$)	15.4	11.6[a]	3.8
	INT ($N = 10$)	16.1	11.7[a]	4.4

[a] $p < .01$ For the difference between number of concrete and abstract stimuli recognized by each of the four experimental groups.

screened. Table 4 also shows the mean difference scores (number of concrete minus abstract stimuli recognized) for the two discrepant groups of imagers. Results confirmed the predicted effect for good imagers but not for poor imagers. Vivid imagers showed an appreciably higher recognition of concrete as opposed to abstract stimuli in INC as compared to INT learning. For test of the significance of the discrepancy in difference scores between the two instructional groups: $t = 2.27$, $df = 18$, $p < .025$ for good imagers; and $t = 0.42$, $df = 18$, $p > .10$ for poor imagers. Frequency analysis of false positive responses for the good imagers showed no variation between instructional groups in the magnitude of difference scores ($\chi^2 = .22$, $df = 1$, $p > .10$) indicating that the predicted effect pertained to correct rather than to incorrect stimuli recognized. The larger sample of 80 subjects was used to test the hypothesis concerning sex differences. Results for the 22 females in the sample of 40 high imaging subjects showed a significant association between the nature of learning instruction and magnitude of difference score (Fisher Exact Test, $p < .05$). Data for the remaining 18 males in the selected sample of good imagers, although there was a trend for their actual mean difference scores to go in the predicted direction, showed no appreciable association (Fisher Exact Test, $p > .10$). Most of the greater difference scores were associated with INC instruction for the female group. Looking across sexes, though, results were not entirely in accord with the "individual differences" hypothesis. For the sexes combined, good imagers clearly differed appreciably from poor imagers in the magnitude of the predicted INC effect but only when the very strongest and the very weakest visual imagers in the sample were considered. The originally selected samples of 40 good and 40 poor imagers did not differ appreciably in the effect shown.

Evidence from this final study again replicated the predicted effect and extended the phenomenon to show that imagery aptitude is relevant to its occurrence. Findings are consistent also with the implication of Ernest and Paivio's evidence that INC learning effects are relatively rare among high imaging males. The variable "vividness of imagery," though, as measured by the Betts QMI is distinct from high imagery ability as defined by Ernest and Paivio (1971). Vividness indexes a distinct sensory dimension of imagery, whereas Ernest and Paivio were concerned more with imagery ability defined in terms of the aid that imagery gives to solution of particular problem-solving tasks. Also, the absence of the predicted effect among poor imagers (male and female) does not necessarily negate the previous occurrences of the effect in unselected samples of imaging subjects (as in Studies I and II). In this experiment the nonvivid imagers were a highly stratified sample of a general population of imagers; such subjects would be tested rarely when drawn in a nonbiased fashion from the population at large. In conclusion, it appears from this series of studies that the adaptive role of imagery in unexpected recall is not only related to the quality of imagery aroused by the stimuli presented to the subject within the setting itself, but also to the quality of imagery the subject typically brings with him to the experimental setting.

Some Conclusions and Explanatory Comment

This chapter has aimed at studying a particular phenomenon of mental imagery—one that argues for visual imagery functioning adaptively in the remembering of material learned incidentally. The chapter has reviewed both historical and contemporary evidence supporting the phenomenon and has examined in some detail a particular research program directed at isolating the effect. The adaptive role imagery may play has been shown in three separate experiments all of which present evidence that imagery should be reckoned with as a mediator of learning in the unexpected recall situation. Certainly, verbal mediators such as meaningfulness and word frequency cannot explain the significance of the imagery effect since these variables were controlled in all of the studies conducted.

The incidental recall situation seems somewhat akin to the "struggle or delay in consciousness" which the early introspectionists uniformly reported as especially prone to enrichment by imagery. Vivid imagery at the moment of recall appears to be one established index of this enrichment. Appeal to subjects' introspections indicates that imagery of a vivid kind does characterize recognition in INC learning but the role imagery plays at the moment of unexpected recall appears to be dependent ultimately on the nature of subjects' differential responses when the stimuli are orginally perceived.

Taking up the theoretical framework behind the research methodology that has been adopted, the empirical function of imagery in INC learning seems best conceptualized in terms of "representational responses" aroused in the incidental learning situation. The representational response analysis of imagery as outlined early in this chapter appears to fit the data well. Imagery responses as judged from subjects' ratings were evoked by concrete items independently of instructions to learn and representational responses of a nonverbal kind were made at inspection regardless of the nature of subjects' orienting activity. It remains an interesting question whether the apparent enrichment of imagery at the time of recall could lead to adaptive performance if imagery were not at first present at inspection. Evidence gathered by Bower (1972) implicitly supports the opposite view. Bower asked INC and INT subjects to rate the vividness of their imagery at the time they constructed imaginal links between word stimuli. His data reinforce the notion that imagery at inspection is a critical factor in efficient INC learning. For INC (as well as INT) groups each subject gave a higher mean vividness rating to pairs he later recalled than he did to nonrecalled pairs. Apparently, the INC subjects had available at the moment of imaginal elaboration information which was predictive of whether they would recall the pair.

Evidence from the series of three studies supported the prediction that *more* of one kind of material compared to another would be recognized in INC as opposed to INT learning. In his comprehensive review of INC learning studies McLaughlin (1965) concluded that there is no justification for the implication that there are two types of learning: incidental and intentional. But it does seem that INC learning, defined as a situation where the subject does not expect to be asked to recall, is a situation relatively more prone than INT learning to benefit from the use of mental imagery. This is not to say that verbal mediators are in anyways unimportant in unexpected recall. Images are certainly far from being an army of helpers rushing to our aid (as is frustratingly obvious to an inveterate imager), but when the stimuli to be recalled arouse images easily and the inspection conditions are appropriate then nonverbal modes of representation clearly may function adaptively to mediate accurate memory. The surprising thing is that they can do it so well in a situation where we are at a loss to know just what to remember. To some it seems the problem is not just "what" to recall, it is also a problem of "how" to recall. Not surprisingly, perhaps, at least some aptitude for imaging appears to be necessary for imagery to serve its adaptive purpose in the incidental learning situation.

Many explanations have been offered for the mediating role imagery appears to play in verbal learning. Imagery may enhance recall by increasing the probability that individual items will be retrieved or serve its adaptive purpose by facilitating interitem organization among the stimuli to be learned. Or, imagery may differentiate the stimuli to be recalled and serve its function more indirectly by reducing intralist interference. These and many other explanations of the way imagery works in recall are possible (for detailed discussion of them see Chapter 11). Any adequate explanation of findings in the three studies reported above, seems to require special emphasis on the recognition process since it was in test of recognition and not test of free recall that the predicted effect emerged. The code-redundancy hypothesis (Paivio, 1971), the organizational (Bower, Lesgold, & Tieman, 1969), and differentiation (Dominowski & Gadlin, 1968) accounts of imagery seem hard put to explain this special distinctiveness of the recognition situation if such may be assumed.

Close perusal of the current literature indicates some degree of support for the position that nonverbal modes of representation are implicated especially in recognition effects. Cohen and Granström (1968), for example, offer strong evidence for a major nonverbal component in short-term recognition memory. They studied the retention of visual figures by manipulating the mode of recall and type of material interpolated during the retention interval. The only significant interference effects present for recognition occurred where the interpolated task contained at least some *visual* material. The pattern of data for reproductive memory, on the other hand, was entirely explicable in terms of interference effects arising from interpolated material preventing rehearsal indicating the influence of verbal modes of representation. Clark (1965) investigating recognition memory for random shapes as a function of their complexity, found that high recognition accompanied low verbal encoding. Subjects claimed they had to rely on remembering uncoded imagery of the entire contour of simple forms. It seems reasonable to argue that much of subjects' recognition reported in both these experiments was in the absence of memory traces and recall of verbal mediators. Data indicate that some instances of recognition at least are almost entirely dependent on pure S-perceptual traces (Adams, 1967), "internal representations," or mental images. The view that imagery can be especially relevant to recognition is reinforced by the evidence of Craig and Raser (1969). In the better controlled of two studies investigating the effect of instructions on memory, their data showed that imagery instructions had less effect on recognition (as compared to no-imagery instructions) than on free recall, suggesting imagery was already playing a significant role in the former test of memory. Not all data are consistent, however. Subjects, for example, who were instructed to learn line drawings by naming each one performed better in recognition than subjects asked to imagine the stimuli during learning (Robinson, 1970).

An imagist-oriented account of recognition seems the most adequate theory to explain the obtained INC effect. Introspectively speaking, it does seem possible for one to be exposed to a stimulus, evoke an image to the item and recognize the stimulus on the basis of that image without ever having to recall a particular response. This view of recognition implies that free recall and recognition involve quite different processes. Assuming this is correct, recognition would facilitate the predicted effect since the nature of recognition memory may rely more directly upon the mediating role of imagery than do other forms of memory such as free recall. Mental images provide convenient internal representations which would lead to the appropriate judgment of familiarity without the necessity of response retrieval. The crucial element in a test of recognition is the sensory presence of the item to be recognized. A subject in order to make the necessary familiarity judgment requires only to match an item with the internal representation in order to make the correct judgment "old." If in recognition, imagery aids memory without the presence of errors arising from retrieval, it is through this method of recall that imageable stimuli might best serve an adaptive purpose in a situation (like INC learning) where memory is especially difficult. If all a subject can remember about an item is an image that the stimulus has aroused this is enough for him to identify the item, providing, of course, that none of the other items in the recognition list arouse the same mediator. Such an image, however, would not necessarily lead the subject to reproduce the correct item on a recall test. In support of this argument, Yavuz and Bousfield (1959) have shown that subjects can learn mediational responses even though they cannot recall the items arousing them. In opposition to recognition, if imagery is used to mediate correct responses in free recall the subject must solve first the problem of decoding before he can produce the appropriate verbal output.

The above theoretical explanation must perforce be tentative. It may be too much to assume the INC predicted effect is recognition specific since the absence of the effect in the free recall test situation in Study I may have been just a chance occurrence. However, the repeated replication of the effect in three tests of recognition and its absence in the only test of free recall deserve some comment. It is much more controversial perhaps to assume by way of explanatory comment that recognition and free recall are not indicators of the same underlying memory state. The present chapter by no means attempts to resolve such a hotly debated issue (see Bahrick, 1965; Kintsch, 1968; Murdock, 1968; Tulving & Thompson,

1971; for just some of the arguments); it asserts only that the obtained effect is consistent with a process distinction. Only further work can really decide these and other questions raised by the phenomenon. The research methodology discussed in this chapter did not yield an effect of great magnitude but the differences which emerged, though relatively small, were reliable. Maybe other paradigms of research could tap the effect and in their own style add more insights into what the introspectionists were apparently saying a very long time ago.

References

Adams, J. A. *Human memory.* New York: McGraw-Hill, 1967.

Bahrick, H. P. The ebb of retention. *Psychological Review,* 1965, **72,** 60–73.

Bartlett, F. C. The relevance of visual imagery to the process of thinking. III. *British Journal of Psychology,* 1927, **18,** 23–29.

Berlyne, D. E. *Conflict, arousal and curiosity.* New York: McGraw-Hill, 1960.

Betts, G. H. The distribution and functions of mental imagery. *Columbia University Contributions to Education Series,* 1909, **26,** 1–99.

Bobrow, S. A., & Bower, G. H. Comprehension and recall of sentences. *Journal of Experimental Psychology,* 1969, **80,** 455–461.

Bower, G. H. Mental imagery and associative learning. In Lee Gregg (Ed.), *Cognition in learning and memory.* New York: Wiley, 1972. In press.

Bower, G. H., Lesgold, A. M., & Tieman, D. Grouping operations in free recall. *Journal of Verbal Learning and Verbal Behavior,* 1969, **8,** 481–493.

Bugelski, B. R. Words and things and images. *American Psychologist,* 1970, **25,** 1002–1012.

Butter, M. J. Differential recall of paired associates as a function of arousal and concreteness-imagery levels. *Journal of Experimental Psychology,* 1970, **84,** 252–256.

Clark, H. J. Recognition memory for random shapes as a function of complexity, association value and delay. *Journal of Experimental Psychology,* 1965, **69,** 590–595.

Cohen, R. L., & Granström, K. Interpolated task and mode of recall as variables in STM for visual figures. *Journal of Verbal Learning and Verbal Behavior,* 1968, **7,** 653–658.

Comstock, C. On the relevance of imagery to the processes of thought. *American Journal of Psychology,* 1921, **32,** 196–230.

Craig, J. R., & Raser, G. A. Imagery and interference in paired-associate learning. Paper presented at the Midwestern Psychological Association Conference, Chicago, Illinois, 1969.

Deese, J. Behavioral effects of instructions to learn: Comments on Professor Postman's paper. In A. W. Melton (Ed.), *Categories of human learning.* New York: Academic Press, 1964. Pp. 202–209.

Dominowski, R. L., & Gadlin, H. Imagery and paired-associate learning. *Canadian Journal of Psychology,* 1968, **22,** 336–348.

Ernest, C. H., & Paivio, A. Imagery ability in paired-associate and incidental learning. *Psychonomic Science,* 1969, **15,** 181–182.

Ernest, C. H., & Paivio, A. Imagery and sex differences in incidental recall. *British Journal of Psychology,* 1971, **62,** 67–72.

Farrimond, T. Retention and recall: Incidental learning of visual and auditory material. *Journal of Genetic Psychology,* 1968, **113,** 155–165.

Finkenbinder, E. O. The remembrance of problems and of their solutions: A study in logical memory. *American Journal of Psychology,* 1914, **25,** 32–81.

Fox, C. The conditions which arouse mental images in thought. *British Journal of Psychology,* 1914, **6,** 420–431.

Galton, F. *Inquiries into human faculty and its development.* London: Dent, 1911.

Jenkin, A. M. Imagery and learning. *British Journal of Psychology,* 1935, **26,** 149–164.

Kintsch, W. Recognition and free recall of organized lists. *Journal of Experimental Psychology,* 1968, **78,** 481–487.

Kuhlman, C. K. Visual imagery in children. Unpublished doctoral dissertation, Radcliffe College, 1960.

Kurtz, K. H., & Hovland, C. I. The effect of verbalization during observation of stimulus objects upon accuracy of recognition and recall. *Journal of Experimental Psychology,* 1953, **45,** 157–164.

Leask, J., Haber, R. N., & Haber, R. B. Eidetic imagery in children: II. Longitudinal and experimental results. *Psychonomic Monograph Supplements,* 1969, **3,** 25–48.

McLaughlin, B. "Intentional" and "incidental" learning in human subjects: The role of instructions to learn and motivation. *Psychological Bulletin,* 1965, **63,** 359–376.

Murdock, B. B. Modality effects in short term memory: Storage or retrieval? *Journal of Experimental Psychology,* 1968, **77,** 79–86.

Paivio, A. Mental imagery in associative learning and memory. *Psychological Review,* 1969, **76,** 241–263.

Paivio, A. *Imagery and verbal processes.* New York: Holt, 1971.

Paivio, A., Smythe, P. C., & Yuille, J. C. Imagery *versus* meaningfulness of nouns in paired-associate learning. *Canadian Journal of Psychology,* 1968, **22,** 427–441.

Paivio, A., & Yuille, J. C. Changes in associative strategies and paired-associate learning over trials as a function of word imagery and type of learning set. *Journal of Experimental Psychology,* 1969, **79,** 458–463.

Paivio, A., Yuille, J. C., & Madigan, S. A. Concreteness, imagery and meaningfulness values for 925 nouns. *Journal of Experimental Psychology Monograph Supplement,* 1968, **76,** (No. 1, Part 2). Pp. 1–25.

Pear, T. H. The relevance of visual imagery to the process of thinking. I. *British Journal of Psychology,* 1927, **18,** 1–14.

Postman, L. Short-term memory and incidental learning. In A. W. Melton (Ed.) *Categories of human learning.* New York: Academic Press, 1964. Pp. 145–201.

Postman, L., Adams, P. A., & Phillips, L. W. Studies in incidental learning: II. The effects of association value and of the method of testing. *Journal of Experimental Psychology,* 1955, **49,** 1–10.

Robinson, J. P. Effects of verbal and imaginal learning on recognition, free-recall, and aided recall tests. *Journal of Experimental Psychology,* 1970, **86,** 115–117.

Sheehan, P. W. A shortened form of Betts' Questionnaire Upon Mental Imagery. *Journal of Clinical Psychology,* 1967, **23,** 386–389. (a)

Sheehan, P. W. Reliability of a short test of imagery. *Perceptual and Motor Skills,* 1967, **25,** 744. (b)

Sheehan, P. W. The role of imagery in incidental learning. *British Journal of Psychology,* 1971, **62,** 235–243. (a)

Sheehan, P. W. Individual differences in vividness of imagery and the function of imagery in incidental learning. *Australian Journal of Psychology,* 1971, **23,** 279–288. (b)

Sheehan, P. W. The role of imagery in incidental learning: Replication and extension of an effect. *Journal of Experimental Psychology,* 1972, in press.

Sheehan, P. W., & Neisser, U. Some variables affecting the vividness of imagery in recall. *British Journal of Psychology,* 1969, **60,** 71–80.

Shepard, R. N. Learning and recall as organization and search. *Journal of Verbal Learning and Verbal Behavior,* 1966, **5,** 201–204.

Tulving, E., & Thomson, D. M. Retrieval processes in recognition memory: Effects of associative context. *Journal of Experimental Psychology,* 1971, **87,** 116–124.

Whimbey, A. E., Mechanic, A., & Ryan, S. F. Individual differences in incidental learning and intentional learning. *Journal of Psychology,* 1968, **70,** 77–80.

Woods, E. L. An experimental analysis of the process of recognizing. *American Journal of Psychology,* 1915, **26,** 313–387.

Yarmey, A. D., & Ure, G. Incidental learning, noun imagery-concreteness and direction of associations in paired-associate learning. *Canadian Journal of Psychology,* 1971, **25,** 91–102.

Yavuz, H. S., & Bousfield, W. A. Recall of connotative meaning. *Psychological Reports,* 1959, **5,** 319–320.

Yuille, J. C. Does the concreteness effect reverse with delay? *Journal of Experimental Psychology,* 1971, **88,** 147–148.

8 JEROME L. SINGER AND JOHN S. ANTROBUS[1]

DAYDREAMING, IMAGINAL PROCESSES, AND PERSONALITY: A NORMATIVE STUDY

Introduction

In view of the degree to which daydreaming reports are actually employed by clinicians to make judgments about the content and magnitude of personality conflicts, it is surprising how little is known of the formal structure of daydreams and related imaginal processes in normal functioning. A series of studies by the senior author has sought to obtain more adequate information as to the role of daydreaming in the structure of personality and its relationship to normal patterns of response (Singer, 1966; Singer & McCraven, 1961; Singer & McCraven, 1962; Singer & Schonbar, 1961). Early in the 1960's Singer and Antrobus (1963) carried out an extensive interview and questionnaire study of a great variety of scales of daydreaming along with other personality measures and Guilford's measures of Divergent Production, employing as subjects a group of 100 Columbia College freshmen. The results of this study suggested that daydreaming patterns could be reasonably well described by about seven factors which at the second order level seemed to form one bipolar dimension that might be termed a form of thinking introversion in which the more fanciful aspects of imaginal behavior loaded at one pole and more controlled thoughtfulness at the other.

[1] This study was supported in part by a grant from the National Institute of Mental Health MH-10956. The authors acknowledge with gratitude the help of Professor Sigmund Tobias for statistical and computer programming consultation; Miss Jane Tucker, for assistance in planning and administering the test battery; and Mr. Lawrence Krasnoff for computational and computer services.

The present report describes some of the major findings of a replication and extension of the earlier study. The main thrust of this presentation will be an examination of specific scales of imaginal processes administered to a large sample of male and female college students with a view to ascertaining the normative aspects and patterning of these different modes of inner response. If we regard daydreaming and the stream of consciousness as a special ongoing manifestation of man's image-making capacities it is reasonable to inquire about the degree to which different features of structure or content of fantasy processes relate to each other and to broader aspects of personality structure in young adults.

Most research on imagery has employed some variation of the psychophysical methods or the methods for studying perception. This has led increasingly to a degree of precision which is evident in the other chapters of this volume. At the same time, the ordinary imagery output of the individual takes place in a context of ongoing interaction in work or social situations with complex demands for shifts of attention from external to internal processes. Emphasis here is more upon the continuous processing of internally generated material which takes place even as we are engaged in directed tasks, either motor or cognitive, than upon the precise measurement of specific images. Daydreaming represents one manifestation of the ongoing stream of consciousness some of which undoubtedly involves fairly vivid imagery in visual or auditory modalities but some of which also is carried out in the form of an interior monologue.

Most people learn to ignore the degree to which they are ordinarily processing internally generated material from a long-term memory system or engaging in playful or fearful reorganizations of such material in the form of fantasies. Some of our experiments have used signal detection methods and frequent interruptions of Ss engaged in such tasks for reports of their "task-irrelevant" or "stimulus independent ideation" (Antrobus, Singer, Goldstein, & Fortgang, 1970; Antrobus, Singer, & Greenberg, 1966). The data make it clear that a great deal is going on in the way of internal processing, sometimes parallel with, sometimes sequential with the major task of detecting the signals. When content reports are obtained, they include a good deal of visual imagery, scenes from the past or anticipated future events or fanciful possibilities as well as some auditory imagery, remembered conversations, etc. When one considers that in our experiments subjects are often processing signals at rates as fast as one every .5 seconds, the amount of internally generated material reported and its complexity are impressive indeed. Imagery thus needs to be seen within this context—it is not simply produced under conditions of demand by tasks of learning or recall, but it almost continuously emerges into consciousness, probably as a feature of the very nature of the brain's function and of man as a plan-making organism.

This chapter will consider a particular study which represents an attempt to establish a normative basis for the content and structure of daydreaming. *What are the major dimensions of ongoing fantasy? What relation do they bear to other normal or pathological personality dimensions? What relationships exist between reported recall of dreams and daydreams, between visual and auditory imagery and frequency of reported daydreaming? Is daydreaming related to certain types of curiosity or distractibility?* These and many related questions are approached in the type of study described here. Still others remain to be answered such as the relationship between well-established cognitive styles such as Witkin's "Differentiation" of "Field Dependence–Independence" and the dimensions which emerge from questionnaire scales of daydreaming.

The approach adopted in the present study involves development of a large number of scales of daydreaming and imaginal processes which are then examined in relation to relevant personality variables and scales. Other, more formally experimental approaches are possible of course. It should be noted that a study by Antrobus, Coleman, and Singer (1967) did find a relationship between frequency of reports of task-irrelevant imagery during a signal detection task and daydream scale scores, e.g., high daydreamers gave more stimulus-independent mentation reports.

Development of Imaginal Processes Scales

In order to move beyond private experience to a description of patterns of daydreaming and imaginal processes shared commonly by normal persons a first step involves the generation of a set of scales tapping diverse facets of these inner processes. The earlier study (Singer & Antrobus, 1963) paved the way for the present approach by indicating through a factor analysis of dozens of daydreaming scales what major clusters emerged and which scales loaded differentially upon each. A revised Imaginal Processes Inventory (IPI) was then developed following item analyses and this new scale formed the basis for the inventory to be described in this chapter. A new factor analysis involving a larger number of subjects, male and female, and a wider range of personality measures was carried out to provide a clearer basis for interpreting the scales of imagery and fantasy. Detailed material on the factor analytic material is available elsewhere. Our concern in this chapter will be primarily the specific imaginal processes scales and their implications for the study of imagery and daydreaming.

The subjects in this study were 206 college students, 130 males and 76 females who volunteered participation in large elementary psychology lectures. They made up an extremely homogeneous group as far as age (18–19) and socioeconomic level (lower middle class) were concerned.

Specific Questionnaires Employed

In discussing the measures administered, our main focus will be upon the IPI since the direction of our concern will be with the interplay of these inner characteristics in their relation to each other and to major personality dimensions. This inventory deriving from a series of earlier instruments, but considerably revised and extended, consists of 400 items to be responded to on a 5-point scale. The inventory includes 29 subscales of which 22 have to do specifically with either content or structure of daydreaming and imaginal processes, while 7 represent measures of curiosity and patterns of attention. At least two of the scales, the "General Daydreaming Scale" and the "Absorption in Daydreaming Scale," had been extensively studied in earlier research and were drawn largely from the previous studies based on their factorial composition (Singer & Antrobus, 1963; Singer & McCraven, 1961). The remaining scales were drawn in part from previous scales but a number of items were added to clarify the scales as well as to improve their wording and to include some negatively phrased items in order to avoid acquiescent response sets.

The following is a list of the specific scales of the IPI. It should be noted that the items from these scales were not presented in order within the inventory itself. Items were randomized and spread around in the actual inventory and were assembled only later by a scoring key. Most of the scales had 12 items with Scales 1, 2, 23 and 24 somewhat longer.

Scale 1	General Daydreaming
Scale 2	Absorption in Daydreaming
Scale 3	Acceptance of Daydreaming
Scale 4	Positive Reactions to Daydreams
Scale 5	Frightened Reactions to Daydreams
Scale 6	Visual Imagery in Daydreams
Scale 7	Auditory Imagery in Daydreams
Scale 8	Problem-Solving in Daydreams
Scale 9	Present Orientation in Daydreams
Scale 10	Future Orientation in Daydreams
Scale 11	Past Orientation in Daydreams
Scale 12	Bizarre Improbable Daydreams
Scale 13	Mindwandering

Scale 14   Night Dream Frequency
Scale 15   Daydream Frequency
Scale 16   Achievement-Oriented Daydreams
Scale 17   Hallucinatory Vividness of Daydreams
Scale 18   Fear of Failure in Daydreams
Scale 19   Hostile Aggressive Daydreams
Scale 20   Sexual Daydreams
Scale 21   Heroic Daydreams
Scale 22   Guilt Daydreams
Scale 23   Curiosity: Interpersonal
Scale 24   Curiosity: Impersonal-Mechanical
Scale 25   Boredom
Scale 26   Mentation Rate
Scale 27   Distractibility
Scale 28   Need for External Stimulation
Scale 29   Self-Reporting Tendencies

In addition to the IPI scales the subjects also responded to the Maudsley Personality Inventory (Eysenck, 1959) which yields the two dimensions of Neuroticism and Introversion–Extraversion. These scales had been employed in the earlier factor analysis along with the Guilford-Zimmerman Temperament Survey (1949) and both were employed again for replication purposes and to establish more precisely the relation between scales of daydreaming and measures of emotional stability or sociability. To strengthen interpretation of general personality implications of the daydreaming scales Gough's California Psychological Inventory (CPI) was also included (1964). This inventory with its 18 scales was believed to have special advantages for use with normal subjects and would point up the more "favorable and positive aspects of personality rather than . . . the morbid and pathological [Gough, 1964, p. 2]." It includes scales such as Sociability, Sense of Well Being, Achievement via Conformance, and Achievement via Independence which might help clarify certain imaginal processes scales.

A final measure included was the Stein-Craik Activity Preference Inventory. This instrument has been used in several studies by Stein and Craik (1965) in the effort to separate out through a listing of patterns of activity those subjects that are predominantly oriented towards mental and ideational activities and those whose preference is for direct motor engagement with the environment. Stein and Craik's findings suggest rather interesting differences in patterns of preference for these types of activities when the inventories have been applied to various pathological groups. It was felt that this scale, yielding two measures, Motor and Ideational Preference, would indicate more precisely the meaning of some of the various factors.

All in all there were a total of 63 variables scored in the study and the final factor analysis was based upon the intercorrelation of scores on these 63 variables as well as biological sex. A correlation matrix of 64 variables was therefore generated. Patterns of response for each of the daydreaming scales will be examined alone in connection with a discussion of the item analysis. Because the various correlates of the CPI, Guilford-Zimmerman and Maudsley are relatively well-established, less attention will be paid to their interrelationships except insofar as these throw light upon the daydreaming material.

The data were analyzed by a Varimax Analytic Solution carried out on a PLDT program for the IBM-360 computer. Specific detail on variances and rotation of the original unrotated factor matrices will be discussed briefly before describing the results for the specific scales.

Major Factors

Nine factors accounting for 56% of the total variance emerged from the Varimax analytic solution of the correlation matrix. Of these, four specifically involved daydreaming and imaginal processes and a fifth was

TABLE 1

Factor 2: "Neuroticism-Anxious Absorption in Daydreaming"[a]

Highest loading scales

Variable number	Name	Loading
43	CPI Good Impression	− .68
30	MPI Neuroticism	.65
55	G-Z Emotional Stability	− .63
56	G-Z Objectivity	− .59
13	IPI Mindwandering and Daydreams	.55
2	IPI Absorption in Daydreaming	.51
25	IPI Boredom	.51
27	IPI Distractibility	.50
15	IPI Daydream Frequency	.49
38	CPI Sense of Well-Being	− .45
45	CPI Achievement via Conformance	− .43
5	IPI Frightened Reactions to Daydreams	.33
48	CPI Psychological-Mindedness	− .32
20	IPI Sexual Daydreams	.32
1	IPI General Daydreaming	.31
9	IPI Present Orientation in Daydreams	− .31
12	IPI Bizarre Improbable Daydreams	.31

[a] Total sample, $N = 206$.

TABLE 2
Factor 3: "Obsessional-Emotional Daydreaming"[a]

Highest loading scales

Variable number	Name	Loading
22	IPI Guilt Daydreams	.83
18	IPI Fear of Failure in Daydreams	.76
19	IPI Hostile Aggressive Daydreams	.65
5	IPI Frightened Reactions to Daydreams	.60
21	IPI Heroic Daydreams	.60
16	IPI Achievement-Oriented Daydreams	.54
17	IPI Hallucinatory Vividness in Daydreams	.53
1	IPI General Daydreaming	.49
20	IPI Sexual Daydreams	.40
12	IPI Bizarre Improbable Daydreams	.39
2	IPI Absorption in Daydreaming	.31
8	IPI Problem-Solving through Daydreams	.28
38	CPI Sense of Well-Being	−.26
3	IPI Acceptance of Daydreaming	−.25
9	IPI Present Orientation in Daydreams	−.25
41	CPI Self-Control	−.25
25	IPI Boredom	.24
56	G-Z Objectivity	−.24
47	CPI Intellectual Efficiency	−.23

[a] Total sample, $N = 206$.

Social Extraversion. The daydream factors essentially replicated the findings of the earlier factor analysis. The factors are labeled Factor (2) Neuroticism-Anxious Absorption in Daydreaming; Factor (3) Obsessional Guilty-Emotional Daydreaming; Factor (4) Positive-Vivid Daydreaming and Factor (8) Controlled Thoughtfulness. When additional statistical manipulation is performed on the unrotated nine factors, in order to maximize loadings on the initially emerging three or four factors, the results suggest that in addition to the powerful Social Extraversion Factor the data break down into either two or three major Imaginal Processes factors. These include, in each case, a potent Neuroticism-Anxious Absorption in Daydreaming factor and either separate Positive-Vivid Daydreaming and Obsessional-Emotional Factors of (in the three factor solution) a bipolar Positive vs. Negative Affect Daydreaming factor. In both cases the controlled Thoughtfulness Factor (number 8, above) blends with the Positive Daydreaming factor. Tables 1, 2, 3, and 4 indicate the major imaginal processes and personality measures loading on the four original daydream factors and Tables 5 and 6 indicate the three and four factor solutions that involve the more compressed and perhaps somewhat more psychologically meaningful outcomes.

Since our emphasis in the balance of this chapter is upon normative features of each scale we shall not dwell at length on the separate factors. One is tempted to the conclusion that for our sample and for the particular battery of tests employed the major dimensions of personality and imaginal processes which emerge herein are best described by something between the three and four factors summarized in Tables 5 and 6. It would appear likely that people can be characterized as far as their daydreams or imaginal processes are concerned into three groups: (1) Those who (by scoring high on the scales loading highest on each of these factors) are given to distractibility, worry, absorption in daydreams, poor sense of well-being, mindwandering and a high degree of anxiety; (2) those who engage in a good deal of tortured self-concern, doubt, ethical rumination, fantasies of achievement, failure and heroism with much negatively toned emotional content; and, finally, (3) those who acknowledge frequent, vivid, and ab-

TABLE 3
Factor 4: "Positive-Vivid Daydreaming"[a]

Highest loading scales

Variable number	Name	Loading
6	IPI Visual Imagery in Daydreams	.60
2	IPI Absorption in Daydreaming	.59
7	IPI Auditory Imagery in Daydreams	.52
3	IPI Acceptance of Daydreaming	.52
4	IPI Positive Reactions in Daydreams	.51
15	IPI Daydream Frequency	.48
20	IPI Sexual Daydreams	.48
8	IPI Problem-Solving through Daydreams	.44
13	IPI Mindwandering and Daydreams	.40
29	IPI Self-Reporting Tendencies	.38
10	IPI Future Orientation in Daydreams	.37
28	IPI Need for External Stimulation	.35
26	IPI Mentation Rate	.31
17	IPI Hallucinatory-Vividness in Daydreaming	.30
11	IPI Past Orientation in Daydreams	.28
1	IPI General Daydreaming	.27
23	IPI Curiosity: Interpersonal	.21

[a] Total sample, $N = 206$.

TABLE 4
Factor 8: "Controlled Thoughtfulness"[a]

Highest loading scales

Variable number	Name	Loading
58	G-Z Thoughtfulness	.63
52	G-Z Restraint	.52
10	IPI Future Orientation in Daydreams	.45
63	S-C Ideational Activity Preference	.44
16	IPI Achievement-Oriented Daydreams	.34
23	IPI Curiosity: Interpersonal	.33
25	IPI Boredom	− .31
26	IPI Mentation Rate	.27
56	G-Z Objectivity	− .26
1	IPI General Daydreaming	.23
46	CPI Achievement via Conformance	.22
55	G-Z Emotional Stability	− .22
13	IPI Mindwandering and Daydreams	− .21
30	MPI Neuroticism	.21

[a] Total sample, $N = 206$.

sorbing daydreaming or general reflectiveness which they view positively, with content oriented toward the future; they express considerable curiosity about people and manifest a high rate of mental activity and preference for ideational activities. The second group seems largely to be oriented psychologically toward traditional masculine interests, while the last is more oriented toward feminine concerns; both men and women are widely dispersed, however, among all three factors.

More detailed discussion of the separate factors is available elsewhere (Singer & Antrobus, 1970) and copies of a revised IPI based upon the findings reported herein is available upon request from the authors. We shall turn now to an examination of the specific daydream scales and will refer further to the factor analytic material as we examine each scale.

Daydreaming Scales and Their Correlates

Each scale of the Imaginal Processes Inventory was constructed to tap a dimension that clinical experience as well as prior empirical research

TABLE 5

Three Factor Solution of Total Principal Components Matrix[a]

| Factor 1 | | Factor 2 | | Factor 3 | |
| Neuroticism-Anxious absorption in daydreaming | | Social extraversion | | Positive frequent daydreaming vs. guilt, negative daydreaming | |
Name	Loading	Name	Loading	Name	Loading
CPI Self-Control	−.77	CPI Socialization	.83	CPI Femininity	.46
CPI Sense of Well-Being	−.74	CPI Dominance	.80	IPI Absorption in Daydreaming	.43
CPI Tolerance	−.73	CPI Self-Acceptance	.77	IPI Daydream Frequency	.43
IPI Absorption in Daydreaming	.73	G-Z Ascendance	.78	G-Z Thoughtfulness	.42
G-Z Objectivity	−.71	MPI Extraversion	.74	IPI Acceptance of Daydreaming	.41
MPI Neuroticism	.67	G-Z Sociability	.71	IPI Self-Reporting Tendencies	.41
CPI Intellectual Efficiency	−.64	G-Z General Activity	.65	S-C Ideational Activity Preference	.40
IPI General Daydreaming	.62	S-C Motor Activity Preference	.51	CPI Flexibility	.38
G-Z Emotional Stability	−.61	IPI Need for External Stimulation	.46	CPI Achievement via Independence	.37
IPI Frightened Reactions to Daydreams	.60	IPI Boredom	−.40	IPI Guilt Daydreams	−.46
IPI Hostile Aggressive Daydreams	.59	G-Z Friendliness	−.40	IPI Heroic Daydreams	−.43
IPI Sexual Daydreams	.59	CPI Intellectual Efficiency	.39	G-Z Masculinity	−.38
IPI Daydream Frequency	.58	CPI Femininity	−.37	IPI Fear of Failure in Daydreams	−.37
IPI Mindwandering and Daydreams	.56	IPI Acceptance of Daydreaming	.36	IPI Hostile Aggressive Daydreams	−.37
IPI Fear of Failure in Daydreams	.53	IPI Curiosity: Impersonal-Mechanical	.36		
IPI Boredom	.41	S-C Ideational Activity Preference	.34		
IPI Distractibility	.40	CPI Achievement via Conformance	.31		
		IPI Problem Solving Through Daydreams	.30		
		CPI Sense of Well-Being	−.22		

[a] Total sample, $N = 206$.

TABLE 6

Four Factor Solution of Total Principal Components Matrix

Factor 1 Neuroticism-Anxious absorption in daydreaming		Factor 2 Social extraversion		Factor 3 Guilty-Obsessional emotional daydreaming		Factor 4 Positive-Vivid daydreaming	
Name	Loading	Name	Loading	Name	Loading	Name	Loading
CPI Tolerance	.78	CPI Socialization	.80	IPI Guilt Daydreams	.73	IPI Absorption in Daydreaming	.60
CPI Intellectual Efficiency	.72	MPI Extraversion	.79	IPI Hostile Aggressive Daydreams	.69	IPI Daydream Frequency	.54
CPI Responsibility	.71	G-Z Ascendance	.77	IPI Fear of Failure in Daydreams	.68	G-Z Thoughtfulness	.49
CPI Sense of Well-Being	.71	G-Z Sociability	.73	IPI Achievement-Oriented Daydreams	.61	IPI Self-Reporting Tendencies	.47
CPI Self-control	.71	G-Z General Activity	−.65	IPI Frightened Reactions to Daydreams	.60	S-C Ideational Activity Preference	.45
CPI Achievement via Conformance	.71	S-C Motor Activity Preference	.52	IPI General Daydreaming	.58	IPI Acceptance of Daydreaming	.42
CPI Achievement via Independence	.65	IPI Need for External Stimulation	.46	IPI Hallucinatory Vividness in Daydreams	.47	IPI Curiosity: Interpersona	.42
G-Z Objectivity	.63	IPI Boredom	−.41	IPI Bizarre Improbable Daydreams	.42	CPI Femininity	.42
MPI Neuroticism	−.51	CPI Femininity	−.39	G-Z Flexibility	−.34	MPI Neuroticism	.42
G-Z Emotional Stability	.50	IPI Acceptance of Daydreaming	.36	G-Z Objectivity	−.32	IPI Future-Orientation in Daydreams	.41
IPI Mindwandering & Daydreams	−.47	IPI Bizarre Improbable Daydreams	−.31	CPI Self-Control	−.31	IPI Visual Imagery in Daydreams	.38
IPI Absorption in Daydreaming	−.45	G-Z Emotional Stability	.31			G-Z Masculinity	−.37
IPI Daydream Frequency	−.42	G-Z Restraint	−.31			IPI Positive Reactions in Daydreaming	.36
		IPI Problem Solving Through Daydreaming	.27				

[a] Total Sample, $N = 206$.

in this program suggested might be an interesting facet of man's ongoing stream of thought. The scales each consisted generally of 12 items, written so that Ss could respond (on the "Daydream Frequency" measure, for example) on a 5-point scale from "never had the daydream" through "frequently, as often as once a week." Changes in direction of phrasing were built into the scales to avoid any excessive impact of acquiescent response sets. Our discussion will center primarily on those scales especially bearing upon imagery and fantasy processes. Space prevents a detailed examination of each separate scale. We are especially concerned here with examining the major implications of specific scales which may be of interest for future research on the nature of the daydream and the individual differences in fantasy patterns.

A word about the scales in general. The internal consistencies as measured by Cronbach's Alpha were quite satisfactory for the scales in the IPI. Only three scales fell below .75 in their coefficients and most were well into the .80's. Since some items were written in negative form to avoid response set and since it is clear that there is variation of a reasonable kind in the size of means for scales (with more pathological types of fantasies yielding lower means), the subjects were apparently exercising some discrimination in their pattern of response. The two scales in the total test battery which were included as checks on careful response, the Eysenck-Maudsley and the Guilford-Zimmerman "Question-Mark" responses both loaded together on a common factor but no correlation emerged between these scales and the daydream scales.

Let us now take a closer look at some of the more interesting scales. We shall present the Means, Standard deviations and Cronbach's Alpha for each Variable using its number in the IPI for identification. The reader should be alerted, however, to the fact that the very data presented here has served as a basis for a further revision of the IPI and the newest version of the questionnaire, available on request from these authors will reflect a somewhat different numbering of scales.

Variable No. 2: "Absorption in Daydreaming" (30 items)
Mean: 95   S.D.: 18.8   Cronbach's Alpha: .90

This scale is a remnant of the earlier daydream questionnaire employed in the Singer-Antrobus (1963) factor analysis. Items chosen for the present scale all loaded at least +.50 on the Neurotic Daydreaming factor in that study. Examination of these items suggests that they include indications of frequent intense daydreaming with considerable absorption in the content of one's fantasies. Of interest is the relatively high mean for this sample on this scale. This result seems in accord with the indications that this sample also scores at the upper end for normal groups on the Maudsley Neuroticism scale, well above the scores for other American college students. The scale itself seems highly reliable based on its alpha.

The items correlating highest with total scale score include: "I often have the same daydream over and over" (.72); "I tend to get pretty wrapped up in my daydreaming" (.71); "I get considerable emotional 'kick' out of my daydreams" (.69); "Some of my daydreams are so powerful that I just can't take my attention away from them" (.68).

While the content of the items in this scale is not clearly pathological in the sense of reference to bizarre fantasies or obvious emotional disturbance, the scale shows a pattern of correlations which indicates its association with emotional instability at least in self-report. While it correlates most highly among other daydream scales with Daydream Frequency (.67); Mindwandering during Daydreaming (.59); Positive Reactions in Daydreams (.57); and Sexual Daydreams (.62), it is not associated particularly with Guilt Daydreams or Heroic Daydreams. It is associated more highly (in the .40's) with General Daydreaming, Problem-Solving in Daydreams, and Hallucinatory Vividness of Daydreams. More modest positive correlations exist with Boredom and Distractibility.

This scale stands out from all the others by virtue of its especially substantial correlations with the Maudsley Neuroticism Scale (.61), and the California Sense of Well-Being Scale (−.46). Although some other daydream scales show comparable trends, only this scale is so decidedly linked with the personality test measures of neurotic tendency or emotional instability, especially in relation to anxiety. From this standpoint, it seems valuable for further use in any research seeking to establish groups characterized by an absorption in fantasy that has clear pathological implications. This scale loads highly on the Neuroticism-Anxious Absorption in Daydreaming Factor (see Tables 1, 5, and 6) but also has a substantial loading on the Positive-Vivid Daydreaming Factor (see Tables 3 and 6).

Variable No. 4: "Positive Reaction to Daydreams" (12 items)
Mean: 39   S.D.: 7.3   Cronbach's Alpha: .79

This scale, especially constructed for the IPI, was included in an effort to tap indications of very positive emotions occurring as a consequence of daydreaming. It has a fairly high mean score compared to other daydream scales and seems reasonably consistent. Highest correlations with total score were obtained for items such as, "My daydreams often leave me with a warm, happy feeling" (.79); "My daydreams often cheer me up when I feel blue" (.72) and "My daydreams are often stimulating and rewarding" (.67).

This scale does not show a strong pattern of intercorrelations except with the other daydream variables. It is most strongly associated with Absorption in Daydreaming (.57) and Sexual Daydreams (.50) and more modestly with General Daydreaming, Acceptance of Daydreaming, Problem-Solving in Daydreams, Daydream Frequency, and a few others. It is not associated with daydream scales involving strong negative emotion such as guilt or fear. In the factor analysis, it loads positively (.51) on the Positive-Vivid Daydreaming factor and more modestly on the Neuroticism-Anxiety factor. It would appear to be a useful scale for any further studies seeking to delineate normal samples with "upbeat" reactions to their fantasy lives.

Variable No. 5: "Frightened Reactions to Daydreams" (12 items)
Mean: 29   S.D.: 9.3   Cronbach's Alpha: .87

This scale was devised for the inventory to elicit indications of anxiety or fearful reactions provided by daydreaming in the respondents. It yields a lower mean than most of the daydreaming scales, suggesting that for this sample such frightened outcomes of daydreaming are not common but, of course, do occur. Highest correlations with total scale score include "My daydreams have such an emotional effect on me that I often react with fear" (.78); "Some of my fantasies are so terrifying I shake and shiver" (.74); and "Sometimes a passing thought will seem so real that I would shudder and feel uneasy" (.74).

This scale correlates most highly with Absorption in Daydreaming, Bizarre Daydreaming, Hallucinatory Vividness of Daydreaming, Fear of Failure Daydreams, Hostile, Sexual, and Guilty Daydreaming. Among the other variables, it is associated most with Maudsley Neuroticism (.46), California Sense of Well-Being (−.35), California Self-Control (−.40), and Guilford Emotional Stability (−.44), and Objectivity (−.43). In the factor analysis, this scale loads only moderately on the Neuroticism factor, but much more strongly (.60) on the Guilt-Emotional Daydream factor. It may prove a valuable scale as part of a group of scales in selecting subjects for research who are not grossly pathological but characterized by strong negative emotional reactions to their fantasies.

Variable No. 6: "Visual Imagery in Daydreams" (12 items)
Mean: 38   S.D.: 9.6   Cronbach's Alpha: .86

The intent in establishing the scale was to estimate the degree to which a visual imagery component was important in daydreaming. The scale yields a fairly high mean, supporting previous findings that daydreams involved a good deal of visualization. Internal consistency is high with no items correlating below .46 with total scale score and seven of the twelve items correlating more than .60 with total. "Visual scenes are an important part of my daydreams" (.78), and "The pictures in my mind seem as clear as photographs" (.75), are examples of scale items with highest correlations with total scale score.

The pattern of intercorrelations suggests that this scale correlates primarily with Absorption in Daydreaming, Positive Reactions to Daydreams, Auditory Imagery in Daydreams, Daydream Frequency, Hallucinatory Vividness of Daydreams and Sexual Daydreams. There are few other correlations of any magnitude although the general trend is toward very small positive associations with Neuroticism and negative correlations with measures of psychological stability. The neurotic component is not critical in this scale and on the factor analysis it loads only on the Positive-Vivid Daydreaming factor (.60). It would appear to be a useful scale in studies of relatively normal daydreaming patterns where there is a desire to examine other components related to visual imagery. It might fruitfully be applied to usage along with the Betts-Sheehan and Gordon scales of vividness of imagery and control of imagery (See Richardson, 1969 and Chapter 5, this volume).

Variable No. 7: "Auditory Images in Daydreams" (12 items)
Mean: 39   S.D.: 5.2   Cronbach's Alpha: .39

This scale was included to complement Scale 6. There were indications from the Singer-Antrobus study (1963) that auditory imagery was more characteristic of certain fantasy styles of a more schizoid nature. It was felt that a more carefully worked-out scale might contribute to a better understanding of the role of verbal or sound imagery in fantasies.

The scale has a high mean suggesting that Ss in this sample did indeed report considerable auditory imagery in their fantasies, more so than in previous studies. The low internal consistency of the scale presents a problem. It has therefore been revised for future use. High correlating items are "The sounds I hear in my daydreams are clear and distinct" (.65); and "In a daydream I can hear a tune almost as clearly as if I were actually listening to it" (.58). Perhaps as a consequence of its unreliability the scale correlates with almost no other scales except for Visual Imagery in Daydreams (.51), Acceptance of Daydreaming (.30), Past-oriented Daydreams (.27) and Hallucinatory Vividness of Daydreams (.26). It loads significantly only on the Positive-Vivid Daydream factor (.52). At least for this sample one is led to conclude that auditory imagery may be associated with a relatively constructive or healthy psychological orientation.

Variable No. 8: "Problem-Solving in Daydreams" (12 items)
Mean: 34   S.D.: 7.6   Cronbach's Alpha: .78

This scale was especially constructed for the IPI. The objective was to establish what role daydreams might play in practical problem solution for respondents and what some of the correlates of such a use of fantasy might prove to be. In a certain sense, one might argue that all daydreaming (unless it is viewed as an epiphenomenon) must serve some adaptive function or be related to the solution of the major problems in an individual's life. Nevertheless, it is unclear whether there is an extensive application, by some people, of daydreaming in practical problem solution and this scale might point to directions for further work in the area.

The data for this sample suggest that there is a widespread use of daydreaming for problem solution. The internal consistency of the scale is satisfactory. Items with very high correlations include "I can get a fresh approach to an old problem almost at once during what begins as a daydream" (.75); "Sometimes an answer to a very difficult problem comes to me during a daydream" (.75); and "My daydreams offer me useful clues to tricky situations I face" (.72).

This scale correlates significantly, chiefly with other daydream scales: Absorption in Daydreaming, Acceptance of Daydreaming, Positive Daydreaming, Achievement Daydreams, Hallucinatory-Vividness of Daydreams, Hostile Daydreams, and Sexual Daydreams. There are indications that persons scoring high on Problem-Solving Daydreams are more Self-Representing, more Ascendant, less Objective, and less Self-Controlled but more Thoughtful. This scale loads, therefore, primarily on the Positive-Vivid Daydreaming factor (.44) and somewhat lower on Obsessional-Emotional Daydreaming factor (.28) but on no other. It would appear to be a useful component in any broader study of positive daydreaming.

Variable No. 10: "Future-Oriented Daydreams" (12 items)
Mean: 43   S.D.: 7.6   Cronbach's Alpha: .79

The very high mean for this scale suggests that most *S*s experience daydreams as future-oriented and have such daydreams frequently. Highest correlating items include "I seldom think about what I will be doing in the future" (.67, keyed negatively); "I picture myself as I will be several years from now" (.65); and "I daydream about what I would like to see happen in the future" (.64).

This scale correlates primarily significantly with Acceptance of Daydreaming, Positive Reactions to Daydreams, Achievement-Oriented Daydreams, Mentation Rate, Guilford-Zimmerman Thoughtfulness and Stein-Craik Ideational Activity Preference. It loads on two factors, Positive-Vivid Daydreaming (.37) and Controlled Thoughtfulness (.45). It would thus appear to be a useful component in a set of scales designed to tap more positive and constructive aspects of inner experience.

Variable No. 12: "Bizarre Improbable Content in Daydreams" (12 items)
Mean: 31   S.D.: 8.3   Cronbach's Alpha: .83

This scale was included to elicit daydreams clearly divorced from practical, realistic, or probable occurrences and problems in the respondents' lives. The scale proves to be quite reliable. The lower than average mean indicates that for most persons daydreams are related to realistic situations in life. At the same time, the mean is not so low that one can assert that improbable daydreams are rare or characteristic only of severely disturbed persons. Thus, "I often have thoughts about things that could rarely occur in real life," has a mean rating of 2.74 out of five and correlates .75 with total scale score. "My daydreams are fairly matter-of-fact and down-to-earth" (keyed negatively) correlates .74 with total scale score and "I daydream about utterly impossible situations," correlates .71 with total and yields a mean of 2.43 which is still well above a minimal score.

This scale has only very modest correlations with the other scales. It is most highly associated with Absorption in Daydreaming (.31), Frightened Reaction to Daydreams (.31), Present-Oriented Daydreams (−.39), Fearful Reactions to Daydreams (.31), Boredom (.45), Maudsley Neuroticism (.30), California Well-Being (−.28), and Guilford Emotional Stability (−.30). It loads primarily on two factors: Obsessional-Guilty Emotional Daydreaming (.39) and Neuroticism (.31). Interestingly enough it also loads very modestly on a predominantly CPI scale Flexible-Achievement by Independence (.23). It appears to be a useful scale for further research particularly as part of a group of items dealing with greater emotionality or distress in the daydreaming sphere.

Variable No. 13: "Mindwandering" (12 items)
Mean: 41   S.D.: 8.8   Cronbach's Alpha: .86

This scale was included to tap the often reported relationship between mindwandering and daydreaming. It is often assumed that the two behaviors are identical, but actually one could have one's attention shifting to other perceptual responses without any awareness of inner content in many situations where one reports "mindwandering" or distraction.

For this sample, shifts of attention are clearly quite common judging by the high mean score for the scale. The internal consistency of the scale is good. "I am the kind of person whose thoughts often wander" (.77), and "No matter how much I try to concentrate, thoughts unrelated to my work always creep in" (.74), are examples of highly correlated items with total scale score.

This scale proves to have many modest but significant correlations with a variety of scales in the total battery. Especially high are correlations with Absorption in Daydreaming (.59), Daydreaming Frequency (.58), Boredom (.58), Distractibility (.60), Maudsley Neuroticism (.48), Well-Being (—.39), Achievement by Conformity (—.36), Intellectual Efficiency (—.36), Psychological-Mindedness (—.35), Emotional Stability (—.41), and Objectivity (—.37). Clearly the scale ties in well with related processes as measured by other instruments. It loads very highly on Neuroticism (.55) and also somewhat lower on Positive-Vivid Daydreaming (.40). Thus, it appears to be a useful addition either to scales attempting to tap neurotic components of fantasy or to a more generally positive daydreaming scale. It is likely that daydreaming is indeed experienced as mindwandering but that for some persons this awareness is part of a sense of anxiety while for others it is tolerated as one of the expected concomitants of a positive daydream experience.

> Variable No. 14: "Night Dream Frequency" (12 items)
> Mean: 32   S.D.: 8.4   Cronbach's Alpha: .85

This measure was especially devised to evaluate the role that recall of night dreams plays in relation to waking fantasy experience. A number of earlier studies had indicated modest but significant correlations between report of daydreaming frequency and recall of night dreams. The Singer-Antrobus (1963) study had also suggested that emphasis on night dream recall was more particularly associated with a factor apparently representing schizoid tendencies. A new Night Dream Frequency was therefore devised for this study.

The mean for Night Dream Frequency is somewhat lower than most in the daydream questionnaire but still substantial. Clearly night dreams are less well recalled or felt to be less frequent than daydreams. The reliability of the scale itself is good.

This scale correlates with only a few of the other scales. It has a small significant association with Daydreaming Frequency (.33), about what has generally been found in other studies. There is a negative correlation (—.30) with CPI Sense of Well-Being and Self-Control (—.35); and a positive association with Stein-Craik Ideational Activity Preference (.30). It loads negatively (—.32) on the Controlled Social Orientation factor (which is based largely on the CPI and Guilford Scales) and its only other loading worthy of notice is (.21) on the Positive-Vivid Daydreaming factor. One might conclude that recall of night dreams does have some subtle relationship to self-awareness and inner sensitivity but is more characteristic of a kind of social withdrawal syndrome—a finding curiously like a result in the earlier Singer-Antrobus factor analysis. Probably the use of only one scale of dream recall limits generalizations. A more intensive study of the correlates of a set of scales of night dream recall, vividness, etc. is in order.

Variable No. 15: "Daydream Frequency" (12 items)
Mean: 37   S.D.: 8.5   Cronbach's Alpha: .89

Earlier studies in this series had measured Daydream Frequency chiefly by summing frequencies assigned to specific daydream content. This scale was devised to determine if a more direct approach would yield comparable findings and to ascertain the value of an approach like this for future research use. The mean for this scale clearly indicates a reasonably high Daydream Frequency for this sample. The internal consistency of the scale is quite good.

The Daydreaming Frequency scale correlates .51 with General Daydreaming (content); .67 with Absorption in Daydreaming; .34 with Positive Reaction to Daydreaming; .37 with Visual Imagery; .58 with Mindwandering; .45 with Sexual Daydreams; .41 with Boredom; .31 with Distractibility; .50 with Maudsley Neuroticism; —.45 with CPI Sense of Well-Being; in the low —.30's with CPI Responsibility, Socialization and Tolerance; —.41 with Self-Control; —.42 with Achievement by Conformity; —.48 with Emotional Stability; —.32 with Objectivity; and .29 with Thoughtfulness. It has strong loadings on Neuroticism (.49) and Positive-Vivid Daydreaming (.48) and a small negative loading (—.27) on Controlled Social Orientation. Obviously, the scale has interesting linkages and seems basically to represent tendencies of normal or pathological potential depending upon context. There seems little doubt that for many subjects an admission of frequent daydreaming goes along with other admissions of anxiety and personal distress. At the same time for many other individuals reports of active daydreaming are merely parts of a report of an active, welcome inner life that is not particularly linked to emotional stress. The new scale can probably be used more effectively than the earlier general daydreaming scale as part of a battery of scales either to measure neurotic fantasy or (with other tests) to tap positive active fantasy.

Variable No. 17: "Hallucinatory-Vividness in Daydreaming" (12 items)
Mean: 24   S.D.: 8.8   Cronbach's Alpha: .87

This scale was devised to establish a degree of vividness in daydreaming that might border on hallucination. It was felt it might yield clues as to schizoid trends in combination with other daydream or personality scales. As can be seen from the very low mean score for this sample on the scale there were few subjects who reported anything better than a minimal frequency for this type of experience. The scale is quite reliable with the lowest correlation of an item with total being .49. "Voices in my daydreams are so distinct and clear that I'm tempted to answer them," correlates .79 with total scale score. "The people in my daydreams are so true to life I often believe they're in the same room with me" (.79); and "My daydreams are so clear that I often believe the people in them are in the room" (.78), are also at the top in correlations with total scale score. "My thoughts seem as real as actual events in my life" (.58), yields the highest mean score for an item on this scale, 2.81, suggesting that this sample does report almost an intermediate level of acceptance of that degree of vividness.

This scale correlates primarily with other daydreaming scales: Absorption in Daydreaming (.47), Frightened Reaction to Daydreams (.52), Visual Imagery in Daydreams (.46), Problem-Solving (.36), Fear of Failure (.39), Hostile Daydreams (.37), Guilt in Daydreams (.41). It shows a pattern of negative correlations with many items on the CPI but the magnitudes are low. This scale loads highest on the Obsessional-Emotional Daydream factor (.53) and also obtains a modest loading (.30) on the Positive-Vivid Daydreaming factor.

Variable No. 18: "Fear of Failure in Daydream Content" (12 items)
Mean: 23   S.D.: 8.4   Cronbach's Alpha: .87

This scale was included for possible combined use at a later date with Achievement Daydreams since evidence from elicited fantasy studies suggests the importance of both Achievement and Fear of Failure in predicting actual achievement. This is a content rather than structural scale. It yields a low mean for this sample, markedly lower than the Achievement Daydream scale. The scale is quite reliable and 10 of 12 items correlate above .60 with total score. "I imagine myself failing those I love" (.73); "In my daydreams I lose my job and am financially in debt and feel worthless" (.72); and "I daydream of being interviewed for an important job and giving a bad impression" (.69), are examples of items correlating well with total scale score.

This scale correlates negatively with Acceptance of Daydreaming (−.31); positively with Frightened Reaction in Daydreams (.55), Bizarre Daydreams (.30), Hallucinatory-Vividness (.39), Hostile Daydreams (.58), Sexual Daydreams (.35), Heroic Daydreams (.38), but most dramatically with Guilt Daydreams (.77). It shows a pattern of low positive correlation with Boredom and Neuroticism and negative correlations with CPI scales, especially Sense of Well-Being (−.38), Tolerance (−.34) and Intellectual Efficiency (−.39). It also correlates negatively (−.36) with Guilford-Zimmerman's Objectivity. It loads only on one factor: Obsessional-Emotional Daydreaming, where its loading is one of the highest of all (.76). Clearly, this scale is tapping a profound self-doubting, "tortured self-concern" manifestation in daydreams which, while not strongly related to the type of neurotic trend measured by scales like Eysenck's or Guilford's, must certainly reflect a deep sense of malaise. It seems to be a useful scale for use in almost any future work on Obsessional Neurosis or negatively-toned emotional content in fantasy.

Variable No. 19: "Hostile-Aggressive Daydreams" (12 items)
Mean: 28   S.D.: 9.2   Cronbach's Alpha: .85

This scale was included as a content scale specifically built around hostile, revenge, or aggressive fantasies. While its mean for this sample is lower than most of the other daydream scales, the fact remains that a sizable number of students admit at least a moderate occurrence of this type of daydream. The scale's internal consistency is good with eight items correlating above .54 with total. Highest correlating items include "I imagine myself getting even with those I dislike" (.81); "In my fantasies I see myself seeking revenge on those I dislike" (.79); "I daydream of ways of 'rubbing it in' or annoying certain people I dislike" (.74).

This scale shows a fairly interesting pattern of correlations. It is associated with Absorption in Daydreaming (.32), Frightened Reaction in Daydreams (.44), Problem-Solving in Daydreams (.32), Achievement Daydreams (.38), Fear of Failure (.58), Hallucinatory Vividness (.37), Sexual (.41), Heroic (.51), and especially Guilt Daydreams (.65). Correlations with the CPI scales are generally negative with especially notable correlations with Sense of Well-Being (−.33), Self-Control (−.48), Tolerance (−.34), Good Impression (−.37), Intellectual Efficiency (−.31) and Guilford's Objectivity (−.36) and Friendliness (−.45). This scale has its major loading on the Obsessional-Emotional Daydreaming factor (.65) and has small but intriguing loadings on Neuroticism (.27) and Masculinity (.23). It would appear to be a useful scale especially for any further studies of highly emotional or obsessional aspects of fantasy.

Variable No. 20: "Sexual Daydreams" (12 items)
Mean: 35   S.D.: 9.6   Cronbach's Alpha: .87

This scale was included for obvious reasons since so much daydreaming is presumably sexual and certainly so in an adolescent sample. The high mean suggests a considerable amount of such fantasy but the variability is somewhat greater for this scale suggesting that some students report only small amounts and others considerable amounts of these fantasies. The internal consistency of the items is quite good. "While reading I often slip into daydreams about sex or making love to someone" (.83); "Sometimes on the way to work I imagine myself making love to an attractive person of the opposite sex" (.80); and "Sometimes in the middle of the day I will daydream of having sexual relations with someone I am fond of" (.77), are examples of high-correlating fantasies.

Sexual daydreams show a high number of correlations with other day-dream scales, including General Daydreaming (.53), Absorption in Daydreaming (.62), Positive Reactions to Daydreams (.50), Frightened Reactions to Daydreams (.44), Visual Imagery (.40), Problem-Solving (.38), Mindwandering (.39), Daydream Frequency (.45), Achievement (.31), Hallucinatory-Vividness (.31), Fear of Failure (.35), and Guilt (.32). On other scales, there is a pattern of association with Boredom, Distractibility, and Neuroticism (.35) as well as negative associations with CPI Sense of Well-Being (−.33), Self-Control (−.35), Tolerance (−.32), Guilford's Emotional Stability (−.31) and Objectivity (−.27).

As might be suspected, therefore, the Sexual Daydreams scale for this sample has complex meaning. It loads on three factors: Positive-Vivid Daydreaming (.48), Obsessional-Emotional Daydreaming (.40), and Neuroticism (.32). It seems clear that the occurrence of sexual daydreams cannot, in isolation, be given a meaning implying serious disturbance. Certainly for some subjects it fits into a pattern of healthy positive fantasizing, for others into a constellation of doubt and obsessional rumination, while for others it is part of an anxiety-ridden, clearly neurotic picture. Probably future research should include not only relatively "normal" sexual fantasy patterns but a variety of other types to ascertain whether these might load differentially on the kinds of factors cited above.

Variable No. 21: "Heroic Daydreams" (12 items)
Mean: 29   S.D.: 10.8   Cronbach's Alpha: .91

This is a content scale that represents the well-known "Walter Mitty" daydreams of heroic achievement. Previous studies have suggested it to be one of the few scales that differentiates between the sexes since women are less likely to generate such fantasies. The mean for such fantasies is fairly low for this sample with a sizable variability. Internal consistency is quite good with no item falling below .58. "I imagine myself receiving honorary mention for having performed actions beyond the call of duty" (.82), and "In my fantasies I demonstrate great heroism and win a medal" (.79), are examples of high correlations with total scale score. The daydream, "I picture myself risking my life to save someone I love," has a particularly high mean for this sample.

Heroic Daydreams are related to General Content Daydreaming (.33), Achievement Daydreams (.58), Fear of Failure in Daydreams (.38), Hostile Daydreams (.51), Guilt Daydreams (.48), Curiosity: Impersonal-Mechanical (.30), CPI Femininity (−.29), Guilford Friendliness (−.31) and Motor Activity Preference (.34). The scale loads on two factors: Obsessional-Emotional Daydreaming (.60) and Masculinity (.37). This is one of the few scales that correlates significantly with the actual sex of the respondents (—.35). Clearly it has two components of which the association with vivid but guilt-ridden, obsessional fantasy is of major interest in the sphere of daydreaming, while the association with masculinity is an obvious reflection of identification with the traditional male role.

> *Variable No. 22:* "Guilt Daydreams" (12 items)
> Mean: 21   S.D.: 8.3   Cronbach's Alpha: .88

This scale was developed because the previous factor analysis by Singer and Antrobus had yielded a factor strongly indicating a facet of daydreaming tied to obsessional rumination, self-doubt, and guilt. Most of the scores in the earlier study were derived from interview ratings. This scale was developed to encompass similar material in a questionnaire form. The low mean for this scale with this sample suggests that the guilty daydream is not especially common. The scale's reliability is good, however, and 11 of 12 items correlate above .60 with total and the remaining item correlates at .59. Highest correlating items include "In my daydreams I am always afraid of being caught doing something wrong" (.73); "I imagine myself running away from someone who is going to punish me" (.72); and "In my fantasies a friend discovers I have lied" (.70).

The pattern of intercorrelations of this scale is interesting. It is associated very highly with Fear of Failure in Daydreams (.77), Hostile Daydreams (.65) (support for a Freudian linkage of agression and guilt, perhaps?), Frightened Reaction to Daydreams (.54), Achievement Daydreams (.34), General Daydreams (.37), Hallucinatory-Vividness (.41), Sexual Daydreams (.31), and Heroic Daydreams (.48). On the CPI it is negatively associated with Sense of Well-Being, Self-Control, Tolerance and Intellectual Efficiency; and on the Guilford there are low negative correlations with Objectivity and Friendliness. This scale proves to be a key scale in the matrix loading only on one factor and the highest there: Obsessional-Emotional Daydreaming (.83). Clearly the scale is a critical one for future research since it seems to tap the "tortured self-concern" factor found mainly with interview data in the earlier factor analytic study. Its 12 items seem well-related and should be a useful part of any future inventory as well as part of a group of tests designed to study the correlates of predominantly guilt-ridden obsessional fantasies.

This concludes a review of some of the 22 scales specifically developed to tap facets of daydreaming. The next group of measures formed part of the Curiosity-Attention Battery, scales designed to tap the relation of fantasy processes in the first 22 scales to Mindwandering, Distractibility, etc. In discussing these scales, emphasis will be placed only upon major factor loadings.

Variable No. 23: "Curiosity-Interpersonal" (16 items)
Mean: 52   S.D.: 10.6   Cronbach's Alpha: .84

This scale includes items reflecting curiosity about people and their relationships. It was developed because it was felt that an important feature of daydreaming might be its representation internally of a strong exploratory tendency. The separation into Interpersonal and Impersonal-Mechanical Curiosity scales reflects earlier experiences which suggest that the former pattern of curiosity is more associated with more fanciful daydreaming and the latter with more controlled thoughtfulness. The data from the present study support the notion that Interpersonal Curiosity is indeed associated with daydreaming of a generally positive type (see Table 6). It also seems associated with a more feminine orientation psychologically, in contrast with Impersonal-Mechanical Curiosity. One might speculate that one function of daydreaming as manifested in scales loading on a Positive-Vivid Daydreaming factor is a kind of internal searching out and exploring of the future, especially in relation to people and personal situations. The more curious one is about how others live or what goes on inside windows of apartments or homes or about the lives of other passengers on a bus the more likely one is also to develop fairly elaborate fantasies and to weave the strangers into them.

Variable No. 27: "Distractibility" (14 items)
Mean: 47   S.D.: 8.5   Cronbach's Alpha: .78

This scale emphasizes concentration difficulty, distraction by noises, and inability to concentrate fully. It was included to ascertain what types of daydreaming might be especially associated with this type of negative self-report.

The high mean suggests that many students are plagued by this experience. The scale is somewhat less reliable than others. "I am not easily distracted" (keyed negatively) (.70); "My ability to concentrate is not impaired by someone talking in another part of my apartment or house" (keyed negatively) (.69); and "I find it hard to read when someone is on the telephone in another room: (.65), are examples of high correlating items.

The scale correlates highest with Mindwandering and Boredom as might be anticipated. It loads only on the Neurotic-Anxious Absorption in Daydreaming factor (.50). It helps clarify the close tie of the Neuroticism Factor to anxiety and differentiates it from the more obsessional or constructive aspects of daydreaming.

Variable No. 29: "Self-Report Tendency" (14 items)
Mean: 4   S.D.: 9.6   Cronbach's Alpha: .79

This scale was designed specifically for this study to tap the degree to which reporting or talking about daydreaming or inner experience was viewed negatively or positively by the respondents. In a sense, it was a kind of control variable. The scale is fairly satisfactory from the standpoint of reliability. Highest correlating are "I like to talk about personal things" (.74); and "I enjoy talking about my personal feelings—the things that make me happy—the things that make me sad" (.78). This scale loads on two factors: Social Extraversion (.34) and Positive-Vivid Daydreaming (.38). Its specific pattern of correlations with individual scales suggests that it is associated with a kind of friendly, sociable, ascendant and outgoing quality. Its link to Positive-Vivid Daydreaming helps clarify that scale as a constructive aspect. The fact that it does not load highly on Neuroticism or the Obsessional-Emotional Daydream scales, for example, indicates that the distress manifested in these scales may not merely be a consequence of greater self-report tendencies, but may rather reflect a more profound experience.

Some Implications

Let us now review some of the generalizations to be drawn from our examination of the IPI scales and the factors on which they load. The scales that tap general Frequency of Daydreaming and Absorption in Daydreaming both emerge as loading highly on two separate factors, one closely linked to neurotic symptomatology and manifestations of anxiety, the other relatively less weighted for measures of emotional instability and presumably reflecting more positive and constructive uses of daydreaming. It should be clear that one cannot cavalierly talk of a person as a "daydreamer" without more careful examination of the pattern of his fantasies. Thus an examination of Tables 5 and 6 suggests that one major dimension associated with considerable daydreaming involves also considerable self-report of low well-being, lack of objectivity, emotional instability, intolerance, much mindwandering, feeling of boredom and distractibility, and frequent sexual, hostile-aggressive and fearful daydreaming. By contrast, another dimension which involves frequent and absorbing daydreams is also associated with thoughtfulness, acceptance and positive content in daydreams, a preference for ideational activities, an attempt to achieve in independent fashion rather than through conformity—all in all a more constructive and creative orientation. A third major dimension, or perhaps the opposite pole of the second (depending on the statistical solution) represents clearly an inner life characterized by guilt, fear of failure, and hostility as well as some heroic or achievement striving.

Clearly the patterns of imagery and fantasy fall into groups that correspond to the major dimensions of personality and psychopathological classification that have been developed in other empirical research (Buss, 1966; Eysenck, 1959; Shapiro, 1965). The Neurotic-Anxious Absorption in Daydreaming factor suggests a personality style characterized by much anxiety, attempts at repression, fleeting and poorly organized intrusive thoughts, images from the past that haunt and distract one. This closely resembles the Anxiety-Hysteria syndrome or the pattern characteristic perhaps of the anxiety neurotic so extensively studied by Eysenck. The other pathological grouping seems clearly to represent the Obsessional Neurotic, much oriented to striving and achievement but also tormented by guilt, fears of failure and hostile wishes—a classical superego conflict pattern. Here the person representing a high scorer on the major scales of this factor might be considerably oriented towards processing imagery and inner experience, but much of the fantasy would have a dysphoric quality and involve great repetition of a small number of themes of a somewhat bizarre nature often emerging with a near hallucinatory vividness (see Table 6). This person would take little satisfaction in his fantasies and daydreams and would report much effort at maintaining control or at maintaining a rigid inflexible pattern of life. Traditional masculine interests would also be evident in this person as values irrespective of actual sex.

The third major category is that which was referred to in the earlier paper where a comparable factor emerged (Singer & Antrobus, 1963) as the "happy daydreamer." A person scoring high on the scales loading this factor might be characterized by frequent, relatively vivid imagery (both auditory and visual), and a preference for ideational kinds of activities or work. He might be speculative and thoughtful, very curious about people, perhaps somewhat overtly anxious but also highly self-aware with an extensive use of daydreaming for exploration of the future. Such a person might indeed enjoy his inner life and risk the consequences of occasional "missed signals" (Antrobus, Coleman, & Singer, 1967) because of the value placed on generating imagery or attending to the ongoing reverberatory processing of material from his long-term memory storage. While statistically one cannot support this view it does seem as if this pattern represents the true Thinking Introvert, a factor that contrasts with the Social Extravert factor which also emerges clearly in all of our studies (Factor 2 in Tables 5 and 6). Both patterns suggest normal *styles,* one oriented to extensive involvement and processing of the stimuli from the environment and from social interactions, the other valuing more self-generated images and fantasies, but both essentially adaptive and free of severe disturbance or personal distress. In this sense, one might be led to think of Jung's Introvert-Extravert ordering of man's consciousness.

The data from the study described here make it abundantly clear that very important individual differences in structure and content of daydreaming and related imaginal processes do characterize a normal college sample. The fact that the results essentially replicate earlier studies and extend them to both sexes indicates that any future research on imagery or ongoing fantasy must take into account differing styles. The specific scales described above, while suffering from the same limitations as any self-report or questionnaire procedures do, seem reasonably reliable and interpretable and may be of value to other investigators exploring the various dimensions of imagery. It also seems clear that daydreaming or various manifestations of frequent, vivid imagery need not be regarded as necessarily pathological eruptions. Rather imagery and fantasy are perhaps best regarded as fundamental human capacities or cognitive skills that can reflect serious pathology or distress but that can also be employed as valuable tools for self-gratification, planning, or creative activity, "experimental action," as Freud put it, but in a most adaptive way.

References

Antrobus, J. S., Coleman, R., & Singer, J. L. Signal detection performance by subjects differing in predisposition to daydreaming. *Journal of Consulting Psychology,* 1967, **31**, 487–491.

Antrobus, J. S., Singer, J. L., Goldstein, S., & Fortgang, M. Mind-wandering and cognitive structure. *Transactions of the New York Academy of Science,* 1970, **32**, 242–252.

Antrobus, J. S., Singer, J. L., & Greenberg, S. Studies in the stream of consciousness: Experimental enhancement and suppression of spontaneous cognitive processes. *Perceptual and Motor Skills,* 1966, **23**, 399–417.

Buss, A. *Psychopathology.* New York: Wiley, 1966.

Eysenck, H. J. *Maudsley personality inventory.* London: Univ. of London Press, 1959.

Gough, H. *California psychological inventory.* Palo Alto, California: Consulting Psychologists Press, 1964.

Guilford, J. P., & Zimmerman, W. S. *The Guilford-Zimmerman Temperament Survey.* Beverly Hills, California: Sheridan Supply, 1949.

Richardson, A. *Mental imagery.* New York: Springer Publ., 1969.

Shapiro, D. *Neurotic styles.* New York: Basic Books, 1965.

Singer, J. *Daydreaming.* New York: Random House, 1966.

Singer, J. L., & Antrobus, J. S. A factor analytic study of daydreaming and conceptually-related cognitive and personality variables. *Perceptual and Motor Skills,* (Monograph Supplement 3-V17) 1963.

Singer, J. L., & Antrobus, J. S. Dimensions of daydreaming: A factor analysis of imaginal processes and personality scales. *NIMH Progress Report,* 1970, (Mimeograph Report).

Singer, J. L., & McCraven, V. Some characteristics of adult daydreaming. *Journal of Psychology,* 1961, **51,** 151–164.

Singer, J. L., & McCraven, V. Patterns of daydreaming in American subcultural groups. *International Journal of Social Psychology,* 1962, **8,** 272–282.

Singer, J. L., & Schonbar, R. Correlates of daydreaming: A dimension of self-awareness. *Journal of Consulting Psychology,* 1961, **25,** 1–6.

Stein, K. B., & Craik, K. H. Relationship between motoric and ideational activity preference and time perspective in neurotics and schizophrenics. *Journal of Consulting Psychology,* 1965, **26,** 460–467.

9 SYDNEY JOELSON SEGAL[1]

ASSIMILATION OF A STIMULUS IN THE CONSTRUCTION OF AN IMAGE: THE PERKY EFFECT REVISITED

Introduction

How can the phenomenological experience we call imagery be defined and measured? The history of psychology is strewn with the failures of those who tried to reduce this evanescent and subjective experience into a verbal report or a drawing, to quantify the resulting product according to some scalar values, and then to assert that the result is a definition of imagery. When the results are compared to psychophysical measurements or definitions of perception, they seem to fall far short of the goal.

It is true that the statement, "I imagine that I see tiger lilies in the backyard, orange and yellow with little yellow specks of pollen and brown specks all inside the flower" is difficult to classify. It is also true that one cannot be certain that this statement correctly describes the image experi-

[1] This paper was prepared during the initial months of my tenure as a research scientist, under the NIMH Development Awards program, Grant No. 1 KO2 MH13324-01. Some of the preparation and much of the work was accomplished with the support of the AFOSR, contract No. F44620-68-C-0093; The City University of New York Faculty Research Award, 1154E also provided support. Some of the experiments were supported under NIMH Grant No. 5-R01-MH-06733 to the Research Center for Mental Health, New York University. I wish especially to acknowledge the inspiration of George S. Klein, who first introduced me to Perky's phenomenon, and who long encouraged me to pursue the present issues. Professors J. L. Singer and R. R. Holt provided suggestions and guidance at various points, which are gratefully acknowledged. I thank also the assistants who worked on different phases of these projects, rendering invaluable assistance: Arnold Wiener, Thomas Todd, Pearl-Ellen Gordon, Vincent Fusella, and Wanda Rapaczynski.

enced by the observer. However, it is possible that the problems involved in first reducing an image to such a statement and then classifying the statement in order to measure it, have been somewhat overestimated.

The measurement of imagery is actually quite similar to the measurement of perception. In both instances there is a phenomenological experience based on patterns of response within the optic tract and the brain, in both instances the observer reports on the phenomenological experience and the neural substrate is obscured. The main difference is that the perception is characterized by the presence of a clearly defined physical stimulus against which verbal report or other behavioral measures can be scaled, but no clearly relevant external stimulus characterizes the image. However, if the image could also be matched against the objective standard of a physical stimulus, then it could be measured in much the same way.

In this chapter, it will be shown that imagery may depend on relevant physical stimuli that are concurrently present, and not only on stored information. Demonstration of this dependence will in turn reveal stable characteristics of the image, and indicate how contemporaneous physical stimuli are processed and assimilated to a constructed image. Piaget's (1962) analysis of the role of assimilation and accommodation in sensory-motor development provided the essential theoretical distinction underlying this concept. Piaget noted that an individual may identify the properties of a stimulus and *accommodate* his behavior to them, or he may focus on a generated idea and *assimilate* relevant properties of the stimulus to that idea. Thus in accommodation, a child might report an apple to be round, reddish-green, smelling fresh, and good to eat; but in the assimilational behavior characteristic of imaginary play, the child might pretend that the apple is a royal feast or a magic egg, assimilating only the edibility or roundness, according to the needs of his imagination. In assimilation, the characteristic properties of the stimulus may be ignored unless they can be appropriated to the generated idea, whereas those same properties are basic to accommodative behavior. In perception, the observer typically accommodates his behavior to the stimulus, but a stimulus is assimilated to the image. Thus, processing of the stimulus during imagery may be quite different than it is during perception. With that distinction in mind, however, it is possible to study the image by relating the subject's verbal report or other data to the physical stimulus.

Some studies have already indicated the feasibility of such an approach. Certain unusual subjective experiences have been reported by subjects under hypnosis, in drug states, during alcoholic intoxication, and in psychotic fugues, and it has sometimes been possible to specify the endogenous stimuli which formed the nidus or basis for these hallucinations (Horowitz, 1964; Klüver, 1966; Saravay & Pardes, 1967). Also, subjects' images and pseudohallucinations obtained during sensory isolation sometimes seem to be related to specific endogenous and even exogenous stimuli (Silverman, Cohen, Bressler, & Shmavonian, 1962). The effect of a stimulus on images and dreams has been carefully studied by Pötzl (1917) and by later explorers of this phenomenon of "subliminal perception" (Fisher, 1954; Klein, Spence, Holt, & Gourevitch, 1958; Shevrin & Luborsky, 1958). If we go back to Würzburg or Cornell, even more relevant data can be found. Külpe (1902) asked subjects to report on any "objective" or "subjective" events that they experienced consciously as they were relaxing in a darkened room. From time to time a square, varying in size, brightness, and location, was projected onto one of the walls. Külpe observed a blending or fusion of this physical stimulus with the observer's imaginal elaborations, and noted that the final product was experienced as a complete and integrated event and often classified as subjective, but the observer could not analyze it back into its "objective" and "subjective" sources. Perky (1910), in her classic experimental sequel to Külpe's work, concluded that an undetected but supraliminal physical stimulus may be "mistaken for and incorporated into an image of imagination, without the least suspicion on the observer's part that any external stimulus is present to the eye [p. 450]."

The work of Külpe and Perky is specifically addressed to the question of whether imagery may depend not only on stored information, but also on stimuli which happen to be present contemporaneously and which are processed as part of the image. If the findings of Külpe and Perky can be verified and replicated, then imagery does depend on the stimulus. In this case, it may be possible to study imagery just as perception is studied: a stimulus can be introduced and the product can be evaluated, and any transformations of the stimulus may be analyzed to determine properties of the intervening processes.

In Perky's experiment, subjects were simply asked to "imagine a banana" (or a book, or a leaf) and describe the image as it appeared to them. A colored form, shaped like a banana and colored yellow, was permitted to oscillate briefly before the subject's gaze while he was describing his image, and "all the observers noted that the imaged banana was on end and not as they had been supposing they thought of it [ibid., p. 432]." Thus the stimulus did register, it partly determined the final appearance of the phenomenally experienced image, and yet the subjects did not for a moment realize that a supraliminal stimulus had in fact been present. If Perky's finding is true and can be replicated then it follows that stimuli may be determining, influencing, and altering images all the time and the image cannot be defined simply as an experience which occurs in the absence of a stimulus.

Perky's experiment was not replicated successfully for about 50 years, until 1964, when Shifra Nathan and I reported a partial replication and extension of Perky's findings (Segal & Nathan, 1964). While we also observed that the images sometimes showed similarities to the stimulus, the assimilation effect did not seem either as clear or as dramatic as in Perky's report. Our subjects reported that their imaged banana was long and yellow, but they did not indicate that it surprised them by appearing in a vertical orientation, as Perky's subjects had. However, when subjects were asked to image a book and an open book in a neutral or white color was projected, virtually all of them described an open book, although it is more usual to image a closed book.

The next study, therefore, provided greater contrast between the stimulus and the image requested. In this experiment, performed in our laboratory in 1965 but never published, subjects were asked to imagine one thing but were shown something quite different. For example, they were told to image a glass of iced tea and shown a stimulus of a gray elephant. One subject reported, "I can see iced tea . . . looks strong and iced . . ." after some delays and prompting, he continued, "the tea has leaves in it . . ." and finally he blurted out, "Everytime I try to visualize the tea, there is a long caterpillar drinking the tea." This subject reported a clearly bizarre image in which certain features of the stimulus: its grayish color, its texture, its animate appearance—perhaps such details as the trunk of the elephant, were noticed. However, the resulting impression was small, too small in relation to the imaged iced tea to be designated as an elephant or any large animal; hence it was inferred to be a small animal and described as a caterpillar.

As dramatic as this was, it was only a single occurrence; nothing else as impressive as this was obtained in this or any subsequent experiment. True, other less dramatic and much more subtle effects were noted, for example, when the elephant was shown, subjects were more likely to report odd images of iced tea with tea bags, mint, spoons, ice, and sugar in them, whereas plain glasses of reddish brown iced tea were reported when a slide depicting a real glass of iced tea was shown. Also, several subjects fused an image of a city skyline to a slide of a red tomato and reported the sun setting behind the skyline of Manhattan. However, these scattered instances were not frequent enough to measure systematically and remained as curious anecdotes.

Gradually it became clear that the effect of the stimulus was generally far more subtle. We had been expecting accommodative changes, and most of the effects obtained were assimilational. In relating a stimulus to the image, it seemed to be atypical or unexpected characteristics of the stimulus which were processed. Therefore, the effect reported by Perky and the occasional dramatic instances observed in our previous work were exceptions. What should be looked for were instances of recruitment of unspecified characteristics of the stimulus to the image. This was clearly not as simple as measuring perception.

The data from eight experiments were reevaluated and analyzed from this viewpoint, and it became clear that the stimulus was at least partially processed, and was assimilated into the generated image according to specifiable principles. This chapter will report on the data from these eight experiments and try to draw out some of these principles. Introspective descriptions were evaluated to try to determine which features of the stimulus were most likely to emerge in the image: the content, the location, the color, or other aspects. In some instances, it was possible to compare assimilational effects when the stimuli were relatively bright or dim, congruent or incongruent to the image, gradual or abrupt in onset. The images were described by verbal reports, and in some instances by drawings, and these products were analyzed in different ways. Many objective analyses were tried, but it was found that a trained judge evaluating these products could locate assimilational effects more effectively than any objective measure.

The Experiments

Experiment 1

The procedure used in this experiment (Segal, 1968b) was followed, with minor variations, in all the subsequent experiments. Subjects were told that we were interested in the quality of their imagery while they were gazing at an unpatterned visual field. Then they were seated in a comfortable chair and a large vinyl hood was lowered over their head and shoulders. Unknown to the subjects, a projector was located behind a window facing them; none of the subjects noticed the window before they were seated under the translucent hood, and it was invisible from within the hood. During the images, slides were back-projected onto the surface of the hood, at about the level of the subject's eyes. The slides were photographs of common objects against an opaque background.

In this first study 46 subjects were tested. Each subject was asked to image 20 different common objects successively: an elephant, a pair of eye glasses, a pack of cigarettes, a book, and so on. Four of the images were never accompanied by the projections, the remaining 16 were always accompanied by slides. The congruence or relationship of the content of the slide to the image was varied systematically. Thus, the image of the elephant was accompanied by the slide of the elephant for half the subjects, but by the slide of the eyeglasses for the other half; the imaged eyeglasses were accompanied by the photograph of eyeglasses for half the subjects, but by a bottle of Coca Cola for the other half, and so on. Subjects' descriptions of their images were tape recorded, and transcribed from the tapes.

Next, judges evaluated the tapescripts for assimilation. The images during which no stimuli had been shown and also the images during which subjects had correctly detected a slide were excluded. Then all tapescripts of the remaining images of an elephant were placed together, all images of eyeglasses were placed together and so on. The judge was asked to sort the images into two piles: those on which they believed the congruent slide had been shown and those on which they judged the incongruent slide had been present. Five judges were used, and each judge was encouraged to develop his own technique for evaluation.

The mean frequency correct for all five judges combined was 53.5%, and their judgment exceeded chance values to a significant degree ($\chi^2 = 28.13$, $p < .001$). Half of the slides had been shown at a brighter intensity than the other half, with both intensities appearing equally often during each image and also for each subject. Assimilation judgments were slightly more frequent with the brighter stimuli (54% against 51% for the dimmer stimuli). Assimilation scores were 57% with the congruent slides compared to 49% for the incongruent.

The results with congruity were somewhat difficult to interpret. Congruence and incongruence referred to the content (whether the same item was imaged and projected or whether different ones were imaged and projected), but it is not certain that the content was fully processed or coded accurately. To evaluate this, and also to provide some systematic albeit *post hoc* information on what attributes of the stimulus registered, a content analysis was performed on the data. Each subject's verbal description was broken up into small information units, and those categories on which the frequency between congruent and incongruent slide presentations differed by 12% or more were listed. The results of this analysis appear in Table 1. Registration of the general form and color of the stimulus, but not the content, seemed to be the rule.

For example, subjects described the tomato as red when a tomato was shown, but when a pilsner glass of beer was projected subjects described the tomato as shaded or dirty red, as shiny, as a homegrown tomato. Examination of the table will show that the image was more likely to emerge in its most typical or conventional form when the congruent stimulus was projected and it tended to have more idiosyncratic features which sometimes related to the content, but it usually resembled the general form and color of the incongruent stimulus when the latter was projected. It seems as if the individual selected an image that was both congruent with the content requested, and also had a formal resemblance to the shape and color of the stimulus presented or at least utilized chromatic and figural qualities of the stimulus as background or details.

The stimulus seems to be partially processed: it is analyzed for general form, color, and sometimes textural qualities, just as the nonattended auditory input is partially processed in a typical dichotic listening task. The phenomenal appearance of the image is constructed *ad hoc;* it depends in part on previous experiences with the object imaged, but it also partially depends on sensory input which is currently being processed. The image then is experienced as an integrated whole, and the imager is not able to distinguish those features which depend on sensory input from the features which depend on past experience (see also Külpe, 1902). An untrained judge, however, can distinguish these two types of features slightly but significantly more frequently than chance.

Experiment 2

Several modifications of the procedure were introduced in this experiment (Segal & Gordon, 1969), and several additional variables were studied. In the previous experiment it had seemed clear that the content of the stimulus did not register and perhaps was not processed at all; therefore, in this experiment, slides were selected which had more clearly defined physical characteristics but no content or meaning. In the previous experiment, the content of the photographs was either the same as the image or different, that is "congruent" or "incongruent," but any effects obtained were probably artifactual or due to congruence of color and shape, as the content was not processed. Here, each slide consisted of a simple geometric form cut out of a black background: either a circle, a square, a triangle, a crescent (see Fig. 1A), or two circles, squares, triangles, or crescents. A wratten gelatine filter, either blue, yellow, red, or green was mounted behind each shape. Thus each stimulus was precisely defined as to color, shape, and number of elements. These specific elements were sometimes "congruent" and sometimes "incongruent" to the comparable characteristics of the image (e.g., a red circle was "congruent" to a tomato, a green crescent was "incongruent"). Twenty-four subjects were each asked to image 18 items; one-third of the items were accompanied by a congruent stimulus, one-third by an incongruent stimulus, and one-third by no stimulus in a counterbalanced design.

TABLE 1

Differences in Content of Images With a Congruent or Incongruent Stimulus Present: Experiment I

Image	Stimulus[a]	Color			Other effects		
		Description	Frequency (%) Congruent	Incongruent	Description	Frequency (%) Congruent	Incongruent
Parrot	Parrot (C)	Green dominant	62	20	In cage	38	20
	Turkey (I)	Yellow or yellow-green	33	15			
		Many colors	5	55			
Orange juice	Orange juice (C)	Orange-yellow	67	100	Big or medium	60	13
	Soda (I)				Small	13	60
					Wet	53	7
Turkey	Turkey (C)	Brown or brownish	62	12½	Thanksgiving	31	12½
	Coke glass (I)	Golden-brown	12½	37½	Table set	6	37½
Tomato	Tomato (C)	Red	80	29	Shiny	13	29
	Beer (I)	Red with shading	13	47	Homegrown	6½	29
					Plant	0	12
Beer	Beer (C)	Gold or goldish	18	0	Handle	6	35
	Milk (I)	Brown	6	20	Thicker cut glass	0	35
					Foam down sides	6	20
					(No foam)	18	40
Iced tea	Iced tea (C)	Transparent	22	0	Lemon	55½	95
	Elephant (I)	Red or red-brown	16	0	Sugar	5½	40
					Spoon	28	50
					Mint/teabag	0	15

Stimulus	Response			Response		
Coffee (C) / Parrot (I)	Bright colors in trim background	5	29	Cup of special design	0	15
				Spoon or sugar bowl	33	10
Eyeglasses (C) / Coke (I)				Sunglasses or bifocals	0	14
				No lens	18	0
Elephant (C) / Eyeglasses (I)	Bright colors in details or background	0	18	In jungle	0	
				Walt Disney		$31\frac{1}{2}$
Coke glass (C) / Coffee (I)	Dark	24	5	In usual coke glass	38	24
	Bright color in details or background	5	24	In container	5	29
Butterfly (C) / Onion (I)	Orange and black	0	23	Designs on it	23	38
				Antennas	31	8
				In collection	15	0
Onion (C) / Orange juice (I)	Yellow/orange	0	24	Prepared in kitchen	0	19
	Pink/purple/maroon	25	0	Raw-out with others	16	0
Ice cream soda (C) / Butterfly (I)	Black and white soda	8	36			

[a] C, Congruent; I, Incongruent.

Several other changes were made in the experimental method to increase the likelihood that the stimulus would register. The large diffuse surface of the *ganzfeld*-type hood was replaced by a translucent plastic cone with a screen at the apex. The screen subtended a visual angle of 26°, so it partially restricted the range of the subject's potential eye movements and made it more likely that the stimulus would be detected. Half of the experiment was conducted like the last one, with the projector hidden and no information that stimuli might be shown. Then, the subjects were informed that slides would be shown during their images; and for the last nine images they were asked after each one if a slide had been projected. Thirty-eight percent of the subjects detected the stimuli in the first half, although there were 15% false alarms; in contrast, 66% detected the stimuli in the second half, with only 4% false alarms.

The judging procedure was similar to Experiment 1. Each judge studied all the subjects' descriptions for each image and guessed for each whether the congruent stimulus, the incongruent stimulus, or nothing had been present. As those images on which the stimulus was correctly detected were excluded, half of the images judged were accompanied by nothing, a quarter by a congruent, and a quarter by an incongruent slide; hence chance guessing was only 26%. The three judges were correct 34%, 34%, and 63% of the time. These values were significantly greater than chance ($\chi^2 = 42.83$, $p < .001$).

The mean assimilation score was 46% with the incongruent stimuli and 40% with the congruent stimuli. This difference was not significant and went in the opposite direction from comparable data in Experiment 1.

However, it appeared that the image had somewhat more idiosyncratic characteristics when an "incongruent" stimulus was present and so judges were more likely to guess correctly. For example, subjects were asked to image an orchid: some were shown a blue triangle (considered congruent), while others were shown two yellow circles. One subject's tapescript began with his asking whether to image "a green or purple kind?" Told he could choose either, he said, "think I'll describe the green type. It has a thin stem. At the end of the stem was the flower with two different shapes . . . the one on the right has a leaf shape, the other has a petal which looks like wooden shoes or a slipper. The color ranges between white and—has stripes, pale green, white, and light brown—in the middle a whitish area with yellow pistils." This subject had been shown the two yellow circles. Another subject, shown the blue triangle, reported it as "purple—long purple leaves joined together at one end—in the middle very delicate."

The judgments were also analyzed to compare assimilation in the first half of the experiment when subjects were naive, to the second half where subjects had been informed that slides would be projected. All judges were more accurate in their assimilation judgments in the second half; they were correct 35% of the time in the first half, and 53% in the second ($\chi^2 = 11.95$, $p < .05$). When subjects expected a stimulus, it was processed more fully, and thus had more influence on the image even when it was not detected.

Experiment 3

The apparatus and procedure in this experiment (Segal & Gordon, 1969) were similar to the previous one, except that all subjects were informed from the beginning that stimuli would be shown and asked after each image if they had detected a slide. Each image was accompanied by one geometric shape for half the subjects and by nothing for the other half. For twelve subjects (Experiment 3a) the stimuli were so bright that they were detected 86% of the time; for another twelve subjects (Experiment 3b) the stimuli were only slightly above threshold and 57% of these were detected.

Judges reviewed these images for assimilation, using the procedure established previously. For the brighter stimuli, chance guessing was 34% correct,[2] and the three judges were correct on 41%, 45%, and 50%; the difference was significantly greater than chance ($\chi^2 = 14.96$, $p < .01$). With the dimmer stimuli chance guessing was about 50% and the three judges were correct on 51%, 58%, and 63% ($\chi^2 = 29.20$, $p < .001$). While it is not possible to compare these rates directly, especially as different judges were involved, judges seemed slightly more accurate in detecting assimilation with the brighter stimuli as had been found also with Experiment 1.

Descriptions of images in this experiment revealed how a stimulus-accompanied image compared to a spontaneously generated image. One spontaneous image of a bird was "a sparrow—brownish and it's sitting on a fence and looking around." But a subject who was shown a blue crescent first commented that he did not see any slide and then described "a parakeet, blue with blue on the front of its breast. The back is alternate shades of white and gray. It has an unusually long tail. The colors are blue, various shades of blue, varying from light to dark, almost blackish blue. The head is white."

Asked to image a pack of cigarettes, subjects shown a green square re-

---

[2] Excluding all those images on which subjects had detected slides meant that there were about twice as many "blank" as slide-accompanied images.

ported Salem or True brand cigarettes (green pack) a quarter of the time, whereas subjects' spontaneous images did not include these brands. Subjects who imaged eyeglasses when two green circles were projected often described black frames and lenses which were extra thick, or dirty, or tinted (sunglasses). When a red circle was projected during the image of a clock, subjects often described the clock as orange or brass; but their spontaneous images of clocks were usually of grandfather clocks, cuckoo clocks, or other special antique clocks.

Experiments 4 and 5

In Perky's original experiment, the stimuli were gradually brightened from a clearly subliminal intensity up to threshold brightness; then the observer's attention was distracted and the stimulus was removed. In Experiments 2 and 3 the stimulus was projected at a single uniform level of brightness. It seemed possible that there would be a difference between assimilation judgments depending on the mode of onset of the stimuli, so two modes (gradual and abrupt onset) were directly compared in the next two experiments (Segal & Fusella, 1969).

Our method of providing *gradual onset* was to brighten the stimulus gradually over 3 seconds and then to dim it over the next 3 seconds; at its starting intensity the stimulus could not be detected on a photometer and the peak value was about 0.8 foot candles brighter than its surroundings. This method was used in both Experiments 4 and 5. In the *abrupt onset* or immediate conditions, the stimulus was projected at the peak intensity (0.8 foot candles) and maintained at that level for a few seconds, 3 seconds in Experiment 4, 2 seconds in Experiment 5.[3] The procedure of these experiments was similar to that of the previous experiment, although a revised hood with a smaller screen (16° visual angle) was used. All subjects knew that stimuli would be shown, and they were asked after each image if a stimulus had been projected. Thirty-two subjects were used in each experiment.

Some of the stimuli used were the squares, circles, triangles, and crescents of the earlier experiments, but also some newer, more complex geo-

---

[3] The reason for changing the duration of the stimulus in Experiment 5 is that if Bloch's Law was operating the observer might effectively respond to the stimulus by treating duration and brightness reciprocally. This reciprocity seemed to influence detectability, for the gradual onset stimulus was detected slightly more often than the 2-second uniform-intensity stimulus, slightly less often than the 3-second stimulus. However, mode of onset per se had no effect on detection.

metric forms were introduced. They had more contours and were quite distinctive, some even had a certain amount of "content" or meaning (see Fig. 1, B and C). The items which subjects were asked to image represented broader categories than in the previous experiments, e.g., flowers, a costume, and could be conceptualized in several different colors or forms. Perhaps use of more general image categories and stimuli with more distinctive properties would increase the salience of assimilational effects.

The judgment procedure was similar to that used previously. Only those images accompanied by undetected stimuli were evaluated by the judges and each judge had to decide which of two stimuli accompanied each image. Five judges were used for each experiment, and all judges were correct at better than chance in both Experiment 4 ($\chi^2 = 47.63$, $p < .001$) and in Experiment 5 ($\chi^2 = 51.64$, $p < .001$). Mode of onset seemed to influence assimilation. Four out of five judges were more often correct with the gradual onset stimuli in Experiment 4, and all five judges had more correct assimilation judgments with gradual onset stimuli in Experiment 5 (the latter effect, but not the former, was significant by a sign

FIG. 1. *Stimuli used in the experiments. All appeared in colors, as described in the text. Experiments 2 and 3 used the designs in A; Experiments 4 and 5 used the designs in A, B, and C. The design in D was used only for Experiment 6, and the design in E was used only for Experiment 7. Experiment 8 used the designs in B.*

test, $p < .05$; for the latter, $\chi^2 = 9.46$, $(.10 > p > .05)$. Table 2 presents these data. Apparently gradual onset, which did not alter the detection rate at all, did affect assimilation. During gradual onset, the stimulus is present over a longer time period and perhaps more retinal cells are activated; this may lead to the partial processing which seems to characterize assimilation.

Introspective data provided further support for the assumption that the image is constructed by integrating concurrently processed sensory input. Asked to image a street and shown two red triangles, gradual in onset, one subject reported, "it's very narrow—where the cars could come down—and there are lots of houses on both sides—along each side of the street each group of houses are the same—except for one house and that's big and red and the porches are of different colors also, some of them are green and some are red, some are tiled and some are cemented." The other stimulus shown during images of a street was a group of nine brown dots in a circular array. One subject described his image,

> it's night time, it has just rained. If you look at the sewer, there's lots of garbage strewn over the sewer because the water pulled it down—it's a very, very dirty street—there are lots of old tenement houses on it, some are boarded up and some aren't—there's a house at the beginning of the block that's just going to be torn down because you can see the wooden doors of the building erected outside it—and there's a little bit of scaffolding—at the end of the block there's a fire house and that's about the only modern thing on the block—there are lots of garbage cans thrown all about—the stoops are filthy—and there are lots of people with their heads out the window presumably because it's a hot night.

Several other images of a street, described by other subjects who were shown the brown dots, also included comments on dirt and holes, that dirty papers and candybar wrappers were on the street, or that there were many potholes in it.

When the image was of a bicycle and the stimulus was the same pattern of nine dots, but colored red, one subject reported, "yes, I see an old beat-up bike—fenders are all dented—and it's sort of a reddish color—just generally beat up." Another said, "it's a boy's bike, small—red—the kickstand is up—it has a horn on it—it's rusty in some spots—the tires are whitewall, but they are a little dirty." In contrast, when the stimulus was two large blue circles, side by side, four out of six subjects said the bicycle was blue. One pictured a "two-wheeler—a big one, about 24 or 26 inches, blue in color, leaning against a fence." Another described a "two-wheeler—and it has thin wheels and spokes, and it's blue—it has a high seat and high handle bars—and it's not moving."

Several of the descriptions given by subjects in these two experiments

TABLE 2
Assimilation Judgment According to Mode
of Onset of Stimuli

	Gradual onset	Abrupt onset	Combined
Experiment 4			
Judge			
EK	.530	.519	.525
SS	.550	.525	.539
VF	.585	.544	.567
RJ	.721	.687	.700
WR	.533	.587	.556
Mean	.584	.572	
Experiment 5			
Judge			
SS	.614	.560	.586
VF	.620	.494	.556
RJ	.617	.603	.608
PB	.595	.560	.577
WR	.797	.722	.759
Mean	.649	.588	

seemed to be unusually long and detailed, as is apparent in some of the examples cited here. These appeared especially with the gradually brightening stimuli. Also, some of the stimuli seemed to have more complex effects than just determining the color and form of some details: they had an almost physiognomic influence on the content of the images. A blue crescent might signify a sunny day; a curving line (Fig. 1C, top center) might signify activity—a flying butterfly, a running fox. This effect was especially clear with the images of a doll. When the image was accompanied by two red squares, several subjects emphasized the rigidity of the figure: "it's in a rigid position with its arms at its side—and it's a female doll with a red dress with polka dots on it." Shown the green spiral, another subject described her doll as "very pliable—tiny—very twisty arms and legs and head—it's got goofy little clothes on, and it's got a funny expression."

Thus, certain new effects of the stimulus were observed in this experiment, making it difficult to make clear advance predictions of the effect of a stimulus. Sometimes results obtained with one image and one stimulus were repeated when the same image and stimulus were used with a second group of subjects, but not always. Sometimes the same stimulus had the same effects on two separate images, but at other times it varied. When subjects were asked to image a volcano and shown the red telephone, many described lava or said it was starting to erupt; however, when a blue crescent was shown, almost a third specified that it was not erupting and several commented on the blue sky. When subjects were asked to image a ship and shown a red circle they often referred to smokestacks and observed that it was a rough day; when a blue snakelike curve was shown, subjects usually commented that there were ropes on the ship and said it was a nice day. The imaged elephant had tusks and was in a jungle when two green triangles were shown; but when a brown "telephone" (Fig. 1C, top right) was shown, the elephant was in a zoo.

However, when I tried to generalize and formulate rules of how a stimulus is transformed to qualify an emergent image, I was at a loss. The problem is illustrated by the four images reported by four different subjects in Experiment 4 who were asked to image "flowers." In three of these images, the stimulus was a pattern of two red crescents. One subject described "roses, long stemmed, like buds—a lot of them." Another described "tiger lilies in the backyard, orange and yellow with little yellow specks of pollen and brown specks all inside the flower." The third reported "3 or 4 tulips right in the middle of the picture—surrounded by grass—they're kind of bending—yellow and purple and red." The fourth subject was shown a slender curving line; he described "one flower opening up—a carnation—green, green sepals—green—green stems—thorns—a white carnation." The influence of the *colors* of the stimuli seemed distinctive, yet the carnation was white, only the leaves and thorns were green like the stimulus. With the red stimulus present, most of the flowers were not red: the roses were not described in color, the tiger lilies were orange, yellow, and brown, the tulips were yellow and purple and red. The effect on the general *form* of the stimuli seemed to emerge in the images, as the bending tulips reflected the crescent shape; yet rosebuds, tulips, and tiger lilies hardly have the same form, and the carnation was very different from the slide. *Number* of stimulus objects at least seemed an unmistakeable feature here, but although there was clearly one carnation, all that could be said of the other images that were generated during projection of the two crescents is that there was *more than one* of each: "a lot" of roses, "tiger lilies," "3 or 4 tulips." Not surprisingly, all five judges were able to discriminate which stimuli accompanied which of the four images without error; nevertheless, this example shows clearly how difficult it is to state any general rules concerning the precise effect of a physical stimulus on the emerging image.

Furthermore, while all these data provided convincing evidence of the phenomenological existence of assimilation, it was difficult to move beyond simple demonstration to clear parametric analysis. While there were always a few individual images which seemed clearly to be constructed around the sensory input, there were always some images which did not clearly relate to the stimulus at all; in addition, there were usually a few images which seemed to relate to one stimulus—but actually occurred when another stimulus or no stimulus had been present. For example, the image of the street with potholes included a red firehouse on the block: at least one judge was led by that to guess that this image had been accompanied by the stimulus of two red triangles. Individuals showed enough variability in their stored experiences and in the characteristics of the images they reported that these individual differences were often more pronounced than the effects of the stimuli. It was thought, therefore, that clearer results might be obtained if two productions by the same subject could be compared when a stimulus was present during only one.

Experiments 6, 7, and 8

In these three studies, each subject reported on only four or five images. Two or three were for practice, and two were critical: a stimulus was present during one and the judge had to decide which one. The same hood with the smaller (16° visual angle) screen was used. In these experiments subjects did not know that stimuli would be shown, and with only a single exposure of the stimulus very few detections were obtained: only 13% in Experiment 6 and none in the other two.

In Experiment 6, (Segal, 1968a) subjects were asked to image either a plant or a violin, and a red angular geometric shape was used (Fig. 1D). Three judges evaluated the productions of 29 subjects and tried to guess during which one the slide had been shown. The judges were correct only 44%, 44%, and 48% of the time. This is the only instance where judges were clearly below chance in their scoring; the reason for their poor showing here is not immediately apparent.

In Experiment 7 (Segal, 1970) 64 subjects described their images of a tree or a parrot and the slide, a geometric shape roughly resembling a fir tree (Fig. 1E), was projected during one of them. This time subjects not only described their images but also drew sketches of them. Horowitz (1964) had found some interesting differences between subjects' descriptions and their drawings of images and I hoped these drawings might reveal some additional information about the phenomenal appearance of the image. The subjects were asked to make a simple sketch, not a finished

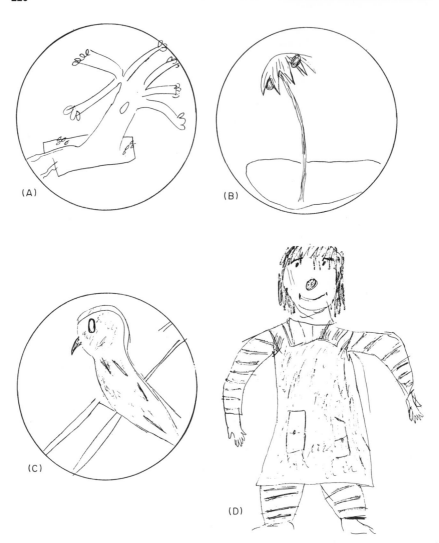

FIG. 2. *Subjects' sketches of their images. A and B were images of trees drawn with the stimulus present in Experiment 7; C was a parrot drawn in the same experiment with the same stimulus present. D is a doll drawn by a subject in Experiment 8 with the stimulus present. In the original drawings, green crayon was used for the leaves (both on the tree and on the ground) in A, and for the trunk and palm fronds in B. The parrot in C was colored blue with a yellow beak. The doll in D had yellow hair, a red mouth and jumper, blue eyes, nose, and stripes on arms and legs.*

Subjects' descriptions of images. (A) It is a very large tree and like very old, and looks like on a flat. It has got one of those big holes in it and it has got a lot of leaves and the branches sort of like topple over the house. It is inside drawing, and they were given a lead pencil and four colored pencils (red, blue, green, and yellow) to work with.

The drawings also served another purpose in this study. Subjects were asked to draw their image within a circle (see Fig. 2) which represented the end of the screen. The slide had deliberately been projected on the lower left-hand portion of the screen and we evaluated whether the images were seen in this location.[4] On examining the protocols, however, location of the sketches did not seem to be a reliable indicant that the stimulus was present for individual subjects. Also, when data from all 64 subjects were combined, it seemed that the stimulus had no effect on the left–right orientation of the images drawn; if anything, there was a bias toward the right among subjects who had been shown the stimulus. However, 32% of these subjects' images appeared in the same horizontal plane as the stimulus, compared to 27% in this plane with no stimulus present. In contrast, for the other three horizontal planes, more images filled them when the stimulus was *not* present. Thus, location of the stimulus had a very minimal effect on inferred location of the image.

Again, the main data of this experiment depend on judges' decisions. Four judges compared the two images drawn by each subject and guessed on which one the stimulus appeared. The judges were correct on 50%, 55%, 56%, and 61%, respectively ($\chi^2 = 4.63$, n.s.).

Although none of the subjects' images of a tree was a fir tree, many of the images of the tree resembled the stimulus. The parallel lines were

[4] Professor William Ittelson is gratefully acknowledged as the source of this suggestion.

---

out, one of those cement-slab things; and its roots go out a long way. (B) It is a palm tree and it is very tall and thin and it leans over to one side, and green leaves on top very long and pointed. There are a few coconuts on the tree and it is on an island. (C) It is a rather large bird, sitting on a limb. It is blue and it has got a yellow beak. I see it from a side; it is so pretty; its head back to me. Looks very soft. A light shade of blue and big dark eyes. It's like my parrot. (D) A doll? well, it's one of those ah raggedy ann sort of dolls, with the long straggly kind of reddish hair and the cloth face. It's a cloth doll, it's all cloth stuffed with—I don't know, odds and ends some kind of, and it's very floppy and it's been around a long time. It's very well used, worn. It's about a foot and a half long, I guess seven or eight inches wide, and when you hold it all the arms and legs flop inward. It's probably hand made because it has the features of a hand made doll, it has a button for a nose, and all that, and has a blue and white striped dress and a white apron like they do, and some kind of—ah—colored stockings, little and brown shoes but they aren't really shoes, they are just different colored cloth and it's got a painted kind of smile on its face.

often incorporated into the drawings, as in Fig. 2A. In Fig. 2B, the circle at the top of the stimulus display was perceived as a coconut on a palm tree. The stimulus was not assimilated so readily to the image of the parrot, although sometimes the upper circle appeared as an eye or a head of the parrot, with the bottom parallel appearing as a perch, the middle lines as the body of the parrot, as in Fig. 2C.

The drawings were often quite different from the descriptions of the images: sometimes they showed aspects of the stimulus which were not revealed in the descriptions; at other times they seemed to deny some of the assimilational effects which emerged in the descriptions. The image is developed over time, it was described while it was still phenomenologically present but it was drawn a minute or so later, so there may have been some changes in the image, some falsifications of memory. It is also possible that some of the drawings were partly conventionalized representations (see Bartlett, 1932).

In Experiment 8, a recent experiment not yet reported elsewhere, subjects were asked to evoke images while a stimulus was shown. Their protocols were set aside if they detected the stimulus or if they were unable to detect it, in a subsequent discrimination task, with at least 80% accuracy (most subjects achieved 100% accuracy). Twelve of the subjects (Experiment 8a) described and drew their images of a tree and a bicycle, and the pattern of dots, in blue, was shown during one; another twelve subjects (Experiment 8b) described and drew their images of a doll and a garden, and the green spiral was shown during one (see Fig. 1B). These geometric shapes were used, as they had led to fairly extensive assimilation effects in Experiments 4 and 5.

In all the previous experiments, there had been considerable variability among judges, so in this study 18 separate judges were used to control for this variability. Their mean frequency of judged assimilation was 56% judging the green spiral, and 57% with the stimulus of blue dots.

Judgments were based both on the descriptions and the drawings. Judges probably tended to rely more on the drawings, as they were clearer and more dramatic. However, in many instances (as before), the drawings and the descriptions were quite different. One subject described her tree as "an oak tree, very old tree . . . must be at least 100 years old, and it's dark and the bark is scratchy and the leaves are bright green and—very long roots and they go out very far and deeply and ah, the tree must be 50 or 60 feet high, and there is a woodpecker in it pecking away." Yet most judges did not guess that the blue dots had been present during this image, in part because the tree that was drawn did not look old, the bark did not look scratchy, the roots were small, and the woodpecker had flown away!

Two samples of drawings are reproduced in Fig. 3. The bicycle and tree images of two subjects are shown; for one the pattern of blue dots accompanied the tree, for the other it accompanied the bicycle. In these examples the drawings, even in achromatic reproductions gave clearer evidence of assimilation than the descriptions.

Assimilation of the spiral to the garden usually resulted in a clearly circular pattern either characterizing the entire garden or repeated in individual plants. The spiral generated pronounced red afterimages, and these sometimes appeared as small red flowers. In Experiments 4 and 5, the spiral seemed to have some physiognomic effects on the doll-image. This was less apparent here, perhaps because the stimulus had an abrupt onset, or it may have been partially masked by the use of drawings. The circular form appeared in the flamenco dress which clothed one doll, who also had high heels, black hair, one arm above her head, and very vivid eyes. Another subject described an image of a Raggedy Ann doll; the curve of the spiral was reflected in the curved arms, and the repeated circles emerged as repeated stripes (see Fig. 2D). Many judges, however, were not sensitive to these nuances of assimilation and did not recognize the influence of the spiral in these images.

This study showed very clearly a point which had been gradually becoming apparent through the series of experiments: the problem of selection of judges. In this experiment 18 judges were used in the hope of controlling interjudge variability, but unexpectedly the variability followed a bimodal distribution. One mode occurred at chance, with 12 out of 24 judgments correct: 8 judges ranged from 11 to 13 correct, while one more had 10 and one had 14 correct. The other mode was at 15.5 or 65% correct, with 4 judges correct on 15, 4 more on 16. This latter group of eight judges seemed especially skilled at detecting signs of assimilation for both of the stimuli. This reinforced an observation that had been increasingly clear: the signs of assimilation were not obvious nor did they follow simple rules of color, form, or location. Complex transformations of the stimulus were involved, and a rather intuitive judge, sensitive to nuances of color and shading, unusual aspects of an image, its details or background, special qualities in the mood, would be more likely to relate these effects to the stimulus.

Several of the more skilled judges were asked to describe their basis for evaluating the images, and all of them had difficulty in specifying their criteria. One referred to the appearance of unusual or unexpected features in the description, but most of them seemed to be making an intuitive judgment on the basis of factors which they were unable fully to explain. It is interesting that comparing two images by the same subject (as in Experiments 6, 7, and 8) seemed to give less information than comparing

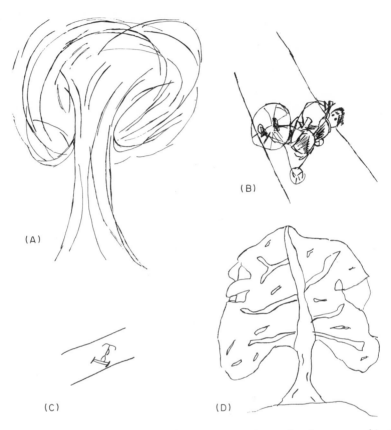

FIG. 3. *The tree and bicycle, A and B, were drawn by the same subject in Experiment 8: the stimulus (pattern of blue dots) was present during the image of the bicycle. C and D were also drawn by one subject, but the stimulus was shown during the image of the tree. Colors were only used in the bicycle (B), where the bicycle was drawn in very light red crayon, the hair was yellow, the street, the clothes, the hands, legs, and eyes were colored blue.*

Subjects' descriptions of images. (A) *Tree: I see a large sturdy oak tree—very wide base and it's very leafy like it would be in the middle of the summertime, very green, very bright, very healthy tree.* (B) *Bicycle: I see a little child's red tricycle—it's um—there's a little boy sitting on it and he is going down a city street—it's red and also white.* (C) *Bicycle: I, I . . . tried to imagine a bicycle at first, but the first picture that came into my mind at first was actually a tricycle, and—ah—it was a black tricycle, not very distinctive in any way. (q) describe it. (S) Well it was—ah—it was laying on the ground as if someone has fell off it.* (D) *Tree: The, the tree I see it's—ah—it's a weeping willow and it has, ah . . . ah, natural features of a weeping willow, it's very large and the—ah—branches extend out in all directions and the—ah—leaves, the leaves—ah—it's a very fading green color. I don't know what's going to happen to them, I . . . don't suppose they fall, maybe they do.*

TABLE 3
Summary of Assimilation Findings

Experiment	Number of judges	Judges' scores	Mean percent correct	Chance	Percent above chance	χ^2	p
1	5	.49 .49 .52 .51 .65	.54	.50	.04	28.13	< .001
2	3	.34 .34 .63	.44	.26	.18	42.83	< .001
3a	3	.41 .45 .50	.45	.34	.11	14.96	< .01
3b	3	.51 .58 .63	.57	.50	.07	29.20	< .001
4	5	.53 .54 .57 .70 .56	.58	.50	.08	47.63	< .001
5	5	.59 .56 .61 .58 .76	.62	.52	.10	51.64	< .001
6	3	.44 .44 .48	.45	.50	− .05	—	—
7	4	.50 .55 .56 .61	.56	.50	.06	4.63	n.s.
8a	18	.33 (1) .42 (2) .50 (6) .58 (6) .75 (2) .83 (1)	.56	.50	.06	Z = 3.55	< .001
8b	18	.33 (2) .42 (2) .50 (6) .58 (2) .67 (1) .75 (3) .83 (2)	.57	.50	.07	—	—

many images of the same *thing* by *different* subjects (as in all the previous experiments). It appears that images have a normative or conventional form, which begins to be clear if a large sample of subjects reports an image of the same item. The influence of the stimulus seems to emerge as the judge evaluates ways in which a particular image tends to diverge from the norm.

Summary of Studies

Thus, while there was tremendous variability in the judgments for different experiments, depending in part on who the judges were, certain clear trends were gleaned by combining the results.

Table 3 provides a summary of the data from all eight experiments. Significant assimilation effects were obtained in six of the eight, with a trend in the same direction for Experiment 7. Only Experiment 6 showed no assimilation whatever. This provides clear evidence that assimilation is a real, reliable, and replicable effect. It does not seem to be very strong,

TABLE 4
Assimilation Summary: Percent Above Chance in Different Conditions

Experiment	Informed (expecting stimuli)	Naive (uninformed regarding stimuli)	Brighter stimuli[a]	Dimmer stimuli[a]	Congruent	Incongruent
1	—	.04	.04	.01	.07	− .01
2	.27	.09	.18	—	.14	.20
3a	.11	—	.11	—	—	—
3b	.07	—	—	.07	—	—
4	.08	—	—	.08	—	—
5	.10	—	—	.10	—	—
6	—	− .05	—	− .05	—	—
7	—	.06	—	.06	—	—
8a	—	.06	—	.06	—	—
8b	—	.07	—	.07	—	—
Mean	.126	.045[b]	.11	.05	.105	.095

[a] When the experiment did not include two levels of intensity, stimuli were considered "bright" if the detection rate (d') exceeded 3.25; it was considered "dim" if the d' was between 2.0 and 2.65.

[b] Informed vs. naive is significant, Mann-Whitney U-Test, $p < .01$.

however, as the mean effect ranged from 4 to 18% above chance, and even if we concentrate on the best judges' ratings, they never exceeded 37% and usually were about 10–15% over chance. This effect is much slighter than had been anticipated from Perky's original report. From her discussion, we had anticipated finding assimilation to be almost universal. It is possible that this was obtained because Perky's subjects, trained introspectionists, gave complete reports of their phenomenal images; our subjects were selected randomly and some gave very sparse and limited comments, although others were quite elaborate in their reports. Considering the extent of the present data, however, it is most probable that the subtle and infrequent assimilation effects we have found are more characteristic than Perky's.

Moreover, assimilation showed a certain lawfulness, changing slightly according to the experimental variations. For example, Experiments 4 and 5 revealed more assimilation for stimuli with gradual onset. Table 4 shows some of the factors that tended to raise or diminish the occurrence of assimilation. Congruence had no clear effect, but more assimilation tended to occur with brighter stimuli. Subjects' expectancies had an important and significant effect: when a subject knew stimuli might be shown, he was much more likely to assimilate the stimulus. Presumably the subjects were more attentive to the stimuli, therefore processed them more completely, completely enough that their images evidenced derivatives of the partial processing, but not fully enough for detection to occur.

Discussion

During imagery the individual forms or constructs an image: he may search for it intentionally, as when he tries to count the windows in his house or to recall what his old history professor looked like; or it may emerge autonomously, as when a song, a phrase, or the image of someone's face suddenly rises to his "inner eye." In either case, sensory input currently being processed may, by chance, be in accord with the image (it is even possible that such partially processed sensory input triggers off the seemingly autonomous image). If the stimulus is concordant in form and color with the image, it may be assimilated in relatively unchanged form; if the stimulus is quite different from the intended or conventional image, it may be quite radically transformed during assimilation—or be somehow rejected. Not only were there many images where no assimilation effects were obtained, there were also some that seemed almost to deny assimilation, stating that "a parrot is usually green" (the color of the stimulus) but "I will image a yellow one," or "the tree is bare, there are no leaves, no green at all."

Bruner (1957) considered that sensory input can be processed more rapidly and accurately if it accords or conforms to the expectancies, but it may be processed more slowly, less accurately, and less completely if it differs in important respects from the expectancies. While Bruner's analysis was concerned with perceptual processes, the argument seems equally applicable in studying the processing of input during imagery.

Any source of light energy that is transmitted to the retina of an observer will activate some retinal cells; with a highly contoured figure, with gradual increments in light energy, with a greater total brightness more cells and also more and larger receptive fields may be activated. This could mediate a more complex or patterned degree of sensory input, which in some instances might trigger off a "recognition" response eventuating in a "perception." At other times the partially processed input may merge or fuse with images which are simultaneously aroused centrally. The input may be assimilated to the ongoing image, modifying, elaborating, or shaping the color, shading, details, background, sometimes even the mood or affect of the image, but rarely affecting its content.

Parallels to the processing of auditory input in a typical dichotic listening task are suggested. Treisman (1969) reported that sounds which enter through the nonattended ear in a dichotic listening task are partially processed. The subject can tell whether it is a male or a female voice, can localize it, can sometimes detect some of the voice qualities (if it is nasal, high or low, speaking slow or fast), but he is usually unable to identify the content or even to tell what language is being spoken.

In the experiments reported here, the visual stimulus, like the nonattended auditory input in dichotic listening, is processed for peripheral attributes. When the subject is attending to his image low-level analyzers process the stimulus; such processing does not require any central attention, it does not depend on meaning, and it can go on entirely outside of conscious awareness. Stimuli are always impinging on the cells of the retina, and some integration and analysis transpires as this sensory input mounts successive levels in the nervous system. The incompletely coded products of the stimulation seem able to modify conscious cognitive experiences. Presumably all perceptions, hallucinations, images, even ideas, may be similarly affected by partially processed stimuli, both exogenous and endogenous in origin.

The emergence of an image does not depend entirely on the revivification of past traces, nor is it a replay of previous experiences as some theorists have believed (see Penfield & Roberts, 1959). Rather, it is an active process in which the observer constructs an image out of past experiences and memories, but uses concurrent sensory input to "flesh it out." According to Neisser (1967; 1970; see also Chapter 10, this volume), each time an individual experiences a percept, a memory, or an image, he constructs it anew. Data from these experiments tend to confirm this. Any currently available sensory input may be recruited toward the formation of the image. In the experiments cited here a source of light of a specific shape and color has been transmitted to the eyes of an imaging subject, and it is clear that some of the time that stimulus—although undetected—has a demonstrable effect on the subject's phenomenological description of his conscious image. The effects of this unique light source have been traced and seem to emerge, partly transformed, in his experienced image. Other unknown stimuli may also have affected the image, past experiences common to the culture or unique to the individual's life and other stored information. The data reported here do not yield a comprehensive or exhaustive delineation of the formation of an image, they are merely a simple model of how images may incorporate partially processed stimuli, and demonstrate how this method may be used to study some of the processing and transformations that typically occur.

References

Bartlett, F. C. *Remembering.* London: Cambridge Univ. Press, 1932.

Bruner, J. S. On perceptual readiness. *Psychological Review,* 1957, **64,** 123–152.

Fisher, C. Dreams and perception. *Journal of American Psychoanalytic Association,* 1954, **2,** 389–445.

Horowitz, M. The imagery of visual hallucinations. *Journal of Nervous and Mental Disease,* 1964, **138,** 513–523.

Klein, G. S., Spence, D. P., Holt, R. R., & Gourevitch, S. Cognition without awareness: Subliminal influences upon conscious thought. *Journal of Abnormal and Social Psychology,* 1958, **57,** 255–266.

Klüver, H. *Mescal and mechanisms of hallucinations.* Chicago, Illinois: Uni. of Chicago Press, 1969.

Külpe, O. Ueber die Objectivirung und Subjectivirung von Sinneseindrücken. *Philosophische Studien,* 1902, **19,** 508–556.

Neisser, U. *Cognitive psychology.* New York: Appleton, 1967.

Neisser, U. Visual imagery as process and as experience. In J. S. Antrobus (Ed.), *Cognition and affect.* Boston: Little, Brown, 1970. Pp. 159–178.

Penfield, W., & Roberts, L. *Speech and brain-mechanisms.* Princeton, New Jersey: Princeton Univ. Press, 1959.

Perky, C. W. An experimental study of imagination. *American Journal of Psychology,* 1910, **21,** 422–452.

Piaget, J. *Play, dreams and imitation in childhood.* (Translated by C. Gattegno and F. M. Hodgson.) New York: Norton, 1962.

Pötzl, O. The relationship between experimentally induced dream images and indirect vision. (Translated by J. Wolff, D. Rapaport, & S. Annin from *Zeitschrift fur die Gesamte Neurologie und Psychiatrie,* orig. publ. 1917, **37,** 278–349.) *Psychological Issues,* 1960, **2** (7, Whole No. 3). Pp. 41–120.

Saravay, S., & Pardes, H. Auditory elementary hallucinations in alcohol withdrawal psychosis. *Archives of General Psychiatry,* 1967, **16,** 652–658.

Segal, S. J. The Perky effect: Changes in reality judgments with changing methods of inquiry. *Psychonomic Science,* 1968, **12,** 393–394. (a)

Segal, S. J. Patterns of response to thirst in an imaging task (Perky technique) as a function of cognitive style. *Journal of Personality,* 1968, **36,** 574–588. (b)

Segal, S. J. Processing of sensory input relative to a constructed image. Paper presented at the Meeting of the Psychonomic Society, San Antonio, 1970.

Segal, S. J., & Fusella, V. Effects of imaging on signal-to-noise ratio with varying signal conditions. *British Journal of Psychology,* 1969, **60,** 459–464.

Segal, S. J., & Gordon, P. The Perky effect revisited: Blocking of visual signals by imagery. *Perceptual and Motor Skills,* 1969, **28,** 791–797.

Segal, S. J., & Nathan, S. The Perky effect: Incorporation of an external stimulus into an imagery experience under placebo and control conditions. *Perceptual and Motor Skills,* 1964, **18,** 385–395.

Shevrin, H., & Luborsky, L. The measurement of preconscious perception in dreams and images: An investigation of the Pötzl phenomenon. *Journal of Abnormal and Social Psychology,* 1958, **56,** 285–294.

Silverman, A. J., Cohen, S. I., Bressler, B., & Shmavonian, B. M. Hallucinations in sensory deprivation. In L. J. West, (Ed.) *Hallucinations,* New York: Grune & Stratton, 1962. Pp. 125–134.

Treisman, A. M. Strategies and models of selective attention. *Psychological Review,* 1969, **76,** 282–299.

The Nature of Imagery

10 ULRIC NEISSER

CHANGING CONCEPTIONS
OF IMAGERY

If memory and perception are the two key branches of cognitive psychology, the study of imagery stands precisely at their intersection. Our images must be based on what we remember, and in another sense what we remember is often based on images; nevertheless imaging is somehow like perceiving so that we speak of "seeing with the mind's eye." Historically this has meant that conceptions of imagery have been derivative from conceptions of memory and perception. The commonly accepted metaphor that images are "mental pictures" which are "summoned up" or "come to mind" simply reflects the classical theories of perception and memory in which perceiving is like looking at pictures, and remembering is like looking at them a second time.

Some years ago I argued that the processes of imagery were closely related to those of perception itself (Neisser, 1967), and that both were instances of active construction rather than passive registration and recall. Since that time there have been several important developments. One of these is the increasing influence of, and evidence for, the new approach to perception based on the work of J. J. Gibson (1966). Another is a startling turn of events in the study of memory, where long-held axioms and assumptions are being abandoned with almost unseemly haste in favor of a cognitive position. By taking these new developments into account, it may be possible to go beyond the mere assertion that remembering and imaging are constructive processes and begin to study the nature of the construction in more detail.

In what follows, I will try to show how Gibson's account of visual perception differs from the classical one, and I will explore the implications of this account—or my version of it—for imagery conceived of as a process related to perceiving. I will also make some general remarks about the differences between cognitive and content-oriented conceptions of the mind. It will be argued that mental processes cannot be studied primarily by introspective methods, and evidence will be presented that the introspective study of imagery is prey to the very difficulties which a cognitive psychologist might expect. New developments in the study of memory will be reviewed, partly as examples of contemporary cognitive psychology and partly because the study of images has played such a central role in them. Then I will attempt to state a more specific definition of imagery as a quasiperceptual process, and try to show why such a definition might be useful. Finally, I will show how these notions lead to particular experimental predictions and present data which support them.

The Senses Considered as Perceptual Systems

My heading is the title of a book by J. J. Gibson (1966), which sharply challenges the assumptions on which most perceptual psychology has been based for more than a century. According to those assumptions, vision begins with a two-dimensional mosaic of sensations somehow produced in the brain as a result of nerve impulses from the eyes. In this display of sensations there are no objects, no distances, no permanence, and no meaning. All such properties of the perceived world were thought to be added by higher processes in the brain; processes which Helmholtz named "unconscious inference." The act of perceiving the real three-dimensional world of objects was seen as very similar to the act of perceiving a painted *picture* of the world. Both acts required the brain to go beyond the information in the stimulus in much the same way: the visual picture was simply supplemented with stored associations. Although occasional lip service was paid to such "cues" as motion perspective or relative motion, which make it impossible for painted pictures to deceive any viewer for long, they occupied a very minor place in perceptual theory. The difference between seeing objects and seeing pictures appeared so insignificant that pictures and drawings were used as stimuli in most perceptual experiments. Even when the Gestalt psychologists rebelled against Helmholtz, rejecting unconscious inference in favor of spontaneous figural organization in the brain, they still used line drawings to make most of their arguments. It is little wonder, then, that images have so often been called "mental pictures." What else could they be?

Gibson, on the other hand, begins with the notion that the primary adaptive function of vision is to provide information about the layout of the *environment*. Most typically—i.e., throughout the evolutionary history of the visual system—the environment consists of a textured ground on which there are objects of various sorts, stationary or in motion. Light rays, reflected off the ground and the objects, may be sampled at various places by an observing eye. More often than not, that eye is itself moving so that it obtains a continuously changing input. What information about the layout exists in the light available to this kind of pickup? When the question is asked in this way it becomes apparent that the static "cues" used by painters and emphasized in psychology textbooks (linear perspective, relative size, etc.) are among the least important aspects of stimulation. Far more important are facts like the "occlusion" of one object by another as the eye shifts position and the corresponding deletion of the former object's microtexture (Gibson, Kaplan, Reynolds, and Wheeler, 1969), or the radial expansion of every contour in the field away from the point toward which the eye is moving (Gibson, 1955). Even the more classical sources of information, such as binocular disparity, appear in a new light when considered directly as sources of optical information (Lee, 1971).

For Gibson, these kinds of optical information do not give rise to "sensations"; generations of introspection did not discover them. They are perceived *directly*. He rejects all mediational theories of perception and distinguishes only three realms of discourse: the real environment (usually made up of objects on a terrestrial ground), the optic array of light which provides rich information about that environment to any eye that knows how to look, and the perceiver's experience (almost always veridical) of that environment, i.e., his perception. There are no sensations, or, if they occur, they are irrelevant to the act of perception. There is no internal flat mosaic which must be supplemented by unconscious inference or by Gestalted brain processes. Nothing remotely like a two-dimensional display ever exists in either the stimulating light or the mind of the observer. Of course, an exception occurs if the observer is actually looking at a painting or a photograph; Gibson (1966, 1971) has dealt extensively with this case, but it is not relevant here. What *is* relevant is the notion that one normally perceives layouts, not pictures. If this is true, we should stop talking about images as mental pictures and try to understand what a mental layout might be.

Intent on refuting the sensation-mediated theory of perception, Gibson goes so far as to reject *all* accounts of the perceptual process, whether neurological or psychological. For him perception is direct; the only thing he will say about the brain is that it "resonates" to the information in the optic array. He is particularly adamant in denying that perception might be "constructive," because this suggests the old notion that sensations are supplemented by some associative process. For me, this is like throwing the baby out with the bath water. Between the existence of information in an optic array and the perception of the layout which it specifies there is a long step. Only a brain—and not all brains—can take that step, which must require very elaborate processes indeed. These processes result in a representation of the environment, available to consciousness, which has been constructed on the basis of the specifying information. The perceiver can construct, or reconstruct, such representations even in the absence of stimulus information; when he does so, we say that he is imaging. I take Gibson's refusal to discuss mental processes and representations as a mistaken overreaction to the simplistic accounts of perception that were accepted for so long. But in all fairness, I must admit to a similar reaction, or overreaction, of my own. My particular impatience is with the classical doctrine of mental content and mental activity which has dominated our conceptions of memory for at least as long as the Helmholtzian assumptions have ruled perception. This set of assumptions now requires examination.

Storehouse vs. Process

Most of the history of psychology has been dominated by what may be called the "storehouse" conception of mental life. The mind has long been thought to be a kind of vessel or a place in which various entities such as ideas, feelings, sensations, and images were to be found. These entities had a discrete existence; they could disappear and reappear again and be recognized (in 1967 I called this the "Reappearance Hypothesis"). The task of psychology was to identify, define, or explain them. This was the working assumption of the introspective psychologists who founded experimental psychology around the 1870's and dominated it until the 1920's. They not only believed that the mind was rather like a storehouse, but that its contents could be discovered, classified, and analyzed by systematic introspection. In fact, they could not think of any other way to psychologize at all: for them, it was introspection or nothing. How could a good observer be wrong about the contents of his own mind? How indeed, unless the mind is not a storehouse to begin with?

The founders of psychology were not the only ones who held the storehouse conception. Indeed, it has been so pervasive that psychologists who differ on every other point have adopted it without question. Freud, for example, took it for granted. Although he made the radical suggestion that some of the entities in the storehouse were "unconscious" (in the cellar, more or less) and could not be examined, his cognitive theory was comfortably based on "associations" between continuously existing and potentially conscious "ideas." The believers in psychical phenomena and their successors who try to study extrasensory perception are another example: their only heresy was the belief that the contents of one person's storehouse could occasionally wander over into another's. Even the behaviorists did not avoid the trap; they still believed that the mind was full of mental objects, but insisted that no one discuss these objects during working hours.

The last few years have seen the beginning of a fundamental change in this attitude, a "paradigm shift" in Kuhn's (1962) terminology. Cognitive psychologists are simply no longer very interested in mental contents. The mind does not seem much like a place anymore. Instead we think of it as an organ, analogous to a bodily organ, with a specific function. That function is the processing of information. A staggering wealth of information reaches the sense organs of the body, but only certain aspects of it are truly informative about crucial aspects of the environment. Hence, the input must be analyzed, abstracted, coded, and reworked if the organism is to survive; in many cases it must also be stored for later retrieval and use. The new definition of "mind," then, is the totality of ways that people handle information. Whatever their disagreements, contemporary cognitive psychologists are united in taking these complex processes as psychology's proper study.

A generation ago, such a paradigm would have been unacceptable simply because terms like "abstraction" or "retrieval" seemed to imply the existence of an inner man, a "homunculus," who did the abstracting and retrieving. Today this objection no longer has much weight because we know that analogous functions can be carried out by properly programmed computers in an entirely nonhomunculoid way. If computers can process information, there can be no lurking philosophical danger in attributing the same capacity to the human mind. To be sure, it is at this point that I part company with some of my colleagues who use computer programs not only as a useful analogy but as an explicit model for mental activity. I think it is a mistake to define the mind as a kind of computer and try to flowchart its program (cf. Hunt, 1971); biological organization is different. To me, metaphors of growth and construction are more appropriate for mental processes than the step-by-step sequences of instructions so characteristic of computer modeling. But there is no disagreement on the fundamental assumption that mental processes are far more subtle than was once envisaged. There are not simply "sensations," supplemented by "association" to form "perceptions" which are stored and recovered. Instead there is a vast array of stages, activities, and processes at every level.

The Problems
of Introspection

This change in our conception of the mind, from a storehouse to an organ, requires corresponding changes in our conception of what introspection can accomplish, particularly where images are concerned. Images are no longer mental contents awaiting description. Instead, imaging is one kind of mental activity worthy of separate study because it seems to have something significant in common with the activities of perceiving. It must be immensely complex involving rapid changes and myriad interrelations in many parts of the brain. What an introspector selects out of such a process for introspection and verbal report must be more than a little arbitrary, even if we suppose that all of it is in some sense available to be described. Asking subjects for introspections is then a little like asking them to describe the shifting cloud formations of a stormy sky. Eloquent and interesting as such reports may be, they leave much to be desired in scientific terms. Hamlet's conversation with Polonius shows how readily they are influenced by factors which today would be called demand characteristics or experimenter bias:

> *Hamlet:* Do you see yonder cloud that's almost in shape of a camel?
> *Polonius:* By the mass, and 'tis like a camel, indeed.
> *Hamlet:* Methinks it is like a weasel.
> *Polonius:* It is backed like a weasel.
> *Hamlet:* Or like a whale?
> *Polonius:* Very like a whale.
>
> *Hamlet, Act III, Scene 2*

These difficulties do not mean that clouds do not exist, but only that an observer's metaphoric description of them would be a poor basis on which to build a scientific meteorology.

It is easy to show that problems of just this sort have arisen in the attempt to study images as mental contents. I will illustrate this point with two examples, one historical and one modern. The historical example concerns the role of images in the process of thinking itself. America's most famous introspective psychologist, E. B. Titchener, believed that images played a necessary and essential role in thought; indeed, thought simply *was* a train of images (not just visual ones of course, but auditory, kinesthetic, and other images as well). Unfortunately, some of his contemporaries came to the opposite conclusion. In several influential experiments, the psychologists of the "Wurzburg School" asked their subjects to introspect on the contents of their minds while in the act of trying to answer difficult questions. These subjects (mostly psychologists themselves) were often as vigorous in denying the presence of images as Tichener in affirming it. This dispute—which could not possibly be resolved within the limitations of the introspective method—probably did much to hasten the demise of structuralist psychology.

How can we account for the discrepant reports of these two groups of researchers? In part, it may be necessary to appeal to the irreducible notion of "individual differences." We know that subjects differ widely in the "vividness" of the images which they find in introspection; that is, in the degree to which their images are subjectively like genuine perceptions. These differences, first reported by Galton (1880), were quantified by Betts in terms of a 7-point scale (Sheehan, 1967a). Titchener was surely a vivid imager; perhaps his opponents simply were not. I suspect, however, that another factor was also at work. Titchener and his students were looking for images and expected to find them; the Wurzburgers were not. This must have set up very powerful demand characteristics (Orne, 1959, 1962), i.e., tendencies for the subjects to perform and report as they believed would be appropriate. There is reason to suppose that such effects would be most powerful where the overtly required performance is itself ill-defined, as in many of Rosenthal's (1966) studies. Given the actual complexity of mental processes, the request to describe them as if they were discrete objects is an ill-defined demand *par excellence* and would seem to offer rich opportunities for effects of this kind.

As a modern example of the same difficulties, consider an experiment conducted by Sheehan and myself some years ago (Sheehan & Neisser, 1969). We were trying to follow up some of Sheehan's earlier studies (1966, 1967b), which seemed to show that "vivid" imagery was correlated with accurate recall. As in those studies, we measured vividness with the modified Betts Questionnaire (Sheehan, 1967a), which asks subjects to "summon up" images of various experiences and rate them on a 7-point scale.

As stimulus materials we used designs composed of circles, triangles, squares, and diamonds in any of four colors. The individual forms actually appeared on the faces of 1-inch wooden blocks, so that a design could be composed just by placing, say, three rows and three columns of blocks on the table. Color photographs of such arrays were projected for the subject's inspection. To insure close attention to the design he was required to reproduce it with similar blocks. When he had done so we turned off the slide, broke up his design, gave him something else to do for a minute or so (a different kind of block test), and then asked him to reconstruct the design with the blocks again, this time from memory. We also asked him to rate the vividness of the image he had at the time that he was reconstructing the block design, using Betts' 7-point scale. After going through this procedure with four different block designs (i.e., four different trials), the subject was asked a lot of introspective questions: had the images been complete in every detail, had they been patterned, was there much verbal labeling, etc? After this inquiry he was tested with four more block designs, asked some more questions, unexpectedly tested on the interpolated material, and sent home. The 32 subjects were selected from a pool of about a hundred, all of whom had taken the Betts test to determine how vivid their images were in ordinary life. Sheehan and I asked an associate to select the 16 best and the 16 poorest scorers on that test so that we wouldn't know which subjects were supposed to be the good imagers. This seemed like a useful precaution against experimenter bias which had not been taken in previous work. Moreover, Sheehan ran half the subjects and I ran the others, each of us being allotted eight good imagers and eight poor ones. To keep the procedure consistent, we read the instructions aloud and occasionally observed each other through a one-way screen.

The main variable did not have any effect on recall. The 16 subjects selected for high imagery did no better than those selected for low imagery. Moreover, the subjects who reported good imagery while reproducing the designs were not any better than those who did not (except in an incidental learning task which is outside the scope of this chapter; that finding is explored further by Sheehan in Chapter 7). What *did* produce results, however, were the variables of experimenter and expectancy, as they affected subjective vividness. First, Sheehan's subjects consistently reported better imagery than mine. Second, and even more interesting, we found significant improvements in the rated vividness of images after the introspective inquiry, probably because subjects then had a better idea of what we wanted. These findings confirm in a modern context what was perhaps already obvious: that introspective reports of imagery can be affected by experimenter effects and perceived demand characteristics. This is not because such biasing factors are all-powerful (they had no effect on *accuracy* of reconstruction in our experiment) but because introspection is particularly vulnerable to them.

Learning and Remembering as
Cognitive Processes

As everyone knows, psychologists eventually grew weary of unresolvable disputes over introspective contents. Lacking the concept of process as it exists today, they turned instead to Behaviorism which tried to dispense with mental events altogether. In my opinion, this was an even more dubious enterprise. Difficult as it might be to base meterology on Polonius' metaphoric descriptions of clouds, it would be harder still to begin by denying that clouds exist. And indeed, behaviorism did not work. The study of memory and of thinking, for example, became sterile and uninteresting when it was assumed that only stimulus variables (the nature of the material, the number of trials, the rate of presentation, etc.) were important in determining behavior. The subject's own contributions to the outcome were given short shrift. If his mental processes were considered at all, it was in a pitifully limited way: he was given credit for forming associations, and nothing more.

This state of affairs has changed radically in the last few years. The study of memory has become exciting again, since we have abandoned our fixation on stimulus conditions and begun to ask about what is going on in the subject's mind, i.e., on how the information we present is being processed. Words like "rehearsal," "strategy," "mnemonic device," "encoding," and, of course, "imagery" now dominate the pages of journals where "interpolated material" and "distribution of practice" flourished before. A host of ingenious experiments testify that what matters is not so much what the experimenter does, but what the subject does. While their results are far from providing an adequate account of the richness of mental life, they do suggest that we have begun to look in the right place at last. Some of these studies are explicitly concerned with mental imagery, and I will consider them shortly. First, however, it may be useful to cite some which do not have this focus to show how wide the implications of the new paradigm are. I will describe two, each of which challenges a cherished assumption of the storehouse, noncognitive approach to memory.

The first such assumption is that the more often a stimulus is presented, the better it will be recalled. Consider an experiment in which subjects have to learn a 36-word list by the method of free recall and repeated trials, after first being "pretrained" with eight trials on a preliminary list. For the experimental group, the preliminary list simply consists of half the words which will subsequently appear in the full list; for the control group, it consists of 18 irrelevant words. Thus, the experimental group has eight extra trials with half of the material in the main list. Can anyone doubt that they will learn the main list more rapidly than the controls? In fact, Tulving (1966) performed this experiment and found that the main list is *harder* for the experimental group than for the control group. This paradoxical result has since been replicated in several other laboratories. What can it mean? Tulving's interpretation, which has not been challenged, is that subjects do not absorb words passively but develop an *organization* appropriate to the entire list. The organization constructed to accommodate 18 words is not necessarily an efficient part of the organization best suited for 36 words, even if the 18 are a subset of the 36. Remembering is not the reappearance of individual items with more or less strength, but the partial reconstruction of the mental activity which the original items helped to instigate.

The second recently challenged assumption concerns the method of recognition in which subjects are asked to say whether they have seen or heard a particular stimulus before. It has been supposed that they do this by comparing the presented stimulus with reappearing "traces" of stimuli seen previously. However, Bransford and Franks (1971) have invented a procedure which leads subjects to say that they recognize (with high confidence ratings) sentences that have never been presented to them at all. These sentences represent composite ideas; what the subjects *have* heard are simpler sentences which represent the elements of the composite. Thus a subject who has heard "the ants ate the sweet jelly which was on the table," "The ants were in the kitchen," "The ants in the kitchen ate the jelly," and three other related sentences will be extremely confident that he has heard "The ants in the kitchen ate the sweet jelly which was on the table." In fact, he will be more confident of the composite than of having heard some of the simpler sentences which were actually presented to him! What he really recognizes, of course, is not a stimulus at all but a composite idea (perhaps including an image) which he formed while hearing the original material. Perhaps this result is not surprising to common sense, but in terms of a simple stimulus-response psychology it would be unintelligible.

The Mnemonic
Uses of Imagery

Although many kinds of mnemonic processes and strategies have been studied in recent experiments, none is more striking than the widespread use of mental images. Now that we realize how much the subject's own mental activities contribute to the quality of his performance, we cannot help noticing that visual representation is among the most common and the most powerful of the strategies actually used. This conclusion is supported by at least three lines of evidence: the advantage of concrete over abstract words, the effect of explicit imagery instructions, and the remarkable success of visual mnemonic devices.

In a series of experiments, Paivio (1969; see also Chapter 11, this volume) has shown that concrete words—i.e., nouns which represent easily visualizable things—are easier to learn than abstract words, and that this difference is not simply a byproduct of word frequency or associative potency. His findings strongly suggest that subjects regularly use images in the process of memorization. Their introspective remarks confirm this, but it is important to realize that the basic argument is not introspective; the inference is drawn from differential performance.

Bower's (1970, 1971) methods have been more direct; he tells subjects to form linking images in paired-associate experiments and compares their performance with that of subjects otherwise instructed. The results are clear: imaging is better than any other method. It is spectacularly better than simple repetition, and somewhat better than mnemonics based on sentences or stories. Moreover, the *type* of imaging is important. No facilitation results if the subject imagines the stimulus and response words separately: he must construct a single image which somehow shows them in interaction. Then the presentation of the stimulus word in the recall test can cue him to recreate the combined image, from which the response word will follow. Integrative imaging facilitates memory while separate imagery does not. This finding was replicated in our own study to be described below.

Perhaps the most curious aspect of the recent work in mnemonics is that the strategies being studied are not at all new. Yates (1966) has shown that they have been a part of the intellectual tradition of the west since classical times. In particular, the single most effective mnemonic technique—the method of "loci," or places—was known to the Greeks and Romans. In this method, one establishes a cognitive map of a series of particular locations or places, which one can mentally "visit" in a particular order. Given any arbitrary list of items to memorize, it is only necessary to imagine each deposited on a particular location; near-perfect recall will follow if one then "revisits" the places in the usual order. The effectiveness of this technique has been verified by Ross and Lawrence (1968) and by Crovitz and his collaborators (Briggs, Hawkins, & Crovitz, 1970; Crovitz, 1969). Anyone who wants to take the trouble can easily verify it further in his own experience.

The proliferation of evidence that something called "imagery" is an effective mnemonic device provides both an opportunity and a danger. The opportunity is the existence of a new array of techniques for studying the nature of imagery itself. The danger, which I shall consider first, is the temptation to adopt an oversimplified notion of imagery. This temptation is very real. Paivio, for example, thinks of images and verbal processes as "alternative coding systems [1969, p. 243]" with the strong implication that images have one definite set of properties whenever they occur. This may easily result in a simplistic account of the cognitive possibilities. Bower (1970) seems to take a similar view, which he links to the recent work of Sperry and his collaborators on the different functions of the right and left cerebral hemispheres (Gazzaniga, 1967; Gazzaniga & Sperry, 1967). But probably the most striking example of the theoretical approach is the symposium on "Imagery in children's learning" published recently by *Psychological Review* (Paivio, 1970; Reese, 1970a,b; Palermo, 1970; Rohwer, 1970). In 39 tightly compressed pages there is only the slightest hint of such possibilities as that there may be more than one kind of imagery, or that children's imaging may be qualitatively different from adults', or that different aspects of a complex imaging process may be brought to bear on different tasks and by different kinds of subjects, or that nouns, pictures, real objects, and image-instructions may not all give rise to the same sort of internal events.

We have good reason to believe that the situation is more complicated than this. This processes—and aspects of processes—we call "imagery" vary enormously even within one person, and certainly from one person to the next. It used to be fashionable to distinguish among "memory imagery," "eidetic imagery," "hypnagogic imagery," and other varieties on the basis of introspective reports. While I do not know what these distinctions really mean, or if they can be consistently applied, there can be little doubt that a great range of different phenomena falls under this rubric even in the mental life of a single individual.

If we consider the differences between individuals, it becomes even more obvious that we would be wrong to consider "imagery" a unitary phenomenon (for another account of this position see Chapter 1, of this volume). Even in the restricted range of persons who have been called "eidetikers," the differences are almost more striking than the similarities. The 12 children studied by Haber & Haber (1964) at Yale maintained images over only a few seconds or minutes, but had high accuracy scores compared with controls during this period; after that their memory was ordinary. The 14 children classified as eidetic by Leask, Haber, & Haber (1969) a few years later did not have higher accuracy than controls even while their images persisted. Luria's remarkable subject *S,* however, (Luria, 1968) could recover any desired image after 15 *years* or more, making virtually no errors at all. A great deal of his remembering was done in terms of special mnemonic images which he constructed for the purpose of remembering otherwise meaningful material. Also, *S*'s imagery was vividly synesthetic, involving a rich blend of visual, tactual, gustatory, auditory, and other experiences even if the event to be remembered had been purely visual or purely auditory. Finally, Stromeyer's (1970; see also Stromeyer & Psotka, 1970) equally remarkable eidetiker "Elizabeth" can summon up a sufficiently clear image of a 10,000-dot random stereogram, first seen some days before, fuse it with a second, directly presented stereogram and perceive depth. She is also said to be able to summon up an image of a page printed in a foreign language and copy it out as fast as she can write. On the other hand, she does not seem to construct artificial images for mnemonic purposes (perhaps she does not need to!) and gives no reports of synesthesia.

Imagery and Perception

If differences such as these appear among persons who are all classified as "eidetic," we must expect an even greater variety when every kind of imagery is considered. What definition can possibly cover such a wide range? I have already hinted at the answer: imaging has something to do with perceiving, considered as a process, but it need not be reflected in any introspective report of picturelike mental contents. A subject is imaging whenever he employs some of the same cognitive processes that he would use in perceiving, but when the stimulus input that would normally give rise to such perception is absent. In some cases, these processes may include forming representations of an entire environment, while in other cases they may be more fragmentary. Since these activities are complex and multilayered, the subject's introspections may take many different forms and will be easily influenced by extraneous factors. Imaging is a constructive process in the sense that while it depends on information stored earlier it does not simply revive that information. Instead, the subject carries out a new activity, perhaps forming a new representation, more or less consistent with what he did before.

A definition of imagery as related to perception has several advantages. First, of course, it seems to cover the range of phenomena that have generally fallen under this rubric. Second, while not based on introspection, it is at least consistent with most introspective reports. It gives us a way of interpreting what people mean when they say they have an image: that a process somewhat like perceiving is now going on in their minds, and that *one aspect* of that process can be described in such-and-such a way. Of course, it also allows us to insist that other people may be imaging even when they themselves deny it; this may lead to confusion, but it cannot be helped. Such subjects may not attend to, or not ascribe much importance to those aspects of the ongoing mental process which resemble perceiving. The question is not whether a person says he has images, but whether he is carrying out quasiperceptual activities. By the same token, the usefulness of imaging (e.g., as a mnemonic) should not depend on how "vivid" the subject claims his images are, but on how well they represent the situation to be remembered.

A third advantage of the perceptual definition of imagery is that it can be given an operational interpretation. One way to do this is suggested by Brooks' (1967, 1968) demonstrations that there are modality-specific interferences in mental activity. Brooks showed that visual imagery suffers when it is put in direct competition with visual perception, while auditory/verbal imagery suffers from competition with listening and speaking. In one of his experiments (Brooks, 1968) the subjects were shown a large block letter and asked to remember what it looked like. After it was removed from view they were asked to describe the sequence of corners that one could encounter in moving around the figure clockwise: to respond "yes" for each corner or indentation that was either on the top or the bottom of the letter and "no" for each one that was not. This task, which seems to require the construction and use of a visual representation, proved to be easy if the subject could respond "yes" and "no" orally, but much harder if he had to point (in a visually guided way) to the words "yes" and "no" on a printed sheet. In another condition, the subject had to respond "yes" for each noun and "no" for each word not a noun in a previously memorized sentence. Most subjects use some form of verbal/auditory representation for this task. As a result, the pattern of difficulty obtained was just the opposite of that in the other condition: spoken response was appreciably more difficult than pointing. This interaction between the response mode and the mental operation has now been demonstrated in many different ways. In another experiment, Brooks (1967) asked subjects to remember sentences which referred to a spatial layout, and found much poorer performance when the sentences had to be read than when they were presented aurally. More recently, Atwood (1971) has shown that similar modality conflicts can interfere with the use of visual imagery as a mnemonic device. Moreover, Segal and Fusella (1970) have demonstrated selective increases in the detectability of stimuli in different modalities as a function of simultaneous imaging in those modalities. All of these findings illustrate the close relation between imaging and perceiving, and thus provide credibility for a definition of imagery as a quasiperceptual process.[1]

An Experimental Demonstration of Nonpictorial Imagery

If imagery is akin to perception and perception is more basically concerned with picking up information about spatial layout rather than with forming pictures, then subjects should be able to imagine layouts which could not be pictured: for example, layouts in which one object is concealed behind or within another. Such "nonpictorial" imagery should be equivalent in every functional way to images generated by "mental picture" instructions. In particular, it should be effective as a mnemonic, provided that the imagined objects were in some real spatial relation to one another and not kept separate as in Bower's (1971) experiment. Subjects who have been accustomed to thinking of images as mental pictures may well report that nonpictorial imaging is difficult, or that the resulting images are not "vivid," but such reports should not be correlated with any objective measure of performance. These predictions have been tested in a recent experiment conducted at Cornell by Neisser and Kerr (1972).

We asked our subjects to imagine a variety of spatial situations, each of which involved a pair of critical items. Some of these situations could easily have been pictured (a cradle dangling from the beak of a pelican, a revolver mounted on an airplane propellor, a daffodil protruding from Napoleon's outside pocket); these were called "pictorial" images. Others, equally picturable, were designed to keep the mental representations of the objects separate and thus reduce the mnemonic effectiveness of the image (you look out one window and see a cradle, and out another window you see a pelican; on your left is a revolver and on your right a propellor; in one room is a daffodil and in another room Napoleon); these we termed "separate" images. The crucial condition utilized "concealed" images designed so that the two objects could not have been represented together in any ordinary two-dimensional picture. In this condition the subject might be asked to imagine a cradle inside the closed beak of a pelican, or a revolver tied to a rapidly rotating propellor, or a daffodil concealed in

---

[1] Since this chapter was written, Shepard and Metzler (1971) have provided a new and particularly elegant demonstration of the same point. Using a reaction-time method, they showed that objects can be rotated in a three-dimensional imaginary space at a fixed rate of speed.

Napoleon's inside pocket. Each subject was asked to form six images of each type (plus a few others for practice). Instances of the different types were presented in a randomized order and the particular critical items used for each type were systematically varied across subjects.

Although our experiment was really a study of the mnemonic effectiveness of the various types of images, the 24 subjects did not think of it as a memory experiment. They were simply asked to form a number of images, taking as long as they wished for each one, and to rate the "vividness" of each one on the 7-point Betts scale. When they had finished, we went through the list again and asked them to describe the image they had formed "of the pelican," or "of the propellor," or "of Napoleon." In each instance, we cued them with one of the critical items from the sentence and scored them correct if their description included the other. We also made detailed notes of their description for subsequent analysis.

There were three specific hypotheses to be tested in the data. If we are right about the nature of images, the "concealed" and "pictorial" conditions should be equally susceptible to mental representation and thus lead to equally good recall. If Bower is right about the importance of integrative as opposed to separate images, our "separate" condition should produce substantially poorer recall than either of the others. Finally, if ratings of subjective "vividness" are based more on what subjects expect images to be than on well-defined aspects of their mental processes, the "pictorial" condition should yield better ratings than the "concealed" even though it does not produce better memory.

Analysis of the results indicates that these expectations were confirmed. The mean number correct for the "pictorial" condition was 5.21 (of 6) which is not significantly different from the 4.83 obtained in the "concealed" condition. Both are very significantly ($p < .01$) better than the 3.96 obtained with "separate" images. In terms of rated vividness, however, the "concealed" and "separate" condition were substantially alike (3.46 and 3.30 on the 7-point scale) while the "pictorial" images were significantly better (2.90).

We also made an attempt to analyze the protocols obtained when subjects were explicitly asked how they had coped with the "concealed" condition. Of the 144 (6 sentences by 24 subjects) instances, there were 19 in which the subject simply disregarded the instructions and made the object visible anyway, 32 in which he used some metaphor like "x-ray vision" to indicate that he imagined himself "seeing through" the concealing surface, 46 in which he reported imagining some movement or change of position which brought the object in view, and 27 in which he "just knew" that the object was there. (The remaining 20 were not analyzable.) It would be unwise to take these categories too seriously, based as they are on the kind of introspection which has proven so un-reliable in the past. Nevertheless, it may be of some interest to note that accuracy of recall did not vary significantly among these categories. This further supports the view that the mnemonic effectiveness of an image depends only on the spatial layout which it represents, not on the pictorial quality of that layout.[2]

Conclusion

The results of our experiment are hardly revolutionary. While we believe it demonstrates something important about the nature of images, its main purpose was not to prove a point but to illustrate a pair of basic ideas. First, imaging is a constructive activity related to perceiving. Second, perception itself is not the examination of a mental picture, but the pickup of information about the layout of the environment. At the very least, these propositions suggest a change from one familiar metaphor to another. Instead of referring to images as mental pictures, we would do better to fall back on the traditional description of mental life as an "inner world." Such a usage may at least remind us that the inner world of imagery is constructed in much the same way as the real world is perceived, and may keep us from underestimating its dimensionality and complexity.

References

Atwood, G. An experimental study of visual imagination and memory. *Cognitive Psychology,* 1971, **2,** 290–299.

Bower, G. H. Analysis of a mnemonic device. *American Scientist,* 1970, **58,** 496–510.

Bower, G. H. Mental imagery and associative learning. In L. Gregg (Ed.) *Cognition in Learning and Memory.* New York: Wiley, 1971, in press.

Bransford, J. D., & Franks, J. J. The abstraction of linguistic ideas. *Cognitive Psychology,* 1971, **2,** 331–350.

Briggs, G. G., Hawkins, S., & Crovitz, H. F. Bizarre images in artificial memory. *Psychonomic Science,* 1970, **19,** 353–354.

Brooks, L. R. The suppression of visualization by reading. *Quarterly Journal of Experimental Psychology,* 1967, **19,** 289–299.

[2] Since this chapter was written, a full replication of this experiment has been conducted, using a more standardized format for the sentences which described the scene to be imagined. The principal results (equivalent accuracy of recall but unequal ratings of "vividness" for pictorial and concealed conditions) were replicated completely. This second experiment is also described in Neisser and Kerr (1972).

Brooks, L. R. Spatial and verbal components of the act of recall. *Canadian Journal of Psychology*, 1968, **22**, 349–368.

Crovitz, H. F. Memory loci in artificial memory. *Psychonomic Science*, 1969, **16**, 82–83.

Galton, F. Statistics of mental imagery. *Mind*, 1880, **5**, 301–318.

Gazzaniga, M. A. The split brain in man. *Scientific American*, 1967, **217** (2), 24–29.

Gazzaniga, M. A., & Sperry, R. W. Language after section of the cerebral commissures. *Brain*, 1967, **90**, 131–148.

Gibson, J. J. The optical expansion pattern in aerial locomotion. *American Journal of Psychology*, 1955, **68**, 480–484.

Gibson, J. J. *The Senses Considered as Perceptual Systems*. Boston, Massachusetts: Houghton, 1966.

Gibson, J. J. The information available in pictures. *Leonardo*, 1971, **4**, 27–35.

Gibson, J. J., Kaplan, G. A., Reynolds, H. N., & Wheeler, K. The change from visible to invisible: A study of optical transitions. *Perception and Psychophysics*, 1969, **5**, 113–116.

Haber, R. N., & Haber, R. E. Eidetic Imagery: I. Frequency. *Perceptual and Motor Skills*, 1964, **19**, 131–138.

Hunt, E. What kind of a computer is man? *Cognitive Psychology*, 1971, **2**, 57–98.

Kuhn, T. S. *The structure of scientific revolutions*. Chicago, Illinois: Chicago Univ. Press, 1962.

Leask, J., Haber, R. N., & Haber, R. B. Eidetic imagery in children: II. Longitudinal and experimental results. *Psychonomic Monographs* 1969, **3**, No. 3 (Whole No. 35), 25–48.

Lee, D. N. Binocular stereopsis without spatial disparity. *Perception and Psychophysics*, 1971, **9**, 216–218.

Luria, A. R. *The mind of a mnemonist*. New York: Basic Books, 1968.

Neisser, U. *Cognitive psychology*. New York: Appleton, 1967.

Neisser, U., & Kerr, N. Spatial and mnemonic properties of visual images. 1972, in preparation.

Orne, M. T. The nature of hypnosis: Artifact and essence. *Journal of Abnormal and Social Psychology*, 1959, **46**, 213–225.

Orne, M. T. On the social psychology of the psychological experiment: With particular reference to demand characteristics and their implications. *American Psychologist*, 1962, **17**, 776–783.

Paivio, A. Mental imagery in associative learning and memory. *Psychological Review*, 1969, **76**, 241–263.

Paivio. A. On the functional significance of imagery. *Psychological Bulletin*, 1970, **73**, 385–392.

Palermo, D. S. Imagery in children's learning: Discussion. *Psychological Bulletin*, 1970, **73**, 415–421.

Reese, H. W. Imagery in children's learning: A symposium; Introduction. *Psychological Bulletin*, 1970, **73**, 383–384. (a)

Reese, H. W. Imagery and contextual meaning. *Psychological Bulletin*, 1970, **73**, 404–414. (b)

Rohwer, W. D. Images and pictures in children's learning: Research results and educational implications. *Psychological Bulletin*, 1970, **73**, 393–403.

Rosenthal, R. *Experimenter effects in behavioral research*. New York: Appleton, 1966.

Ross, J., & Lawrence, K. A. Some observations on memory artifice. *Psychonomic Science,* 1968, **13,** 107–108.

Segal, S. J., & Fusella, V. Influence of imaged pictures and sounds on detection of visual and auditory signals. *Journal of Experimental Psychology,* 1970, **83,** 458–464.

Sheehan, P. W. Functional similarity of imaging to perceiving: Individual differences in vividness of imagery. *Perceptual and Motor Skills,* 1966, **23,** 1011–1033 (Monograph Supplement 6-V23).

Sheehan, P. W. A shortened form of Betts' "Questionnaire upon mental imagery." *Journal of Clinical Psychology,* 1967, **23,** 386–389. (a)

Sheehan, P. W. Visual imagery and the organizational properties of perceived stimuli. *British Journal of Psychology,* 1967, **58,** 247–252. (b)

Sheehan, P. W., & Neisser, U. Some variables affecting the vividness of imagery in recall. *British Journal of Psychology,* 1969, **60,** 71–80.

Shepard, R. N., & Metzler, J. Mental rotation of three-dimensional objects. *Science,* 1971, **171,** 701–703.

Stromeyer, C. F. Eidetic images. *Psychology Today,* 1970 (Nov.), 76–79.

Stromeyer, C. F., & Psotka, J. The detailed texture of eidetic images. *Nature (London),* 1970, **225,** 346–349.

Tulving, E. Subjective organization and effects of repetition in multitrial free-recall learning. *Journal of Verbal Learning and Verbal Behavior,* 1966, **5,** 193–197.

Yates, F. A. *The art of memory.* London: Routledge & Kegan Paul, 1966.

11 ALLAN PAIVIO

A THEORETICAL ANALYSIS
OF THE ROLE OF IMAGERY
IN LEARNING AND
MEMORY[1]

Introduction

A volume of research, most of it appearing within the last 8 or 9 years, has firmly established that imagery variables are among the most potent memory factors ever discovered (for reviews, see Bower, 1971; Bugelski, 1970; Paivio, 1969, 1971; Reese, 1970; Rohwer, 1970). It is extraordinarily important, therefore, to understand precisely *why* the independent variables that define imagery are so effective. That question is the primary concern of this chapter. We will turn to it following a brief review of operational approaches to imagery and its effects.

Operational Approaches to Imagery

Three basic operations have been used to define or manipulate imagery, namely, stimulus attributes, experimental manipulations, and individual differences. As a stimulus attribute, imagery has been defined in terms of the image-arousing value or concreteness of the stimulus material. This can be viewed as a dimension ranging from objects or their pictures at the high imagery end, through concrete words, to abstract words at the low end of the scale. Among words, the dimension has been defined by the average rating that a group of subjects assigns to a word on a low

[1] Preparation of this chapter, and the author's research summarized in it, have been supported by grants from the National Research Council of Canada (APA-0087) and the University of Western Ontario Research Fund.

imagery-high imagery scale (Paivio, Yuille, & Madigan, 1968). So defined, imagery has been found to be positively effective in paired-associate (PA) learning, free recall, serial learning, verbal discrimination learning, and the Brown-Peterson short-term memory (STM) task (see Paivio, 1969; Paivio & Rowe, 1970; Paivio & Smythe, 1971). These effects are consistent and often very large, typically exceeding the effect of other commonly used empirical attributes such as meaningfulness. The only clear exceptions to this generalization are sequential memory tasks, such as immediate memory span (Paivio & Csapo, 1969), and perceptual recognition (Paivio & O'Neill, 1970)—exceptions with important theoretical implications, as we shall see.

Instructions or training on the use of imagery has been the most common method of manipulating the variable experimentally (e.g., Bower, 1971; Bugelski, Kidd, & Segman, 1968; Paivio & Yuille, 1967, 1969). Other experimental manipulations include the use of pictures as mediators (e.g., Davidson, 1964; Reese, 1965; Rohwer, Lynch, Levin, & Suzuki, 1967), and variation in presentation rate, which presumably influences image formation or utilization time (e.g., Bugelski et al., 1968; Paivio & Csapo, 1969). Generally consistent and often striking, these effects, too, demand theoretical explanation.

Finally, individual differences in imagery have been investigated using both ratings of the subjective vividness of experienced imagery (e.g., Sheehan, 1966) and spatial manipulation ability tests (e.g., Ernest & Paivio, 1969) as predictors of task performance. Individual differences in effective imagery modalities have also been inferred from sensory deficits such as blindness (e.g., Paivio & Okovita, 1971). Inasmuch as individual differences are covered in considerable detail in this volume elsewhere (see Chapter 4; and also Chapters 5 and 7), they will not be discussed further in the remainder of this chapter except where they are particularly relevant to a theoretical issue under consideration. However, the stimulus attribute and experimental approaches to imagery will receive more detailed attention in the context of the theoretical discussions that follow.

Theoretical Interpretations of Imagery
Effects on Memory: An Outline

In considering alternative interpretations of the effects of imagery variables two possible but unlikely hypotheses will be ignored, one stressing motivational factors as the basis of the effectiveness of imagery mnemonics, and the other emphasizing verbal processes to the exclusion of imagery. A motivational interpretation was considered and rejected for various reasons by Bower (1971) and Paivio (1969). It is unimportant here to consider all of the arguments and it is sufficient simply to point out that a motivational interpretation is ruled out by the fact that imagery effects are undiminished under incidental as compared to intentional learning conditions (Bower, 1971; Yarmey & Ure, 1971; Yuille, 1965). A purely verbal interpretation of imagery effects has been definitively ruled out by the research program conducted by Paivio and his associates (see Paivio, 1969). Thus item attributes such as m and frequency, which can be regarded as measures of verbal meaning, are clearly weaker in their effects than imagery concreteness and inconsistent in the direction of their effects (e.g., Paivio & Madigan, 1970; Paivio, Smythe, & Yuille, 1968; Paivio, Yuille, & Rogers, 1969). Similarly, the relations between mediation instructions, subjects' reports concerning the type of mediator used in learning, and learning scores can be consistently interpreted in terms of imagery mediation or a combination of imagery and verbal processes, but not verbal mechanisms alone (e.g., Paivio & Yuille, 1969). Accordingly, although an exclusively verbal hypothesis will be mentioned again later, it will be generally assumed in the following discussion that both imagery and verbal processes are effective coding and mediating mechanisms, and the emphasis will be on interpreting the unique contribution of imagery to mnemonic effects.

The theoretical analysis is divided into two major sections, the first dealing with *encoding,* and the second with *storage* and *retrieval* processes.

Encoding Factors

This section deals with the effects of imagery that are attributable to factors operating at the encoding stage, when the imaginal memory code or mediator is generated or discovered. Attention centers on the ease or speed of such encoding, which determines whether or not the mnemonic process is available to the subject in the experimental situation. The crucial factors affecting image discovery appear to be *item concreteness, instructional sets* (or other conditions designed to prime imaginal encoding), and *rate of presentation.*

Item Concreteness and Instructional Sets

A two-process approach proposed by Paivio (e.g., 1969) states essentially that the ease of generating images to stimulus items varies directly with item concreteness, whereas verbal coding or mediation would be independent of concreteness and related instead to such factors as verbal associative meaningfulness. The hypothesis has been supported by reaction time data, which showed that the arousal of images to single words or imaginal mediators to pairs of words is faster for concrete than for abstract items, whereas the latency of verbal associations or mediators is relatively unaffected by concreteness (e.g., Colman & Paivio, 1970; Ernest & Paivio, 1971; Paivio, 1966; Simpson & Paivio, 1968; Yuille & Paivio, 1967). The hypothesis implies that memory effects attributable to imagery can be explained partly in terms of ease of image discovery. Paivio and Foth (1970) obtained support for this interpretation in a PA experiment in which subjects were required to generate imaginal or verbal mediators to pairs of concrete or abstract nouns. The mediators were overtly produced in the form of crude drawings in the case of images and written phrases or sentences in the case of verbal mediators. Two aspects of the results are relevant here. First, as in the association studies cited above, it took longer to generate images to abstract than to concrete pairs but verbal mediators were not similarly affected. Second, subjects recalled fewer abstract pairs under the imagery than under the verbal mediation condition. A correlational analysis of mediator latencies and PA performance revealed a negative relation, so that long image-production latencies were associated with lower recall, but verbal mediation latencies and recall were uncorrelated. Moreover, the superiority of the verbal set over the imagery set with respect to average recall was reduced to nonsignificance when the analysis was based only on abstract pairs for which mediators had been discovered during the 15 second interval allowed for mediator generation to each pair.

The above findings suggest that the relative effects of imaginal and verbal mediation instructions with abstract pairs result from differences in the speed of imaginal and verbal encoding. They also suggest that images might be as effective with abstract as with concrete pairs under conditions that facilitate the discovery of images to the former. This suggestion is supported by Marshall's (1965) experiment in which pictures supplied by the experimenter (for example, a picture of a baby to mediate the pair *formula-innocence*) were superior to their concrete-noun labels as mediators of PA learning for abstract pairs, presumably because the mediators were provided and encoding so facilitated. However, controlling for encoding differences does not explain the *superiority* of the pictorial condition in Marshall's experiment any more than it explains why imagery mnemonics are sometimes better than verbal ones with concrete pairs (e.g., Bower, 1971; Raser & Bartz, 1968; Rimm, Alexander, & Eiles, 1969; Taylor & Black, 1969). Paivio and Foth (1970), for example, showed consistent superiority of imagery over verbal mnemonic sets with concrete noun pairs. Since they also found that, on the average, imaginal and verbal mediators were discovered equally quickly for such pairs, the PA recall effect must be due to factors other than ease of encoding. Accordingly, this aspect of their data and similar findings by others (including Marshall's results) will be considered in detail in the sections dealing with storage and retrieval mechanisms.

The data considered thus far illustrate the effect of concreteness on imagery encoding and also show the relative effects of verbal and imaginal instructions on encoding latency. The effects of both factors are further revealed by post-learning mediation questionnaire data (e.g., Paivio, Smythe, & Yuille, 1968; Paivio & Yuille, 1969), which show that subjects report frequent use of images to mediate noun pairs in which at least one member is concrete and high in rated imagery, but infrequent use of imagery with abstract pairs. By contrast, the frequency of verbal mediation and other learning strategies is relatively unaffected by item concreteness.

The pattern of reported mediators was modified in interesting ways by instructional sets used by Paivio and Yuille (1969). For the first PA learning trial following instructions, their subjects reported frequent use of the learning strategy they were asked to follow. Thus, instructions to use imagery, verbal mediation, and rote repetition differentially enhanced reported frequency of the corresponding strategies relative to uninstructed control conditions. On trials following the first, however, *the frequency of rote repetition decreased sharply despite prelearning reminders to subjects to continue to use the same strategy.* Imagery and verbal mediation, on the other hand, increased in frequency over trials even in the case of subjects instructed to use rote repetition. Finally, regardless of instructional sets, the frequency of both reported imagery and PA performance scores varied systematically with stimulus and response concreteness, with both dependent measures being highest for concrete–concrete pairs, followed in decreasing order by concrete–abstract, abstract–concrete, and abstract–abstract pairs. Taken together, these data show that, while the subjects' encoding or learning strategies can be modified by instructional sets, *the meaning attributes of the items themselves override the instructional sets as learning trials progress.* More specifically, imagery appears to be a preferred strategy when at least one member of the pair is concrete and high in image-arousing value. It is important to note at the same time that *both* imaginal and verbal mediators apparently are easily discovered when pairs are concrete but only verbal mediators are readily available for abstract pairs. Thus both processes might be simultaneously implicated in effects of concreteness and imagery mnemonic instructions on performance. This possibility is relevant to the following discussion as well as to later considerations of processes occurring during storage.

Presentation Rate

Presentation rate is the third variable affecting the discovery of imaginal as well as verbal mediators. Studies by Bugelski *et al.* (1968) and Gruber, Kulkin, and Schwartz (1965) showed that study trial presentation rate modified the effectiveness of imagery mnemonics. Since test trial rate was held constant in both studies, the observed effects can be attributed to events occurring during the image formation or encoding stage rather than storage or retrieval, although they obviously must persist throughout the latter stages as well. Bugelski *et al.* (1968) found the rhyming (one-bun) mnemonic to be superior to control conditions at rates of 4 or 8 seconds per item, but not at 2 seconds. Gruber *et al.* (1965), however, found that imagery mnemonic instructions facilitated standard PA recall at rates as fast as 1 second per pair when recall was tested by presenting the stimulus noun as a retrieval cue. The discrepancy may be due to the extra coding step involved in the rhyming mnemonic. Thus, if the first item is "pencil," the subject is presented "one-pencil" and he must implicitly generate "one-bun-pencil" and then transform the verbal relation into an image. The PA analogue would involve presentation of the pair "bun-pencil" and the subject is therefore not required to generate the peg word "bun" from long-term memory before imagining the relation. This difference in the number of encoding steps involved seems to be the most parsimonious explanation of the differing rate effects in the two experiments, but more direct empirical support is obviously needed to confirm the hypothesis.

Rate would also be expected to interact with concreteness and mnemonic instructions. Despite the obviousness of such implications, little direct evidence is available at this time on the issue and apparently none that permits one to conclude that the observed effects are due entirely to events occurring during encoding. Paivio and Csapo (1969) investigated the interaction of rate, item concreteness, and type of memory task in a study designed to test the hypothesis that verbal and imaginal memory codes are differentially effective in sequential but not in nonsequential memory tasks. The hypothesis implicates assumed differences in the nature of organization processes during storage or retrieval (or both) and it will be discussed again later in that context. The relevant feature of the study at this point is a prediction from the hypothesis that verbal and imaginal codes are differentially available for pictures, concrete words, and abstract words. Specifically, it was hypothesized that both codes are readily available for easily named pictures and concrete words, but only (or primarily) the verbal memory code is available for abstract words. Pictures and concrete words were further differentiated in terms of the relative availability of the two codes: It takes more time to name a picture than to read a word (e.g., Fraisse, 1968), therefore the verbal code is less available in the former case; the nonverbal (concrete image) code is directly aroused by pictures but only indirectly (associatively) by concrete words, therefore imaginal coding is more available in the case of pictures. Moreover, it was assumed that the verbal code is generally more available (aroused more quickly) to pictures than images are to concrete words. Thus the summative availability of *both* codes was assumed to be highest for familiar pictures, next for concrete words, and least for abstract words. On the further assumption that both codes can enhance memory performance, it was predicted that the effect of presentation rate would be greatest for pictures and least for abstract words.

The experiment involved sequential presentation of nine pictures, concrete words, or abstract words for free recall, recognition, immediate sequential recall, or serial learning at a rate of either 5.3 or 2 items per second. Ignoring the task effects, which will be dealt with later, the results yielded a strong interaction of rate and item attribute that precisely confirmed the predictions: pictures were inferior to words in the sequential memory tasks at the fast rate but not at the slow rate. Pictures and words did not differ in free recall or recognition memory at the fast rate, but the typical ordering, with pictures being remembered best and abstract words most poorly, occurred at the slower rate. As stated earlier, the possibility that the effects are due to events occurring during storage or retrieval cannot be ruled out conclusively, but the encoding or trace-formation hypothesis is certainly favored by the data. The faster of the two rates was explicitly intended to eliminate verbal coding to pictures during input but it presumably also precluded image arousal to concrete words. The slower rate apparently allowed sufficient time for associative arousal of the verbal code (i.e., a name) to a picture and an image to a concrete word. It is difficult to suggest an alternative hypothesis that would account equally parsimoniously for all features of the observed interaction.

A somewhat different interaction of presentation rate and concreteness occurred in a PA learning experiment by Csapo (1968). The study trial rates were 0.8 and 2.0 seconds per pair for different groups of subjects. The learning material consisted of nine homogeneous 12-pair lists resulting from the factorial combination of pictures (P), concrete words (C), and abstract words (A) on the stimulus and response sides of pairs. Thus one list consisted of P–P pairs, a second, P–C, a third P–A, and so on. A significant interaction of stimulus-term attribute, rate, and trials showed that overall performance was best with P stimuli at both rates, and C tended to be superior to A words, but less so at the fast rate—indeed, no difference occurred on the first two trials. Taking performance with abstract stimuli as the baseline, these data suggest that there was insufficient time at the fast rate for concrete items to evoke images that could effectively mediate learning, especially on the first two trials. The effectiveness of pictures was relatively less affected by increased rate, however, presumably (according to the present theory) because they arouse images more directly than do concrete words.

Note that the results and the conclusion for the PA task contrast directly with the ones arising from the Paivio and Csapo (1969) study of sequential and nonsequential memory tasks, where the rate effect was greatest for pictures. The difference could be due to the slower rates used in the PA experiment (0.8 and 2.0 seconds per pair rather than the .188 and .5 seconds per item for fast and slow rates in the Paivio and Csapo study). Moreover, unlike the other memory tasks, PA learning involves the presentation of an explicit retrieval cue for each response term on the recall trial. Perhaps imaginal associations formed even at the faster of the two rates during the study trial were redintegrated as mediators of recall by the highly concrete (pictorial) stimulus terms. Given that such images function as effective mediators of PA learning, the rate dependent availability of verbal labels to pictures during input may have been relatively less important in that task than in the memory tasks that involved no explicit retrieval cues. Note, however, that this suggestion contrasts with Rohwer's (1970) hypothesis that the effective use of picture-evoked images as mediators depends on the learner's ability to store a verbal tag along with the image. The contrasting proposals remain to be tested. Moreover, these speculations hinge on assumptions concerning storage and retrieval processes, to be considered next.

Storage and Retrieval Processes

These two processing stages will be discussed together because it is difficult often to determine which stage is implicated by effective variables. The distinction is theoretically important, however, and in some instances the locus of an effect can be specified. This section is concerned with the following hypothetical processes as they are related to imagery effects: (a) properties of the memory trace such as strength or vividness; (b) code redundancy; (c) organizational processes occurring during either or both stages; (d) interference, or freedom from it, during storage or retrieval; and (e) retrieval mechanisms related in particular to the attributes of effective retrieval cues. The following sections deal with the relevance of these factors to such findings as the facilitating effect of imagery (as defined operationally) over control conditions, the superiority of imagery over verbal mediation, and the evidence that interference effects involving imagery do occur for some items (although the overall effect of imagery may nonetheless be facilitative when the subject is required to learn a list of items).

Effective Properties of the Memory Trace

Vividness. The ancient wax-tablet model (see Gomulicki, 1953) related memory to the vividness of the trace or image of what has been perceived. This view held that perceptions are impressed on the mind like the tracings of a signet ring on a block of wax, to be maintained in memory as long as the impression lasts, and manifested itself in the emphasis on vividness of experienced images in early imagery research (Betts, 1909; Fernald, 1912). While devoid of assumptions concerning subjective (perceptual) vividness of memory images, contemporary strength theories of memory (see Wickelgren, 1970) could be regarded as analogues of the wax-tablet theory and, as such, they may help to restore some of the pristine respectability of the latter.

The crucial problem in the present context is the operational definition of vividness independent of memory performance. The defining operations, moreover, should permit direct comparisons of nonverbal images and verbal memory representations. Presumably the only way the latter can be accomplished is to assume with the early researchers that verbal representations are also images—generally acoustic or kinesthetic, although visual word images could also be accommodated in such an approach. This seems plausible in principle, at least for short-term memory, given the contemporary emphasis on acoustic or articulatory coding in short-term or primary-memory (e.g., Baddeley, 1964; Conrad, 1964; Sperling, 1963; Wickelgren, 1965). It is difficult, however, to see how different memory modalities could be scaled on vividness in such a way that cross-modal comparisons of relative effectiveness would be possible. Such comparisons in any case have not been made and the only available relevant evidence comes from attempts to vary vividness of imagery within a given modality and determine the relation between vividness and independently measured memory performance. Measures of individual differences in reported vividness, however, generally have not been very successful as predictors of memory, although the recent series of studies by Sheehan (e.g., 1966; Sheehan & Neisser, 1969) have yielded some positive evidence (see also Chapter 4, this volume).

Apart from the context of individual differences, Bower (1971) found that rated vividness of imaginal scenes suggested by noun pairs was predictive of the later recall of the pair: More vivid "scenes" were better remembered. This occurred even under incidental-learning conditions, suggesting that the relationship was not simply an artifact of some kind of relative learning set that influenced both vividness and recall. One aspect of an experiment by Anderson and Hidde (1970) similarly required subjects to form an image of the event described by each of a series of sentences and then rate the vividness of each image. The subjects were then given a surprise recall test in which they attempted to recall the verb and object of each sentence given the subject as a retrieval cue. That the imagery manipulation was effective was indicated by the fact that these subjects recalled over three times as many words as subjects who rated the sentences for pronunciability rather than image vividness. In addition, sentences rated as evoking vivid imagery were better recalled than ones that evoked vague images, although the relation was not especially strong.

The above findings are suggestive, but image vividness needs to be operationally distinguished from other possible correlates before the observed relations can be precisely interpreted, particularly in view of Paivio's (1968) finding that rated vividness of imagery correlated highly with imagery latency and its analogue, rated ease of image arousal. Until such variables are teased apart we cannot be sure of the conceptual or empirical status of the vividness concept in relation to memory research.

Vividness aside, it would be possible to compare the strength or efficacy of imaginal and verbal memory codes using pictures or their verbal labels as stimuli, provided that the availability of the two codes can be equated while preventing the associative arousal of one code when the stimulus for the other one is presented. For example, it would be desirable to prevent an implicit labeling response to a picture while still allowing the latter to be recognized. An appropriately fast rate of presentation, such as that used by Paivio and Csapo (1969) in the study described above, achieves these aims. These results from that experiment showed that, in tasks requiring only item retrieval, pictures and words were equally well remembered even at the fast rate. This suggests that item information is stored effectively in either system. The results also showed that false positives (erroneously saying that a new item had been in the input list) in the recognition memory task were fewer for pictures than for words, suggesting that some aspects of item information are better retained in the nonverbal than the verbal memory system.

The Dual-Coding Hypothesis

The above approaches to storage mechanisms emphasize variation in the potency of the memory image and the relative strengths of imaginal and verbal codes. An alternative is the dual-coding, or trace redundancy hypothesis, which states that high imagery conditions are so effective in learning and memory because they increase the probability that *both* imaginal and verbal processes will play a mediational role in item retrieval. This offers a parsimonious explanation of the superiority of pictures over concrete words and of the latter over abstract words in various memory tasks. Thus, in free recall of pictures, the subject presumably will implicitly name at least some of the items during input. Such items may be stored in both codes. Assuming that the required verbal response can be retrieved from either code, such dual coding would enhance the probability of recall because one code could be forgotten during the retention interval without complete loss of the nominal item. Concrete words similarly are more likely to arouse images during input than are abstract words, enhancing the probability of dual coding and recall in the case of the former. Dual coding would be more likely in the case of easily named pictures than in the case of concrete words, however, presumably because a naming response is more likely to pictures than an image is to the words.

The dual-coding hypothesis is supported by several kinds of evidence. Procedures designed to encourage verbalization of familiar pictures during their presentation have been shown to enhance subsequent verbal recall (e.g., Bahrick & Boucher, 1968; Kurtz & Hovland, 1953; Wilgosh, 1970). Instructions to image to words or phrases similarly have been found to facilitate free recall (Gupton & Frincke, 1970; Kirkpatrick, 1894; Rogers, 1967). Strong support can also be found in the results of the Paivio and Csapo (1969) study described above. Recall that, at a very fast presentation rate (which presumably precluded implicit naming of pictures as well as imaging to words), there were no differences in free recall or recognition memory for pictures and words. At a slower rate, which presumably permitted the alternative code to be evoked by at least some items during input, free recall and recognition scores increased from abstract words, to concrete words, to pictures. These data favor the dual coding interpretation over one that stresses superiority of images over verbal representations because the latter hypothesis cannot account for the absence of differences at the fast rate. Specifically, if images of pictures were simply easier to remember than verbal representations, the advantage should show up even at the fast rate, unless one assumes further that such a rate somehow interferes more with image encoding of pictures than verbal encoding of printed words. Such an assumption is gratuitous and unparsimonious, although it probably warrants a direct test before we can reject it firmly. Pending the results of such a test, the code redundancy hypothesis appears to be favored, particularly in tasks requiring a verbal response during output.

It is also possible that nonverbal imagery alone contributes to the superiority of pictures in recognition memory, as indicated by the infrequent occurrence of false positives in picture recognition even at the fast presentation rate in the Paivio and Csapo experiment (see above). False positives were also found to be rare in picture recognition at fast rates by Potter and Levy (1969), and Cohen and Granström (1970) found that verbal coding contributed to reproduction but not recognition of visual forms. Such data suggest that dual coding may account for some aspects of memory performance but not for others. Just as the verbal code was found to be essential for sequential memory (Paivio & Csapo, 1969), nonverbal images may be superior in other tasks, especially those involving figural (spatial) information. This leads to a consideration of organizational processes in regard to the relative effectiveness of imaginal and verbal codes.

Organizational Processes during Storage or Retrieval

The theoretical distinction between imaginal and verbal processes in terms of their relative capacity for spatial and sequential organization of items in memory is particularly relevant here. The finding (Paivio & Csapo, 1969) that sequential memory for pictures suffers when items are presented sequentially at such a fast rate that they can not be implicitly named clearly indicates that temporal order information is poorly retained in the image system alone, although item information is retained imaginally at least as well as verbally. That study, however, did not test for *spatial* organization, for which imagery is presumably specialized.

Evidence for the effect of spatially organized images on free recall has been presented by Bower, Lesgold, and Tieman (1969) and Mueller and Jablonski (1970). Bower *et al.* asked their subjects to form mental pictures combining more than one item in a single image. The items were nouns presented simultaneously in groups of various sizes. The effectiveness of imagery organization was demonstrated, for example, by the findings that recall suffered if subjects were forced to regroup items from trial to trial, and was facilitated by conditions that encouraged the formation of larger imagery groups over trials. The findings are consistent with an interpretation in terms of spatially organized imagery, but the study included no comparison with analogous verbal mnemonics. Mueller and Jablonski, however, demonstrated directly that instructions to combine items in imagery result in higher recall than standard free recall or sentence mediation conditions.

The above findings suggest that the picture > concrete noun > abstract noun ordering in free recall performance might be attributable to organizational processes based on imagery. If this is true, then measures of subjective organization (Tulving, 1962) or intertrial repetitions (Bousfield, Puff, & Cowan, 1964) should also vary with concreteness and recall performance in free recall. This has indeed been the case in some experiments (Paivio & Csapo, 1969; Tulving, McNulty, & Ozier, 1965) but not in others (Frincke, 1968; Paivio, & Madigan, 1970; Paivio, Yuille, & Rogers, 1969). Thus it is difficult to account for the concreteness effect in free recall entirely in terms of differential interitem organization, although the Bower *et al.* and Mueller and Jablonski data clearly suggest that imagery organization can facilitate recall. Of course, the two sets of findings are not incompatible. That concreteness sometimes facilitates recall without concomitant variation in organization is consistent with the dual-coding hypothesis, which suggests that imagery facilitates *item* retrieval by providing an alternative memory code. Thus imagery presumably can enhance free recall either by increasing the probability that individual items will be correctly retrieved, or by providing an organizational scheme whereby recall of one item will tend to redintegrate others from the same spatial cluster.

Somewhat more evidence on imagery organization is available in relation to PA learning, where such organization has been the major explanation of facilitative effects attributable to manipulation of imagery variables. The idea goes back to the ancient Greek mnemonists, but modern examples that have influenced research can begin with Köhler (1929). He suggested that pairs of nouns such as *lake-sugar, boot-plate, girl-kangaroo,* and so on, are easier to learn than pairs of nonsense syllables because the nouns can be imagined as a series of pictures that constitute well-organized wholes. The lump of sugar might be seen as dissolving in a lake, the boot resting on a plate, and so forth. Köhler's formulation influenced Epstein, Rock, and Zuckerman (1960), who demonstrated that pictures of paired objects were learned better when each pair was presented as a meaningful unit (for example, a hand in a bowl) than when the members of pairs were presented as separate units (a hand beside a bowl). Similar effects were obtained using verbal analogues of the pictorial conditions. The imagery-mediation hypothesis of concreteness effects in associative learning (Paivio, 1969) similarly emphasizes the arousal of compound images by both members of a concrete noun pair during the study trial, and the redintegration of the compound by the stimulus member on the recall trial.

Such a conceptualization implies that the degree of figural unity or integration of the mediating image would be an important determinant of its effectiveness. A number of recent studies have confirmed this expectation. Wollen (1969) presented subjects with concrete noun pairs accompanied on the study trial by drawings depicting the referent objects either in some kind of interaction (e.g., a cigar on a piano) or side by side without interaction (a cigar beside a piano). On recall trials only the stimulus noun was presented. The results showed that recall under the interacting picture condition was more than double the recall under the noninteracting condition. Bower (1971) gave one group of subjects standard instructions in which they were asked to image a scene of two objects interacting in some way. A second group was given "separation" instructions in which they were asked to image the two objects one at a time separated in their imaginal space, like two pictures being seen on opposite walls of a room, with one object picture not being influenced in any way by the contents of the other object picture. The cues for the images were concrete-noun pairs. The recall test showed that recall was much higher under the interactive imagery than under the separated imagery condition. Results supporting the same conclusion have been obtained by a number of other investigators using different procedures (e.g., Atwood, 1969; Eiles, 1970; Taylor, Josberger, & Prentice, 1970; Winograd, Karchmer, & Russell, 1971; see also Chapter 10, this book).

Figural organization may also be the basis of the superiority of imagery mnemonics over verbal mediation conditions with concrete noun pairs in the Paivio and Foth (1970) experiment described earlier, as well as several other studies (e.g., Bower & Winzenz, 1970; Colman & Paivio, 1970; Raser & Bartz, 1968; Rimm, Alexander, & Eiles, 1969). Assuming that the stimulus-response association is stored in the form of a compound image and that this image is reliably reinstated by the stimulus cue on recall trials, it presumably can be quickly "inspected" and decoded to yield the verbal response. On the other hand, verbal mediators together with the to-be-associated words must be stored sequentially as a string of "mental words," resulting in a relatively greater memory load during storage or longer search time and less efficient retrieval of the relevant response from the mediator during recall, or both. These hypotheses are consistent with latency data from the Paivio and Foth study. Those findings showed, on the one hand, that the latency for generating imaginal and verbal mediators to concrete pairs did not differ, indicating that differences in recall under the two conditions could not be attributed to processes operating during encoding. On the other hand, concrete pairs were recalled more quickly in the imagery than in the verbal-mediation condition, indicating that the former was more effective than the latter for information storage or retrieval.

An alternative or additional possibility (a variant of the coding redundancy hypothesis) is that the imagery mnemonic increases the availability of *both* imaginal and verbal mediators during recall, whereas the verbal mediation condition primarily affects the availability of verbal mediators. Indeed, although the emphasis in this section has been on the differential properties of imaginal and verbal processes that might affect memory, it is likely that the two systems interact continually in tasks that are assumed to involve imagery, at least when the to-be-learned items are words. Any use of mediating imagery under such conditions obviously requires word-to-image coding during input and the reverse during recall. Moreover, it is probable that in many instances the generation of an imaginal mediator might be on the basis of a sentence or phrase first aroused by the test items.

The above evidence in any case permits us to conclude that imagery enhances memory even for verbal units beyond a level that can be explained on the basis of verbal processes alone. The effect might be attributable in part to functional differences between the two systems, but it is likely that it also reflects their interaction. As I have suggested elsewhere (Paivio, 1971, Chapter 11), the image system may contribute flexibility and speed to the transformations involved in mediated learning, whereas the logical verbal system keeps the transformations on track, i.e., relevant to the learning task and the items involved in it.

Interference and Distinctiveness

One of the cardinal principles of the ancient art of memory was that mnemonic images should be novel or bizarre in order to be effective (see Paivio, 1971, Chapter 6). In the context of contemporary interference theory, this prescription could be viewed as an effort to increase the distinctiveness of items and reduce interitem interference effects. This feature of imagery mnemonics has been investigated directly in only a few studies and the results are contradictory. While positive results were reported by Delin (1968), the results have been entirely negative in other studies (e.g., Atwood, 1969; Wollen, 1969; Wood, 1967). These contrasting findings leave the role of bizarreness or novelty in some doubt, and further research on the problem is clearly needed, particularly since the studies to date have used various procedures and different retention intervals.

Regardless of the outcome of research on the effect of bizarreness, an interference or distinctiveness interpretation of imagery effects remains plausible. One possibility is that facilitative effects that have been attributed to imagery, as in the case of the superiority of concrete over abstract nouns in memory tasks, are actually due to differential intraverbal interference. Another possibility is that, regardless of their bizarreness, images are generally less susceptible to interference effects than are verbal processes. Although the first of these—differential verbal interference—may be a relevant factor, it can be ruled out as a sufficient explanation of imagery effects on the basis of several empirical findings. Mentioned earlier were the findings that measures of verbal meaning, such as frequency and associative meaningfulness, which presumably could constitute a potential basis for differential verbal interference, cannot account for the effect of imagery concreteness. More direct evidence comes from two other studies. Paivio (1965) investigated differential verbal-associative overlap as a possible explanation of the strong effect of stimulus concreteness in paired-associate learning and found no support for such an interpretation. Paivio and Begg (1971) investigated a claim (Wickens & Engle, 1970) that the superior memorability of concrete items over abstract items in the Peterson and Peterson (1959) distractor STM task can be explained in terms of differential semantic or verbal-associative overlap. They systematically varied interitem associative overlap within and between noun triads, which varied in imagery concreteness. High imagery nouns were, as usual, recalled significantly better than abstract nouns, and this effect was not qualified by either between- or within-triad overlap. These experimental findings together with logical considerations indicated that differential interference attributable to interitem semantic or associative relatedness cannot account for the superior recall of high imagery nouns in STM or in other memory tasks.

The negative findings in regard to verbal interference do not rule out the alternative possibility that imagery itself is the source of distinctiveness and resistance to interference among concrete items, or when imagery is manipulated by mnemonic instructions. In the case of the latter, Bugelski (1968) found that the one-bun rhyme mnemonic could be used with six successive lists of ten items each without any evidence of negative transfer from one list to the next, and with recall being uniformly high in each case. Similar evidence that imagery mnemonics reduce interitem interference, particularly proactive interference, has been found by others (e.g., Bower, 1971; Crovitz, 1970; Ross & Lawrence, 1968). In contrast, however, Wood (1967) reported negative transfer when the same noun pegs were used as stimuli for successive word lists. Keppel and Zavortink (1969) reported retroactive interference with the one-bun mnemonic when subjects were tested for recall of all lists following the learning of four sets of lists using the mnemonic.

While the conditions under which imagery mnemonics do and do not reduce interference obviously need clarification, the evidence to date suggests that, under some conditions at least, the technique does reduce interference. It is reasonable, therefore, to suppose also that the facilitative effect of concreteness in various memory tasks results in part from the increased resistance to interference provided by the availability of imagery as an alternative memory code. Precisely why imagery should have such an effect is unclear at the moment, but the coding redundancy hypothesis provides a possible explanation. That is, the availability of imagery as a mediator or alternative memory code permits reconstruction of the target item even if the verbal code is forgotten because of verbal interference. Alternatively, images may be particularly resistant to interference because of their distinctiveness as figural units.

The above reasoning raised the somewhat paradoxical possibility that images may in some cases be the *cause* of interference. This would be the case in paired-associate learning when, for example, concrete noun responses have synonyms whose recall could be mediated by the same response-term image. Thus the image of an adult female may generate "lady" or "woman" as a response. This possibility is very important theoretically because it permits one to predict that, while performance under high imagery conditions may be generally superior to performance under low imagery conditions, there may be more decoding or synonym errors in the high imagery case. Evidence for such contrasting effects has been obtained in paired-associate learning (e.g., Anderson & Hidde, 1970; Bower, 1971; Lockhart, 1969; Yuille, 1971). Strong evidence for such effects has also been obtained in recognition memory tasks by Begg and Paivio (1969), who found that alterations that changed the meanings of sentences were well recognized but changes in wording which did not affect meaning were poorly recognized when the sentences were concrete, whereas the reverse occurred in the case of abstract sentences. Prompted by the Begg and Paivio finding, Wirtz and Anisfeld (1970) tested for synonym and antonym errors of recognition using concrete and abstract adjective-noun phrases. They found that synonym errors exceeded antonym errors in the case of concrete but not abstract phrases. All of these studies consistently support the conclusion that images are better remembered than verbal material alone, but that decoding errors are more likely in the case of the former.

The above hypothesis and the supportive findings clarify a puzzling result that was briefly reported by Paivio (1965). As indicated above, in that study associative overlap did not explain a facilitative effect of stimulus concreteness in the learning of noun–noun pairs. However, associative overlap scores for concrete noun stimuli alone correlated significantly with recall, the correlation value being —.69, whereas the relation for abstract stimuli was only .02. Thus the greater the associative overlap between a given concrete stimulus noun and the other concrete nouns in the list, the poorer the associative recall; no such relation occurred with abstract stimuli. This finding now seems completely reasonable if we assume that the relation for concrete stimulus nouns reflects interference created by similarity among images aroused by such items.

Retrieval Mechanisms and the Conceptual-Peg Hypothesis

The role of imagery in learning and memory is both conceptually and empirically clearest in associative retrieval. Attention in this section centers on the assumption that the ease of image-mediated association is related to the concreteness of the to-be-associated events, particularly the one that must serve as the retrieval cue. This view was stated long ago by Quintilian and was accepted by later mnemonists such as Feinaigle, who suggested that, "sensible objects have a powerful effect in recalling to mind the ideas with which it was occupied when those ideas were presented [1813, cited in Paivio, 1971, p. 170]." The assumption extended to word meaning, since the names of objects were proposed as cues for the arousal of the images that were to serve as memory localities for the items that were to be recalled. The implied importance of the abstractness–concreteness of the retrieval cue was made explicit in Paivio's (1963) conceptual-peg hypothesis of paired-associate learning, according to which the stimulus term functions as a "peg" to which its associate is hooked during learning trials and from which it can be retrieved on recall trials. The more concrete the stimulus, the more "solid" it is as a conceptual-peg and the better the recall. The most important implication of the hypothesis is that the concreteness or imagery value of stimulus terms should have a greater effect on associative learning than the same degree of variation in the concreteness of the response terms. It must be emphasized that this prediction applied to the standard paired-associate learning situation in which the stimulus and response functions of paired members are explicitly distinguished. The hypothesis is essentially a *retrieval* theory—a high imagery item is especially effective as a retrieval cue for the associated member. The formation and the storage of the compound mediating image during the study trial presumably depend equally on the concreteness of both members of the pair, but the imagery value of the response member is assumed to be less important than that of the stimulus during the recall trial.

The evidence for the hypothesis as applied to paired-associate learning has been reviewed in some detail elsewhere (e.g., Paivio, 1969, 1971) and here we need only reiterate that a strong positive effect of item imagery is consistently stronger on the stimulus than on the response side of pairs. The effective dimension ranges from highly abstract words to pictures. That is, pictures are superior to their labels, which in turn are superior to abstract words as stimulus items in the paired-associate task.

The implications of the conceptual-peg hypothesis for tasks other than standard paired-associate learning have also been uniformly supported. The theory implies that, if no retrieval cue is explicitly presented and the subjects are instead asked to free recall both members of each pair, there should be no differential facilitative effect of concreteness favoring either the left- or the right-hand member of the pair. This prediction has been confirmed in experiments by Yarmey and Ure (1971) and Yuille and Humphreys (1970). Another implication is that the differential concreteness effect should be obtained for the nominal "response" member (i.e., the right hand or second member of the pair) when it serves as the retrieval cue, as in a test of backward association. This prediction, too, has been confirmed (e.g., Lockhart, 1969; Yarmey & O'Neill, 1969). Still another implication is that no differential effect favoring concreteness of either member should be obtained when a matching test, rather than recall, is used to assess associative learning, inasmuch as either the nominal stimulus or the nominal response could function as the retrieval cue. Evidence consistent with this hypothesis can be found in studies by Paivio and Rowe (1971) and Raser and Bartz (1968).

While the above findings are fully in accord with the conceptual-peg hypothesis, the stated results do not in themselves constitute direct evidence that imagery mediation is involved. It has been argued alternatively that the superiority of pictures as retrieval cues might be explained in terms of stimulus differentiation or recognition rather than association (Dominowski & Gadlin, 1968; Wicker, 1970). That is, high imagery stimuli may be more effective as retrieval cues simply because they are easier to discriminate from each other or to recognize as units. Without denying that such a process could contribute to the effects, the available evidence permits us to conclude that it is not a sufficient explanation of the stimulus imagery effect. The Paivio (1965) study, described above in connection with interference factors, tested the stimulus differentiation hypothesis using associative overlap between a given item and other items in the list as the index of distinctiveness or discriminability. Although concrete stimulus terms produced much better learning than did abstract stimuli, concreteness did not relate significantly to overlap scores. While the finding does not preclude a differentiation interpretation of the efficacy of pictures as stimulus cues, it does restrict the generality of the interpretation at most to picture-word comparisons.

Other recent studies provide positive evidence that stimulus imagery effects are indeed attributable to mediating images. Paivio and Yuille (1969) gave their subjects instructions to use one of several learning strategies, including imagery. Different groups were given one, two, or three learning trials followed by a cued recall test and then a questionnaire asking about the extent to which they used different learning strategies to learn each pair. The results showed the typical stimulus superiority of item imagery along with facilitating effects of both imagery and verbal mnemonic instructions. The relevant result in the present context was a striking similarity in the pattern of results for reported imagery mediation and learning scores as a function of stimulus and response imagery-concreteness. That is, frequency of reported imagery and learning were highest for concrete–concrete pairs, next for concrete–abstract, abstract–concrete, and abstract–abstract, in descending order. The fact that a similar pattern was not obtained for reported verbal mediation although subjects had an equal opportunity to choose accordingly in describing their strategies suggests strongly that the reported mediators are in fact valid indicators of the associative strategies actually used by the subjects.

Also relevant here is the study by Bower (1971), which showed that imagery instructions in which subjects are asked to imagine the objects suggested by noun pairs as interacting in some way resulted in much better cued recall than instructions in which the objects are separated in their imaginal space (see above). That experiment demonstrated further that the advantage of interactive imagery remains substantial even when only recognized stimulus items are considered. The finding indicates that interactive imagery indeed has its effect through associative mediation rather than stimulus recognition or differentiation.

The clearest evidence that stimulus evoked imagery has its associative effect via mediation, while demonstrating at the same time that imagery can facilitate discrimination, comes from a recent study by Rowe and Paivio (1971). The subjects were presented a verbal discrimination learning task involving pairs of concrete nouns. The most relevant feature of the study in the present context was a comparison of the effects of two kinds of imagery instructions. In one imagery condition, the subjects were asked to image to the correct member of each pair; in the other, they were required to image to both members of each pair but to differentiate the pair members by imagining the correct "object" as being larger than the incorrect one. The results showed that discrimination learning was best when subjects imaged only to the correct pair member, whereas subjects who imagined both pair members performed no better than an uninstructed control group. In sharp contrast to the discrimination data, the results of an associative recall test that unexpectedly followed the discrimination task showed recall to be highest for the subjects who had imaged to both members of each pair during discrimination learning. Thus imaging to *one* member of each pair indeed facilitated discrimination learning, whereas imaging to both members did not; conversely, imaging to *both* members facilitated incidental associative recall of the pairs more than did imaging to only one member. These results clearly indicate that imagery can facilitate both discrimination and association, but the kind of imagery activity that is maximally effective differs markedly in the two tasks.

Further Convergent Evidence on Effective Imagery

The data we have reviewed in the course of this theoretical analysis provide consistent, strong support for an imagery interpretation of the effects of imagery mnemonic instructions and imagery as a scaled attribute of stimulus units, particularly words. In the case of the latter, we have relied essentially on correlational data involving long-established word attributes, and the skeptic can still question the validity of describing such relations in terms of the imagery construct. This final section summarizes conclusive evidence from two further operational approaches to the concept: one involving the experimental development of effective imagery, and the other involving an imagery deficit associated with blindness.

A number of writers (e.g., Mowrer, 1960; Sheffield, 1961; Skinner, 1953; Staats, 1961) have interpreted images as conditioned sensations or perceptual responses, with words functioning as one important class of conditioned stimuli. Paivio (1969) suggested that such an interpretation might be appropriate in the case of concrete, high imagery words. In any case, whether one accepts the classical conditioning model or not, there seems to be no alternative to some kind of associative explanation of the acquisition of word imagery. Until recently, however, the interpretation had not been directly tested in the sense that *effective* concreteness or image-arousing value was shown to be acquired by previously neutral stimuli. Philipchalk and Paivio (1971) did so using a transfer design and the well-established stimulus effect of word imagery in PA learning as the criterion of effective imagery-concreteness. The successful procedure involved a meaning-acquisition phase in which nonsense syllables were repeatedly paired with pictures of familiar objects, or names of objects, or abstract words. This was followed by a transfer task in which the syllables served as stimuli for new meaningful response words. The acquisition phase involved PA anticipation trials in which the subject either produced the response (wrote the words or drew a crude drawing of the picture), or was told simply to "think about" the associate. In the transfer task, some subjects were told to use the associations learned in the first phase as mediators; others were not told this. For subjects given the mediation instructions, learning in the transfer task proved to be best for pairs in which the syllable stimuli had previously been associated with pictures, next best for those previously associated with concrete nouns, and poorest for those that had been associated with abstract nouns. Note that this is precisely the ordering of effectiveness that is found for the referent stimuli (pictures, concrete nouns, abstract nouns) in PA learning. The experimental group not given the mediation instructions did not show the same effect, presumably because the acquisition phase was too brief to develop effective imagery without the additional priming provided by the instructional set. The problem requires further research to determine the most effective conditions for the acquisition of word imagery, but even as they stand Philipchalk and Paivio's (1971) findings provide strong experimental support for the imagery interpretation of stimulus concreteness effects.

The other source of convergent support is a study by Paivio and Okovita (1971) comparing blind and sighted subjects in paired associate learning involving words varying in imagery modality. The hypothesis was that the congenitally blind, presumably lacking in visual imagery, could not take advantage of the image-arousing value of purely "visual" words such as *lightning, shadow,* and *sunset* to mediate learning; such words should be effectively abstract. On the other hand, they should be able to use the auditory imagery evoked by words like *whistle, trumpet,* and *laughter.* Sighted subjects, on the other hand, should profit more from visual than from auditory word-imagery because of the importance of the visual modality in their experiences with words and their referents. Two paired associate learning experiments yielded results completely consistent with the hypothesis: the blind showed superior learning for pairs of words that were high in auditory imagery than for low-auditory pairs, even if the latter were high in visual imagery. Conversely, the sighted subjects benefitted from visual but not auditory word imagery. It is difficult to explain these findings in any other way except in terms of the theory that learning was mediated by modality specific images.

In summary, the theory that nonverbal images can function as powerful mediators of learning and memory is supported by the results of studies involving a number of different converging operations: scaled attributes of stimulus items, subjective reports, mnemonic instructions, experimentally acquired concreteness, and individual differences in imagery as inferred from sensory deficits as well as tests of imagery ability. More than a beginning has also been made in the study of the effective attributes of imagery, and its modus operandi in the encoding, storage, and retrieval stages of different memory tasks. For those students of memory that have become involved in the exciting rediscovery of an ancient approach to memory, it is fortunate that much theoretical and empirical work remains to be done.

References

Anderson, R. C., & Hidde, J. L. Imagery and sentence learning. Unpublished manuscript, University of Illinois, 1970.

Atwood, G. E. Experimental studies of mnemonic visualization. Unpublished doctoral dissertation, University of Oregon, 1969.

Baddeley, A. D. Semantic and acoustic similarity in short-term memory. *Nature* 1964, 204, 1116–1117.

Bahrick, H. P., & Boucher, B. Retention of visual and verbal codes of the same stimuli. *Journal of Experimental Psychology*, 1968, **78**, 417–422.

Begg, I., & Paivio, A. Concreteness and imagery in sentence meaning. *Journal of Verbal Learning and Verbal Behavior*, 1969, **8**, 821–827.

Betts, G. H. *The distribution and functions of mental imagery.* New York: Teachers College, Columbia University, 1909.

Bousfield, W. A., Puff, C. R., & Cowan, T. M. The development of constancies in sequential organization during repeated free recall. *Journal of Verbal Learning and Verbal Behavior,* 1964, **3**, 489–495.

Bower, G. H. Mental imagery and associative learning. In Lee Gregg (Ed.), *Cognition in learning and memory.* New York: Wiley, 1971, in press.

Bower, G. H., Lesgold, A. M., & Tieman, D. Grouping operations in free recall. *Journal of Verbal Learning and Verbal Behavior,* 1969, **8**, 481–493.

Bower, G. H., & Winzenz, D. Comparison of associative learning strategies. *Psychonomic Science,* 1970, **20**, 119–120.

Bugelski, B. R. Images as mediators in one-trial paired-associate learning. II: Self-timing in successive lists. *Journal of Experimental Psychology,* 1968, **77**, 328–334.

Bugelski, B. R. Words and things and images. *American Psychologist,* 1970, **25**, 1002–1012.

Bugelski, B. R., Kidd, E., & Segmen, J. Image as a mediator in one-trial paired-associate learning. *Journal of Experimental Psychology,* 1968, **76**, 69–73.

Cohen, R. L., & Granström, K. Reproduction and recognition in short-term visual memory. *Quarterly Journal of Experimental Psychology,* 1970, **22**, 450–457.

Colman, F., & Paivio, A. Pupillary dilation and mediation processes during paired-associate learning. *Canadian Journal of Psychology,* 1970, **24**, 261–270.

Conrad, R. Acoustic confusions in immediate memory. *British Journal of Psychology,* 1964, **55**, 75–84.

Crovitz, H. F. *Galton's walk.* New York: Harper, 1970.

Csapo, K. The effects of presentation rate and item attributes in paired-associate learning. Unpublished M.A. thesis, University of Western Ontario, 1968.

Davidson, R. E. Mediation and ability in paired-associate learning. *Journal of Educational Psychology,* 1964, **55**, 352–356.

Delin, P. S. Success in recall as a function of success in implementation of mnemonic instructions. *Psychonomic Science,* 1968, **12**, 153–154.

Dominowski, R. L., & Gadlin, H. Imagery and paired-associate learning. *Canadian Journal of Psychology,* 1968, **22**, 336–348.

Eiles, R. R. Effects of mediational and motivational instructions on forward and backward recall of concrete paired-associate nouns. Unpublished doctoral dissertation, Arizona State University, 1970.

Epstein, W., Rock, I., & Zuckerman, C. B. Meaning and familiarity in associative learning. *Psychological Monographs,* 1960, **74** (Whole No. 491).

Ernest, C. H., & Paivio, A. Imagery ability in paired-associate and incidental learning. *Psychonomic Science,* 1969, **15,** 181–182.

Ernest, C. H., & Paivio, A. Imagery and verbal associative latencies as a function of imagery ability. *Canadian Journal of Psychology,* 1971, **25,** 83–90.

Fernald, M. R. The diagnosis of mental imagery. *Psychological Monographs,* 1912, **14,** No. 58.

Fraisse, P. Motor and verbal reaction times to words and drawings. *Psychonomic Science,* 1968, **12,** 235–236.

Frincke, G. Word characteristics, associative-relatedness, and the free-recall of nouns. *Journal of Verbal Learning and Verbal Behavior,* 1968, **7,** 366–372.

Gomulicki, B. R. The development and the present status of the trace theory of memory. *British Journal of Psychology Monograph Supplement,* 1953 (Whole No. 29).

Gruber, H. E., Kulkin, A., & Schwartz P. The effect of exposure time on mnemonic processing in paired-associate learning. Paper presented at the Eastern Psychological Association meeting, Atlantic City, 1965.

Gupton, T., & Frincke, G. Imagery, mediation instructions, and noun position in free recall of noun-verb pairs. *Journal of Experimental Psychology,* 1970, **86,** 461–462.

Keppel, G., & Zavortink, B. Further test of the use of images as mediators. *Journal of Experimental Psychology,* 1969, **82,** 190–192.

Kirkpatrick, E. A. An experimental study of memory. *Psychological Review,* 1894, **1,** 602–609.

Köhler, W. *Gestalt psychology.* New York: Liveright, 1929.

Kurtz, K. H., & Hovland, C. I. The effect of verbalization during observation of stimulus objects upon accuracy of recognition and recall. *Journal of Experimental Psychology,* 1953, **45,** 157–164.

Lockhart, R. S. Retrieval asymmetry in the recall of adjectives and nouns. *Journal of Experimental Psychology,* 1969, **79,** 12–17.

Marshall, G. R. The effect of concrete noun and picture mediation on the paired-associate learning of abstract nouns. Paper presented at the Eastern Psychological Association Meeting, Atlantic City, 1965.

Mowrer, O. H. *Learning theory and the symbolic processes.* New York: Wiley, 1960.

Mueller, J. H., & Jablonski, E. M. Instructions, noun imagery, and priority in free recall. *Psychological Reports,* 1970, **27,** 559–566.

Paivio, A. Learning of adjective-noun paired-associates as a function of adjective-noun word order and noun abstractness. *Canadian Journal of Psychology,* 1963, **17,** 370–379.

Paivio, A. Abstractness, imagery, and meaningfulness in paired-associate learning. *Journal of Verbal Learning and Verbal Behavior,* 1965, **4,** 32–38.

Paivio, A. Latency of verbal associations and imagery to noun stimuli as a function of abstractness and generality. *Canadian Journal of Psychology,* 1966, **20,** 378–387.

Paivio, A. A factor-analytic study of word attributes and verbal learning. *Journal of Verbal Learning and Verbal Behavior,* 1968, **7,** 41–49.

Paivio, A. Mental imagery in associative learning and memory. *Psychological Review,* 1969, **76,** 241–263.

Paivio, A. *Imagery and verbal processes.* New York: Holt, 1971.

Paivio, A., & Begg, I. Imagery and associative overlap in short-term memory. *Journal of Experimental Psychology,* 1971, **89**, 40–45.

Paivio, A., & Csapo, K. Concrete-image and verbal memory codes. *Journal of Experimental Psychology,* 1969, **80**, 279–285.

Paivio, A., & Foth, D. Imaginal and verbal mediators and noun concreteness in paired-associate learning: The elusive interaction. *Journal of Verbal Learning and Verbal Behavior,* 1970, **9**, 384–390.

Paivio, A., & Madigan, S. Noun imagery and frequency in paired-associate and free recall learning. *Canadian Journal of Psychology,* 1970, **24**, 353–361.

Paivio, A., & Okovita, H. W. Word imagery modalities and associative learning in blind and sighted subjects. *Journal of Verbal Learning and Verbal Behavior,* 1971, **10**, 506–510.

Paivio, A., & O'Neill, B. J. Visual recognition thresholds and dimensions of word meaning. *Perception and Psychophysics,* 1970, **8**, 273–275.

Paivio, A., & Rowe, E. J. Noun imagery, frequency, and meaningfulness in verbal discrimination. *Journal of Experimental Psychology,* 1970, **85**, 264–269.

Paivio, A., & Rowe, E. J. Intrapair imagery effects in verbal discrimination and incidental paired-associate learning. *Canadian Journal of Psychology,* 1971, in press.

Paivio, A., & Smythe, P. C. Word imagery, frequency, and meaningfulness in short-term memory. *Psychonomic Science,* 1971, **22**, 333–335.

Paivio, A., Smythe, P. C., & Yuille, J. C. Imagery versus meaningfulness of nouns in paired-associate learning. *Canadian Journal of Psychology,* 1968, **22**, 427–441.

Paivio, A., & Yuille, J. C. Mediation instructions and word attributes in paired-associate learning. *Psychonomic Science,* 1967, **8**, 65–66.

Paivio, A., & Yuille, J. C. Changes in associative strategies and paired-associate learning over trials as a function of word imagery and type of learning set. *Journal of Experimental Psychology,* 1969, **79**, 458–463.

Paivio, A., Yuille, J. C., & Madigan, S. Concreteness, imagery, and meaningfulness values for 925 nouns. *Journal of Experimental Psychology,* 1968, **76** (1, Pt. 2).

Paivio, A., Yuille, J. C., & Rogers, T. B. Noun imagery and meaningfulness in free and serial recall. *Journal of Experimental Psychology,* 1969, **79**, 509–514.

Peterson, L. R., & Peterson, M. J. Short-term retention of individual verbal items. *Journal of Experimental Psychology,* 1959, **58**, 193–198.

Philipchalk, R., & Paivio, A. Acquired stimulus imagery and associative learning. Research Bulletin No. 183, Department of Psychology, University of Western Ontario, 1971.

Potter, M. C., & Levy, E. I. Recognition memory for a rapid sequence of pictures. *Journal of Experimental Psychology,* 1969, **81**, 10–15.

Raser, G. A., & Bartz, W. H. Imagery and paired-associate recognition. *Psychonomic Science,* 1968, **12**, 385–386.

Reese, H. W. Imagery in paired-associate learning in children. *Journal of Experimental Child Psychology,* 1965, **2**, 290–296.

Reese, H. W. Imagery and contextual meaning. In H. W. Reese (Chm.), Imagery in children's learning: A symposium. *Psychological Bulletin,* 1970, **73**, 404–414.

Rimm, D. C., Alexander, R. A., & Eiles, R. R. Effects of different mediational instructions and sex of subject on paired-associate learning of concrete nouns. *Psychological Reports,* 1969, **25**, 935–940.

Rogers, T. B. Coding instructions and item concreteness in free recall. Unpublished Master's thesis, University of Western Ontario, 1967.

Rohwer, W. D., Jr. Images and pictures in children's learning: Research results and instructional implications. In H. W. Reese (Chm.), Imagery in children's learning: A symposium. *Psychological Bulletin*, 1970, **73**, 393–403.

Rohwer, W. D., Jr., Lynch, S., Levin, J. R., & Suzuki, N. Pictorial and verbal factors in the efficient learning of paired-associates. *Journal of Educational Psychology*, 1967, **58**, 278–284.

Ross, J., & Lawrence, K. A. Some observations on memory artifice. *Psychonomic Science*, 1968, **13**, 107–108.

Rowe, E. J., & Paivio, A. Effects of imagery and repetition instructions in verbal discrimination learning. Paper presented at the meeting of the Eastern Psychological Association, New York, April, 1971.

Sheehan, P. W. Accuracy and vividness of visual images. *Perceptual and Motor Skills*, 1966, **23**, 391–398.

Sheehan, P. W., & Neisser, U. Some variables affecting the vividness of imagery in recall. *British Journal of Psychology*, 1969, **60**, 71–80.

Sheffield, F. D. Theoretical considerations in the learning of complex sequential tasks from demonstration and practice. In A. A. Lumsdaine (Ed.), *Student response in programmed instruction*. (NAS-NRS Publ. No. 943) Washington, D.C.: National Academy of Sciences–National Research Council, 1961.

Simpson, H. M., & Paivio, A. Effects on pupil size of manual and verbal indicators of cognitive task fulfillment. *Perception and Psychophysics*, 1968, **3**, 185–190.

Skinner, B. F. *Science and human behavior*. New York: Macmillan, 1953.

Sperling, G. A model for visual memory tasks. *Human Factors*, 1963, **5**, 19–31.

Staats, A. W. Verbal habit families, concepts, and the operant conditioning of word classes. *Psychological Review*, 1961, **68**, 190–204.

Taylor, A. M., & Black, H. B. Variables affecting imagery instruction in children. *Research Monograph No. 6*. Audio-Visual Center, Indiana University, April, 1969.

Taylor, A. M., Josberger, M., & Prentice, J. L. Imagery organization and children's recall. Paper presented at the American Educational Research Association Convention, Minneapolis, March, 1970.

Tulving, E. Subjective organization in free recall of "unrelated" words. *Psychological Review*, 1962, **69**, 344–354.

Tulving, E., McNulty, J. A., & Ozier, M. Vividness of words and learning to learn in free-recall learning. *Canadian Journal of Psychology*, 1965, **19**, 242–252.

Wickelgren, W. A. Acoustic similarity and intrusion errors in short-term memory. *Journal of Experimental Psychology*, 1965, **70**, 102–108.

Wickelgren, W. A. Multitrace strength theory. In D. A. Norman (Ed.), *Models of human memory*. New York: Academic Press, 1970. Pp. 65–102.

Wickens, D. D., & Engle, R. W. Imagery and abstractness in short-term memory. *Journal of Experimental Psychology*, 1970, **84**, 268–272.

Wicker, F. W. On the locus of picture-word differences in paired-associate learning. *Journal of Verbal Learning and Verbal Behavior*, 1970, **9**, 52–57.

Wilgosh, L. R. Interaction between pictures and their labels in the memory of four-year-old children. Unpublished doctoral dissertation, McMaster University, 1970.

Winograd, E., Karchmer, M. A., & Russell, I. S. Role of encoding unitization in cued recognition memory. *Journal of Verbal Learning and Verbal Behavior*, 1971, in press.

Wirtz, J., & Anisfeld, M. Imagery, synonymity, antonymy, and false recognition of phrases. Unpublished manuscript, Yeshiva University, 1970.

Wollen, K. A. Variables that determine the effectiveness of picture mediators in paired-associate learning. Paper presented at the meeting of the Psychonomic Society, St. Louis, November, 1969.

Wood, G. Mnemonic systems in recall. *Journal of Educational Psychology Monographs*, 1967, **58** (6, Pt. 2).

Yarmey, A. D., & O'Neill, B. J. S-R and R-S paired-associate learning as a function of concreteness, imagery, specificity, and association value. *Journal of Psychology*, 1969, **71**, 95–109.

Yarmey, A. D., & Ure, G. Incidental learning, noun imagery-concreteness and direction of associations in paired-associate learning. *Canadian Journal of Psychology*, 1971, **25**, 91–102.

Yuille, J. C. Effects of noun imagery and meaningfulness on latencies of mediators and on learning. Unpublished Master's thesis, University of Western Ontario, 1965.

Yuille, J. C. Reported mediation, noun imagery, and delay in paired-associate learning. Unpublished manuscript, University of British Columbia, 1971.

Yuille, J. C., & Humphreys, M. S. Free recall and forward and backward recall of paired-associates as a function of noun concreteness. Paper presented at the meeting of the Canadian Psychological Association Winnipeg, May, 1970.

Yuille, J. C., & Paivio, A. Latency of imaginal and verbal mediators as a function of stimulus and response concreteness-imagery. *Journal of Experimental Psychology*, 1967, **75**, 540–544.

12

MARDI J. HOROWITZ[1]

IMAGE FORMATION:
CLINICAL OBSERVATIONS
AND A COGNITIVE MODEL

Much current imagery research consists of experimental investigation of the use of images in perception, information processing, and memory using largely normal subjects and a variety of ingenious and diverse methods. As a complement to the data from such studies, clinical observations may provide useful criteria for a cognitive model of image formation. The task of this chapter is to review these criteria and offer a conceptual model that seems to meet them. Since I have reviewed much of the relevant literature elsewhere (Horowitz, 1970), and intend to allow for a certain amount of speculation, I will take the liberty of referring to my own clinical research and experience. In doing so I must indicate that the observations to be made are not original but rather a part of dynamic psychiatry and clinical psychology. My sole purpose is to marshal certain observations about image experiences in summary form and see what they suggest about the process of image formation. In a sense, my concern is more theoretical than empirical.

[1] Research Psychiatrist and Assistant Chief, Department of Psychiatry, Mount Zion Medical Center and Associate Clinical Professor of Psychiatry, University of California School of Medicine. The research upon which this chapter is based was supported by grants from the United States Public Health Service through the National Institute of Mental Health (Research Scientist Development Award, K2-MH-22,573 and Research Grant MH-17,373). The author thanks Stephanie S. Becker and Marilyn Jones for important help throughout this research and in preparation of this chapter.

Framework for a
Cognitive Model

Definitions

Because of the multiple use of important terms, I shall begin with how I will use the words *image, image formation*, and *image encoding*. I shall use the word "image" to mean a representation of information that has a sensory quality when that representation is consciously experienced. For precise terminology the image quality must be designated—for example, one should refer to a visual, auditory, or olfactory image. In what follows, however, I shall refer to visual images when using the term "image" unless otherwise specified. While a person can describe image experiences, he usually is unaware of all the underlying processes or motives which may lead to "image formation." A person describes an image by reporting on the contents and form of a particular representation. Describing image formation, however, involves explaining how, when, and why the image was formed, a process description that accounts for more than subjective experience.

I will employ in this chapter a third term, "image encoding" to clarify and separate the issues of subjective experience and retention. By image encoding I mean a coded form of an image, a form which could reproduce that image if activated but which need not be in the same units or organizations as the image. As an external example, if a face on the television screen is analogous to an "image," the inch of recorded magnetic tape which can reproduce that face on replay is an "image encoding." Thus, "images" and "image encodings" are both representations of information and "image formation" is the *process* through which representation, encoding, and experiencing of images takes place.

Approach Strategy

What are the boundaries and central concerns of a cognitive model of image formation? It is easier to begin by saying what it is not. First, a cognitive model of image formation will not consist merely of a categorical system for classifying the wide variety of subjective image experiences, although such a model would facilitate development of a rational classification. Second, a cognitive model will not be a neurophysiologic model of what anatomical structures and electrochemical changes are essential to subjective image experience, although a cognitive model should be consistent with neurobiological possibilities. Instead, a cognitive model of image formation will consider the stages involved in the transmission, transformation, and expression of information about external reality and internal ideas and feelings. A central concern will be the regulation of flow of information within a system of sequentially or simultaneously organized processes.

Cognitive processes are not ordinarily part of subjective experiences and hence are approached largely by inferences based on outcomes or products. Inferences about cognitive processes can be most optimally based on observations of relevant experiences. Normal experiences are not necessarily the experiences of highest relevance because they are outcomes of blended, integrated, overlapping, and well synthesized cognitive functions. Instead, the most relevant experiences might be those products that occur when the underlying cognitive processes are in a state of stress or strain, when regulatory functions are less likely to be smooth and harmonious. Following this line of reasoning, I have selected to study image experiences associated with a subjective sense of loss of control. This decision is supported by the fact that such experiences are key problems in both clinical research on psychopathological forms of imagery, and clinical research on psychopathological forms of response to stress. This strategy is traditional in clinical medical research: in deviation from normal function we often see a fragmentation of processes that are otherwise so synthesized that delineation of parts or sequential operations is difficult. Thus, study of the cleavage points and forms of fragmentation may reveal processes involved in normal as well as abnormal functioning.

In reporting the results of this approach, I find it useful to break the material down in terms of two issues, even though any clinical syndrome will contain elements relevant to both points of view (and others as well). One issue concerns the formal properties of images, especially their intensity and the problem of differentiation of fantasy and perception. Failures in this differentiation are commonly called a loss of reality testing. The person may not only experience a fantasy image as intensely as if it were a perception, he may experience as well a subjective sense that both perception and fantasy have escaped his volitional control: that fantasy has intruded on the assessment and appraisal of external reality.

The second issue concerns the loss of control over what contents are depicted in image form. In discussing this, I will use the term "unbidden images" to designate episodes in which images appear in conscious awareness that are subjectively experienced as intrusions. This term focuses on the subjective sense of loss of volitional control over contents and can thus be used to refer to imagery along various dimensions of intensity—to hallucinations and pseudohallucinations as well as to thought images, to images of memory or fantasy as well as illusions, and to wakeful images as well as hypnagogic or dream images.[2] The study of unbidden images is especially relevant to a model of psychological regulation of image formation since clinical experience suggests that, whatever the cause of increased image formation or the increased intensity of subjective experience, the image contents have psychodynamic determinants. That is, even though hallucinatory states may be evoked by neurophysiologic or environmental factors such as drugs, dreaming sleep, sensory deprivation, intoxications, vascular accidents, tumors or brain stimulation, the contents of the hallucinations will relate to the motives and recent experiences of the person (Horowitz, Adams, & Rutkin, 1968).

Loss of Control over
Intensity of Images

I have reviewed and summarized elsewhere (Horowitz, 1970) evidence for two types of subjective loss of control over the intensity of images. In one type, the person experiences exceedingly intense images and is unable to avoid or dispel these experiences. In the other type of loss of control the person is unable to form images that he subjectively wishes to have. Sometimes both types of lessened control blend together: there is excessive intensity of some images and inadequate intensitv of others.

Excessive Intensity

Subjective experiences in which images become more intense than a person consciously desires include images containing immediate information from both external and internal sources. For example, perception of horrible external events may be accompanied by a subjective sense of nonvolitional fascination, reflected in such typical statements as, "I couldn't take my eyes off it" and in behavioral situations where it is necessary to literally pull a person away from looking at a disturbing scene that is overwhelming

---

[2] Gordon (1949, 1950, see also Chapter 3, this volume) uses the term "autonomous imagery" to delineate the same concept. I avoid her term only because it might be confused with the concept of ego autonomy in psychoanalytic theory.

him. We are more familiar, however, with episodes which involve excessive vividness of images representing information of immediate internal origin. There are several types of such imagery phenomena (see Chapter 2, this volume) of which hallucinations and pseudohallucinations are the most striking.

In hallucinations, images that represent information of internal origin rival perceptions in intensity and the person experiences the images as if they represented reality. The progressive development of hallucinatory episodes can be traced in clinical research by comparing reports of subjective experience at different times. Two common sequences can be abstracted from such reports. In one progression into hallucinations, the person first experiences certain memory or fantasy images as unusually vivid and peremptory although his sense of what is external (i.e., perception) and what is internal (i.e., thought) is unimpaired. Next, some of the fantasy or memory images seem quasi-real in subjective experience and the person uses checking maneuvers to stabilize his sense of reality. These maneuvers include changes in perception (looking "harder," closing the eyes, looking away) and in thought (trying to suppress the image, trying to think of something else, evaluating the probability of such events being real). In the next stage, the thought images may resemble perceptual images in experienced intensity but the person still labels them as nonperceptual by applying a cognitive counter such as "I know it can't be so," "I'm only dreaming or hallucinating." In the most advanced stage of hallucination, the person regards or reacts to the intense images of internal origin as if they were real.

A second type of progressive loss of differentiation between external and internal sources of information begins with an alteration of perceptual images rather than intensification of fantasy or memory images. The initial stage may be blurring, graying, bending, halo effects, shimmering, seeing reduplication of forms, or other types of perceptual distortion. Next, vivid entoptic images may be experienced subjectively including spots, flashes, elaborate patterns, and "hallucinatory constants" (Klüver, 1942). Finally, pseudohallucinations or hallucinations may be elaborated out of these basic forms (Horowitz, 1964; Jackson, 1932). This type of loss of differentiation of source of information is noted in the onset of psychotic or toxic hallucinations, in the progression of imagery experience with LSD, and in experimental evocation of imagery experiences by electrical stimulation of the human brain (Horowitz, Adams, & Rutkin, 1968; Penfield & Rasmussen, 1950). This particular kind of loss of differentiation is also noted in the development of idiosyncratic illusions, that is, those that are not consensually validated as are geometric or figural illusions. Such illusions occur more frequently with increases in wishful and fearful expectancy, with fatigue, and with decrease in clarity of the externally available perceptual field. Indeed, the elaboration of an entoptic image, such as wiggly lines into a vision of "terrible snakes," is a special form of illusion.

Both types of hallucinatory progression, and the clinical phenomenology of illusions, indicate that images based on internal information can gain the same subjective status and intensity as images based on external information. These observations suggest also that any image experience can be composed of information from external and internal sources. Any model of image formation should account for this and should include a description of operations that lead to a subjective sense of "knowing" the source of the information. The model would have to explain ordinary ("normal") functioning in which there is correct (consensually validated) differentiation between external reality and thought reality and out-of-the-ordinary ("abnormal") functioning in which this differentiation is lost. This criterion indicates that a model should posit a dual input of information into a common image-formation process or, in other words, overlapping channels for processing external and internal information. This criterion has long been noted by investigators of clinical phenomena (Arlow, 1969; Freud, 1900) and has also been indicated by recent experimental work (Antrobus & Singer, 1970; Neisser, 1967; Segal, 1968a,b, 1970; West, 1962).

Inadequate Intensity

As mentioned, loss of control over intensity includes the inability to form images of sufficient subjective intensity. This inability may involve perceptual images, as in hysterical blindness or scotomata (blind spots). Hysterical scotomata may involve a given portion of the visual field or may be object specific, as in blindness for certain persons or parts of persons such as for the area of sexual organs. The specificity that occurs in such symptoms indicates that the subjective properties of the incoming stimulus information modify the processing of that information prior to the subjective experience of perceptual images. Inability to generate images of sufficient intensity may also involve memory or fantasy functions. Clinically, some persons are unable to form certain consciously desired memory images, such as the face of a person, although other visual images are easily formed. Psychotherapeutic investigation often uncovers conflicted motives about the perceptions, memories, or fantasies that are volitionally but unsuccessfully attempted. Such observations suggest that any model of image formation should include operations in which motives can affect the regulation of both internal and external inputs of information.

Loss of Control over
Image Contents

While a variety of unbidden image experiences occurs in everyday life, I selected to study unbidden images as a major complaint in psychiatric patients, patients who reported recurrent intrusions of the same image contents. By providing a repeated event for study, this tactic increased the likelihood of discovery of the meanings and implications of the content and the dynamic function of image formation. The methods and detailed results of such clinical research are reported elsewhere (Horowitz, 1970). Here, I shall present only brief vignettes and a summary of explanatory principles.

Recurrent unbidden images may occur in various diagnostic categories. For example, I have encountered such symptoms in patients with both hysterical and obsessive-compulsive neurosis, and with various forms of psychosis including schizophrenia, depression, and hysterical psychosis, as well as organic brain syndromes. Recurrent unbidden images may, indeed, be more closely related to cognitive and experiential contexts than to the standard psychiatric diagnostic categories. For example, perceptual involvement in a stress event appears to be one important precursor or context for syndromes of recurrent unbidden images as illustrated in the following vignette.

Example 1

John,[3] a veteran of the Vietnamese war, complained of recurrent frightening and unbidden images of a face contorted by pain. The images were much more intense than his ordinary thought images, but he knew they were not real even during the image experience. He could not prevent formation of the images nor dispel them, once formed, from his conscious experience. The face was that of a Vietnamese woman he had killed during a night patrol. The patrol had been fired upon earlier and John was feeling extremely fearful when he saw, dimly, a moving figure at close range. He fired a burst with his automatic rifle and struck his target. A flare, fired later, illuminated the prostrate figure. It was a woman, dying from extreme abdominal wounds. The recurrent image represented her pain-contorted face as she struggled vainly to crawl away.

The unbidden image recalled a perception, registered during a period of intense fear, that depicted a terrible scene. The repetition of trauma

[3] Names and some details are changed in this example and those to follow.

as intense, unbidden images is clinically well known and Freud (1920) was sufficiently impressed by this phenomenon to attribute it to an instinctual compulsion to repeat trauma. In uncomplicated situations, unbidden images after stress are experienced less and less with time. This tendency towards gradual reduction in frequency, intensity, and peremptory quality has significant exceptions, however. Extraordinarily traumatic perceptions, such as those of concentration camp survivors, may persist for decades even after a free period of several years duration (Niederland, 1968). Also, associated emotional conflict may perpetuate the tendency to compulsive repetitions as unbidden images. For example, John had been forced by circumstances to be involved in an act that he considered horrible. But he and his buddies had committed such acts as killing men and women before, they had rationalized more stressful episodes with such concepts as "they're all gooks," "it's them or us," "the kids and women'll shoot you too."

Ordinarily, even a terrible sight, such as seeing the woman die, would have faded gradually in intensity of imagery and in recurrent awareness. But the episode had been associated with another sensation and memory which John found more unacceptable than killing in combat and which he avoided remembering and communicating for some time. While watching the woman writhe in pain, and her efforts to escape, he felt sexually aroused (a feeling reported occasionally by other combatants such as fighter pilots). While having a sense of confusion as to the rightness of the war, he felt that he had to kill because of his role as soldier and the context of danger to himself and his friends. But to be aroused sexually by looking at a woman he had shot was especially horrible to him and he felt intense guilt. Probably because of this aroused conflict between sexualized aggression and guilt (which had prior determinants) he was less able to work through the painful memories and fantasies.

Unbidden Images as a Cognitive Response to Stressful Perceptions

As illustrated above, recurrent unbidden images may follow stressful perceptions. That is, in persons complaining of recurrent images, there is a high likelihood that the image contents will be derived from prior stressful perceptions. Also, in persons exposed to stressful perceptions, there is a tendency to subsequent episodes of intrusive and repetitive thought.

This clinical hypothesis has been confirmed in a series of experimental studies (Horowitz, 1969a, 1970; Horowitz & Becker, 1971a,b,c, 1972). The results indicate that intrusive and repetitive thinking is a more general response to stress than heretofore realized. Such repetitions in content, and unusual vividness and intrusiveness of subjective experiences, apparently occur after mild to moderate stresses as well as "psychic traumas," and in persons without psychiatric illness.

When the stress itself, and associations to the stress, are worked through (either with time or with the adjunct of psychotherapy) then the images of the event lose their peremptory and intensive quality. Thus, a model of image formation should explain why stress related images may tend to persist and return to awareness episodically over extended periods of time with unusual intensity and an intrusive quality. Also, the model should explain cessation of such phenomena.

The foregoing observation of recurrent unbidden images after highly stressful *external* events can be supplemented with observation of a similar phenomenon after highly stressful *internal* events. That is, the information, represented in the image that is later repeated, may be derived from immediately internal sources. For example, a fantasy or a nightmare may act as a stress event and return to awareness again and again in a peremptory manner. I have suggested that certain flashbacks may follow this pattern (Horowitz, 1969b).

Flashbacks, as follow from the use of LSD for example, may include spontaneous return of perceptual distortions or increased awareness of mental imagery (Freedman, 1968). But here I refer only to recurrent unbidden images as a relatively less common subcategory of flashbacks. These recurrent images repeat a hallucinatory image that the person recalls experiencing first during the drug-induced hallucinatory episode, as in the following example.

Example 2

    Ted was a 16 year old who had enjoyed his first nine LSD trips. His tenth trip was "bad." He recalled the worst moments when he had an hallucinatory image of himself drowning by being sucked into the vortex of a whirlpool. After a three week symptom-free period, not on drugs, he experienced intrusive repetitions of the same image. The experience was a vivid one but less than hallucinatory in intensity and sense of reality. Fear accompanied each image experience. Partly this was a fear of dying, partly it was a fear he was losing his mind. It appeared that the image condensed and symbolized several themes that he was concerned with but also avoided thinking clearly about: his fear of being smothered by others if he related closely to them, despair after being kicked out of a communelike situation because of uncooperative behavior, apprehension that he was being "sucked-down" by reliance on drugs. The flashbacks subsided during a period of brief psychotherapy which dealt with these issues that he had avoided conceptualizing in clear form.

As in the illustration on page 289, during the hallucinatory episode there may be emergence of extremely frightening memories and fantasies, of ideas, impulses, and fears ordinarily repressed from conscious thought. These frightening images may then tend to be repeated compulsively, as is observed following perception of stressful external events. Thus, as suggested in the foregoing section, compulsive repetitions also may follow stressful images of either internal or external origin.

These observations suggest additional criteria for a model of image formation. The model should account for how percept-related images of unusual intensity may be stored for long period after termination of the event, far longer than the ordinary storage of short-term or iconic memory. The model should account for episodic and nonvolitional entries of such images into awareness, and it should also account for termination of such unbidden images with resolution of attendant conceptual and emotional conflicts.

Other criteria for a model are suggested by further evidence from clinical research on recurrent unbidden images. Of great importance, while the contents of unbidden images may be derived from stressful events once perceived, the image-formation process need not be the result of the kind of "compulsive repetitiveness" described above. Sometimes the image-formation process may serve other motives such as the need to provide a screen to express, partially, yet conceal partially, warded-off ideas and feelings (Glover, 1929; Malev, 1969, Reider, 1960) or to activate a sense of impending danger and hence motivate defensive readiness (Murphy, 1961; Schur, 1953). The following vignettes from clinical research on patients with syndromes of recurrent unbidden images illustrate such psychodynamics.

Example 3

Isabel required psychiatric hospitalization for a syndrome of hallucinations, extraordinary agitation, and cognitive confusion. She had recurrent images of the face of an old man either dead or screaming angrily at her. The intensity of these images as well as her state of consciousness and appraisals of reality varied so that the images, while identical in content, might be labeled at different times as hallucinations, pseudohallucinations, illusions (seeing real persons as the old man), hypnagogic visions, or nightmares. In each instance she regarded the images as a kind of haunting accusation and responded with intense guilt and fear.

The old man had been seen in previous stressful situations as she now experienced him in subjective images. He had screamed angrily at her, "You are trying to kill me!" and somewhat later she had discovered him dead in his bed. But the images were not simply a return of these stressful perceptions.

Not only had a year elapsed since his death,[4] but other emotional dangers precipitated the onset of the recurrent images. These dangers centered around the threat of strong aggressive impulses towards her children.

To condense considerably an explanation of the psychodynamics, Isabel was currently involved in a highly frustrating relationship with a daughter and she had terrifyingly strong impulses to hurt her physically. The images of the old man, while stressful in and of themselves, were intrinsically linked with the dangerous rage and impulse to hurt her daughter. The image formation had two defensive functions. Instead of excessive rage, the dreaded emotional state, the experience of the images activated intense guilt and fear.[5] Also, the image formation reversed the interpersonal role structure of the dreaded ideas. Instead of depicting the most dangerous situation—herself as the aggressor and her daughter as victim—the image encoding depicts the old man as the aggressor who haunts her, and she as the victim. Of interest, this interpersonal role structure in which she is fearful and guilty, and another person is angry and violent relates to traumatic childhood memories of her mother beating her for minor misdeeds. Her own rage, poor control, identification with her mother, and desire for revenge contributed to her current dangerous impulses to injure her daughter. The recurrent image synthesized defensive and expressive motives. The images expressed the concept of one angry and potentially hurtful person but it avoided designating that person as her: it is not her, but the old man. This transformation allowed a fearful emotional response to the images and this fearful state protected her, somewhat, from experiencing an out-of-control rage. The images also served to motivate self-control, she warned herself that someone may be killed or hurt. Also, the images mitigated the demands of conscience; she punished herself in advance by hurting herself with the images, by remembering how guilty she felt when the old man died. Finally, from a social interaction standpoint, she developed a symptom that removed her from dangerous proximity to her daughter to the comparative safety (and dependency) of a hospital ward.

[4] Symptom-free intervals not uncommonly precede development of compulsive cognitive repetitions of traumatic events so this alone would not contraindicate such an explanation.

[5] As pointed out by Jones (1929) fear, guilt, and hate stand in relation to each other in that generation of one can reduce the experience of another. A person in a given interpersonal situation may make himself angry to avoid feeling guilty, or may generate guilty feelings to avoid experiencing anger. I am suggesting that selective image formation is the operation through which some persons accomplish such transformations in affective states. The details of such transformation and much more clinical evidence are provided elsewhere (Horowitz, 1970).

While the psychodynamics cannot be fully elucidated in so short a space, the above example illustrates the frequent clinical observation that unbidden images conceal as well as express ideas and feelings. For instance, patients in psychoanalytic treatment may report vivid intrusive images during the course of free associations. While these images contain meaningful contents, the shift in thought to exclusively visual representation often occurs as a resistance to further emergence and expression of ideas and feelings in words. And, in such circumstances, the experience of the images may serve to activate defensive affects. A patient attempting unconsciously to ward off anger at the analyst may develop an anxiety-provoking image representing punishment just as Isabel used the old man image to provoke guilt and avoid experiencing the arousal of rage.

This type of observation indicates that image formation may be used to generate emotion, as well as to respond to or to express emotion. Also, one constellation of encoded images can be facilitated to inhibit awareness of another set of encoded images (or other forms of encoded information). Thus, the subjective properties of encoded images apparently can motivate regulation of image formation even before images are consciously experienced. Another case example will illustrate this issue further.

Example 4

> Shortly after bearing a child, Mary attempted suicide and required psychiatric hospitalization because of extreme withdrawal punctuated with temper tantrums, cognitive confusion, and recurrent unbidden images. Two varieties of images occurred in separable clinical phases. In the first set she experienced "earthquakes," her label for an experience consisting of feelings of catastrophic fear, sensations of shaking movements, and images of the ceiling falling in, her head being crushed, or her abdomen as hollow or defective. A second set of images emerged in a later phase of her hospital course. The contents involved visualizing herself with guns, knives, or bombs. She used these weapons to destroy the abdomen of other people or to blow up their buildings or cars. These aggressive images were not as peremptory as the "earthquakes," while she regarded the image formation in a passive way she also said she enjoyed the images in "a smirky, evil way."
>
> The two sets of images occurred during separate clinical phases, either one or the other predominating—they did not coincide. There were also intermittent symptom-free phases.

As in the previous example of Isabel, the unbidden images have a covert but basic role structure consisting of a victim, an aggressor, and an aggressive action or injured state. Mary could alter her identification with either role by shifting the images she experienced. In her dilemma she felt hurt and emptied—victimized by others; she also felt enraged and wanted revenge. Her thought was dominated by these themes and her strong emotional responses to them threatened to become overwhelming. She responded to this affective threat (an internal source of stress) by unconscious defensive processes in which there was a splitting of the ideational-emotional complex into separate components. Relative facilitation of one component aided in suppressing the second component. Thus, when an external or internal stimulus tended to trigger a train of thought evocative of an excessively unpleasant affective state, encoded images evocative or supportive of an alternative set of thoughts and feelings could be activated. For example, if she were in danger of viewing herself as cruel and mean because she was not caring for her baby, she could form the earthquake images in which she viewed herself as dependent victim. On the other hand, if she were in danger of feeling excessive despair because she was deserted by the father of the child, by her parents, and by the baby (she was yielding it for adoption), she could form the shooting and exploding images and feel like the active aggressor.

Although Mary had both sets of motives, she did not form the aggressive images when she was in danger of feeling most aggressive but, rather, when she was in danger of feeling most injured. In injury, she needed a compensatory or defensive maneuver to avoid feeling passive despair and helplessness. The aggressive images expressed valid ideas and feelings, but they also served defensive motives and allowed regulation of her affective state. Because she wished to ward off this entire complex of mental contents, there were efforts at suppression and repression of any representation of relevant ideas and feelings. But the unfinished emotional issues, revolving associatively around the childbirth and adoption, were problems pressing for solution. Although partially defended against by the additional unconscious defensive operations of splitting, reversal, and denial, some of the ideas and feelings emerged.

Because of the association of the emergent ideas with the complex of ideas and feelings warded off through defensive maneuvers, the subjective experience of the images had an intrusive quality. This intrusive quality, the subjective sense of loss of control over image formation, could be attributed to a combination of factors. First, there was a strong tendency to express ideas related to an uncompleted and important life crisis. Until the crisis was worked through, related ideas tended towards expression. Second, expression of the ideas would evoke extremely unpleasant affective states and this subjective property of the ideas led them to be experienced as unwelcome, and motivated defensive avoidance of their expression. Third, episodic expression (albeit partial expression only), in spite of defensive operations, was subjectively experienced as a loss of control. In addition, a specific defensive avoidance—nontranslation of image meanings into word meanings—lent the images a mysterious or ego-alien quality that also contributed to the sense of their intrusiveness.[6]

In the above clinical vignettes, psychodynamics were compressed into incomplete summary statements. These vignettes are sufficient, however, to illustrate how image formation is affected by impulsive and defensive aims. The first important point is that even unbidden images, those not controlled by conscious choices, are the result of nonconscious constructive processes involving control and regulation of both the form and content of the emergent experience. The second important point is that image-formation processes have a transactional relationship with emotions. The immediate emotional state influences image formation, is reflected in image forms and contents (directly or indirectly), and is influenced by the image experience. This latter factor, the modification of emotional state by image experience, means that emotional learning may take place. That is, images that tend to "successfully" transform emotional states (reduce displeasure, increase pleasure, or modulate tension within desirable limits) will tend to be repeated. This association of image with emotional effect can be conditionally learned, and the repetition may occur without any necessary conscious association between the images and the modifications of emotion or tension levels.

To conclude, these clinical observations and inferences suggest that any model should account for nonconscious as well as conscious influences on image formation as a way of processing ideas and affective states. The model should allow for operation of a variety of nonconscious defensive maneuvers and should account for episodic emergences of unbidden images into consciousness in spite of unconscious defenses or conscious control efforts.

List of Criteria for a
Model of Image Formation

Clinical observations and inferences based on syndromes of loss of control over intensity of image experiences and over content of image experi-

---

[6] Of interest, this resistance to translation into word meanings retards the assimilation of and accommodation to the life crisis. Inhibition of translation into words thus preserved the tendency to repetition of ideas as images. As recently reexamined by Klein (1967), repression preserves ideas and, paradoxically, increases the likelihood of peremptory ideation.

ences have been summarized above. The criteria for a model of image formation developed in the text above will now be listed, and then a model meeting these criteria will be described.

1. The first set of criteria are obtained largely from consideration of loss of control over intensity, the second from loss of control over content.

(a) The subjectively experienced image may encode information derived from both immediately external and immediately internal sources.

(i) The sources of information can often be subjectively discriminated correctly.

(ii) The sources of information may at times be incorrectly or incompletely differentiated. Immediately internal information may be subjectively experienced as if it were external information and sometimes a perception can be appraised incorrectly and be experienced as if it were a fantasy. A model should explain how internal and external information can be blended, as well as how internal or external sources may be correctly or incorrectly discriminated.

(b) Attitudes towards the meaning and implication of information influences the sampling and processing of that information (whether or not the information is available from immediately external or internal sources). In other words, a model of image formation should include a way in which the emotional and ideational implications of information might affect the processing of that information.

2. Images related to a stressful event (of internal or external origin) may be stored for long periods after the event and repeatedly return to awareness with unusual intensity and a subjective experience of intrusiveness.

(a) The storage and compulsive-repetition period is longer than that usually considered for short term or iconic memory in ordinary circumstances.

(b) The repetitiousness, intrusive quality, and unusual intensity can at times be reduced with working through of the conceptual and emotional implications of the images.

(c) Nonconscious defensive operations influence the form and content of subjectively experienced images.

(d) There is a complex relationship between image formation, images, and affect. Images are not formed simply in response to emotions; they do not merely express or discharge emotions or drive derivatives; and emotions are not simply responses to imagery experiences. Image contents, and the processes of image formation, are influenced by affective states and the imagery experiences in turn influence affective states. Emotions act as *motives* for the image formation. Emotions are *ex-*

pressed in the imagery experience. And images evoke emotional *responses.*

A Conceptual Model of
Image Formation

A model to meet the criteria suggested by clinical observation could be developed from multiple points of view. Here, I shall consider only an information processing point of view and discuss three topics: (a) the use of the image as a mode of representation of information; (b) the construction of an image from immediately external and immediately internal sources of information; and (c) the processing of an image after it is constructed and experienced. Modeling the patterns for information processing through image formation, under these three topics, is analogous to formulating the program by which a computer is steered in its information processing task. This viewpoint of cognitive processes follows the theoretical lead of Miller, Galanter, and Pribram (1960), and the examples of Klein (1967) for ideational processes and Neisser (1967) for perceptual processes. This model is not, to my knowledge, incompatible with current neurophysiologic models.[7]

[7] As suggested by Sperry (1969, 1970), neurophysiologic processes, cognitive processes, and subjective phenomena such as images can be considered within a "holistic system," one in which conscious experience emerges out of certain neurophysiological processes *and also* one in which conscious experiences play a causal role in organizing and regulating the neural activity.

Sperry refers to a command hierarchy of causal controls in this holistic system, one in which there are forces within forces extending from the level of atoms and molecules through the levels of neurons and nerve circuits, cerebral processes, and finally conscious phenomena. He uses a wheel rolling downhill as a simple example: the displacement in time and space—and the ultimate fate—of components from atoms to the spokes, rim, and hub are determined by the holistic properties of the wheel as a unit: its shape, size, weight and so forth in relation to the relevant environment. Similarly, Sperry suggests that a subjective experience such as a visual image possesses holistic properties which may influence the component processes of image formation. That is, the subjective properties of an image will influence the formation, sensation, storage or retrieval of that image through such control operations as facilitation, inhibition, and perseveration. These control operations could be described at any level from the "highest" order or function (those involved potentially with conscious experience) to the "lower" orders of function (the basic electrochemical and neurophysiologic changes). My model will involve only the "higher" order regulatory functions and the subjective properties of images that influence the direction and force of these regulatory functions.

The Use of the Image as a Mode of
Representation of Information

So far this chapter has concentrated on the nature and psychodynamic importance of image contents, and the immediate sources of information contained in an image. However, image *contents*—the theme and sequence of describable events—can be conceptually separated from the mode of *representing* those contents of thought (e.g., in the visual or auditory or lexical modes). Thus, we arrive at a larger, more basic issue: why is certain thought content represented in images and not in other modes of representation? This separation of content and mode is made strictly for purposes of analysis. In natural circumstances, the "mode of thought" and "thought content" interact in time according to the motives for thought representation at any given moment.

If the goal is to simply sample external stimuli, it is probably most efficient to retain perceptual images derived from the modality similar to the stimulus configuration. Information embodied in light waves will be optimally sampled by vision, in sound waves by hearing. Thus the use of image formation to form perceptual images is often guided by the immediate perceptual quality of the orignal external stimuli, and the same is often true of memory images. Sometimes, however, the mode of representation is not guided by the nature of the immediately available external stimuli. For example, the form of thought representation may also be influenced by the organization of a person's representational systems: while most people retain sound information simply as auditory images, a few claim that they transform sound into color and retain a synesthetic experience (for discussion of this phenomenon see Chapters 2 and 6, this volume).

Another example of external sources of information not directly determining image formation occurs with fantasies, which may be new constructions whose content and motives are derived from immediately internal sources. Often very complex emotional and cognitive motives operate to influence the mode of representing thought contents. For example, why did Mary experience an image of herself machine-gunning someone rather than simply experiencing a thought in lexical form such as "I'd like to shoot someone?" From an information processing point of view it is insufficient to consider just the sampling of visual stimuli, neurophysiologic capacity, or habitual cognitive styles as affording a full explanation for representational selection. We must consider also the question "why is image formation sometimes selected as the preferred representation of information derived from immediately internal sources?" The chosen mode of thought representation can contribute much information about the *functional psychodynamics* of thought.

We can begin to answer some of these questions by formulating and comparing the available modes for representation of thought.

Image formation has been postulated as one of the earliest forms of cognitive representation, one which is gradually replaced in development with lexical representation (Freud, 1900; Piaget, 1930; Schilder, 1942). More recently, Bruner (1964) has posited three systems for processing information and constructing inner models of the external world: enactive, iconic, and symbolic systems of representation. As suggested by Neisser (1967), a given system such as the visual organizing system can have both iconic and symbolic properties, and I have therefore modified Bruner's terms somewhat.

I hypothesize three interrelated representational systems: enactive thinking, image thinking, and lexical thinking. While described in detail elsewhere (Horowitz, 1970), we could briefly define enactive thinking as "thought through action" using micromovements as well as gross action. Image thinking consists of any quasi-sensory representation; there are different subsystems, each in a sensory organizing system: visual, auditory, tactile, etc. Lexical thinking uses verbal and symbolic representations; here, there is a major reduction in sensory quality so that words are not visualized, "spoken" subvocally, or experienced as auditory images.

Each mode has special areas of effectiveness in organizing information. Visual images are efficient representations of information with spatial or simultaneous characteristics; words are efficient representations for sequential information and specific communicational meanings as well as for expression of logical and abstract relationships. For brevity, samples of the special areas of effectiveness for each system are indicated schematically in Table 1.

Each system of representation has different schemata for organizing the units within the system. Units are assembled into subsets of units according to such schemata. Schemata developed in one system could, of course, be used in another system so that when clear sequential organizations are developed, with acquisition of lexical capacity, it will be possible to use a clearer form of sequential organization in image formation as well.[8] Similarly, organization schemata, developed in preverbal thinking, will be used to organize lexical representation as word meanings are acquired during

---

[8] This "retrospective use" for image representation of an organizational capacity developed during acquisition of lexical representation may account for data such as that of Rohwer (1970) which indicates that children, performing learning tasks, do not profit much from use of images until after they have developed the capacity to profit from use of lexical mediators of information.

TABLE 1
Modes of Thought Representation[a,b]

Mode	Sample of units	Sample of sets of units	Sample of schemata	Sample of relationships of units
Enactive	Anticipatory: movements tensions kinesthesia	Acts Gestures Postures Facial expressions	Direction and force	This does that
Images	Images: tactile gustatory olfactory visual auditory	Signs Body image Fantasies Introjects	Space Volume Simultaneity Signs and signals	This is there This is like that This and that happen together
Lexical	Morphemes	Grammar (phrases, sentences, paragraphs)	Linearity Sequential schemata Syllogisms	First x then y, then z x Leads to y if w but not if not w

[a] The figure starts at a high level of functioning. It could start with smaller units such as particulate sensations for imagery (e.g., geometric forms, colors, and so forth) or with phonemes (units of sound) for lexical constructions.

[b] From M. J. Horowitz (1970); reproduced with permission.

cognitive development. Normal thought will blend all forms of representation and organization but, in abnormal functions such as states of psychologic or physiologic stress, lines of cleavage may be noted.

The efficient representation of spatial information in the visual image mode means that image formation will be especially useful to represent self and object relationships as found in the external world through perception, or as fantasied in the trial perception and trial action of thought. I shall not focus here on the utility of image formation in solving neutral spatial problems, but on the importance of object relationships to the arousal of emotions and the utility of image formation in regulating affective states.

Images interrelate closely with affective states for several reasons. The overlapping channels for processing perceptual information and immediately internal information make it possible for a person to generate an image from memory and yet regard that image "as if" it were perceptual (by a reduction of reflective self-awareness; Schafer, 1968). Also, primitive "preverbal" memories, in addition to traumatic memories at all levels of development, may be recorded in a particularly sensory manner. Recollection of such memories is likely to occur in imagery and to evoke associated affective states. Of great importance, images represent both self and object (e.g., another person) and the relationship between self and object in a simultaneous format. This quality of simultaneity allows condensation of multiple meanings into a single image format. Such condensation permits a wide variety of shifts and transformations in emphasis including symbolizations, reversals, reaction formations, and also shifts in which role, in a bipolar relationship, is regarded as the self (as illustrated in the transformation between active and passive role in the case illustrations). As a result of condensation, symbolization, and displacement the person may not subjectively understand his own image experiences although they may influence his state of emotional arousal.

How can we conceptualize this close relationship between image formation and emotion? Assume for the moment that emotional systems can be separated from representational systems but that the separable systems are intimately interconnected. Activation of any system at any point would constitute "information" and processing this information might follow habitual routes as acquired in cognitive and affective development (Rapaport, 1957). A physiological state might constitute a drive (sexual tension, for example). This emotion-arousing state will influence the regulation of the representational systems. It will influence, for example, what types of information are facilitated, inhibited, and perseverated. This influence of emotional state on thought is what is meant by regarding emotions as motives. In order for feelings to be subjectively experienced, they must be represented in some way. While image formation is not the only way of representing emotion, it is an apt way, for the person with an average cognitive style. Thought, however, is not simply epiphenomenal; it does not float on the surface of emotional or physiological changes. The course of thought influences the emotional states that are influencing thought and are represented in it. This is what is meant by emotions as responses to thought.

In summary, images may be selected as a preferred mode of representation for several reasons. In addition to neurophysiologically determined capacities, and in addition to acquired cognitive styles, image formation may be used because of its special attributes in representing and processing information. It is close to perception and close to affect, and it allows memories to be treated almost as if they were current experiences. Image formation also serves the adaptive function of permitting disguises and shifts of meanings which, if represented in words, might be too difficult to disguise, and might evoke anxiety.

Construction of an Image from Immediately External and
Internal Sources of Information

According to the first set of criteria summarized earlier, a model of image formation would include a dual set of information: (a) a way in which the source of information might be correctly or erroneously differentiated in subjective experience, and (b) a way in which emotional or ideational implications of information might affect the processing of that information.

To meet this first set of criteria we will assume that there is informational input from outside and inside into a "series of matrices" for encoding images. Representation of information on these matrices would be essential for any subjective experience of "an image" to occur but the encodings would not necessarily be a part of conscious awareness. By "a series of matrices" I mean only that there may be multiple formats for duplication and representation of the same information, *not* any particular kind of structure. Each representation of information could be slightly different in emphasis. While information might eventually be encoded on any matrix, certain matrices might be, in effect, oriented more to input from perception, others oriented more to input from memory or fantasy sources of information. In states of relatively high intensity of input, information from one source might gain encoded form on a matrix usually encoding information from the second source. This might lead to failures in differentiation of reality from thought, as suggested by Freud (1900) in his topographic regression model.

The dual inputs, the transitions between matrices, and the matrices would be interrelated with feedback process through which checking, testing, and revisions of information would occur. This feedback would include provisions for matching perception images with schemata and with memory images, and searching for a "best fit" compromise image (see Neisser, 1967, for elaboration of this aspect of a model). It would also interrelate with sensorimotor control systems, especially those involving schemata for eye movements, head position, proprioception, vestibular sensation and other sensory input. Regulatory operations for facilitation, inhibition, perseveration, and so forth would affect the inputs into and between the matrices. These control operations could work in concert or conflict, with greater or less capacity, with discrete or general application.[9]

[9] Such reciprocal control models have been suggested in neurophysiology (Hernandez-Peon, 1964) and in psychoanalytic metapsychology (Gardner, 1969; Holt, 1968).

In ordinary cognition, perceptual images are readily distinguishable from memory or fantasy images, and this differentiation is, as far as subjective experience is concerned, instantaneous and fully automatic (i.e., apparently effortless). But differentiation of information input into an image experience may not be, subjectively, either instantaneous or effortless if one part of the triad of subjective intensity (e.g., vividness) is incongruent with the other two (e.g., localization and/or plausibility). Suppose, in the model, there is a large scale activation of matrices usually oriented towards perceptual input. A very vivid image may be experienced. But if the image is appraised as implausible, and if there is absence of indications that the information had entered from perceptual sources, then the person may wonder if his vivid image represents reality or is a product of thought. He can check the image by modifying regulatory control over the sources of information input. If perception is facilitated (e.g., by "looking harder"), does the image increase in subjective intensity? Does it disappear with closure of the eyes, or with attempts to think of something else? Note that, as checking becomes extended in time, there is a sequential process initiated which involves complex appraisals of the meaning and implications of the image experience.

So far, the model meets the first set of criteria in that it allows a dual input and the possibility of either differentiation, confusion, or fusion of information from both sources. Progressive changes, as in the onset of hallucinosis, might occur with progressive loss of regulatory capacity. For example, as suggested by Jackson (1932), progressive disinhibition or disruption of regulatory controls could allow elementary perceptual information, such as pattern recognition input, to gain too prominent a place in encodings leading to subjective experience of entoptic phenomena or perceptual distortions. Disinhibition of internal input could lead to the fusion of wishful or fearful expectancies with perceptual information resulting in the occurrence of illusions. Wishes and fears, as well as defensive needs, may serve as motives for altering the regulation of one or another source of input. Such inhibition or facilitation could affect an entire function (e.g., perception or recollection) or could affect that function only in processing certain information content (e.g., that related to a particular psychological conflict).

Once an image (or series of images) has been formed through the processes outlined above, the experienced image may require additional information processing as suggested by the second set of criteria. This relatively sequential aspect of a model is considered in what follows. It is reported in greater detail elsewhere in relation to experimental findings (Horowitz & Becker, 1972).

The Processing of an Image after It Is Constructed

We will assume that registration of an image, whatever the composition of input sources, sets in motion a programmatic sequence with a tendency for directional processing to a point of completion. This tendency is an intrinsic property of the sequence, that is, the program has a built in tendency to complete successive steps (Miller, Galanter, & Pribram, 1960). If such a task plan is interrupted, the uncompleted portion remains stored in "working memory" or as encoded images (Mandler, 1964). If we assume further that cognitive processes have a finite capacity, then some types of information (e.g., stressful information) may overload the capacity for rapid information processing. The information of the incompletely processed images will remain in encoded form as a kind of holding operation. The encoded images, when triggered, would lead to reformation of the experienced image.

The sequential aspect of information processing would begin with the formation of the image. The following steps in the sequence would extend interpretation of meaning by association with other visual images, images of other sensory types, and with word meanings. Images at every level of development would be retained as information encodings. Checking, rechecking, and revision would take place between images at the various phases of information processing. This sequential operation seems to be acceptably identical with Neisser's (1967) model of *iconic images* (an early phase of image formation), *symbolic images* (a programmatically later phase), and the checking and rechecking of images coincides with his *analysis by synthesis*.

Once information has been coded at the symbolic level of representation, another sequential step is possible—appraisal of the implications of the information. This appraisal would follow many branching routes of associational connections. These branching routes would include assessment of threat, appraisal of coping alternatives, and reappraisal of threat based on the flow of events and reflection (Lazarus, 1966). As these assessments of the information were completed, another phase of processing would include storage in memory of the new information according to multiple associational categories. During the process of comparing the new information with preexisting expectancies and schemata there would be change in both the information and the preexisting expectancies and schemata. Hence the result might be a revision of the person's world model, his body image, his expectation of future events, or his current action plans—in short, adaptation through assimilation and accommodation (Piaget, 1930).

We can add to this programmatic sequence the "test" portion of the Miller *et al.* (1960) "TOTE" model. This would be an operation that functions according to the question, "Are the above processes completed?" If they are completed, then image encodings would be cleared from the holding operations. But under the types of internally or externally imposed stress conditions described earlier, the processing of information is difficult to complete. If it is uncompleted, the program remains nonterminated, and image encodings remain in the holding operations at the various sequential levels of processing. *Note that, in this model, the erasure of images from encoded form is an active process and that images are retained in the holding operation until this active process is instituted.*

A given topic will have to compete with other topics for the available cognitive capacities. Hence, some system of priorities would be assigned to information encoded at various levels of processing. That is, some higher order program would assess the importance and relative urgency of a topic and regulate the dominance hierarchy of programs. An uncompleted program assigned a relatively low place on the hierarchy would not "vanish," it would retain its tendency to complete. The images would be retained in encoded form until processing could be again resumed. The competition for available cognitive capacities or channels would include the branching programs for appraising a given image, the many different topics encoded as images and requiring image formation, and the programs and capacities for representing and processing information encoded in other modes such as in other systems of imagery (e.g., auditory rather than visual) or in words.

This leads us to the special consideration of images that encode stress-related information. Stress-related information is (by definition of psychological stress) of great subjective importance. But it is also (again by definition of stress) difficult to process. That is, stress-related information is harder to assimilate in terms of all of its associated meanings *and* it is harder to accommodate existing schemata, expectancies, attitudes, and action plans to the stress-related information.

Suppose, then, that processing the stressful information (of internal or external origin) activates ideational or emotional conflicts. Running the program then creates a danger situation because of the possible evocation of such responses as intense fear, anxiety, guilt, shame, despair, or other negative affects. Subjective appraisal of the information—the knowledge that such affects can be generated—causes inhibition of the processing of this information. In other words, defensive motives may lead to alteration of the place of a given program for information processing in a hierarchy of programs and, also, the warded-off information may be inhibited at various phases in the programmatic sequence. Less dangerous programmatic sequences may be facilitated or run over and over again (perseveration) as an avoidance maneuver.

As an example of the consequences of inhibition of information processing, consider a visual image that contains stressful information. Suppose translation of the meanings from image representations to lexical representations is inhibited because the increase in clarity of signification (meaning) leads to evocation of intolerably strong negative affects. The program for processing the visual image is left in an unconsummated state. The tendency to go to the next phase (e.g., translation into words) persists and the image is held in encoded form. If inhibitory capacity wanes, if there is a shift in priorities, or if that information is primed by relevant input, then the encoded image might be reactivated with resumption of attempts to process the information.

Where, in this model, is conscious experience? So far, we have presumed that conscious experience, or at least, that conscious experience which can be recalled, is not essential to processing information. Also, we have presumed that images might be encoded during the holding operation in a form other than that of images in conscious experience. When the incompleted program is reactivated (or disinhibited), then these encoded images might be activated into a form accessible to conscious experience and images containing important information are likely to enter awareness.

It is in this context that stress becomes an especially relevant concept for understanding images experienced as intrusive. Perception is oriented towards adaptation to the environment. Perceptual information, i.e., perceptual images, that imply some potential stress to the organism have a high priority for attention deployment. An animal, for example, will have to interrupt eating behavior if perception of a predator triggers a need for flight or fight. As suggested earlier in the dual input consideration, images representing internal information are processed in a manner similar (in some ways, at least) to the processing of perceptual images. Hence, images representing potentially stressful internal information are also important, by definition, and command a high place on vigilance hierarchies. Reactivation of a program involving such stress-relevant images would lead to a conscious experience and, perhaps, to images of unusual intensity in subjective experience. This tendency for stress-related images to become conscious has an adaptational utility. Stress occurs when automatized ways of processing information are inadequate to resolve a current problem. Through acquisition of conscious status, new forms or routes of information processing can be established and routine attitudes or arrangements can be revised.

Stressful information of internal origin has another subjective property. Since such information would indicate a problem not readily solved (it would not be stressful, otherwise), representation and appraisal would lead to affects such as anxiety, shame, guilt, despair, or a sense of helplessness (Freud, 1926; Lazarus, 1968). Excessive levels of such affects are disorganizing while appropriate levels of such affects may motivate organization of defensive and coping strategies. This is one way in which the regulation of image formation can modulate immediate levels of emotion. Inhibition may be instituted to avoid disorganizing or poorly tolerated levels of affect. On the other hand, facilitation can be used to generate signal affects, such as signal anxiety. Thus, there are motives for both facilitating and inhibiting programs that process stress-related information.

We may thus formulate three sets of forces. The first is the intrinsic property of the program—it tends towards completion. The second and third are motives for and against permitting representation of the information being processed in the program. These motives affect the regulation and control of the rate and direction of information processing along the branching sequences of the program.

By reason of these forces, stress-related images are likely to be difficult to process, and regulation of the processing will be affected by conflicting motives. A stymied program involving stress-related encoded images would be reactivated whenever there was a reduction in inhibitory capacity, whenever a program of higher place in the hierarchy was completed and therefore terminated, or whenever the encoded information was primed by associational connection to other information under active processing. In each instance, a stress-related image would enter conscious experience. The images might seem unrelated to the conscious experience just preceding their entry into awareness, they might evoke an unpleasant affect, they might seem uncanny because of inhibition of translation into word meanings, and they might repeat information associated with suppressive efforts. As a result of these properties, the image experience would be accompanied by a subjective sense of intrusiveness. Because processing would be difficult to complete, the program might be once again inhibited leading to repetitive returns (see also Klein, 1967 on ideomotor cycles that repeat due to inhibition and Singer, 1970, on the assignment of priorities to "unfinished business").

It seems to me that this sequential aspect of a model of image formation meets the criteria required by the second set of clinical observations. The model indicates that relatively intense and incompletely processed images may be retained as encodings for long periods of time after stress events of internal or external origin. It explains how these images will tend toward repetitive and intrusive entry into awareness, and how such syndromes of unbidden images might terminate on completion of the programmatic sequence. The model also formulates how the subjective properties of encoded images affect the regulation of programmatic sequences and how and when images might be subjectively experienced as a loss of control over thought.

The conceptual model put forward in this chapter is stated in general form and is by no means intended to be exhaustive. One might also comment, for instance, on the important issue of individual differences—in styles of encoding and storing information, in assigning priorities, in tolerance for emotion, in capacity for inhibition, facilitation, or perseveration, in appraisal of implications, and so forth. Discussion of the question of individual variations in cognitive style, however, together with other issues are beyond the scope of this chapter.

References

Antrobus, J. S., & Singer, J. L. Mindwandering and cognitive structure. *Transaction of the New York Academy of Sciences,* 1970, **32,** 242–252.

Arlow, J. Unconscious fantasy and disturbances of conscious experience. *Psychoanalytic Quarterly,* 1969, **38,** 1–27.

Bruner, J. S. The course of cognitive growth. *American Psychologist,* 1964, **19,** 1–15.

Freedman, D. X. On the use and abuse of LSD. *Archives of General Psychiatry,* 1968, **18,** 330–347.

Freud, S. (Orig. publ. 1900.) The interpretation of dreams. In J. Strachey and A. Freud (Eds.), *The complete psychological works of Sigmund Freud.* London: Hogarth Press, 1953. Vols. 4–5.

Freud, S. (Orig. publ. 1920). Beyond the pleasure principle. In J. Strachey and A. Freud (Eds.), *The complete psychological works of Sigmund Freud.* London: Hogarth Press, 1953. Vol. 18, Pp. 7–64.

Freud, S. (Orig. publ. 1926). Inhibition, symptoms, and anxiety. In J. Strachey and A. Freud (Eds.), *The complete psychological works of Sigmund Freud.* London: Hogarth Press, 1953. Vol. 20, Pp. 75–175.

Gardner, R. W. Organismic equilibration and the energy, structure duality in psychoanalytic theory: An attempt at theoretical refinement. *Journal of the American Psychiatric Association,* 1969, **17,** 3–40.

Glover, E. The screening function of traumatic memories. *International Journal of Psychoanalysis,* 1929, **10,** 90–93.

Gordon, R. A. An investigation into some of the factors that favour the formation of stereotyped images. *British Journal of Psychology,* 1949, **39,** 156–167.

Gordon, R. A. An experiment correlating the nature of imagery with performance on a test of reversal of perspective. *British Journal of Psychology,* 1950, **41,** 63–67.

Hernandez-Peon, R. Psychiatric implications of neurophysiological research. *Bulletin of Menninger Clinic,* 1964, **28,** 165–185.

Holt, R. R. "Psychoanalytic theory of the instinctual drives in relation to recent developments." A panel report by Dahl, H. J. *Journal of the American Psychoanalytic Association,* 1968, **16,** 613–637.

Horowitz, M. J. The imagery of visual hallucinations. *Journal of Nervous and Mental Disease,* 1964, **138,** 513–523.

Horowitz, M. J. Psychic trauma: Return of images after a stress film. *Archives of General Psychiatry,* 1969, **126,** 565–569. (a)

Horowitz, M. J. Flashbacks: Recurrent intrusive images after the use of LSD. *American Journal of Psychiatry,* 1969, **126,** 4. (b)

Horowitz, M. J. *Image formation and cognition.* New York: Appleton, 1970.

Horowitz, M. J., Adams, J., & Rutkin, B. Visual imagery on brain stimulation. *Archives of General Psychiatry,* 1968, **19,** 469–486.

Horowitz, M. J., & Becker, S. S. Cognitive response to stressful stimuli. *Archives of General Psychiatry.* 1971, **25,** 419–428. (a)

Horowitz, M. J., & Becker, S. S. Intrusive thinking after stress. *Journal of Nervous and Mental Disease.* 1971, **153,** 32–40. (b)

Horowitz, M. J., & Becker, S. S. Cognitive response to stress and experimental demand. *Journal of Abnormal Psychology.* 1971, **78,** 86–92. (c)

Horowitz, M. J., & Becker, S. S. Cognitive response to stress: Experimental studies of a "compulsion to repeat trauma." *Psychoanalysis and Contemporary Science,* Vol. 1. 1972, in press.

Jackson, J. H. (Orig. publ. 1932.) *Selected writings.* In J. Taylor (Ed.), Vol. 2. New York: Basic Books, 1958.

Jones, E. Fear, guilt and hate. *International Journal of Psychoanalysis,* 1929, **10,** 383–397.

Klein, G. S. Peremptory ideation: Structure and force in motivated ideas. In R. Holt (Ed.), *Motives and thought: Psychoanalytic essays in honor of David Rapaport (Psychological Issues,* 1967, 18–19, Pp. 80–128).

Klüver, H. Mechanisms of hallucinations. In Q. McNemar and M. A. Merrill (Eds.), *Studies in personality.* New York: McGraw-Hill, 1942. Pp. 175–207.

Lazarus, R. S. *Psychological stress and the coping process.* New York: McGraw-Hill, 1966.

Lazarus, R. S. Emotions and adaptation: Conceptual and empirical relations. In W. J. Arnold (Ed.), *Nebraska symposium on Motivation,* Lincoln: Univ. of Nebraska Press, 1968. Pp. 175–266.

Malev, M. Use of the repetition compulsion by the ego. *Psychoanalytic Quarterly,* 1969, **38,** 52–71.

Mandler, G. The interruption of behavior. In D. Levine (Ed.), *Nebraska Symposium on Motivation.* Lincoln: Univ. of Nebraska Press, 1964, **12,** 163–219.

Miller, G. A., Galanter, E., & Pribram, K. H. *Plans and the structure of behavior.* New York: Holt, 1960.

Murphy, W. F. A note on trauma and loss. *Journal of the American Psychoanalytic Association,* 1961, **9,** 519–532.

Neisser, U. *Cognitive psychology.* New York: Appleton, 1967.

Niederland, W. G. Clinical observations on the 'survivor syndrome.' *International Journal of Psychoanalysis,* 1968, **49,** 313–315.

Penfield, W., & Rasmussen, T. *The cerebral cortex of man.* New York: Macmillan, 1950.

Piaget, J. *The child's conception of physical causality.* New York: Harcourt, 1930.

Rapaport, D. (Orig. publ. 1957). Cognitive structures. In M. Gill (Ed.), *The collected papers of David Rapaport.* New York: Basic Books, 1967. Pp. 631–664.

Reider, N. Percept as a screen: Economic and structural aspects. *Journal of the American Psychoanalytic Association,* 1960, **8,** 82–99.

Rohwer, W. D. Images and pictures in children's learning. *Psychological Bulletin,* 1970, **73**, 393–403.

Schafer, R. Aspects of internalization. New York: International Univ. Press, 1968.

Schilder, P. *Mind: Perception and thought in their constructive aspects.* New York: Columbia Univ. Press, 1942.

Schur, M. The ego in anxiety. In R. M. Lowenstein (Ed.), *Drives, affects, behavior.* New York: International Univ. Press, 1953. Pp. 67–103.

Segal, S. J. The Perky effect: Changes in reality judgments with changing methods of inquiry. *Psychonomic Science,* 1968, **12**, 393–394. (a)

Segal, S. J. Patterns of response to thirst in an imaging task (Perky technique) as a function of cognitive style. *Journal of Personality,* 1968, **36**, 574–588. (b)

Segal, S. J. Imagery and reality: Can they be distinguished? In W. Keup (Ed.), *Origin and mechanisms of hallucinations.* New York: Plenum, 1970. Pp. 103–115.

Singer, J. L. Drives, affects and daydreams: The adaptive role of spontaneous imagery or stimulus-independent mentation. In J. S. Antrobus (Ed.), *Cognition and affect.* Boston: Little, Brown, 1970. Pp. 131–158.

Sperry, R. W. A modified concept of consciousness. *Psychological Bulletin,* 1969, **76**, 532–536.

Sperry, R. W. An objective approach to subjective experience: Further explanation of a hypothesis. *Psychological Review,* 1970, **77**, 585–590.

West, L. J. A general theory of hallucinations and dreams. In L. J. West (Ed.), *Hallucinations.* New York: Grune & Stratton, 1962. Pp. 275–291.

13 LEONARD W. DOOB

THE UBIQUITOUS
APPEARANCE OF IMAGES[1]

Images are ubiquitous: they appear universally among all peoples and at a very early age among children, and therefore they must reflect a human ability that has survived from an earlier evolutionary stage. This thesis will be defended but, it must be lamented from the outset, it cannot be proven. Like anyone concerned with images, I must note in passing that images can be observed directly only by each person within himself. Being elusive, they tend to be neglected in cross-cultural and developmental research. The term is not even listed among the hundreds of categories in the Outline of Cultural Materials of the Human Relations Area Files (Murdock, Ford, Hudson, Kennedy, Simmons, & Whiting, 1965); and the topic is seldom if ever directly mentioned in conventional or unconventional ethnographies which concern themselves with objectively verifiable facts and behavior. A broad and satisfactory survey of images (Richardson, 1969) fails to include the categories of "age," "children," "culture," "development," and "society" in its otherwise adequate index.

Under these circumstances it is tempting to follow the precedent set by the behaviorists of the 1920's and to abandon the investigation of images related to our central thesis. But I shall not do so: the fruitful studies resulting from the renewed interest of psychologists in imagery (Holt, 1964) and scattered data from the other social sciences at least suggest

[1] Appreciation once again is expressed to the Carnegie Corporation of New York whose encouragement and support in Africa have enabled me to investigate eidetic imagery and related phenomena and to gain whatever cross-cultural insight I have into imagery.

the outlines of a convincing defense. Besides, the topic is too significant to be cast aside: any child knows that images are close to the core of existence.

If we begin with fundamentals, we must agree that "the only safe evidence of the presence of imagery in any mental process is direct introspective evidence [Betts, 1909, p. 7]" and that our concern is with the individual's "phenomenal world [Gibson & Olum, 1960]." The "evidence" and that "world" quite obviously are private and solipsistic and hence cannot be utilized scientifically in behalf of our thesis. Instead we must resign ourselves to one of two operations, *viz.,* to investigate either Reported Images or Inferred Images. In an experiment or investigation images are *reported* when they are mentioned or described verbally by the subjects experiencing them; they are *inferred* by the experimenter or investigator either from the stimulus materials or from the observable responses of the subjects. I learn about your dreams in two ways: from what you tell me when you awaken (Reported Images) and from your Rapid Eye Movements (REM) when you are asleep (Inferred Images). This last example immediately suggests the hazards of inference since the correlation between reported dreams and REM is far from perfect. A Risky Inference is made again and again; for example, according to a writer on Piaget, "if the direct path to a child's goal is blocked, he will take another route; this indicates that the baby now has a mental representation of the world around him . . . [Boyle, 1969, p. 39]." I admit to feeling queasy, however, when types of Reported Imagery are established by such frontal challenges as "Imagine a pan of onions frying on a stove [Brower, 1947]," but my confidence is somewhat convincingly restored by the relatively high reliability of such introspection, at least among question-plagued American students (Sheehan, 1967).

So much for terms, capitalized terms. But another introductory note: the word "images" in the title of this chapter is somewhat misleading because the discussion is confined almost entirely to visual images which have occupied the attention of experimentalists and others. This may well reflect the ethnocentric bias of our own literate society; perhaps we tend to have predominantly visual images and therefore avoid studying auditory, gustatory, olfactory, and tactile images in nonliterate societies.

Evidence for the Primitive
Nature of Imagery

My thesis with reference to infants and children is assumed by many writers without necessarily supplying substantiating or convincing evidence.

Assertions to the effect that there is a primitive quality about imagery have been made by a classical investigator of images (Betts, 1909, p. 11), by a clinical psychologist and Rorschach expert (Schachtel, 1959, p. 16), by textbook writers on child development (Mussen, Conger, & Kagan, 1969, p. 429) and by the author of a goading thesis on visual thinking and art (Arnheim, 1969, p. 255). A Soviet psychobiologist holds a similar view concerning "the highest vertebrates and man [Beritashvili, 1969, p. 631]."

Dreams and Related Phenomena

The primitive quality of imagery, whether Reported or Inferred, seems reasonably evident in a variety of phenomena. Two writers who have analyzed the content of thousands of dreams reported by Americans (Hall & Van De Castle, 1966, p. 19) state that "the experienced dream consists primarily of pictures." According to one summary of relevant research (Roffwarg, Dement, & Fisher, 1964) Rapid Eye Movement periods have been observed during sleep from birth on. In fact these periods composed from 55 to 80% of the total sleeping time in neonates and 40% in young infants; the figures dropped to 20% or less in the third or fourth years where it remained until about 18 years when it then increased to 25%, after which it sank slowly. Since "awakenings in 3–4-year-old children during REM periods elicited clear narratives of visual dreams" the tentative conclusion may be drawn that dream imagery occurs very early in human beings, perhaps before the dreams can be reported verbally after awakening and hence images may be as primordial as any nonphysiological function that can be postulated. The images appearing during "the agonizing struggle" of the nightmare seem to be ones that have originated in childhood, although the immediate reason for their rearousal must be traced to the present problems of the dreamer; and children have nightmares too (Jones, 1950).

In addition to dreams and nightmares, experiences under the influence of drugs and during psychotherapy suggest evidence for the view that "visual imagery often contains information about affect and fantasy that is not carried into consciousness by thought in word representations" and hence "pictorial cognition is viewed as a developmentally more primitive system that has special psychological utility as a carrier of affectively charged memories, ideas, and impulses [Horowitz, 1967, p. 946]." After taking LSD, for example, 11 out of 18 "normal subjects" stated they had "imagery filling the visual world," i.e., "things seen in the three-dimensional space within the subject's field of vision [Hoffer & Osmond, 1967, p. 111]." A British artist under the influence of mescaline experienced "pictures" showing "features well known in the physiologic process of seeing or in pathologic conditions due to organic lesion of the visual apparatus [Maclay & Guttman, p. 137]." Five schizophrenic patients, however, could produce fewer images concerning various stimulus situations after ingesting mescaline, but more generally there was a negative correlation between these induced images and hallucinatory ones (Thale, Gabrio, & Salomon, 1950). In therapy, patients of psychoanalysts are said to have "verbal imagery analogous to the visual images of dreams" which serves the function during free association of regulating "the distance of the patient from the analyst [Kanzer, 1958, p. 482]." The "early memories and fantasies" of childhood are recalled by most analysands and the rest of us in the form of "pictures and scenes"; such "pictorial thinking is nearer the pleasure principle" than action (Lewin, 1968, pp. 9, 22)—although it probably has components other than imagery.

Nonliterate Societies

The anthropological evidence for imagery outside the West can be called semiconvincing only by making perilously Risky Inferences. We may conjecture that the artists responsible for ancient cave drawings may have been guided by eidetic images while reproducing scenes they had actually perceived in real life. When Bushmen, however, creatively drew "two lions with curiously conventional manes . . . in yellow and black" together with "a striped figure with the face missing, wearing a cycad-branch tail and imitating the lions [Goodwin, 1953, pp. 26–27, 36]," they probably could not have stored eidetically such an event whose duration, if indeed it had occurred, must have been brief; rather they may have relied upon memory images or some kind of storage. This latter view was Galton's which he based upon the report of a European who actually observed a Bushman making a drawing: the artist, he felt, must have "had a clear image in his mind's eye of what he was about to draw [Galton, 1883, pp. 102–103]." Was imagery employed as a mnemonic device when the Kikuyu, in view of their belief that counting brought ill-luck to the people, sheep, cattle, or goats being counted, taught their boys "how to be a good observer and to reckon things by observation without counting them?" During the training period, the boy was tested to see whether or not he noted the absence from the flock of a few animals which had been deliberately hidden; if he erred, the elder asked him "to trace back in his memory and explain at what time and place he last saw the missing sheep or goat [Kenyatta, 1962, pp. 99–100]." Are images guiding the play of little Acholi girls in Uganda who "pick up maize-cobs, sticks, or bottles, pretending that these are their babies [Apoko, 1967, p. 56]?" Among the Akan children of Ghana, it seems reasonable to infer the presence of imagery from the fact that many of them who were brought to shrines for cures suffered from "feverish imaginings and terrifying dreams about febrile illness, mostly common malaria [Field, 1960, p. 426]." Over half of a sample of Eskimo adults responded affirmatively to the question, "Are you ever bothered by nightmares (dreams which frighten or upset you) [Murphy & Leighton, 1965, p. 134)?" Apparently Ibo, Yoruba, and Hausa highschool boys were able easily to supply information about their dreams (LeVine, 1966).

A number of caveats, however, must be entered immediately concerning these anthropological materials. Are dreams among non-Western peoples composed of Reported or Inferred Images? A very broad survey suggests that dreams may be universal, but that their content (a) may not be "recognized as images created by the [individual's] own mind" and yet (b) may be more closely related to images in the waking state because "primitives" while asleep engage in "secondary elaboration" that is "not intensive" as a result of the alleged fact that their "repression is only skin deep [Lincoln, 1935, p. 99]." A split second of reflection suggests that every society places some emphasis upon verbal learning which must have an effect upon the utilization of imagery; thus it would be fascinating to learn whether Ngoni adults in what is now Malawi had fewer images or had images evoked less frequently because as young children they were constantly called upon to deliver verbal messages from one part of a village to another (Read, 1960, pp. 43–44). In another generation and with a colonial bias Rivers concluded that "imagery is especially vivid and necessary among savage peoples," a generalization that "fully accords with their almost exclusive interest in the concrete, with the high degree of development of their powers of observation, and with the accuracy and fullness of memory of the more concrete events of their lives." In support of this conclusion one anecdote from Melanesia is related which seems to suggest that the woman testifying at a trial must have been having eidetic images—"she looked first in one direction and then in another with a keenness and directness which showed beyond doubt that every detail of the occurrence she was describing was being enacted before her eyes." It is equally provocative but unconvincing to be told that "people who have to rely on imagery in order to remember will necessarily put their experience into such concrete and imaged form as will enable it to be grasped and held [Rivers, 1918, pp. 393–394]." These necessarily are Inferred rather than Reported Images.

Universality

Now let us take a long, long leap to grant images evolutionary priority by listing what might be universal processes or conditions which are associated with images in our society and which also appear to reflect innate or inevitable human proclivities persisting as part of our heritage from the distant past.

1. *Electroencephalograms.* The presence of images and the tendency to be visualizers or nonvisualizers have been linked to distinctive alpha phenomena (Richardson, 1969, pp. 63–72). Alpha records, however, are ambiguous indices because they are related to other reactions (see Chapter 15, this volume).

2. *Decreasing Dependence upon Environmental Conditions with Increasing Age.* With few exceptions, studies in the West and in the non-West find that susceptibility to the Müller-Lyer illusion decreases with age (Segall, Campbell, & Herskovits, 1966, pp. 196–199), and children between the ages of 5 and 8 seem less influenced by experimental manipulation in drawing a fruit tree than those between 9 and 12 (Adler, 1969). Being bound to the stimulus configuration of the environment so that one "sees" an illusion or a tree and being less susceptible to suggestions, as a result of past experience, may mean that experience is stored in relatively inelastic images.

3. *The Manipulability of Images and other Modes of Storage.* Changes in environmental conditions can markedly affect the arousal and utilization of both Reported and Inferred Images. Here the evidence from our society is voluminous and convincing. Reported imaginal responses have been conditioned under hypnosis so that when the subjects experienced an image in the waking state after perceiving the conditioned stimulus they were "invariably surprised and puzzled [Leuba, 1940]." Similar effects were achieved without hypnosis but only when distractions were eliminated and there was enforced concentration or adequate motivation (Corn-Becker, Welch, Fisichelli, & Toback, 1949). Inferred images have been induced by investigators: subjects who were told during the training session to concentrate on the shape of irregular drawings profited more from that mode of perception and—presumably—of storage than those who were told to concentrate upon the names given the drawings, provided that the memory being tested involved shape (Ranken, 1963); the way in which subjects were led by one stimulus, whether pictorial or verbal, to anticipate how

the information would be utilized then determined their method of encoding (Tversky, 1969).

4. *Sensory Deprivation, Sensory Isolation, and Bordeom.* Under these conditions (although the optimal form is uncertain), the production of imagery has been facilitated (Richardson, 1969, pp. 100–110). In one study the task-irrelevant thoughts of subjects while performing a boring task were related to their self-appraisals on "daydreaming" and "thoughtfulness" scales (Antrobus, Coleman, & Singer, 1967).

5. *Children's Learning the Vocabulary of their Native Language.* Perhaps—and here the leap is truly gigantic—children everywhere are like American children whose vocabulary is reported to be "less abstract" and to contain "many more picturable words" than that of adults (Brown, 1958, p. 277). Whether such concepts are learned because they are associated with images or vice versa is a spiral that need not be straightened here since either way images play a role.

The conclusion to be drawn from these scattered inferences I think is one which Galton himself drew almost 90 years ago: "The visualizing faculty is a natural gift, and, like all natural gifts, has a tendency to be inherited," but there is also "abundant evidence" that this faculty "admits of being developed by education [1883, pp. 100–105]." The modern version of these statements has been made by Richardson (1969, p. 128) whose words probably apply to all or most forms of imagery: imaging, he writes, is "a common human capacity," but it is not "a common human ability," so that "training may even be necessary for some people before they become aware of their after-images."

The Functions
of Imagery

A corollary of our thesis concerning the survival of images from an earlier evolutionary stage must be that they serve significant functions, for otherwise—the scientific Weltanschauung of our age suggests—they would be gradually or quickly extinguished. Each of us knows, to our private joy and sorrow, their vivid importance in crowded or lonely hours (cf. Pinard, 1957). We need no psychiatrist to remind us of their expressive or emotive function. And we do not have to read Titchener in the original or in modern dress to be reminded that they give or help give meaning to our experiences whether they be recollected or anticipated, whether they pertain to work or poetry. Modern psychologists, however, have tended to focus upon their mediating function which means the role they play in the storage of information. And that role is perhaps the most relevant to our thesis: men survive not alone by learning, but learning is critical.

This function, however, cannot be discussed without first indicating that there are diverse images which fall along various continua. A very elaborate classificatory schema has been proposed by Piaget: the two main types refer to reproduction and anticipation, each of which may have kinetic or transformational content; static images are used only in reproduction. In addition, reproductory and anticipatory images may be analyzed with respect to "leur degré d'intériorisation [Piaget & Inhelder, 1966, pp. 11–17]." These distinctions are most operationally useful as Piaget and his collaborators unfold a 461-page description of their characteristically ingenious experiments with French-Swiss children, but they themselves admit at the outset, in connection with the distinction between kinetic and transformational images, as one always must in analyzing behavior, "il y a naturellement tous les intermédiaires [ibid., p. 13]." More generally, then, we are concerned with a continuum; for present purposes no sharp line needs to be drawn between images which reproduce or anticipate stimulus configurations because the function of reproduction is to anticipate reality (if only for the approval or the disapproval of the investigator) and anticipation is partially a function of past experience.

Likewise the four classes of imagery—afterimages, eidetic, memory, and imagination—which Richardson employs in his excellent book is, in his own words, both "convenient" and "somewhat arbitrary," and he too indicates, as others before him have implied (e.g., Susukita, 1937), that "the experience of becoming aware of a particular class of imagery varies, more or less, on a continuum which extends from almost complete determination by the persistence of a stimulus in the relevant sensory receptor to almost complete determination by events that are centrally initiated [Richardson, 1969, pp. 127–128]." That continuum is one of vividness and controllability of imagery; conceivably other criteria, such as richness of details or optimal fixation time (Meenes, 1934), could be employed. The kind of eidetic imagery some of us have been studying recently (Doob, 1966; Leask, Haber & Haber, 1969; Siipola & Hayden, 1965) seems to be much closer to memory images than afterimages, whereas the incredible subject uncovered in the Cambridge, Massachusetts, area has images so vivid (though apparently also controllable) that they must fall closer to afterimages (Stromeyer & Psotka, 1970) which for some unknown reason remain positive and do not quickly become negative.

The evidence for the memory function and hence survival value of imagery is clearest by definition on that part of the continuum allocated to memory images. Many investigations (e.g., Paivio, 1963; see also Chapter

11, this volume) have demonstrated that paired-associate learning is facilitated when the stimulus word is concrete and hence allegedly image-producing rather than abstract. On purely *a priori* grounds it may be asserted that imagination, when it points toward the future, enables the individual to anticipate or create novel solutions or, when it functions as fantasy, it allows him to secure substitute satisfaction. The case for eidetic imagery, most of us who have been toiling in that elusive vineyard now feel, must rest not on efficiency of recall but on the confidence in recall that is engendered by seeing images in front of the eyes. It is reassuring to note, too, that British children who reported more images (presumably of the memory variety) but did less well in reproducing figures than adults stated they felt "confident" concerning their performance (Jenkin, 1935). If so-called afterimages appear some time after perceiving the stimulus configuration, the memory function again seems obvious; it could be that their immediate appearance after exposure, when positive, facilitates the storing process or, when negative, acts as a protective mechanism inasmuch as they are more likely to appear under conditions of intense and hence potentially dangerous stimulation.

Much of the experimental work on imagery assumes some kind of generalization which occurs for utilitarian or biological reasons: persons with a tendency to employ imagery because it has been useful in the past will employ it in future or novel situations. Seventh graders who were dichotomized into visualizers and nonvisualizers on the basis of standard paper-and-pencil tests performed predictively differently when the stimulus words were known to evoke imagery (Christiansen & Stone, 1968). Some of the variance in the results of experiments involving recall, even among relatively homogeneous Australian college students, may be accounted for by both the vividness and the salience of imagery (Sheehan, 1966).

Finally, the reason for the partial or almost complete disappearance of imagery as individuals mature in our society or probably any society is obvious and often repeated: language is usually more efficient than imagery (e.g., Humphrey, 1963, p. 288; Richardson, 1969, p. 40). Abstract concepts can be utilized more frequently as behavior guides than concrete images. Images, in short, come to have less and less survival value.

The Development
of Imagery

There exists one other reason, a double-barreled reason, for asserting that images are primordial: first, ontogenetic development precedes in a sequence from percept to imagery and then to verbal storage; second, imagery itself develops along the continuum from afterimage to imagination. The first part of this proposition is commonly stressed by child psychologists and others interested in socialization (cf. Wallon, 1930; Popescu-Neveanu & Negoescu, 1966), including an "interpretation" by a Soviet writer (Gankova, 1960), though all may differ or quibble here and there about the invariability of the sequence. Relevant evidence is quite abundant and varies (a) from the disclosure that a small sample of British children reported "a greater amount" of imagery than adults in reproducing sensible or nonsensical figures (Jenkin, 1935) to (b) the revelation that with increasing age fewer American children were able to select "concrete" drawings from a group of drawings purporting to "show best what government is [Hess & Torney, 1967, pp. 40, 268]."

Piaget accepts the same postulated ontogeny. Between 2 and 4 years, he maintains, the early "sensori-motor period" ends. "The" child becomes less dependent on his environment as he begins to store internal remnants of his own movements in the external world, some of which are images. At this stage, while "he" gradually exhibits "deferred imitation," language need not play any role whatsoever. Piaget has also demonstrated again and again *and* again that, although "recognition memory is present during the first few months of life [1968b, p. 11]," only after a gradual development is the child able to store with accuracy various configurations confronting him in everyday life; he thus has representations of objects, persons, and events that are no longer perceptually present and that represent his understanding and assimilation of them; an image, as Piaget has stated, is "internalized imitation [1967, p. 90]." At the age of 7 or so, the child's images are static and not kinetic or transformational, and they are more likely to be reproductive rather than anticipatory (Piaget & Inhelder, 1966, which is the definitive publication; a less opaque account in summary form has been given felicitously by Ginsburg & Opper, 1969, pp. 73–78, 152–161). From his data the conclusion is inescapable that to attain memory images requires as much activity, motivation, knowledge, previous experience, and maturation during perception as any other kind of learning. Even though Piaget himself quite unequivocally states that developmental stages are not "le produit d'une prédétermination innée, car il y a une construction continuelle de nouveautés [1968a, p. 289]," two of his distinguished collaborators have tried unsuccessfully, according to their report, to accelerate children's modes of reacting by explaining to them the principles behind various experimental manipulations (Inhelder & Sinclair, 1969).

One possible misunderstanding of the developmental sequence arises from the fact that the various stages overlap and hence individuals in any society are likely to employ or experience images throughout their existence even when they have become, as most of us do, very verbal. The adult in the West who may claim no imagery is of course able to recognize his friends though he admittedly can give no adequate verbaľ description of their faces. Suddenly, moreover, images may play a role in behavior; one subject, for example, seemed to respond to TAT drawings with eidetic images (Sheehan, 1968). It is well to stress the obvious fact that stored images, when rearoused, are likely to interact with other tendencies currently affecting the organism; thus the hallucinations evoked in one mentally disturbed woman by stimulating electrically her temporal lobe were "often related to the patients' mental content before or at the time of stimulation [Mahl, Rothenberg, Delgado, & Hamlin, 1964]."

A semantic point with psychological implications intrudes here. If images precede verbalization, they cannot be reported by very young children; the record of a child who reported afterimages and dreams at the age of 3 and eidetic images a little later (Helson, 1933) is probably not typical. From the fact of non- or inadequate verbalization, however, it does not follow that there are no images before verbalization, rather they must be inferred. Then since it is undoubtedly true that all sentient, normal human beings eventually utilize verbal storage, that storage must have some effect upon whatever imagery continues to be present. It seems highly likely, therefore, that *preverbal* imagery differs from *postverbal* imagery in ways we shall never be able to specify. Ontologically, though, we must not confuse the two.

There are other difficulties confronting the ontogenetic thesis. We do not have cross-cultural studies of imagery comparable to that conducted among the Wolof of Senegal regarding children's concept of identity (Greenfield, 1966) or among the Kpelle of Liberia concerning cognitive style (Gay & Cole, 1967). Even when cultural differences appear, they cannot be explained easily; investigators of the relatively simple phenomenon of susceptibility to visual illusions could not locate, for example, the causal factors within the societies which produced the variations they observed (Segall, Campbell, & Herskovits, 1966). In Kenya Kamba adults with eidetic imagery or "pictorial images" once told me that they could "see" their ancestors most vividly (Doob, 1965); since "a belief that ancestral spirits are active in human affairs" is not fortuitous but (at least in one sample of 47 societies) has been found to be correlated statistically with the presence of "sovereign kinship groups other than the nuclear family [Swanson, 1960, p. 108]," it may well be that imagery or a certain kind of imagery is associated with the modal beliefs and practices of a particular society. Similarly a connection, again only a statistical one, has been established between the function ascribed to dreams—and hence, I add, their content, since ascribed function helps determine the content of the dream image—and societal factors such as type of economy and residence at marriage (D'Andrade, 1961, pp. 322, 326). Also we do not know whether differential performance on memory tests involving geometrical figures—such as the Benton Test, where improved performance has been found to be associated with education in three African societies and in Jamaica (Doob, 1960, p. 295)—is a function of imagery, verbal storage, or both.

Psychologists are often thought to make a significant contribution to their craft by maintaining the opposite of what is generally believed: allegedly we do not run because we are afraid, rather we are afraid because we run; allegedly we look at more car advertisements not only before but also after purchasing a car; allegedly babies are very primitive if the Zeitgeist suggests they are rational, and vice versa. Perhaps similarly some investigators recently have been suggesting that imagery does not precede but follows the development of verbal storage: "the ability to use linguistic or verbal means for storing and preserving information emerges earlier developmentally than the ability to use visual or imagery processes for accomplishing the same ends [Rohwer, 1970, p. 401]." The experiments purporting to support this iconoclastic, new look are stimulating and ingenious, but I venture the opinion that they do not support such a sweeping conclusion for a variety of reasons which follow.

1. *The Method of Paired Associates.*   The "bulk of the available work has been done with paired-associate tasks [Rohwer, 1970, p. 393]," a method which is perhaps both inappropriate and bizarre for the study of imagery. A psychologist in summarizing a recent symposium on "Imagery in Children's Learning" wrote that the possibility of analyzing the child's use of principles to solve problems and the bases for those principles, in imagery or whatnot, "makes paired-associate learning of unrelated pairs of items a rather less interesting task than many others which might be used in an effort to understand learning [Palermo, 1970, p. 419]." Inferred Images have indeed been shown to be more efficient than verbalization when a series of events (e.g., pictures) can be perceived slowly rather than quickly and when they are subsequently recalled freely in any order rather than in the previously exposed order (Paivio & Csapo, 1969). The method of paired associates, then, is obviously sequential rather than spatial in character; and one of the progenitors of the new theory himself (see Chapter 11, this volume) has stated, on the basis of his own research just cited and that of others, that "imagery is specialized for the processing of spatial information, whereas the verbal system is characterized more by its capacity for sequential processing [Paivio, 1970, pp. 386–387]." Actually, I guess, children everywhere must use paired associates on many occasions

to learn the names of objects and the referents of names, but it also seems reasonable to suppose that utilizing at one full swoop a long series of paired associates is not a procedure likely to appear outside the psychological laboratory and that imagery is evoked under far different kinds of circumstances among children in real life and in nonliterate societies. It would be very difficult to contend that after- and eidetic images function only as the response components of paired associates. The very specificity and perhaps ethnocentricity of this laboratory method, moreover, is suggested by the fact that the data supporting the new generalization have been obtained only by testing recall shortly after the learning criterion has been attained; American subjects yielded quite different results when the testing took place 20 minutes or 2 days later (Palermo, 1970), a period of delay which is more lifelike than one of 2 minutes. Similarly other American students could give the response of "same" more rapidly when there was a "physical match" rather than a "name match" between two letters (e.g., *A* followed by *A* rather than by *a*, and not some other letter), but only when the delay between stimulus and response was extremely short and when there was no interpolated activity of a particular sort (Posner, Boies, Eichelman, & Taylor, 1969); but surely from this finding it cannot be argued that all Inferred Images (the investigators themselves do not use the concept of imagery in connection with "physical match") persist for such a restricted time period.

2. *Actuarial Assumption Concerning Imagery-Arousing Stimuli.* To carry on an experiment, the assumption is made that pictures or concrete nouns known in one group of subjects to have elicited many more Reported Images than, respectively, words or abstract nouns will function similarly in the group being tested. Actuarial assumptions may be reasonable, but they are assumptions. "The rated imagery or concreteness of the item" may be "the best single predictor of associative learning involving meaningful material" (Paivio, 1970, p. 389), yet the possibility remains that imagery and concreteness may themselves be only indices of some other factor such as frequency of usage. The same investigator himself suggested that pictures, which ought to be prepotent image-arousers, in fact "hindered learning as responses" since in this role they "pose a decoding problem" among children (*loc. cit.,* p. 390). In addition, the standard deviations of a great many of the words used in experiments (when rated on a 7-point imagery scale by "university students, most of them enrolled in introductory psychology") tended to be relatively large; thus the first two on the list, "abasement" and "abbess," had respective means of 2.03 and 2.97, but with σ's of 1.28 and 1.96 (Paivio, Yuille, & Madigan, 1968). Almost four decades earlier, it was shown that the imagery ratings of words

secured from various groups of Canadian high-school students were very consistent (the r's were .86 and .94), but the correlations between rated visual, auditory, and kinaesthetic imagery of a 135-word list on the one hand and the reproduction of that list by the same students were low and not significant (Bowers, 1931).

3. *The Confounding of Imagery's Arousal and Utilization.* The central thesis of the Young Turks is that only after attaining a certain age, when language is already functioning, are children able to utilize adequately or fully the imagery-producing attributes of stimuli. Thus, for example, it has been shown that "the superiority of concreteness on the stimulus side is less reliable in the case of children" who were Canadians in grades 4, 6, and 8 than it was for adults; yet the investigators themselves also indicate that the nouns which constituted the materials had less "meaning" (which meant operationally that they evoked fewer words in free-association tests) for the younger children (Paivio & Yuille, 1966, p. 87). In addition, the assumed nonutilization of imagery is not equivalent to its absence. When once it is conceded, as these investigators obviously do, that there are intervening responses which mediate between stimulus and response in paired-associate learning, then learning involves not only the type of mediating response, but also the establishment of the necessary bonds. Recall of paired verbal associates as well as the capacity to respond with Reported Images to a verbal stimulus were shown to be significantly greater (as measured by the number of images and the speed of responding) among Canadian children in grade 6 than those in grade 2; nevertheless, the "facilitating effect of concrete stimuli" as well as that of "response concreteness" was greater among the younger children (Yuille & Pritchard, 1969, pp. 462, 464). Thus the general capacity of the younger children to learn and freely to respond with images was less than that of the older ones, but they could utilize the concreteness of words (and hence presumably Inferred Images) more effectively when and only when the experimenter provided that opportunity. In my opinion, in brief, the various theories which have been presented to account for the fact that imagery facilitates paired-associate learning in older children and adults more than it does in younger children (Reese, 1970) refer to differences in general learning ability and do not settle the problem of the relative efficiency of imagery vs. verbal learning; the learning of paired associates as such is probably more difficult at a young age, no matter what the stimulus or the response.

4. *The Limited Sample of Subjects.* The youngest children on whom the generalization is based appear, with very few exceptions, to be of kindergarten age. By then they have literally a speaking acquaintance with

language and some of its uses, and they could well have previously had preverbal images that cannot be tested with the paired-associate technique. With the exception of one reference to a replication in French with French-Canadian children (Paivio, 1970), all the subjects have been speakers of English in North America. One of the somewhat skeptical progenitors of the innovative theory himself offers as "a teasing reference" the asserted fact that trends favoring the view that "a preference for and a capacity to make effective use of visual representation and storage develops later than is the case for verbal modes of representing and storing information" have been derived from his own research based upon middle-class children in Berkeley, California and that these same trends were "reversed for lower-class black children [Rohwer, 1970, p. 401]." This last finding, any anthropologist or cross-cultural psychologist must say, indicates vividly the fact that developmental sequences usually have a vastly significant cultural component.

So much for the brave new theory. Now two afterthoughts. First, the view is surely valid when it is confined to the method and subjects in question. A controlled experiment always suffers from limitations, and maybe the fate of psychology is to be unable usually to attain a level of generalization sufficiently abstract to embrace cross-cultural phenomena. Second, similar objections can be raised concerning imagery in general. When it is maintained, for example, that "initially, fantasy is expressed verbally and coupled with alternation in role-taking in which the child talks aloud for all the characters in the drama" and "later . . . it is internalized in the form of predominately visual imagery [Singer, 1961, p. 396]," we must conclude that the reference is to postverbal images; internal images may well precede verbalization which is first practiced aloud and then internalized.

Conclusions

It seems reasonable, I think, to accept the proposition that children high in Inferred Images excel in some tasks but not in others, as suggested in the widely cited, unpublished study involving the association of verbal labels with pictures *vs.* forming concepts inherent in a set of pictures (Kuhlman, 1966). Then it follows that each child is likely to learn and thus to use the kind of mediating response best adapted to the problems facing him. The sequence of image and language, consequently, will depend upon the cultural and environmental conditions at the age of learning. Since the preverbal child, as Piaget and others quite rightly emphasize, can solve or resolve some of his problems only by internalizing experience and anticipating outcomes, it seems reasonable to infer that some of the storage is accomplished through preverbal imagery. In Kuhlman's study, previously mentioned, Inferred Images may have been more useful at an earlier than at a later age, since their strength correlated positively with school achievement in grades 1 and 2, but only negligibly in grades 3 and 4. In a group of American children the use of fantasy has been shown to be statistically related to various background conditions involving the family (Singer, 1961); environmental factors are certainly a promising way to account for variability. Under appropriate circumstances, as suggested above, verbally inclined adults can utilize their capacity to employ images. When asked to spell the word "Nachahmungsbewegung" backwards, German adults forced themselves to "see" the word written out, but this device was invoked more readily by those more accustomed to employ imagery than by those less accustomed to do so (Hummeltenberg, 1939). It is idle to speculate, though, whether Inferred Images that have been aroused in order to curb exhibitionist sexual urges (Evans, 1968), fetishism (Kolvin, 1967), or children's fears (Lazarus & Abramovitz, 1962) are predominately, partially, or negligibly imaginal in nature.

In Western investigations, imagery has been found to be correlated with personality traits and other behavior, only a few examples of which will be cited: among young and middle age Britains, ability to control visual imagery *and* less stereotyped views concerning nationality groups (Gordon, 1949); among American adults, the themes of reported dreams *and* the paper-and-pencil traits of dominance, self-confidence, and seeking admiration from others (Rychlak & Brams, 1963); among fifth- and eighth-grade American children—but very slightly—dream content *and* some personality traits but not others (Rychlak, 1960); among males but not female adolescents, claims concerning the possession of vivid Reported Imagery or fantasy *and* persuasibility (Janis & Field, 1959, pp. 62–63); among American children between the ages of 6 and 9, fantasy based on Reported and Inferred measures *and* patience, creativity, oedipal conflict, parental control, etc. (Singer, 1961); and among American junior high-school students, visual and eidetic imagery measured on a standard test *and* ability to spell (Pierro, 1967). From such studies it might be argued that reinforcement and extinction among children are a function of other tendencies they possess; if this is so, then whatever developmental sequence is postulated must be in part an epiphenomenon.

Let us now abruptly, finally, and briefly return to the second half of the ontogenetic hypothesis which proposes a developmental shift from afterimages eventually to imaginal ones. It can be argued that afterimages must be more primordial than the others because after involuntary or voluntary exposure they are least subject to control; alas, their presence in infants or very young children cannot be detected or must be indirectly tested or inferred until the subjects "have the means for describing such forms to us" (Werner & Kaplan, 1963, p. 426). Most investigators of eidetic imagery have assumed or presented data indicating a negative relation between the incidence of that imagery and age (e.g., Jaensch, 1930). If this were so, it would be reasonable to assert that with advancing age eidetic imagery gives way to other imagery and verbal storage. The careful studies of American children by the Habers (Leask *et al.,* 1969), however, indicate that this is not the case; and in different African societies the original assertion has been both confirmed and contradicted (Doob, 1970). Piaget's investigations establish trends only for memory images. It seems useful to know that "il n'existe aucune différence systématique entre la formation ou le développement des images reproductrices cinétique et les images anticipatrices" or that "si l'on cherche à rassembler ces stades partiels pour en dégager les stades généraux du développement de l'image, on ne trouve guère que deux moments décisifs et une seule coupure de portée générale [Piaget & Inhelder, 1966, pp. 190, 421]"; but then one is forced to remind oneself of the fact that these conclusions spring from limited numbers of Swiss children—again, the banal if valid indictment, though some of his theories have been vindicated cross-culturally (e.g., among the Tiv of Nigeria by Price-Williams, 1961)—and that the experimental materials consist almost exclusively of neutral wires and geometrical drawings or blocks. Even a hand and a face (ibid., p. 147) are schematic and unrealistic. Likewise the almost censuslike reports on the development of dreams, whether based upon the REM studies already cited or the reports of American children (Ames, 1964), cannot be generalized beyond the samples in question; hence it is useless to compare age norms from analyses of dreams with norms for other images, such as Piaget's, in order to emerge with a proposition concerning sequential development. We simply have, in short, no data on the development of various kinds of imagery in the same samples of children from the same culture. A good theory of images, as Piaget has also noted in another context concerning his own theory (1962, p. 70), must account for the storing of images in the first place. Perhaps afterimages which are part of the genetic potential, may well be the beginning and they in turn may give rise to the other images along the postulated continuum.

As forecast in the opening paragraph, this chapter has had to struggle with the sad fact that imagery in the early years and in non-Western societies more frequently than not must be inferred rather than reported. No single investigation or experiment by itself proves the thesis that imagery is one of the basic human attributes. The cumulative evidence, nevertheless, makes one conclusion seem inescapable: although our experiences are labeled promiscuously and stored literally and figuratively in unified and fragmented sentences, phrases, and words, our images survive and continue to increase stimulation in the present and also to assist us, for better or worse, in reexperiencing and remembering the past.

References

Adler, L. L. Fruit-tree study as a measure of associative thinking and imagery in children of different ages. *Developmental Psychology,* 1969, **1,** 444.

Ames, L. B. Sleep and dreams in childhood. In E. Harms (Ed.), *Problems of sleep and dream in children.* New York: Macmillan, 1964. Pp. 6–29.

Antrobus, J. S., Coleman, R., & Singer, J. L. Signal-detection performance by subjects differing in predisposition to daydreaming. *Journal of Consulting Psychology,* 1967, **31,** 487–491.

Apoko, A. At home in the village: growing up in Acholi. In L. K. Fox (Ed.), *East African childhood.* Nairobi: Oxford, 1967. Pp. 43–75.

Arnheim, R. *Visual thinking.* Berkeley: Univ. of California, 1969.

Beristashvili, I. S. Concerning psychoneural activity of animals. In M. Cole & I. Maltsman (Eds.), *A handbook of contemporary Soviet psychology.* New York: Basic Books, 1969. Pp. 627–670.

Betts, G. H. The distribution and functions of mental imagery. *Teachers College, Columbia University Contributions to Education,* 1909, No. 26. Pp. 1–99.

Bowers, H. Memory and mental imagery. *British Journal of Psychology,* 1931, **21,** 271–282.

Boyle, D. G. *A student's guide to Piaget.* New York: Oxford Univ. Press (Clarendon), 1969.

Brower, D. The experimental study of imagery. *Journal of General Psychology,* 1947, **37,** 199–200.

Brown, R. *Words and things.* Glencoe: Free Press, 1958.

Christiansen, T., & Stone, D. R. Visual imagery and level of mediator abstractness in induced mediation paradigms. *Perceptual and Motor Skills,* 1968, **26,** 775–779.

Corn-Becker, F., Welch, L., Fisichelli, V., & Toback, E. Factors productive of conditioned images or sensations. *Journal of Genetic Psychology,* 1949, **75,** 149–164.

D'Andrade, R. G. Anthroplogical studies of dreams. In F. L. K. Hsu (Ed.), *Psychological Anthropology.* Homewood, Ill.: Dorsey, 1961. Pp. 297–332.

Doob, L. W. *Becoming more civilized.* New Haven: Yale, 1960.

Doob, L. W. Exploring eidetic imagery among the Kamba of Central Kenya. *Journal of Social Psychology,* 1965, **67,** 3–22.

Doob, L. W. Eidetic imagery: A cross-cultural will-o'-the-wisp? *Journal of Psychology,* 1966, **63,** 13–34.

Doob, L. W. Correlates of eidetic imagery in Africa. *Journal of Psychology,* 1970, **76,** 223–230.

Evans, D. R. Masturbatory fantasy and sexual deviation. *Behavior Research and Therapy,* 1968, **61,** 17–19.

Field, M. J. *Search for security.* Evanston: Northwestern, 1960.

Galton, F. *Inquiries into human faculty and its development.* New York: Macmillan, 1883.

Gan'kova, Z. A. (On the interrelation of action, image, and speech in the thinking of children of preschool age. *Voprosy Psikhologii,* 1960, **1,** 69–77). *Psychological Abstracts,* 1962, **36,** 1FC69G.

Gay, J., & Cole, M. *The new mathematics and an old culture.* New York: Holt, 1967.

Gibson, E., & Olum, V. Experimental methods of studying perception in children. In P. H. Mussen (Ed.), *Handbook of research methods in child development.* New York: Wiley, 1960. Pp. 311–373.

Ginsburg, H., & Opper, S. *Piaget's theory of intellectual development: An introduction.* Englewood Cliffs: Prentice-Hall, 1969.

Goodwin, A. J. H. *Cave artists of South Africa.* Cape Town: Balkema, 1953.

Gordon, R. An investigation into some of the factors that favour the formation of stereotyped images. *British Journal of Psychology,* 1949, **39,** 156–167.

Greenfield, P. M. On culture and conservation. In J. S. Bruner, R. R. Olver, P. M. Greenfield *et al.* (Eds.), *Studies in cognitive growth.* New York: Wiley, 1966. Pp. 225–256.

Hall, C., & Van De Castle, R. L. *The content analysis of dreams.* New York: Appleton, 1966.

Helson, H. A child's spontaneous reports of imagery. *American Journal of Psychology,* 1933, **45,** 360–361.

Hess, R. D., & Torney, J. *The development of political attitudes in children.* Chicago: Aldine, 1967.

Hoffer, A., & Osmond, H. *The Hallucinogens.* New York: Academic Press, 1967.

Holt, R. R. Imagery: The return of the ostracized. *American Psychologist,* 1964, **19,** 254–264.

Horowitz, M. J. Visual imagery and cognitive organization. *American Journal of Psychiatry,* 1967, **123,** 938–946.

Hummeltenberg, M. Vorstellungstypus, Gedächtnis, und Gesamtpersönlichkeit. *Zeitschrift für Psychologie,* 1939, **147,** 10–37.

Humphrey, G. *Thinking.* New York: Wiley, 1963.

Inhelder, B., & Sinclair, H. Learning cognitive structures. In P. Mussen, J. Langer, & M. Covington (Eds.), *Trends and issues in developmental psychology.* New York: Holt, Rinehart & Winston, 1969. Pp. 2–21.

Jaensch, E. R. *Eidetic imagery and typological methods of investigation.* New York: Harcourt, Brace, 1930.

Janis, I. L., & Field, P. B. Sex differences and personality factors related to persuasibility. In I. L. Janis *et al.* (Eds.), *Personality and persuasibility.* New Haven: Yale, 1959. Pp. 55–68.

Jenkin, A. M. Imagery and learning. *British Journal of Psychology,* 1935, **26,** 149–164.

Jones, E. *On the nightmare.* New York: Liveright, 1950.

Kanzer, M. Image formation during free association. *Psychoanalytic Quarterly,* 1958, **27,** 465–484.

Kenyatta, J. *Facing Mt. Kenya.* New York: Random House, 1962.

Kolvin, I. "Aversive imagery" treatment in adolescents. *Behavior Research and Therapy,* 1967, **5,** 245–248.

Kuhlman, C. K. Visual imagery in children. Quoted in J. S. Bruner, R. R. Olver,

P. M. Greenfield *et al.* (Eds.), *Studies in cognitive growth.* New York: Wiley, 1966. Pp. 26–29.

Lazarus, A. A., & Abramovitz, A. The use of "emotive imagery" in the treatment of children's phobias. *Journal of Mental Science,* 1962, **108,** 191–195.

Leask, J., Haber, R. N., & Haber, R. B. Eidetic imagery in children: II. Longitudinal and experimental results. *Psychonomic Monograph Supplements,* 1969, **3,** 25–48.

Leuba, C. Images as conditioned sensations. *Journal of Experimental Psychology,* 1940, **26,** 345–351.

LeVine, R. *Dreams and deeds.* Chicago: Univ. of Chicago Press, 1966.

Lewin, B. D. *The image and the past.* New York: International Universities Press, 1968.

Lincoln, J. S. *The dream in primitive cultures.* London: Cresset Press, 1935.

Maclay, W. S., & Guttman, E. Mescaline hallucination in artists. *Archives of Neurology and Psychiatry,* 1941, **45,** 130–137.

Mahl, G. F., Rothenberg, A., Delgado, J. M. R., & Hamlin, H. Psychological responses in the human to intracerebral electrical stimulation. *Psychosomatic Medicine,* 1964, **26,** 337–368.

Meenes, M. The relationship of the eidetic phenomenon to the after-image and to the memory image. *Psychological Bulletin,* 1934, **31,** 739.

Murdock, G. P., Ford, C. S., Hudson, A. E., Kennedy, R., Simmons, L. W., & Whiting, J. W. *Outline of cultural materials.* New Haven: Human Relations Area Files, 1965.

Murphy, J. M., & Leighton, A. H. *Approaches to cross-cultural psychiatry.* Ithaca: Cornell, 1965.

Mussen, P. H., Conger, J. J., & Kagan, J. *Child development and personality* (3rd ed.). New York: Harper, 1969.

Paivio, A. Learning of adjective-noun paired associates as a function of adjective-noun word order and noun abstractness. *Canadian Journal of Psychology,* 1963, **17,** 370–379.

Paivio, A. On the functional significance of imagery. *Psychological Bulletin,* 1970, **73,** 385–392.

Paivio, A., & Csapo, K. Concrete image and verbal memory codes. *Journal of Experimental Psychology,* 1969, **80,** 279–285.

Paivio, A., & Yuille, J. C. Word abstractness and meaningfulness, and paired-associate learning in children. *Journal of Experimental Child Psychology,* 1966, **4,** 81–89.

Paivio, A., Yuille, J. C., & Madigan, S. A. Concreteness, imagery, and meaningfulness values for 925 nouns. *Journal of Experimental Psychology,* 1968, 76 (1, Pt. 2). Pp. 1–25.

Palermo, D. S. Imagery in children's learning. *Psychological Bulletin,* 1970, **73,** 415–421.

Piaget, J. *Plays, dreams and imitation in childhood.* New York: Norton, 1962.

Piaget, J. *Six psychological studies.* New York: Random House, 1967.

Piaget, J. Le point de vue de Piaget. *International Journal of Psychology,* 1968, **3,** 281–299. (a)

Piaget, J. *On the development of memory and identity.* Barre, Mass.: Clark Univ. Press, 1968. (b)

Piaget, J., & Inhelder, B. *L'image mentale chez l'enfant.* Paris: Presses Universitaires, 1966.

Pierro, P. S. An investigation of visual form perception and eidetic imagery in students who read well and spell poorly. *Dissertation Abstracts*, 1967, **27**, 2894–5A.

Pinrad, W. J. Spontaneous imagery. *Boston University Graduate Journal*, 1957, **5**, 150–153.

Popescu-Neveanu, P., & Negoescu, V. (Contribution to the study of the genesis of geometrical designs. *Revista de Psihologie*, 1966, **12**, 89–101.) *Psychological Abstracts*, 1967, **41**, 16243.

Posner, M. I., Boies, S. J., Eichelman, W. H., & Taylor, R. L. Retention of visual and name codes of single letters. *Journal of Experimental Psychology* 1969, **79** (1, Pt. 2). Pp. 1–16.

Price-Williams, D. R. A study concerning concepts of conservation of quantities among primitive children. *Acta Psychologica*, 1961, **18**, 297–305.

Ranken, H. B. Language and thinking: Positive and negative effects of naming. *Science*, 1963, **141**, 48–50.

Read, M. *Children of their fathers*. New Haven: Yale, 1960.

Reese, H. W. Imagery and contextual meaning. *Psychological Bulletin*, 1970, **73**, 404–414.

Richardson, A. *Mental imagery*. London: Routledge & Kegan Paul, 1969.

Rivers, W. H. R. Dreams and primitive culture. *Bulletin of the John Rylands Library*, 1918, **4**, 387–410.

Roffwarg, H. P., Dement, W. C., & Fisher, C. Preliminary observations of the sleep-dream pattern in neonates, infants, children, and adults. In E. Harms (Ed.), *Problems of sleep and dream in children*. New York: Macmillan, 1964. Pp. 60–72.

Rohwer, W. D. Images and pictures in children's learning: Research results and educational implications. *Psychological Bulletin*, 1970, **73**, 393–403.

Rychlak, J. F. Recalled themes and personality. *Journal of Abnormal and Social Psychology*, 1960, **60**, 140–143.

Rychlak, J. F., & Brams, J. M. Personality dimensions in recalled dream content. *Journal of Projective Techniques*, 1963, **27**, 226–234.

Schachtel, E. G. *Metamorphosis*. New York: Basic Books, 1959.

Segall, M. H., Campbell, D. T., & Herskovits, M. J. The *influence of culture on visual perception*. Indianapolis: Bobbs-Merrill, 1966.

Sheehan, P. W. Functional similarity of imagery to perceiving: Individual differences in vividness of imagery. *Perceptual and Motor Skills*, 1966, **23**, 1011–1033.

Sheehan, P. W. Reliability of a short test of imagery. *Perceptual and Motor Skills*, 1967, **25**, 744.

Sheehan, P. W. Color response to the TAT: An instance of eidetic imagery? *Journal of Psychology*, 1968, **68**, 203–209.

Siipola, E. M., & Hayden, S. D. Exploring eidetic imagery among the retarded. *Perceptual and Motor Skills*, 1965, **21**, 275–286.

Singer, J. L. Imagination and waiting ability in young children. *Journal of Personality*, 1961, **29**, 396–413.

Stromeyer, C. F. III, & Psotka, J. The detailed texture of eidetic images. *Nature (London)*, 1970, **225**, 346–349.

Susukita, T. Ueber die wahrnehmungsmässigen Vorstellungsbilder von Wirklichkeitscharakter. *Tohoku Psychologica*, 1937, **5**, 1–20.

Swanson, G. E. *The birth of the gods*. Ann Arbor: University of Michigan Press, 1960.

Thale, T., Gabrio, B. W., & Salomon, K. Hallucination and imagery induced by mescaline. *American Journal of Psychiatry,* 1950, **106,** 686–691.

Tversky, B. Pictorial and verbal encoding in a short-term memory task. *Perception and Psychophysics,* 1969, **6,** 225–233.

Wallon, H. De l'image au réel, dans la pensée de l'enfant. *Revue Philosophique de la France et de l'Étranger,* 1930, **109,** 446–458.

Werner, H., & Kaplan, B. *Symbol formation.* New York: Wiley, 1963.

Yuille, J. C., & Pritchard, S. Noun concreteness and verbal facilitation as factors in imagination mediation and PA learning in children. *Journal of Experimental Child Psychology,* 1969, **7,** 459–466.

14 THEODORE R. SARBIN

*IMAGINING AS MUTED
ROLE-TAKING: A
HISTORICAL-LINGUISTIC
ANALYSIS*[1]

Introduction

In earlier efforts directed toward clarifying psychological theory
(Sarbin, 1950, 1967; Sarbin & Juhasz, 1967) "imagining" emerged as a
central concept. Tacitly assuming that everybody knew what was meant
by "imagining," I employed "imagining" as a primitive concept, a term
the referents for which required no analysis. I must confess to having been
taken in by the assumption. Like everyone else, I talked, uncritically, of
images, imagery, and imagining in much the same way as the mentalistic
psychologists and philosophers. When I had to face the working through
of a theory the better to account for certain forms of self-reports, I began
to question the assumption that everybody shares the same referents for
"imagining."

To introduce the argument, and to provide concrete reference, I list several cases that would be called imagining by the speakers of ordinary
language.

1. In a laboratory experiment, a subject reports a scene that he "sees
in his mind's eye." The usual description of such an event is that
the subject is experiencing visual imagery.

2. In a psychological experiment, a subject announces that he sees

[1] An earlier version of this chapter was prepared during my tenure as a Fellow
of the Center for Advanced Studies, Wesleyan University, 1968–1969. It is slightly
expanded from a draft read to the Fellows of the Center, October 21, 1968. The
first part is an abridgment of a companion paper that provides a more detailed
analysis of models for the study of imagination, especially the notion of man
as actor (Sarbin & Juhasz, 1970).

a visual display when no stimulus is presented. In contemporary psychophysics, this is labeled a "false alarm" or miscall.

3. A patient in a mental hospital reports seeing and communicating with saints. The usual psychiatric practice is to call such reported imaginings "hallucinations."

4. A novelist describes his creative work as imagining the presence of characters in the room with him, "listening" to what they say, "watching" what they do, and writing down their remarks.

5. A 3-year-old boy engages in conversation and makebelieve play with a fictional playmate. Child psychologists refer to such play partners as imaginary companions.

6. A theatre-goer laughs at the supposed antics of a fictional 6-foot rabbit. The playwright and actors are said to have created an illusion to which the imaginative theatre-goer responds.

These reference cases are cited as typical of "imagining." They all attest to the fact that the subjects made use of covert processes, sometimes called imagining, imaging, being imaginative, and kindred names. To some of these reported imaginings observers may apply labels of approval or disapproval. I have argued elsewhere (Sarbin, 1967) that approval or disapproval of reported imaginings depends not on the fact of talking about absent objects as if they were present, but rather upon the surrounding circumstances and the social characteristics of the imaginer.

In these illustrations it is clear that each imaginer had acted or talked in a manner that was *contrary to fact*. Having decided that the utterance of the imaginer is contrary to fact, the theorist is faced with a perplexing problem. If he subscribes to the view that every response must have a stimulus, then he must discover a stimulus for the report, e.g., "I see a dragon," "I hear the voice of God," etc. When the distal (external) ecology provides no consensually validated stimulus events, the theorist concludes that the stimulus events are elsewhere, and turning to the outside–inside dichotomy, he declares that the events are "inside." The "inside" is codified by mentalistic philosophers and psychologists as the mind, thus the handy form: pictures in the mind. Since mind itself is a case of a hypostatized entity—a metaphor turned myth—such a conclusion frustrates our efforts to understand an important feature of human conduct.

If you ask the man in the street to tell you about imagining, he will say it takes place in his mind; he will likely talk in the visual idiom, about visualizing, and about seeing in the mind's eye. The man in the street, of course, uses mentalistic terms with impunity. His friends and neighbors do not challenge such a statement as "I saw it in my mind's eye," but rather appear to understand the sentence. As a result, he continues to act and talk as if there are minds, and that minds, like bodies have eyes and other sense organs.

Psychologists, who should know better, offer similar descriptions; however, they obscure their *naiveté* by employing technical terms, usually of
Greco-Latin origin. The psychologist might say, "I am experiencing an
image." In this respect, he has not advanced beyond the now discredited
efforts of the late nineteenth century introspectionists. Most of the time,
of course, contemporary psychologists avoid talking or writing about
events that do not lend themselves to stimulus-response explanations. In
this connection, beginning about 1940, it was fashionable to talk about
images as "conditioned sensations." However, recent work in my laboratory (and elsewhere) shows that the Pavlovian conditioning paradigm
simply does not apply to stimuli *in absentia* (Sarbin & Juhasz, 1970).

The psychological study of imagination seems to have come to an abrupt
halt about 1910. The usual explanation for abandoning the subject was
(and is) that laboratory methods were too unwieldy to hold down the
phantasmagorical nature of images and imagery. The prevailing dualistic
thought model directed only that the subject look into his shadowy mind
and report his observations. Experimental psychologists were unable to
develop methods that were not contaminated by instructions of the type:
"Tell me what is going on in your mind."

Imagination as a
Reified Metaphor

To understand imagining as a key concept in psychological science, a
bold hypothesis is suggested to replace the mentalistic hypothesis of pictures in the mind. This hypothesis is similar to those used in my earlier
efforts at demythification, a recognition of the docility of psychologists
(and others) toward their conceptual language (for a report of similar
misgivings see Chapter 10, this volume).[2]

[2] For the past decade, I have been engaged in a program of research and writing
that my colleagues have labelled the "demythification of psychology." I have taken
a number of entrenched concepts—concepts central to the theory and practice
of psychology—and subjected them to historical, linguistic and pragmatic analysis.
The general conclusion is that these concepts are the end result of a mythmaking
process, dependent on uncritical (usually tacit) acceptance of Cartesian dualism.
I have tried to show that a central concept for contemporary psychology, anxiety,
is a reified metaphor (Sarbin, 1964; 1968). I have tried also to expose the weaknesses
of the "trance" concept in hypnosis theories. Like the concept of anxiety, the
trance turns out to be a mental state word, fraught with error, the result of an
unrecognized shift from metaphor to myth (Sarbin, 1950; Sarbin & Andersen, 1967).
More recently, I have tried to expose the questionable scholastic and dualistic
underpinnings of such concepts as mental illness (1968), schizophrenia (1969),
and hallucination (1967).

The hypothesis may be sketched as follows: the concept "imagination" was constructed by our linguistic ancestors as the consequence of a category mistake, a metaphor-to-myth transformation. Like most mentalistic words, the early forms of the word "imagination" were first employed as a metaphor to communicate about identifiable instances of human conduct. The metaphor was reified, i.e., given literal status by those authorities who had the power to endow with substantive properties such constructs as soul, psyche and mind. Such reifying of metaphors is a criterial attribute of myth. That is to say, a figure of speech becomes transformed to a myth, a belief unwarranted by empirical observation that serves as a guide to conduct. Thomas Mann (1947) made use of the concept in similar fashion. In writing of Napoleon, he said "we need not doubt that—at least at the period of his Eastern exploits—he (Napoleon) mythically confounded himself with Alexander; while after he turned his face westwards he is said to have declared: 'I am Charlemagne.' Note that: not 'I am like Charlemagne' or 'My situation is like Charlemagne's,' but quite simply: 'I am he.' That is the formulation of the myth [p. 424]."

My argument involves several steps: first is a defense of the claim that "the imagination" is an instance of metaphor-to-myth transformation. To conduct such a defense, I shall demonstrate through historico-linguistic analysis that the substantive "the imagination" is a term the metaphorical qualities of which have been so long submerged that its ontological status has been taken for granted. The commonly held view of imaginings as pictures-in-the-mind is an unwarranted belief developed out of the Cartesian view of the dualistic nature of man. Such a belief was supportable when the requirements of logic and science were less stringent than today. To regard imagining as a process taking place on the shadowy stage of the mind or in the photographic laboratory of the psyche is to reaffirm a demonstrably futile model of human conduct (Ryle, 1949). A review of theories and research designed to clarify the concept of "imagining" makes one fact abundantly clear: the model of pictures-in-the-mind has produced virtually nothing in the way of pragmatically useful or heuristically exciting propositions.

In the following paragraphs I sketch the historico-linguistic happenings whereby the root forms of the word "imagining" were changed from a metaphorical device into a term denoting a "self-evident" belief in a mythical mentalistic entity.

The analysis begins from the proposition that language grows through metaphor. When an event occurs that is sufficiently interesting to talk about, and no ready-made class name is available, then it is likely that a term will be borrowed through metaphor, thus, every man is a poet. Emerson (1903) epitomized the process in the following words: "For though the origin of most of our words is forgotten, each word was at first a stroke of genius, and obtained currency because for the moment it symbolized the world to the first speaker and to the hearer. The etymologist finds the deadest word to have been once a brilliant picture. Language is fossil poetry [p. 329]."

The linguistic borrowing is not whimsical but follows from resemblances observed between the new event and the old. The metaphor-maker may begin by employing the simile "A is like a B" and compress it into the form "A is a B," or he may use a hypothetical form "it is *as if* A is a B"; or "Let A stand for B"; or "Let A symbolize B"; or "Pretend that A is B," etc. Unless the hypothetical (suppositional, assumptive) quality of the transformation is periodically reaffirmed, the metaphorical meaning may be dropped and replaced by a literal quality. Thus, for statements of the type "A is a B" identity rather than similarity might be assumed when the intent is that of marking a resemblance. Such a process is a natural development in language and serves the purposes of convenience and simplicity. However, the observer must always be alert to the possibility that the assumed identity between new and old concepts may be an unwarranted extension or an illicit reification. The following paragraphs are intended to support the notion that "the imagination" is an instance of unacknowledged reification.[3]

According to the Oxford English Dictionary, the etymological root of imagining, *imago,* was derived from a form from which imitate (*imitari*) had been developed. The root metaphor denoted imitating, copying through constructing a graven image, a carved likeness, or a sculptured statue. The etymology suggests that a word was required to communicate about three-dimensional sculpturing and engraving. On the basis of partial similarity between events ordinarily denoted by *imitari* and the copying activities of artisans, the root form of imitate was borrowed to denote the latter. The use of related words, "image," "imago," and similar forms was until the sixteenth century restricted to three-dimensional imitations such as objects of religious worship, sculptured figures, and carvings. When applied in a metaphorical way to those occurrences that are currently called "imaginings" the tenor was an *active* constructive process. That is to say, the pre-Renaissance imaginer was regarded as a fashioner, an image-maker, a fabricator, a doer; no implication was intended that he was a passive registrant of a mysterious process happening in an equally mysterious mind. When the rediscovered concept of mind was used to "naturalize the

---

[3] A more detailed presentation of these ideas is to be found in two of my earlier papers, Sarbin, 1964, 1968. See also Chun & Sarbin, 1970; Schon, 1963; Turbayne, 1962.

soul," i.e., to give philosophical credibility to the soul, human events not easily explained by concurrent rule-following models were assigned to the mysterious domain of mind. (To anticipate somewhat: the theory I shall advance brings back the notion of imitation as an element in imagining.)

A question of interest to linguistic historians is: how did the metaphor of constructing three-dimensional images become transformed into Everyman's "pictures in the mind?" The answer to such a question begins from the apparent similarity between graven images and optical images. Both are copies: one is obviously constructed through action, the other appears just to happen. When the mind was conceptualized as an organ located within the person, it was assigned the job formerly given to its more active predecessor "minding," which included imagining along with thinking and remembering.

What was the bridge between imagining as three-dimensional copying and imagining as two-dimensional (mental) pictures? Such a question can only be answered speculatively. I would suggest that in the distant past, a curious man looked into the eyes of a companion and beheld there a little child, a miniature, a *pupil*. (The locus of the reflection was later designated by the same word.) Unlike ordinary mirror images, the copy was miniaturized. In the absence of optical science, the tiny copy was assumed to lie somewhere behind the eye. Since the mind stuff could be anywhere within the body, the interiorized image could logically be located behind the eyeball, "in the mind." If a person reported "seeing" an absent object and there was no reflection from the body's eye, then the "seen" copy had to be in the mind's eye. Although these speculations may not be confirmable, the fact is undeniable that a shift in metaphor occurred—a shift from imagining as an active three-dimensional imitation to imagining as a passive mechanical mirroring in the mind.

After assigning images to the mind, the next step was the assimilation of imagining as active three-dimensional copying to an interiorized form of seeing. Our language is full of instances of this assimilation—"seeing in the mind's eye," "visualizing," "seeing mental pictures," "having a visual image," etc. These everyday expressions are witness to the fact that we have been taken in by the unlabeled metaphor—we now talk (a) as if there are pictures (sometimes called impressions or representations) and (b) as if there are minds that, like art galleries, provide a place for displaying these pictures.

The error of illicit metaphor-to-myth transformation and the assimilation of imagining to seeing is confounded by the different meanings of the verb "to see." An equivalence is assumed for the verb "to see" when it is used to denote ordinary seeing of objects in space and when it is employed in the special sense of "seeing in the mind's eye." In this connection, mention should be made that at least a score of meanings may be assigned to the verb, to see.

The uncritical acceptance of this particular metaphor-to-myth transformation has produced no fruitful suggestions for the psychological study of imaginings. Instead, it has followed the scholastic path of more and more verbalizations, increasingly remote from observations. That I am not setting up a straw man may be inferred from a statement of Holt (1964) who defined, e.g., image as the "generic term for all *conscious subjective presentations* of a *quasi-sensory* but *non-perceptual* character [p. 255]. Italics are added to emphasize the use of a vocabulary that might stimulate interminable scholastic disputations but not empirical research.

To recapitulate before continuing: In the natural history of the popular model of imagining as pictures in the mind, linguistic factors and metaphysical developments have been responsible for the unwarranted belief that imagining is an interiorized activity, carried on by a mythical organ, and resembling the seeing of spatial objects.

Imagining as Hypothetical Instantiation (*As If* Behavior)

Of course, rejecting the copies-in-the-mind formulation by no means solves the problem of accounting for the behavior normally denoted by the term "imagining."

Mentalism is not the only thought model available to students of silent and invisible processes. An alternate way of conceptualizing begins with guiding postulates quite different from those which conditioned the conclusions of, among others, John Locke (1924), who wrote "For in bare naked perception, the mind is, for the most part, only passive; and what it perceives, it cannot avoid perceiving [p. 73]." The alternate view looks upon man as an active, exploring manipulating, creating, doing creature. In short, man is an actor who, within limits, can construct his world instead of being merely the envelope of a passive mind and at the mercy of a capricious world. Man as actor demonstrates complex systems for acquiring and processing knowings, and most significantly, an aptitude or skill to function at various *levels of hypotheticalness*. ("Supposition," "assumption," and "as-ifness" are synonyms for this awkward term.) This aptitude makes it possible to distinguish between sentences of the form "I heard the voice," "I 'heard' the voice" and "I heard the voice of conscience." That is to say, man has a hierarchy of *as if* skills that liberate him from the constraints of the immediate environment. Through the use of this skill he can interbehave with events that are spatially distant and temporally remote. He can "entertain hypotheses," and relocate himself in different times and places.

Ryle (1949) has made suggestions for a better theory, in addition to exposing the error and lack of utility of the mentalistic view of regarding imagining as pictures in the mind. He argued that imagining is one way of applying the lessons that one has acquired through perceptual learning. Such behaviors as pretending, mocking, play-acting, and fancying are the referents for such expressions as "seeing with the mind's eye," "hearing a tune run through one's head," etc. The pictures in the mind metaphor collapses when proximal events (somesthetic experience) rather than distal events are fancied. The absurdity of the doctrine becomes apparent when we phrase the question: "what mentalistic window of the soul would have to be opened in order to imagine the taste of cheese blintzes, the fragrance of bayberry candles, or the feel of cracker crumbs in bed?"

Valuable as it is, Ryle's analysis is incomplete in that he fails clearly to differentiate imagining from recognition and from thinking, and, more important, the question of empirical confirmation is left open (Ryle, 1949).

The concept that I want to propose and defend is that of *hypothetical instantiation* (synonyms: suppositional instantiation, imitated perception, quasiperception, pretend instantiation, *as if* or metaphorical instantiation). Before describing hypothetical instantiation (*as if* behavior) a few words are in order about the concept instantiation. Borrowed from earlier writers, instantiation has been employed as a central concept in a theory of cognition (Sarbin, Taft, & Bailey, 1960). Among other things, this theory holds that, in the interest of survival, all of us must locate ourselves in our various ecologies. In order to do this we try to make sense out of the jumble of sensory inputs that are spun off from the world of occurrences. Our task is rendered possible by forming and using categories or classes. For simplicity and brevity, let us assume that a creature has but two classes in his catalogue of knowledge into which to sort occurrences in his natural ecology, "hostile things" and "not-hostile things." Suppose the world of occurrences suddenly generates some sensory input in the form of an unidentified sound. If the creature were subhuman, he would display the signs of vigilance characteristic of his species, e.g., distention of the nostrils, visual scanning movements, perking up the ears, reduction in motility, etc. If the creature could talk, he would compress all the behavior of vigilance into a question of the form *what is it?* If he were a philosophically oriented psychologist he might say: of which class of events is this sensory input an instance?

On the basis of resemblances between the unidentified noise and characteristics of, say, the class "hostile," he then constructs an instantiation: The thing emitting that sound is an instance of the class "hostile things," and he simultaneously prepares for action. Instantiation is thus an active process, it calls for sorting, classifying behavior, and for the utilization of concepts.

Through instantiation human beings place themselves with reference not only to objects and events that are present in the world of occurrences, but also with reference to objects and events that are absent. The act of instantiating absent objects and events is the referent for "hypothetical instantiation." Such an act can occur only when the person has achieved the skill of using fictions, such skill following from the acquisition of sign and symbol competences. These linguistic competences have been described by Vaihinger (1925) and by others as skill in using the *as if* grammatical form.

The words "skill" and "competence" are used intentionally to connote that *as if* behavior is subject to variation among individuals, and that it is acquired through commerce with people, things, and events. "Skill" in the present context takes on the same meaning as when employed with such modifiers as motoric, mechanical, verbal, or social. Competence is used here in similar fashion: it is not a mental state word, but a word that signifies ability or readiness to *perform* certain acts.

A three-stage sequence of child development is required to account for the achievement of the *as if* skill. As we know, the child acquires knowledge in a number of ways, one of which is imitation. In the developmental sequence, the first stage is the outright copying of performances of another person. This is the paradigm of imitation. That is to say, to imitate is to copy the actions of a model that can be seen and heard. In the second stage a complexity is introduced. The child imitates the actions of another, but that other is *absent*. The child imitates the motions and the talk of the absent model. This is the paradigm of role-taking. To pretend to be Fido when Fido is out of sight, is a high order achievement. The importance of playing "let's pretend" games in the development of the role-taking skill cannot be overemphasized. As an instance of engaging in suppositional, hypothetical behavior, a child may set up a tea table with limited stage props; she may pour fictional tea into ephemeral cups, and talk to an unoccupied chair as if it were holding a guest.

The third stage is concurrent with another achievement of early childhood: the muting of speech. To talk to oneself rather than aloud at first requires only the skill in controlling the volume of air that passes over the vocal cords. With practice, the child learns to inhibit most of the obvious muscular characteristics of speech. At the same time that he acquires the skill in muting his speech, the child learns to attenuate his role-taking actions, to reduce the amplitude of the overt responses that comprise his let's-pretend roles. For this third stage—muted, attenuated, role-taking—the word "imagining" is appropriate.

The parallel between the semantic analysis sketched before and the three-stage development of skill in imagining is indeed striking. For the root of the word "imagination" the shift in meaning is from three-dimensional imitating to silent internalized "seeing in the mind's eye." For the development of skill in imagining, three-dimensional copying of actual objects comes first—upon this foundation is built the ability to copy *in absentia;* in turn, copying *in absentia* serves as a basis for acquiring skill in muting the role-taking actions.

Experimental Tests of Imagining as Hypothetical Instantiation

The foregoing paragraphs point to the lack of utility of the prevailing mentalistic doctrine of imagining, and introduce a new metaphor, hypothetical instantiation (which I shall henceforth mercifully shorten to *as if* behavior). It now remains to illustrate the utility of the new metaphor. The formulation of imagining as a skill, dependent upon concurrently acquired skill in role-taking and in imitating, has led to a number of experiments. The methods are unlike those employed by psychologists who subscribe to some version of the pictures-in-the-mind doctrine. Such investigators in one way or another ask their subjects to examine their "minds" and report what they "see." Such methods have not been fruitful. Introspection as a method has failed because of the unrecognized transformation of mind from a metaphor to a literal entity.

In a number of studies in my laboratory, we began with a set of tasks that met the traditional requirements for imagery. That is, the subject was asked to perform a task where some object necessary to the completion of the task was absent. To solve the problem, he must, in the older language, have an image: in the present language he must engage in hypothetical behavior, in *as if* behavior. Furthermore, we have not limited ourselves to tasks in the visual mode: we have also used tasks that call for *as if* behavior in the auditory, olfactory, tactile, and gustatory modes, singly and in combination. In our experimental designs, these tasks serve as dependent variables.[4]

[4] The experiment reported below is abstracted from Juhasz, J. B., Imagining, imitation, and role-taking. Unpublished doctoral dissertation, University of California, Berkeley, 1969.

Some of the fourteen tasks that met the criterion of imagery are herewith described. In the first, the experimenter asks the subject to sniff seven vials, in order. He is asked to "keep in mind" the smell of the first two, and to select from the following five the one that is a 50/50 combination of the first two. An important feature in developing this test is to use materials for which the subject has no ready-made code word.

The second task is like the first save that the materials affect taste only—the subject samples drops of liquid.

The third is of the same pattern, except that touch is the medium. The subject must add distances presented by compasslike instruments (one at a time) to the back of the hand.

In another task, the same paradigm is used with musical sounds.

In another task, the subject sees a videotape recording of a model train running around a circular track and passing through a tunnel. Then the subject views five additional videotapes of the same stimulus material, but in four, the speed of the train has been modified during its transit through the tunnel. The subject must select the scene that matches the first.

Another item is a "visualization" task drawn from the early literature. The subject is asked to imagine a 3-inch cube painted red. Then he is to imagine the cube sawed into 1-inch cubes. His task is to report to the experimenter, how many of the cubes have paint on three sides, on two sides, on one side, and on no side.

In another task the subject feels an abstract-shaped tile blindfolded. Then he is asked to pick it out from a group of four other similar ones by visual inspection alone. Then he is reblindolded and is asked to select the one that he had just pointed to on visual inspection.

These are exemplars of the imagining tasks. Performance is scored from 0 to 4 depending upon previously established criteria. Scores for each task are added to make up a composite imagery score.

During the second phase of the experiment, ten imitation tasks are performed before a videotape camera. Each person is asked to imitate a model who performs such simple acts as clapping his hand three times, pinching his ears, and saying "three roses." The subjects' performances are recorded on videotape so that the quality of the imitations can be assessed at a later time by a panel of judges.

After the imitations, ten role-taking tasks are performed. Each subject is asked to portray a role before the videotape camera in one minute, without props or supporting players. Examples of the role playing tasks are "you are a French chef instructing a group of American housewives on the proper way to boil artichokes"; "you are an old lady who has just received a telegram saying that your only son has been killed."

Three judges, without knowledge of performance on the imagery tasks, made differentiated judgments on the quality of the imitations and on various dimensions of role-playing.

It is important to note that the tasks were constructed to test specific hypotheses that were drawn from a set of propositions suggested in part by the foregoing historical-linguistic analysis, namely, that imagining was an active form of conduct, a performance, a doing, that had its origins in the practice of imitating with models present and of imitating with models absent.

With the aid of a high speed computer, multiple regression coefficients were calculated. Nine ratings and scores of the imitation and role-taking tasks were combined in an optimal fashion. This composite score correlated significantly with the sum of the imagery tasks. The magnitude of the multiple correlation coefficient ($R = .65$) is unprecedented for crude variables of this kind.[5]

The results confirm the conjecture that persons who are efficient imitators and convincing role-players are also skilled at imagery tasks. This empirical support for the hypothesis strengthens the underlying theory of action which was offered as a replacement for the traditional mentalistic view.

Degree of Involvement and the "Reality" of Imaginings

In the preceding pages, I have tried to show that the traditional view of imagining is sterile; that the alternate view of imagining as a form of attenuated action is productive in setting conditions for me and my students to generate hypotheses that could be tested empirically. It has been said before that empirical observations alone do not change the course of science. An entrenched but unproductive theory can withstand numerous empirical assaults. It begins to collapse only when challenged by a new metaphor—one more appropriate to the times, more consistent with concurrent developments in political, social, and technological life.

In spite of my arguments some readers will insist on the usefulness of such statements as the following (uttered by a colleague): "In my experience, when I am imagining something, I see pictures. I am a good visual-

---

[5] In a cross-validational study with art students as subjects, Juhasz used a short form of the imagery procedures. Correlations with meaningful dependent variables were promising, e.g., with ratings of students' art work .55, with ratings of originality .61, and with Gottschaldt Figures Test .71. (Personal communication.)

izer. My pictures are not always as clear as good photographs, but they are pictures nevertheless. The mental pictures that I see are *real.*" When questioned regarding what is "real," he replied that for some images there is no question but that they have a "reality not different from actually seeing an object in veridical perception."

In earlier times, the reports of religious leaders have been used to ratify the claim that, under some conditions, what appears as imagining is a veridical perception. In the context of mentalism, the interpretation was offered that the reporter was in fact responding to stimulus events of a superempirical order. Such interpretations are not acceptable to modern scientists.

The problem of what is real turns out to be a pseudoproblem. The word "real" is an excluder word. It tells only what something is not, and then only if the context is known. Linguistic philosophers and philosophers of science have clearly demonstrated that the word *real* has no function in an argument. Cohen (1964) put it cogently:[6]

> If terms that have no genuine negatives are to be condemned as devoid of significance, the word reality should head the list. I am not unmindful of the many attempts to define the unreal. But the question is: What corresponds to these definitions? The Hindoo mystic is deeply irritated when the wise Chinese suggests that the realm of Maya or illusion does not really exist, or that it is not worth while worrying about it. The reality of illusion is the emphatic center of the Hindoo's philosophy, and similarly, of all those who sharply contrast reality and appearance. The difficulty here is classic. What I am more especially concerned about, however, is to call attention to the fact that the word *reality maintains* itself as a term of praise rather than of description. To be "in touch with reality" is our way of expressing what our less sophisticated brothers and sisters do by the phrase "in tune with the infinite." It is an expression which carries an agreeable afflatus without dependence on any definite meaning. Such edification is pleasing and would be harmless if it did not also cause intellectual confusion [pp. 455–456].

The problem contained in those self-reports that declare that the image has the appearance of reality cannot be dismissed merely by informing the reporter that his choice of language is questionable. It is important to recognize that we have just entered the area of degree of belief. "Real" is frequently used as a term to indicate credibility. The posture for the contemporary behavior analyst, then, is to ask questions of the following type: "What does the reporter *mean* when he says that his image was real?" "What are his observations that led him to choose 'real' as an attribute,

---

[6] Austin (1962) has also written a pointed analysis demonstrating the lack of utility of the words "real" and "reality."

rather than some other characteristic?" "What are the observations and inferences that led him to believe his imaginings to be literal events?" The answers to such questions can only emerge from detailed analyses of the reporter's communications, analyses that are semantic, syntactic, and pragmatic.

The more general question is now open; to wit, what are the antecedent and concurrent conditions that account for the metaphors a person employs to communicate about those areas of dim knowledge that are sometimes labeled intuitive, unsystematic, phenomenal, and unconscious?

As a starting point, consider David Hume's selection of the metaphors *lively* and *vivid* (among others) to describe that bit of dim knowledge to which he had assigned other metaphors—"impressions" and "ideas." He was of course writing in the historical period when mentalism was an unquestioned doctrine. The everyday language of vision and spatial relations provided him, as it did his contemporaries, with a framework for a theory of mind. To be consistent with the language of vision he should have employed such descriptive terms as "degrees of clarity," "brightness" and "distinctiveness" when referring to mental contents. Such words were currently available. Instead, he used adjectives more appropriate to a language of action: "lively," "vivid," "vivacious," and "forceful." This inconsistency poses a problem: why did he employ adjectives with a transparent relationship to action rather than the scalar words of vision?

I submit that such terms as lively, vivid, vivacious, and forceful were selected by Hume not because they were appropriate to fictive mental contents but rather because such words denoted high degrees of involvement in cognitive activity. That is to say, in examining his own cognitive behavior, Hume was engaged in a form of action, rather than in the passive reception of sensory stimuli or in the observation of impressions and ideas flitting hither and yon in mental space according to the laws of association. He was struggling to generate new knowledge and expanding effort in the process. So when he examined his own conduct (not his own mind) he noticed the bodily signs of action, of involvement in the intellectual role. Metaphors such as "lively," "vivid," and "active" were more appropriate to the conclusions drawn from his self-examination than the attributes of spatial stimuli. In the intellectual climate of the eighteenth century, the active minding, thinking, and classifying conduct of human beings was easily assimilated to the illusory mechanical motions of mental objects in mental space.

In speculating about Hume's phenomenology, I am suggesting that the action concept "degrees of involvement" is applicable to silent, attenuated, *as if* behavior. To prepare the way for incorporating this concept into the present argument, I refer to a concept that has already demonstrated its usefulness: degree of involvement in role enactment. The referent here is a quantitative one: In overtly enacting a role, the actor may participate with varying amounts of force and vigor. Under some conditions, few organismic systems are activated, self and role remain separate, and we may speak of minimal involvement in the role. Example: a ticket seller at a movie theater during a slow period, who takes the money, pushes the button for the tickets and another for the change. Under other conditions, more of the organismic systems are activated, the role engages the self, so to speak, we refer to moderate involvement. Example: a professional actor who is portraying a role on stage for the thirtieth time; his actions must be convincing, he must be alert to cues from other actors and from the audience. High involvement in role behavior is illustrated in such conditions as ecstasy, mystical experience, religious conversion, and sexual union (Sarbin & Allen, 1968).

Just as we can fruitfully talk of degree of involvement in overt role-enactment so can we talk of degree of involvement in muted role-taking, i.e., imagining. At the minimal level of involvement we might cite the college sophomore who appears as a subject in a required laboratory exercise. He reports tasting salt when a few drops of tasteless distilled water are put on his tongue. He is probably not highly involved in the *as if* behavior of tasting salt.[7] An example of moderate involvement in imagining would be the case of the playwright or novelist struggling to construct a character or a scene—especially if he were facing a deadline. The degree of involvement could be noted in the motoric accompaniment of the creative process such as nervous pacing, heavy pressure of the pencil on the tablet, vigorous striking of typewriter keys, inattention to extraneous stimuli, etc. Perhaps at a similar level of involvement in imagining behavior is the reader of a story who weeps upon reading the tragic destiny of the hero. An unusually high degree of involvement in *as if* behavior is illustrated in the following excerpt. It is taken from the report of an experiment by Feshbach & Feshbach (1963).

> Ten neighborhood boys, ranging in age from 9–12, were invited to a Halloween party at the home of the experimenters. . . . When the boys arrived, they found themselves in a completely darkened house except for one room which was illuminated by a jack-o-lantern. The eeriness of the atmosphere was further enhanced by having the children form a circle and relate ghost stories to each other. Although the diameter of the circle was about

[7] In this experiment, only distilled water was used. Certain subtle demands were made for students to "taste" salt. Many of them reported "salt"—demonstrating that imagining can to a certain extent be manipulated by setting up the proper conditions (Juhasz & Sabrin, 1966).

11 ft. at the beginning of the storytelling, by the time the last ghost story was completed, it had been spontaneously reduced to approximately 3 ft [p. 499].

I have given what may seem like an inordinate amount of space to developing the concept *degree of involvement*. The space is justified if the description is helpful in understanding why some individuals claim their imaginings are "real," why some imaginings are believed to be of the same character as literal happenings in the distal world. The arguments are intended to convey the proposition that when a person claims "reality" for his imaginings, it is likely that he is deeply involved in the *as if* behavior and further, that words such as "real," "lively," and "vivid" would be the metaphors of choice.

Metaphoric Coding

At this point, I recognize a gap in my arguments. It is one thing to say that when a person is deeply involved in his muted role-taking, he is likely to assign descriptive adjectives that convey the notion that his imagining was indistinguishable from his seeing, hearing, tasting, smelling, and feeling of objects in the distal world. It is another thing to point to a principle that would predict that he would use metaphors to describe his self-observations, and, even more important, that would point to the conditions that support the leap from metaphor to myth.

Returning to cognitive theory for a moment, the problem for the actor is to locate himself with reference to the confused mass of sensory inputs that surround him. The inputs are generated in the distal ecology—mediated by the organs of seeing and hearing, and in the proximal ecology—mediated by a number of sense organs which include taste, smell, touch, muscular strain, heat and cold, and others. Inputs must be instantiated in order to be useful in constructing premises and in drawing conclusions. In nontechnical language, the actor must make sense out of the blooming, buzzing confusion of sights, sounds, tastes, feels, etc.

One way of looking at the instantiation process is through the employment of codes. For our purposes, we can identify two kinds of codes, the employment of which enables the actor to go beyond the information given. First, we can identify conventional codes—the arbitrary system of spoken and written symbols which stand for something different from the sensory input contained in the symbol. The peculiar pattern of sound waves "chair" signifies an object of certain characteristics known to all adult members of the English language community. When an actor wants to signify to himself or to others what a certain external object is, he will make use of the conventional code.

When an actor must instantiate inputs for which the conventional system has no symbol, he must rely on his ability to construct an analogy. He notices a resemblance between a feature of an uninstantiable event such as specks on the horizon and a feature of a known event.*flying objects* and borrows the symbol for the previously uninstantiated event. Under benign conditions, when involvement is of a low order, the actor might verbalize his conclusion by using the simile: "The speck is like a flying object." If he has some language sophistication, he might say: "It is *as if* the speck is a flying object." When talking to an audience, he might drop the suppositional modifier and say "It is a flying object." I have already alluded to this process in discussing the etymology of imagining—an unlabeled metaphor comes to serve as a minor premise in a syllogistic argument.

More important than the construction of the *as if* inference in connection with distal events such as imaginary flying saucers, is the use of the metaphor to encode inputs that are generated in the nondistal world. For example, a browser suddenly notices the peculiar musty smell that is characteristic of old book stores. He has no conventional code word to instantiate the olfactory input—such as resinous, 4711, or rosewater. He notices a resemblance to another event: the smell of the interior of a summer cottage by the sea. He might say to himself "it is like the summer cottage" or "it is *as if* I am in the summer cottage," or "I am in the summer cottage." Because of the limitations of print, I have had to illustrate metaphorical instantiation through the use of words. The psychological literature abounds in observations that colors, shapes, sizes, and nonsense sounds may be used for such metaphorization. The taste of lemon juice is instantiated as the sound *bing*, not *bang;* a sudden awareness of an obvious cue in solving a puzzle may be instantiated as *boing* or *aha!;* the discovery of a new metaphor may be instantiated as an electric globe; the noonday heat in Death Valley as *10 tons,* the sound of a flute as the color *blue-white;* the feel of sandpaper as the sound of a *bagpipe* (Sarbin & Quenk, 1964). Because such cognitive outcomes are usually not made public, metaphoric codings tend to be idiosyncratic.

When the actor tries to communicate his hypothetical instantiation to others, under ordinary conditions he tries to make use of the conventional code. In many instances, however, the conventional code words are too feeble to capture the full intent of the speaker. Under these conditions, the speaker becomes a metaphor maker and user and, as I said before, the metaphor may be expressed through other forms than words: gestures and dance, music and sonic rhythm, color and line.

On the Credibility
of Imaginings

My final point is addressed to the degree of belief in imaginary experiences that amounts to complete conviction. In the terms of this chapter, complete conviction is expressed as the metaphor being displaced by a myth. It now remains to suggest how this leap is accomplished. I have already alluded to the degree of involvement in *as if* behavior. My proposal is this: the higher the degree of involvement, the more likely the actor will interpret his metaphors literally. When he formulates them for his relevant audiences, he will use identity terms, rather than *as if* terms. Instead of saying: It was *as if* I heard the word of the Lord, he will say "I heard the word of the Lord!" (The average listener will not ask if quotation marks should be placed around "heard.") In another place, I report an experiment that demonstrates a strong tendency even under conditions of low involvement for people to drop *as if* qualifiers when they reproduce stories. Under conditions of high involvement, more organismic systems are engaged and the imaginer has more sensory inputs of a bodily kind to instantiate. The following autobiographical account, written by George Trosse, a seventeenth century clergyman, is instructive. (Note that he shifts back and forth between the metaphorical and literal.)

> While I was thus walking up and down, hurried with these worldly disquieting thoughts, I perceiv'd a Voice (I heard it plainly), saying unto me, *Who art thou?* Which, knowing it could be the Voice of no Mortal, I concluded, was the Voice of God, and with Tears, as I remember, reply'd, *I am a very great Sinner, LORD!* Hereupon, I withdrew again into the inner-Room, securing and barring the Door upon me, I betook myself to a very proper and seasonable Duty, namely, Secret Prayer. . . .
> For while I was praying upon my Knees, I heard a Voice, as I fancy'd, as it were just behind me, saying, *Yet more humble; Yet more humble;* With some Continuance. And not knowing the Meaning of the Voice, but undoubtedly concluding it came from GOD, I endeavour'd to comply with it. . . . [Hunter & MacAlpine, 1963, p. 154].

Reverend Mr. Trosse was undoubtedly struggling with some important problem. In the course of his meditation, some input (not necessarily generated externally) was instantiated as a voice. Most logically, since there was no one else in the room and since God was everywhere, he concluded that the voice came from God. One does not entertain lightly an experience that concerns one's relationship to the transcendental world. As William James wrote: "For common men 'religion,' whatever more special meanings it may have, signifies always a serious state of mind . . . It [religion] favors gravity, not pertness; it says 'hush' to all vain chatter and smart wit [James, 1902, p. 56]." When one engages in conduct of a religious character, then, he is likely to participate with a high degree of involvement.

The autobiographical statement by the late Bishop James A. Pike lends itself to an interpretation in the present idiom (Pike, 1968). A theological scholar of many accomplishments, Bishop Pike reported communications with his dead son through psychic mediums. Recognizing that my brief description cannot do justice to the detail presented in his book, the account may be summarized as follows. His son, Jim, age 20, killed himself in a New York hotel room. The tragic event occurred at the end of a period during which father and son had shared a sabbatical in England living together and becoming close friends. The setting for the development of their deep relationship was the effort (not successful) of the younger Pike to give up a dependency on psychedelic drugs.

Shortly after the suicide, a series of unexplained events occurred in the apartment which he and his son had shared. These events led Bishop Pike and his two staff members to the conclusion that a poltergeist was at work. For example, objects that had belonged to the younger Pike, or were related to his interests, mysteriously appeared in a geometrical pattern of 140 degrees. The bangs of the hair-do of Bishop Pike's secretary were mysteriously removed by an undiscovered burning instrument. To explain these and similar events, Bishop Pike consulted first one medium, then another, then a third. With all three mediums, communications was established with the spiritually alive (although physically dead) son. A few excerpts establish the basis for regarding his imaginings of the counterfactual conditions (*as if* behavior) as being characterized by a high degree of involvement. For example, when his son's ashes were scattered at sea, Bishop Pike ". . . felt the deep sorrow of having lost not only a son, but also my closest friend [p. 73]." The expectation of occult events is reflected in a number of passages.

> I then made bold to address Jim directly, feeling somewhat strange in doing so since he was of course nowhere to be seen. "Did you know that was going to happen when you left me at the airport?"
> He seemed to reply, "I had a fear of it—because I dreaded your leaving me this last time [p. 123]."

That Bishop Pike was deeply involved over his son's death is easily documented. Like most men with deep parental feelings, in this case reinforced by a period of intense comradeship, the "grief work" was intense and pervasive. That Bishop Pike had feelings of guilt over the suicide is an inference that a reader might safely draw. These conditions set the stage for high involvement, for "seeing" and "hearing" and "feeling" in the absence of sensory input. The will-to-believe, of course, plays a part in the story, particularly since the meassage from the spirit world conveyed the impression that all was well and that the younger Pike would be able to help and inspire the elder.

Briefly, I mention two additional variables that influence the assigning of credibility to imagined, counterfactual, events: ambiguity and risk.

Some Additional Variables

The ambiguity of the setting in which imagining occurs must be taken into account. In experiments where the stimulus intensity is near threshold the subject may interpret a nonexistent stimulus as present, or an existent simulus as absent. In short, ambiguity facilitates *as if* behavior. The subject is called upon to instantiate an event when the amount of information supplied is inadequate. Under conditions of high involvement the subject is likely to assign a high degree of credibility to the hypothetical instantiation.

Further, we cannot ignore the fact that the actor takes into account such factors as risk and the potential value of outcomes if he maintains the metaphor or if he shifts to the myth. Under conditions of cognitive strain, all of us at one time or another have entertained the hypothesis that a supposition be taken as a veridical observation. The soldier assigned to night sentry duty in the jungles of South-East Asia may hear a noise like a footstep, or "hear" a noise like a footstep. He must make a quick decision—whether to say to himself "it is *as if I heard* a footstep," or "I *heard* a footstep." The potential loss to him and his comrades of maintaining the belief that it was an imaginary footstep is greater than the potential loss in mistakenly shouting a challenge. Furthermore, unless there is overwhelming evidence to contradict his literal interpretation, it will continue to be believed.[8]

Summary

In this chapter, I have tried to describe imagining as action. Rejecting the mentalistic model that depended upon "pictures in the mind" and simi-

---

[8] Professors Philip Hallie and Karl Scheibe independently noted the similarity to Pascal's wager: In the absence of certain knowledge, to disbelieve in the existence of God is to take an unnecessary risk of the greatest magnitude.

lar metaphors, I have argued for the use of metaphors more continuous with current efforts to describe social behavior. Arguments are offered to support the hypothesis that imagining may be fruitfully regarded as a form of hypothetical or "*as if*" behavior, namely, muted role-taking.

The present formulation helps illuminate the murky problems generated by the observation that some imaginings are regarded as "real." In the context of social interaction, it is useful to talk about degrees of involvement in the performance of a role. This concept can be applied to muted role-taking as well, where the person is enacting his role silently and in attenuated form. Under high involvement (focused attention and increased physiological arousal), conditions are created for regarding the hypothetical behavior as credible. Thus, when persons talk about the "reality" of their imaginings, they are referring to the high degree of credibility that they choose to attach to their suppositions and hypotheticals.

References

Austin, J. L. *Sense and sensibilia.* London: Oxford Univ. Press, 1962.

Chun, K., & Sarbin, T. R. An empirical demonstration of metaphor to myth transformation. *Philosophical Psychology,* 1970, **4,** 16–21.

Cohen, M. R. (Orig. publ., 1931.) *Reason and nature.* New York: Free Press, 1964.

Emerson, R. W. Essay: The poet. In E. W. Emerson and W. E. Forbes (Eds.), *Complete works.* Boston, Massachusetts: Houghton, 1903.

Feshbach, S., & Feshbach, N. Influence of the stimulus object upon the complementary and supplementary projection of fear. *Journal of Abnormal and Social Psychology,* 1963, **66,** 498–502.

Holt, R. R. Imagery: The return of the ostracized. *American Psychologist,* 1964, **19,** 254–264.

Hunter, I., & MacAlpine, A. (Eds.), *Three hundred years of psychiatry.* London: Oxford Univ. Press, 1963.

James, W. *Varieties of religious experience.* New York: Longmans, Green, 1902.

Juhasz, J. B., & Sarbin, T. R. On the "false alarm" metaphor in psychophysics. *Psychological Record,* 1966, **16,** 323–327.

Locke, J. *An essay concerning human understanding.* London: Oxford Univ. Press, 1924.

Mann, T. Freud and the future (Translated by H. T. Lowe-Porter.) In *Essays of three decades.* London: Secker & Warburg, 1947. Pp. 411–428.

Pike, J. A. (with Diane Kennedy) *The other side: An account of my experiences with psychic phenomena.* Garden City, New York: Doubleday, 1968.

Ryle, G. *The concept of mind.* Oxford: Hutchinson, 1949.

Sarbin, T. R. Contributions to role-taking theory I: Hypnotic behavior. *Psychological Review,* 1950, **57,** 255–270.

Sarbin, T. R. Anxiety: The reification of a metaphor. *Archives of General Psychiatry,* 1964, **10,** 630–638.

Sarbin, T. R. On the futility of the proposition that some people be labeled mentally ill. *Journal of Consulting Psychology*, 1967, **31**, 447–453.

Sarbin, T. R. The concept of hallucination. *Journal of Personality*, 1967, **35**, 359–380.

Sarbin, T. R. Ontology recapitulates philology: The mythic nature of anxiety. *American Psychologist*, 1968, **23**, 411–418.

Sarbin, T. R. Schizophrenic thinking: A role theoretical interpretation. *Journal of Personality*, 1969, **37**, 190–206.

Sarbin, T. R., & Allen, V. L. Role theory. In G. Lindzey and E. Aronson (Eds.), *Handbook of Social Psychology*, Vol. I. Reading, Massachusetts: Addison-Wesley, 1968. Pp. 488–567.

Sarbin, T. R., & Andersen, M. L. Role-theoretical analysis of hypnotic behavior. In Gordon, J. E. (Ed.), *Handbook of clinical and experimental hypnosis*. New York: Macmillan, 1967. Pp. 319–344.

Sarbin, T. R., & Juhasz, J. B. The historical background of the concept of hallucination. *Journal of the History of Behavioral Sciences*, 1967, **3**, 339–358.

Sarbin, T. R., & Juhasz, J. B. Toward a theory of imagination. *Journal of Personality*, 1970, **38**, 52–76.

Sarbin, T. R., & Quenk, A. The rationality of nonsense: Intensity of meaning of non-referential verbal units. *Psychological Record*, 1964, **14**, 401–409.

Sarbin, T. R., Taft, R., & Bailey, D. E. *Clinical inference and cognitive theory*. New York: Holt, 1960.

Schon, T. W. *Displacement of concepts*. London: Tavistock, 1963.

Turbayne, C. *The myth of metaphor*. New Haven: Yale Univ. Press, 1962.

Vaihinger, H. *Philosophy of "as if."* New York: Harcourt, 1925.

15 VLADISLAV ZIKMUND

PHYSIOLOGICAL
CORRELATES OF
VISUAL IMAGERY

Introduction

A common feature of phenomena subsumed under the rather general term of mental imagery is the presence of an experience of sensory nature that is not based on actual sensory input. There exist however, many other characteristics by which various kinds of mental images may differ one from another in a more or less substantial way. The relation of an image to a previous percept may vary from a close bond between sensory stimulation and its mental reflection (e.g., as in an afterimage), to imagery phenomena, where the appropriate perceptual source is hardly detectible (e.g., some fantasies, hallucinations, dreams). Particular kinds of mental images may differ conspicuously in their vividness, duration and the degree to which they can be controlled and influenced at will. Basic differences exist between some mental imagery phenomena as regards the way they are processed by the mind and/or the manner in which an individual deals with them. Some mental images are fairly normal, while others are pathological phenomena. Some of both may be closely related to changes in consciousness. Consequently, a general and comprehensive definition of mental imagery is difficult to shape. This applies equally to its physiological bases.

The majority of physiological studies of mental imagery have been based on the experiential similarity between imaging and perceiving. As early as 1893, Külpe denoted images as centrally excited sensations. Leuba (1940) pointed to their conditioned nature, and Oswald (1962, p. 76) believed that "the neurophysiological *response* (author's italics) present when a real object is perceived by means of one's sense organs is similar to that present when an image, a pseudohallucination or a hallucination is perceived." These views or hypotheses indicate two somewhat different levels at which the physiological mechanisms of mental imagery phenomena may be discussed. The first, which is the basic one, concerns the physiological mechanisms *underlying* particular mental imagery phenomena, that is mechanisms which, under various physiological or pathological conditions give rise to perceptual experience in an individual in the absence of appropriate sensory stimulation from the outer world. Another level of the study of physiological mechanisms of mental imagery concerns rather its physiological phenomenology, that is, the physiological consequents and/or changes *accompanying* various kinds of mental images. Many attempts have been made in recent years to determine those changes in physiological functions which *characterize* the appearance of an image. Most physiological studies of mental imagery, from both points of view, have been concerned with the visual modality. It is this modality that we will also be concerned with in this chapter.

Research data referring to the physiological mechanisms underlying particular mental imagery phenomena have been scant. This is due to the enormous complexity of these phenomena and to the well-known methodological difficulties of the physiological study of mental events in general. Some problems concerning this approach to visual imagery will be briefly illustrated in the examples of afterimages and of hallucinations given in the next section.

In the following sections physiological changes accompanying or characterizing visual imagery will be discussed. The term "to accompany" as used in this connection is meant to convey that certain physiological changes may appear during imagery due to its complex nature. These changes may reflect certain alterations for example in the general arousal of the central nervous system, changes in attention, emotions, etc., which may vary considerably depending on the individual, his attitude to the imagined content, the actual conditions under which an image takes place, and so forth, even if the same visual image has been evoked. Physiological changes which may accompany visual imagery will be briefly reviewed from the most general ones (autonomic changes) to those which may reflect the process of imagining in a rather specific manner (changes in the bioelectric activity of the brain and changes in oculomotor activity).

Finally, data will be presented indicating that following, or pursuit, eye movements may be recorded in some subjects during vivid visual imagery of moving objects. This type of gaze movements, forming the slow phase of the so-called optokinetic nystagmus (OKN) is an inherent component of the mechanisms of visual motion perception and it may be used (as will be shown in the present chapter) as a physiological indicator which characterizes vivid visual imagery under certain conditions. These results allow indirect inferences concerning the physiological processes underlying sensory experience during vivid visual imagery. They support the view that vivid visual imagery is closely related to the reactivation of the complex visual and oculomotor components of previous percepts which have been stored in the brain.

Physiological Bases of Visual Imagery

Present day knowledge about the physiological processes underlying particular phenomena of visual imagery is scant. Available data point to the great complexity of these processes, involving the broad integrative activity of the whole mind, as illustrated by the more precisely defined visual-imagery phenomena such as afterimages and hallucinations. There is no doubt, for example, that visual afterimages are primarily a retinal phenomenon due to physiological changes persisting in retinal cells after visual stimulation has been withdrawn (e.g., Brindley, 1959, 1962; Craik, 1940; Kohlrausch, 1925). Some evidence exists, however, suggesting that the sensory information from an afterimage is elaborated upon to various degrees at the cerebral level. A rather central origin has been presumed for such phenomena as fragmentation and regeneration of afterimages of patterned stimuli (e.g., Bennet-Clark & Evans, 1963; Evans, 1965, 1967; Piggins, 1968). Popov and Popov (1953, 1954) described afterimages as being elaborated on the basis of conditioned reflex mechanisms. The afterimage of a stimulus applied to one eye is known to be perceived also in the nonstimulated eye. Abnormal clarity or persistence of visual afterimages was demonstrated in some patients with a disorder of the occipital lobe (Bender & Teuber, 1947; Herman & Pötzl, 1928) and also in subjects with eidetic imagery ability (e.g., Meenes & Morton, 1936). Observations of afterimages occurring as an aftereffect of vivid visual images of stimuli in the waking state, in dreams and in hallucinations under hypnosis, have recently been reviewed by Richardson (1969).

Abundant neurophysiological, psychophysiological, and clinical data exist that point to the complex elaboration by the brain of hallucinatory experience. Visual hallucinations can be evoked through stimulation of the visual pathways at almost any level (Walsh & Hoyt, 1969). Penfield and his co-workers (Penfield & Jasper, 1954; Penfield & Kristiansen, 1951;

Penfield & Pérot, 1963; and Penfield & Rasmussen, 1950) found that simple visual hallucinations (e.g., lights, colors, shadows) were experienced when the visual, parastriate, and peristriate cortex of the occipital lobe were stimulated, while complex hallucinations of meaningful forms, such as images of people and objects resulted rather from stimulation of the temporal region. Clinical observations report, to a certain degree, similar topographical relations between the type of visual hallucinations and the localization of pathological processes in the brain structures (e.g., Gassel, 1969; Walsh & Hoyt, 1969; Williams, 1969). These hallucinations may also be produced by a lesion of diencephalic structures (e.g., De Morsier, 1969a, 1969b). Sem-Jacobsen, Petersen, Lazarte, Dodge, and Holman (1955) reported hippocampal discharges in psychotics experiencing visual hallucinations. Walsh and Hoyt (1969) support the conclusion of Weinberger and Grant (1940) to the effect that visual hallucinations in cerebrally diseased patients do not have any such precise localizing value as has been attributed to them by many clinicians. The visual mechanisms of these hallucinations are not known. Their resemblance to the visual sensory experience induced by electrical stimulation of the brain merely suggests that the visual sensations which occur in disease may be irritative phenomena, or seizures (Feldman & Bender, 1970). The authors mentioned above (Weinberger & Grant, 1940) even believe that the factors determining whether any lesion at any level of the visual system may arouse visual hallucinations, are the subject's own visual memories and experiences. Horowitz (1964) supposes that the origin of some visual hallucinations may be in the anatomic structures of the eye and the bioelectrical circuits for pattern receptivity in the retinal ganglionic network. The sensory impulses of such an origin are then secondarily elaborated in dependence on the functional state of the higher levels of the brain. Some support for such concepts may be seen in the evidence that almost identical visual hallucinations may arise under very different pathological conditions and that the content of the hallucinations, on the other hand, is markedly influenced by the subject's previous experiences, attitudes, emotions and other mental events. It may be presumed that the less a visual hallucinatory experience depends on the processes affecting the visual system, the more pathological mental events underlie and determine its content.

An attempt has recently been made by Hebb (1968) to analyze the mechanisms of sensory experience in various mental imagery phenomena in physiological terms. The author holds the mechanism of imagery to be an aberrant mechanism of exteroception which is not generated by sensory input, but by the processes in the central nervous system. He speculates that the differences between the vividness and clarity of various kinds of mental images (e.g., memory images, eidetic images, hallucinations) are due to the involvement of hypothesized cell assemblies of various orders in association cortex and related structures of the brain.

Physiological Changes Accompanying Visual Imagery

Since the complex cerebral processes underlying imagery phenomena have offered, like all other mental events, very restricted possibilities for direct physiological study, a more indirect approach has tended to be followed in recent years: one oriented to the physiological concomitants of imagery rather than to the bases of imagery arousal. It was presumed that the physiological changes accompanying any act of imagining could yield some conclusions about its basic physiological mechanisms. However, an important question arose: Do there exist specific physiological correlates of an image which can distinguish this phenomenon from all other mental events, or which could relate it to perceptual processes? Barratt (1956) has concluded that an objective indicator of imagery should comply with the following conditions: (a) it should be specific to the mental phenomenon it is said to indicate; (b) it should appear under all conditions under which the appropriate mental phenomenon is present and should not appear under any other circumstances; and (c) the conditions under which some events operate as indicators of imagery should be specified exactly.

The physiological changes studied from this point of view in visual imagery can generally be grouped into three main categories: (a) changes in autonomic functions; (b) changes in bioelectric activity of the brain; and (c) changes in eye movement activity. The remainder of this chapter will deal with each of these categories in turn. The first category refers to physiological changes accompanying imagery as a complex mental phenomenon implying the presence of many other mental functions, e.g., attention, memory, emotions, etc. The second category refers to the bioelectrical display in the brain of the processes leading to the tendency to imagine and to the production in the mind of the "visual image" as well. Consequently, this category involves both the physiological correlates of integrative mental events on the basis of which an image can be aroused and also the electrophysiological manifestations of the processes in the brain related to the sensory component of an image in the strict sense of the term. The third category is in some way similar to the second, except for the fact that oculomotor activity can directly indicate the perception of particular kinds of visual stimuli, and thus be used also as an eventual specific indicator of their visual imagery.

Changes in Autonomic Functions

Changes in the vegetative functions are an inherent reflection of changes in arousal level in the central nervous system. They are known to be closely related to the emotions (e.g., Dunbar, 1954; Gellhorn & Loofbourrow, 1963), attention, and general orienting reaction (e.g., Lynn, 1966; Sokolov, 1963). Several attempts have been made to describe breathing patterns characteristic of visual imagery and/or of visual imagery ability as compared to the imagery aroused in other sensory modalities (Golla & Antonovitch, 1929; Paterson, 1935; Wittkower, 1934). The conclusion of these studies was that visual imagery seemed to be associated with a regular rate of breathing, while verbal–auditory imagery was associated with a more irregular one. The findings of Short (1953), however, did not support such an inference. Some correlation between a regular–irregular dimension of breathing and visual-imagery scores has been reported recently by Chowdhury and Vernon (1964, as quoted by Richardson, 1969).

In a study of our own using 20 undergraduates (14 men and 6 women of mean age 20 years), polygraphic recordings of autonomic reactions (heart rate, respiration rate and peripheral vasomotor changes measured by mechanical plethysmography of the right hand), EEG, and eye movements were made during a large-scale investigation of visual imagery. The subjects sat in a comfortable chair in a darkened room with eyes closed, except for a 10-second period during which the visual stimulus that was to be imagined was projected on the screen at a distance of 100 centimeters from the subject's eyes. A pattern of horizontally moving vertical black and white stripes served as the basic visual stimulus for imagery. Subjects had been instructed at the beginning of the experiment to visualize this stimulus while a weak tone signal lasting 10 seconds was presented about 40 seconds after each projection. They had to signal the vivid experience of visualizing the stimulus pattern by pressing a key with their right index finger. Eight projections of visual stimulus and consequent tone signals for visualizing were applied at irregular intervals for about 40 minutes. Two 30-second intervals preceding and two such intervals following each tone signal during the whole session were statistically compared in each individual. Statistically significant changes in respiration rate during and after the visualizing interval as compared to the pretone interval were found in only one subject out of the whole group; significant changes in heart rate were observed in two subjects and significant changes in plethysmographical recording were found in three of the 20 subjects tested. Great intersubject and intrasubject differences were found in response to particular signals for visualization, but these differences did not show any clear-cut dependence either on the signalizing of the vivid experience of visualization, or on any of the other parameters evaluated. The autonomic changes resembled much more those observed during orienting reaction (Zikmund, 1967a, 1969).

Figure 1 plots for three subjects (A, B, and C) the mean values of the beat-to-beat heart rate variations for the 10 seconds immediately preceding each of the 8 signals to imagine the visual stimulus, within the period of the visual imagery itself and for 10 seconds after the signals were withdrawn. Thus the heart rate changes reflect the reaction of the autonomic nervous system to a complex of stimuli. Marked intersubject differences may be easily observed.

Further illustrations concern experiments in which the visual stimulus (moving black and white stripes) was projected at the beginning and the subjects were asked to signalize the visual imagery which later appeared, rather spontaneously, without any special mental effort. No external signals to imagine were applied during these experiments which lasted about 20 minutes.

Figures 2 and 3 illustrate the instances in which breathing was stopped when subjects signalized a vivid experience of visualizing the stimulus pattern. Figures 4 and 5 illustrate various recordings in the same subject within the same session. Figure 4 shows suppression of breathing while the subject signalized vivid visual imagery, whereas it may be seen from Fig. 5 that breathing during another imagery experience remains almost unchanged within the same session. Similar contradictory changes were ob-

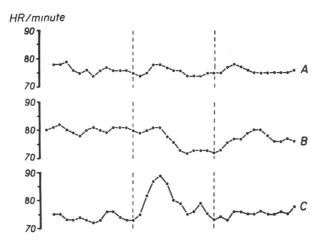

FIG. 1. Beat-to-beat heart rate (HR) changes (averaged from 8 trials) during visual imagery of a moving stimulus pattern in three subjects (A, B, and C). Vertical lines indicate the onset and the end of the tone signal for imagery.

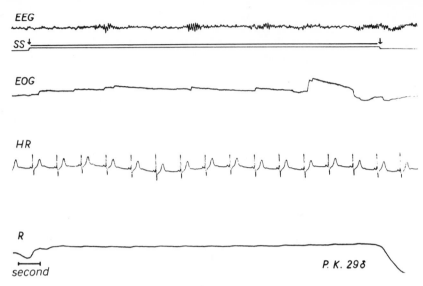

FIG. 2. *Physiological changes during visualization of horizontally moving black and white stripes which were projected at the beginning of the trial. EEG, electro-cenphalogram, derivation parietooccipital left; EOG, horizontal eye movements; HR, heart rate; R, respiration recorded by mechanical pneumogram; SS, subjective signalization of the duration of vivid visual imagery.*

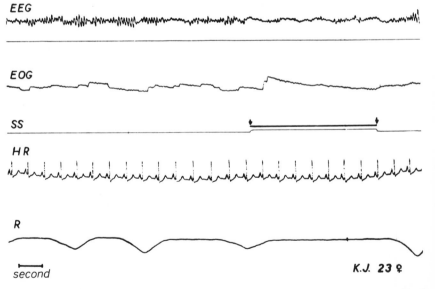

FIG. 3. *Physiological changes during visualization of horizontally moving black and white stripes which were projected at the beginning of the trial. Another subject. Description as for Fig. 2.*

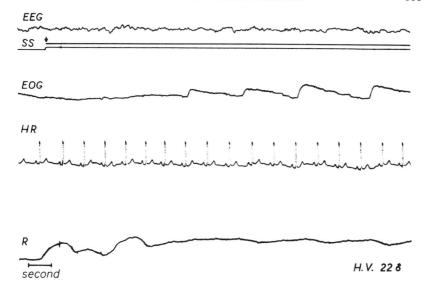

FIG. 4. *Physiological changes during visualization of horizontally moving black and white stripes. Description as for Fig. 2. Note the holding of breathing during the nystagmoid eye movements in EOG.*

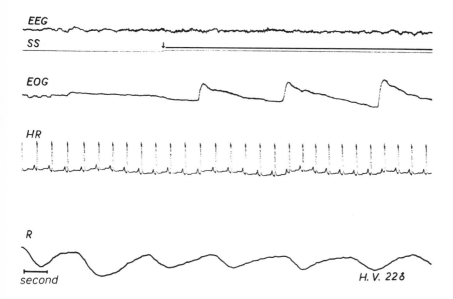

FIG. 5. *Physiological changes during visualization of horizontally moving black and white stripes. Another recording for the same subject as in Fig. 4 (description as for Fig. 2). Note that the respiration remains almost unchanged. Adapted from Zikmund (1966).*

served in many other subjects as well. Thus, we failed to find any consistent autonomic changes which could obviously be related to visual imagery.

Visual Imagery and Bioelectric Activity of the Brain

The discovery of the close association between visual perception and changes in the occipital α rhythm belongs to the early results of research in electroencephalography (Adrian, 1943; Adrian & Matthews, 1934; Berger, 1935; Durup & Fessard, 1935). The first EEG studies of visual imagery, however, were concerned with the relationship between characteristics of the EEG α rhythm and general characteristics of imagery ability (Golla, Hutton, & Walter, 1943; Short, 1953; Short & Walter, 1954). Golla *et al.*, for example, reported that the so-called M (minus) type of the EEG α activity, indicated according to their classification by a very low amplitude of α rhythm, was found to be characteristic of people preferring the visual mode of imagery, whereas the P (persistent) type in which the well pronounced α rhythm remained present under various conditions of arousal, was observed as typical of people preferring the auditory–kinaesthetic mode of imagery. Finally, the so-called R (responsive) type of EEG α rhythm, which was characterized as displaying well pronounced α activity under rest conditions with eyes closed and the suppression or blocking of α with eyes open, was ascribed to the mixed type of imagery. Several other authors, however, threw doubt on to such a categorisation (Barratt, 1956; Drever, 1955; Oswald, 1957). Drever (1958) failed to find either the above types of EEG α rhythm, or any relation between EEG and imagery ability. Slatter (1960) concluded that the so-called M-type and P type of EEG are only extreme types of a continuous spectrum. Simpson, Paivio, and Rogers (1967) and Brown (1968a) reported recently that the EEG recordings of subjects categorized as "non-visualizers" contain little α rhythm.

The suppression or blocking of the EEG α rhythm during reports of visual imagery first described by Short (1953), was reexamined by many other authors with contradictory conclusions. Barratt (1956), Mundy-Castle (1957), Stewart, Smith, and MacFarlane (1959), and Slatter (1960) all reported visual imagery as accompanied by more expressed suppression of α rhythm than the imagery of other sensory modalities, but at the same time emphasized the necessity to take into account other factors which may influence the α rhythm in EEG. Barratt (1956) refused to accept α blocking as an objective criterion of visual imagery because of the number of other mental factors which lead to the same result. Oswald (1957, 1962) concluded that the suppression of an α rhythm may be explicable solely in terms of mechanisms controlling alertness, without reference to visual imagery. He presumed that effortless visual imagery could be unaccompanied by EEG α rhythm blocking, a conclusion which we also substantiated in our own experiments. There has been little evidence supporting the view that it would be possible to control and/or to quantify the proportion of alpha activity blocking due to the process of visual imagery as compared to all other factors influencing α. It is well known that such factors as attention level (e.g., Berger, 1930), emotions (Lindsley, 1951), orienting reaction (Graschenkov & Latash, 1963; Lynn, 1966; Sokolov, 1963), and actual oculomotor activity (Mulholland, 1968, 1969; Mulholland & Evans, 1966) may influence EEG activity α in a very different way.

Within any single session the degree of α blocking during visual imagery of an identical visual stimulus in the same subject may undergo variously marked changes which bear no clearcut relation to signalization (by pressing a key) of vivid visual imagery. This may be seen in Table 1. Table 1 shows the time percentage of signalizing vivid imagery and the time percentage of EEG α blocking (meaning the percent of the 10 second period during which the α was blocked) both within a time interval of 10 seconds

TABLE 1

Time Percentage Values of Signalization of Imagery and
α Blocking in a Sample of 15 Subjects on Two
Different Occasions of Testing

Subject	Age	Time (%) Signalization of imagery		Time (%) of EEG α blocking	
		I	II	I	II
1	20	0.0	0.0	20.8	49.3
2	21	0.0	0.0	58.8	80.4
3	21	0.0	0.0	80.3	69.4
4	19	0.0	4.9	67.9	50.3
5	19	0.0	100.0	100.0	69.3
6	21	20.7	80.4	100.0	73.4
7	23	32.8	50.0	98.7	73.7
8	18	44.3	52.0	51.7	75.3
9	22	50.0	46.6	100.0	36.9
10	22	46.5	15.7	100.0	51.6
11	23	63.7	33.5	97.6	100.0
12	20	78.4	77.6	60.0	16.1
13	18	82.0	79.7	100.0	100.0
14	19	88.8	91.3	9.3	19.6
15	19	100.0	100.0	38.1	28.4

in a group of 15 healthy undergraduates (12 men, 3 women of mean age 20 years) reporting vivid visual imagery ability and displaying well pronounced EEG α rhythm. The I values indicate the first imagining (or attempt to imagine) and the II values the eighth imagining of horizontally moving vertical stripes within one experimental session of about 40 minutes. The experimental procedure is described in more detail above, under the heading of autonomic changes during visual imagery. Results show that the time percentage of α blocking varies independently of the time percentage of signalization of vivid visual imagery when the procedure of imagining is repeated. High time percentage of signalizing vivid visual imagery may be accompanied by high time percentage of α blocking (e.g., subject No. 13) or low (subject No. 15) and vice versa (cf. subjects No. 1 and 3).

Some examples of variations in EEG α blocking during visual imagery may be shown in the following recordings. Figure 6 shows that the EEG α rhythm is markedly suppressed when an imagining accompanied by vivid sensory experience is signalized, whereas during another signalisation by the same subject α suppression is much less marked. Figure 2 illustrates partial suppression of α during signalization of vivid visual imagery in another subject. Figures 4, 5, and 7 illustrate examples in which no distinct EEG α activity was found during the whole recording. In this series of trials (Fig. 2, 4, 5, and 7) an experiment lasted about 20 minutes with the pro-

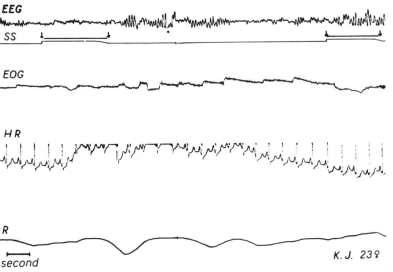

FIG. 6. *Physiological changes during visualization of horizontally moving black and white stripes (description as for Fig. 2). Note the suppression of α during the first signalization of vivid visual imagery, whereas during the second α rhythm is present.*

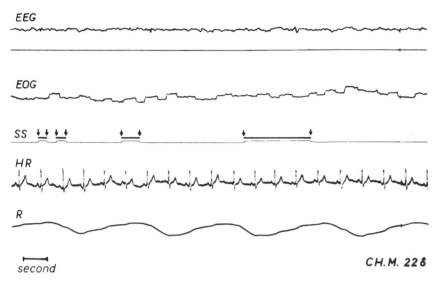

FIG. 7. Physiological changes during visualization of a static scene (description as for Fig. 2). Note the saccadic eye movements in EOG.

jection of the visual stimulus occurring at the beginning only. The subjects were instructed to sit with eyes closed without any special mental effort and when a visual image appeared spontaneously, to signalize the whole duration of sensory experience of "seeing" by slightly pressing the key with the finger tip. Otherwise, they were entirely relaxed.

Mental imagery, either forced or spontaneous, when arising in the waking state, takes place within integrative mental events which underlie or influence the process of imagining and which are, on the other hand, influenced by it as well. Attention, emotions, mental effort and other factors may arouse a mental image, which by its very meaning, perceptual nature, vividness, etc. may evoke a reciprocal hightening of arousal, attention, emotional reactions, a general orienting reaction, and so forth. In some of our recordings (e.g., Fig. 2 and 3) the EEG α rhythm and breathing were suppressed during spontaneous imagery, very probably as a consequence of a perceptual experience, whereas in many other cases similar changes could be instituted by an effort to evoke and retain an image in the mind. It seems, however, that the changes in α rhythm to attention stimuli depend also on its prestimulus level. An increase of α activity during hightened attention was reported as tending to occur in subjects with little α in the resting EEG (e.g., Kreitman & Shaw, 1965; Legewie, Simonova, & Creutzfeldt, 1969; Mulholland & Runnals, 1962). Thus, EEG α suppression can hardly be used as a specific indicator of visual imagery. Its eventual statistical value can be established only after further studies under strictly defined conditions are performed.

Visual Imagery and Gaze Movements

Ocular movements are one of the basic preconditions of normal vision. Even during voluntary fixation of a small point the eyes display several kinds of rather fine movements by which the perceived image is shifted unceasingly throughout the retina. When these movements are artificially eliminated and conditions of the so-called stabilized retinal image are established, visual perception is disturbed in various ways (e.g., Ditchburn, 1955; Ditchburn & Fender, 1955; Evans & Piggins, 1963; Ratliff, 1952; Yarbus, 1956, 1957). There exists, however, another category of eye movements, that provides and determines the direction of the gaze. Four types of gaze movements have been distinguished (Sachsenweger, 1969), all of which need to be taken into account in a study of eye movement changes during visual imagery: (a) command movements which are independent of optical stimuli; (b) guiding or attraction movements occurring in response to optical, sensory, or acoustic stimuli; (c) following, or tracking (pursuit) movements; and (d) compensatory movements, enabling the fixation of an object during rapid movements of the head. The first two types of eye movements are of a saccadic character, that is, in changing fixation from one point in space to another the gaze changes its direction by means of quick jerks. In the other two types the eyes may display a rather slow smooth changing of position relative to the head according to either the velocity of the movement of the object observed, or to the movement of the head when some point is fixed by the gaze. A special kind of pursuit movement arises when contrasts, moving smoothly in one direction, are observed. The smooth pursuit gaze movements are rhythmically interrupted by quick saccadic eye movements in the opposite direction to that of the object's motion. This is the so-called optokinetic nystagmus (e.g., train nystagmus).

Thus gaze movements of a saccadic character may be initiated by various stimuli of a visual or nonvisual nature (e.g., voluntary gaze movements, sensory stimuli of other than the visual modality), whereas the smooth following movement of the gaze under usual conditions appear when the visual perception of moving contrasts takes place, provided, however, that head movements have been eliminated.

Eye Movements and the "Scanning Hypothesis."   Data on eye movements during dreams and during visual imagery in the waking state were collected in very early studies of the physiological changes that occur during these mental events. Ladd (1892) reported that the eyes take various positions as they "control the dream" during sleep. Moore (1903) and Perky (1910) described a similar observation in people imagining some scenes with their eyes closed. About forty years ago Jacobson (1930, 1932) pointed out that the extraocular muscles display contractions during visual imagery of certain objects similar to those which take place during visual perception. Totten (1935) recorded positions of the eyes during the visual imagery of simple patterns and concluded that the eyes follow the contours of the pattern imagined.

The reports published by Aserinsky and Kleitman (1953, 1955), and subsequently by many other authors, dealt with the relationship between rapid eye movements in the paradoxical phase of sleep and dreaming. These studies stimulated research into eye movements during visual imagery in the waking state.

Rapid eye movements (REMs) during the paradoxical phase of sleep have been presumed by some investigators to represent scanning responses of the eyes to the visual dream images (e.g. Berger & Oswald, 1962; Dement & Kleitman, 1957; Dement & Wolpert, 1958). Roffwarg, Dement, Muzio, and Fisher (1962) concluded that rapid eye movements in the paradoxical phase of sleep bear a one-to-one relationship with the dream content, a finding which Moskowitz and Berger (1969) failed to confirm when they repeated the Roffwarg experiment. However, many other observations have appeared casting doubt on the validity of the "scanning hypothesis." The REM's have been observed in the neonate (e.g., Parmelee, Wenner, Akiyama, Schultz, & Stern, 1967; Roffwarg, Dement, & Fisher, 1964) in subjects with life-long blindness (Gross, Byrne, & Fischer, 1965) and in the decorticate human and animal (Jeannerod & Mouret, 1963; Jouvet, Pellin & Mounier, 1961). The basic pattern of REMs during sleep has been found to remain rather constant in animals and in man as well, whereas the imagery of dreams undergoes marked changes (e.g., Aserinsky, 1967). Aserinsky presumes that REM episodes during the paradoxical phase of sleep must be differentiated from those of ocular quiescence in more general terms than are those suggested by the scanning hypothesis. In addition, many observations support the view that the dreams appear during non-REM stages of sleep (e.g., Foulkes, 1962; Goodenough, Shapiro, Holden, & Steinschreiber, 1959; Kamiya, 1961). Frequency of dream recall has been found to be affected by physiological, methodological and psychological factors (Cohen, 1970). Molinari and Foulkes (1969) distinguish within the REM stage of sleep phasic and non-phasic episodes and hypothesize that these two episodes are associated with qualitatively different mental activities. They found for instance that

REM-phasic awakenings were associated with reports of primary visual experience, whereas REM-nonphasic and non-REM sleep awakenings were associated with reports of secondary cognitive elaboration of the dreams. Thus, available data concerning the relationship between eye movements and dreams fail to support the view that eye movements in sleep offer a specific index of dream imagery.

The "scanning hypothesis" has been also examined by several authors with respect to the dreams induced under hypnosis (Brady & Rosner, 1966; Schiff, Bunney, Freedman, 1961; Tart, 1964). These authors concluded that there exists a positive relation between the amount of eye movements and the content of the hypnotically induced hallucinations.

Amount of Eye Movements.   Quantitative aspects of the oculomotor activity in waking imagery and in other mental events have been analyzed recently in some detail. Lorens and Darrow (1962) considered that the marked increase in oculomotor activity during mental arithmetics was possibly related to the eventual visual imagery of the problems under solution. Antrobus, Antrobus, and Singer (1964), and Singer and Antrobus (1965) found that imagining of moving events produced significantly more eye movements than imagining of static scenes. Yet under conditions of spontaneous imagery, subjects reported more visual imagery when interrupted following a period of ocular quiescence than when interrupted following a period of ocular movement. Brown (1968b, 1970) concludes that the general occurrence in visualizers of eye movement activity during both visual recall and mental arithmetics supports the evidence that they do indeed use visual imagery during recall. An absence of eye movements, on the other hand, during attempted visual recall in nonvisualizers indicates that they do not.

Unambiguous interpretation of the quantitative correlation between amount of eye movement and visual information presented in a visual image cannot be made without first the elimination of other factors known to influence oculomotor activity (as suggested earlier). Such factors are namely changes in arousal or attention level, and orienting reaction. Asher and Ort (1951) found increased rate of eye movements as a reaction to stressful words in an association experiment. Amadeo and Shagass (1963) concluded that an increase in rapid eye movement rate is an expression of increased attention level. The decrease in oculomotor activity during "spontaneous" imagery reported by Antrobus et al. (1964) might also be ascribed to a decrease of attention. In a recent study Weitzenhoffer and Brockmeier (1970) reported that attention had no significant effect upon rapid eye movement rate when the eyes were closed, but under open eye conditions even a marked reduction in rapid eye movement rate was observed when attention was heightened. Changes in oculomotor actvity have been observed to be one of the basic components of the orienting reaction in man (e.g., Sokolov, 1963; Zikmund, 1967a, 1969). In our study (Zikmund, 1969) we found that the rate of saccadic eye movements may decrease or increase when acoustic stimuli are applied to subjects keeping their eyes closed, depending on the prestimulus level of the oculomotor activity. Thus, on a merely quantitative basis it is extremely difficult to distinguish the eye movement component of visual imagery from some other nonspecific influences. A closer analysis of amplitude, direction, and the general pattern of scanning eye movements during visual imagery of particular stimuli as compared to their visual perception, however, might find some characteristics of eye movements specific to visualization.

Several reports in recent years have pointed to the possibility that visual imagery can be studied objectively when pursuit eye movements or OKN is adopted as the physiological indicator. Thus, scenes have been used as a basis for visualizing in which smooth movement of objects took place.

Pursuit Eye Movements and Optokinetic Nystagmus (OKN).   In one study where pursuit eye movements were recorded, Deckert (1964) reported that while imagining a beating pendulum 18 out of 20 subjects with eyes closed developed pursuit eye movements of a frequncy comparable to that observed when they had previously watched the pendulum actually beating. Deckert suggested that the necessary prerequisite for the elaboration of pursuit eye movements is not visual input, but the development of an appropriate cerebral image, and that the method described can be used as an objective technique for the identification of certain types of visual imagery. However, Brown (1968b) using Deckert's technique in 52 subjects categorized according to their visual imagery ability as "visualizers" and "nonvisualizers," failed to find such consistent results. Although pursuit eye movements occurred during recall of motion more frequently in individuals who reported experiencing visual imagery than in those who did not, the same type of eye movement was also recorded in subjects who never reported experiencing visual imagery; in addition, eye movements during recall generally under—or over—estimated both the excursions and the timing of the original motion. In a recent study Lenox, Lange, and Graham (1970), reexamining Deckert's notions failed to find that pursuit eye movements could be faithfully reproduced under conditions of imagery with eyes closed. The eye movements that they recorded in 12 subjects were of a saccadic character and overshot markedly the amplitude of eye movements shown while the subjects were actually watching the beating pendulum.

The results of these three studies unfortunately are not strictly comparable. Except for Brown's (1968b) study there is a lack of data in the studies mentioned concerning the subjects' ability to arouse vivid visual imagery, and concerning the method by which the subjective report of the actual experience of vivid imagery was compared to particular parts of the eye movement recording. Thus the reported results do not seem adequate enough to offer a final solution to the problem and the issue remains open for further study.

Roffwarg et al. (1962), when studying correlations between the pattern of eye movements and the content of dreams in the paradoxical phase of sleep, observed a subject in which nystagmoid eye movements appeared in the REM period. When awakened, the subject reported that in his dream he was in a moving subway train and was watching the tunnel lights through the window. Brady and Levitt (1964, 1966) concluded that nystagmoid eye movements may serve as an objective criterion of visual hallucinations of a situation which could ordinarily elicit OKN. The authors recorded nystagmoid eye movements of similar frequency as had occurred during actual visual perception in eight subjects hallucinating under hypnosis that they were watching a rotating drum. In our earlier studies (Zikmund, 1964a; Zikmund & Visser, 1964) nystagmoid eye movements were repeatedly recorded in four out of twenty subjects during visual imagery of previously watched vertical black and white stripes moving horizontally in one direction. In these and in further studies (Zikmund, 1966; Zikmund & Visser, 1966) the facilitative effect of vivid visual imagery of the moving stripes was observed in the elaboration of optokinetic nystagmus as a conditioned oculomotor response to an acoustic stimulus. In all of the above studies vertical black and white stripes 2 and 4 centimeters wide served as the basic visual stimulus which was projected on a screen at a distance of 80 centimeters from the subject's eyes. The speed of movement of the black–white pattern was 3–5 centimeters/second the frequency being, nevertheless, constant for each individual. During the experiment subjects sat in a comfortable chair and while imagining the moving stripes kept their eyes closed. Electroencephalogram and electrooculogram recordings were continuously made on a Visiograph Supra Alvar polygraph. Horizontal eye movements were recorded by means of two disc electrodes placed at the outer canthi of both eyes. AC coupling was used with a time constant of .7 seconds. In some groups of subjects the instruction was given to imagine the visual stimulus during a tone signal following the projection of the stripes, both the projection and the tone being applied repeatedly; in other groups the visual stimulus was applied only once, at the beginning of the experiment, the subjects having been previously instructed either to imagine the stripes during a tone signal, or to imagine it spontaneously. In another group of 30 subjects (6 of them undergraduates studying the graphic arts, Zikmund, 1966) investigations were carried out on repeated spontaneous visual imagination of scenes in which continuous movements in one direction took place, as e.g., watching the country from the window of a car, train or tram, and watching people walking.

In some subjects visual images of static black and white stripes or various scenes lacking motion were also investigated. In all instances subjects were instructed to signalize the duration of vivid visualization of the stimulus by pressing a key, this signal simultaneously appearing on the polygraphic recording.

For the total number of 110 subjects tested, mostly undergraduates of various disciplines, 160 experimental trials were conducted in which visual imagery of the movement in the visual field under various conditions and its physiological concomitants were investigated. It was found that only in about 17% of subjects nystagmoid eye movements were recorded repeatedly when vivid visual imagery of moving contrasts was signalized. In all other subjects nystagmoid eye movements either did not appear at all, or were recorded only occasionally. Most of the results have been already published elsewhere (Zikmund, 1964a, 1964b, 1965a, 1966, 1967b; Zikmund & Visser, 1964, 1966). Following are some illustrations of the recordings made and some discussion of the results that were found.

Figure 8 shows no eye movement activity when a weak tone signal was applied for visualization of the stripes. Here, the EEG α rhythm is suppressed. In Fig. 9 large deviations of eye movements were recorded when the signal for visualization was applied. These eye movements are of a rather voluntary origin and indicate the "searching" of an image by the subject with eyes closed. Saccadic eye movements preceding the visual imagery of moving stripes are illustrated in the left parts of Fig. 3 and 5; Fig. 7 shows the tracing of saccadic eye movements during visual imagery of a still life scene (a vase of flowers on the table). As we have reported elsewhere (Zikmund, 1966), the pattern of saccadic horizontal eye movements during visualizing of a static scene is, as regards the amount of oculomotor activity, mostly indistinguishable from the pattern of eye movements present during heightened attention or during orienting reaction. Typical nystagmoid eye movements during vivid visual imagery of moving contrasts are illustrated in Fig. 2, 3, 4, and 5. Fig. 6 shows that optokinetic nystagmus appeared after the subject had finished signalization by pressing a key, and disappeared when the subject began to signalize again. Thus, the pressing of a key acted as a certain kind of distraction, diminishing the experience of visualization, an observation which was reported by several subjects. The pursuit component of nystagmoid eye movements may be fairly smooth, as for example in Fig 2, 5, and 6, or

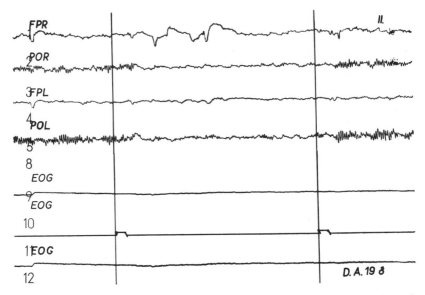

FIG. 8. *Physiological changes during a tone signal to visual imagery of moving stripe pattern when the latter failed to evoke any eye movement response. The α activity is suppressed in EEG. Derivations: FPR, fronto-parietal right; POR, parieto-occipital right; FPL, fronto-parietal left; POL, parieto-occipital left; EOG, horizontal eye movement recording. Reprinted from Zikmund (1966).*

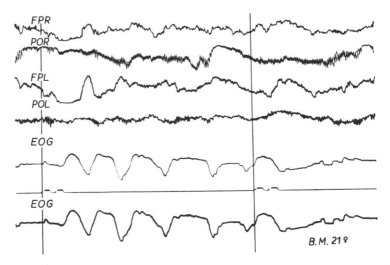

FIG. 9. *EEG and EOG during a tone signal to visual imagery in a case when the latter evoked large deviations of eye movements of a rather voluntary origin (description as for Fig. 8). Reprinted from Zikmund and Visser (1964).*

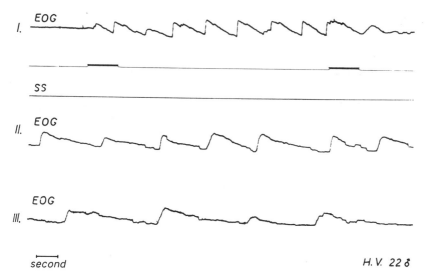

FIG. 10. EOG recording during: I, watching the stripes moving to the right; II, subjective signalization (the line above the tracing) of vivid visual imagery of the stripes moving to the right; III, hallucinating the stripes moving to the right under hypnosis.

saccadic eye movements may be superimposed on the pursuit component. Figure 10 shows: I OKN when the subject watches the stripes moving to the right, II when he signalizes their vivid visual imagery keeping his eyes closed, and III when hallucinating the stripes under hypnosis. In tracings II and III some saccades are superimposed on nystagmoid jerks. On the other hand, in another recording of nystagmoid eye movements during

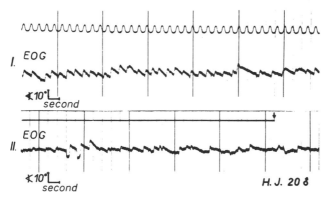

FIG. 11. EOG recording during: I, watching the vertical stripes moving to the right; II, subjective signalization (the line above the tracing) of vivid visual imagery of the stripes moving to the right. At the top is the recording of the projected moving stripes by means of photo cell.

visualizing of moving stripes the saccadic component in the previous subject is much less expressed (See Fig. 4). Figure 11 illustrates: I OKN during visual perception of the projected moving stripes and II during their vivid visual imagery. It may be seen that the direction of nystagmoid eye movements during imagery of moving stripes corresponds with that during visual perception, that is, the fast component of nystagmus is opposite to the direction of the moving stripes. Figure 12 shows the same phenomenon. This relation was regularily observed in almost all of the cases when visualization of the optokinetic situation was signalized and nystagmoid eye movements were recorded. There are other similarities also, although nystagmoid eye movements during imagery are mostly of a lower frequency and amplitude, and are less regular. Figure 13 shows a few nystagmoid jerks occurring as conditioned reflex responses. Here, the conditional stimu-

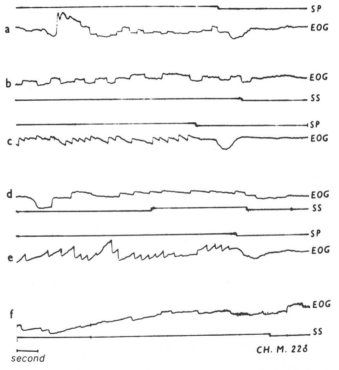

FIG. 12. EOG recording for one subject during: (a) watching the static vertical stripes; (b) visual imagery of the static vertical stripes; (c) watching the vertical stripes moving to the right; (d) visual imagery of the vertical stripes moving to the right; (e) watching the vertical stripes moving to the left; (f) visual imagery of the stripes moving to the left. SP, stripe projection; SS, subjective signalization of vivid visual imagery. Adapted from Zikmund (1966).

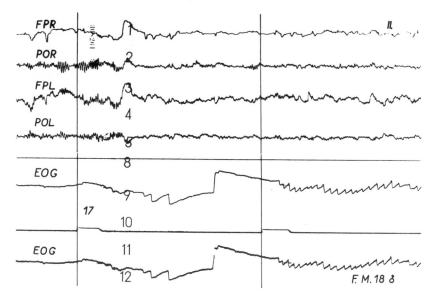

FIG. 13.   EEG (*derivations as for Fig. 8*) *and EOG* (*horizontal eye movements*) *during the seventeenth combination of tone signal with optokinetic stimulus. Tone signal preceded the presentation of the moving stripes by 10 second.*

lus was a tone signal of 20-second duration. This was combined after 10-second duration with the unconditional stimulus, horizontally moving vertical stripes projected upon a glass screen for 10 seconds. The method has been described elsewhere (Guensberger & Zikmund, 1956). Nystagmoid jerks are a purely oculomotor response in this case, not entering into consciousness, nor accompanied by any sensory experience.

The correlation between the signalization (S) of vivid experience of visualizing the moving contrasts and simultaneous tracing of nystagmoid eye movements (N) has shown (Zikmund, 1965a, 1965b) that a positive relationship (S + N +) exists between these two indicators in only 47.6% of cases, whereas in 35.4% of the cases subjects signalized vivid imagining of moving contrasts and showed no nystagmus (S + N —). Finally, in 17% of the cases nystagmus was recorded while no visualization was signalized (S — N +). These correlations were found in 212 trials evaluating 22 subjects. Subsequent analyses, however, have shown (Zikmund, 1966), that when subjects professionally use visual imagery (such as undergraduates studying the graphic arts) and are trained to distinguish imagining as "thinking on" or "trying to reconstruct in the mind" a visual percept in a rather cognitive way from imagination as visualizing the stimulus at a primary perceptual level, the correlation between these two indicators increases markedly. In the above study the S + N + rose up to 74.7%

of trials, the S + N — occurred in 16.0% of trials, and the S — N + decreased to 9.3%.

Conclusion. Returning to Barratt's (1956) criteria of an objective indicator of visual imagery it may be concluded that: (a) OKN is an inherent component of motion perception mechanisms and thus may be regarded as a potential "specific" indicator of the imagining of appropriate visual stimuli. However, nystagmoid eye movements of nonoptokinetic origin must be eliminated as, for example, nystagmus of vestibular origin, or nystagmus due to neurologic disturbance. In exceptional cases nystagmoid eye movements may be observed as a rather generalized pattern of oculomotor activity when the optokinetic stimulation is repeated many times within one session. (b) The correspondence between reported experience of visualization of moving contrasts and the appearance of nystagmoid eye movements depends on the definition as to what is meant by vivid imagining and when and how the visualizing is reported or signalized. The distinction between primary visual experience and secondary cognitive elaboration as proposed in the study of dreams (Molinari & Foulkes, 1969), might be useful in this connection. The experience of visualization should be indicated in such a way, as to enable strict comparison of selected periods of electrooculographic recording. Since the vividness of an image may wax and wane in the interval of a few seconds. (c) Under conditions of regular correspondence between the signalizing of vivid visualization of contrasts moving continuously in one direction and the occurrence of nystagmoid eye movements, this physiological phenomenon may be held to be an objective indicator of visual imagery.

As has been demonstrated saccadic eye movements may be somewhat slower, and similar to pursuit eye movements (e.g., Fig. 9) when the eyes are closed, but there is little doubt that they can be distinguished from true pursuit eye movement recordings. When the eyes are open, tracking eye movements during vivid imagining may interfere with the fixation saccades due to the visual input. However, saccadic eye movements may arise when a vivid image fades and the "searching" activity of the eyes takes place and/or when the eyes are scanning some stationary details of an imagined moving scene.

Theoretical Comment and Conclusion

Variability of autonomic changes accompanying different mental events is rather restricted. These changes predominantly reflect more general reactions of the central nervous system to various kinds of stimuli. Consequently, autonomic changes (heart rate, respiration, plethysmographic changes) do not seem to be suitable for consideration as eventual indicators of visual imagery. The amount of α blocking in EEG and of saccadic eye movements in EOG seem, similarly, to offer only unsatisfactory means of detecting visual imagery at the physiological level. Both these parameters are closely related to different mental events and to more general changes in the functional state of the central nervous system. The presumed similarity between imaging and perceiving necessitates elucidation of physiological changes which are related to visual perception and/or visual imagery in a much more specific way.

Review of evidence on gaze movements has pointed out that OKN is an inherent component of visuo–oculomotor mechanisms responsible for motion perception. It has been shown that under certain conditions this physiological phenomenon can be used as a specific indicator of vivid visual imagery of objects moving smoothly in one direction. In about 17% of 110 subjects under study nystagmoid eye movements were recorded repeatedly when the subjects signalized vivid visual imagery of the optokinetic situation. The correspondence between these two indicators (signalization by the subject of the experience of vivid imagery and simultaneous recording of nystagmoid eye movements) increased markedly when the visual imagery was closely defined and the subjects were trained to signalize only its high vividness and/or intensity. These results suggest that there exists a certain similarity between the physiological processes underlying visual perception and those occurring while sensory experience of vivid visual imagery takes place. Evidence supports the view that during vivid visual imagery complex visual and oculomotor components of visual perception mechanisms are reactivated.

OKN is an inherent component of visual perception of motion in the visual field. It may be elicited in neonates a few hours after birth (Kurtz, 1957) and requires a minimum amount of visual afferentation (Ohm, 1922). OKN represents one of two basic mechanisms of motion perception. The first is motion detection by afferent impulses from moving retinal images; the second is efferent motion detection related to the pursuit eye movements forming the slow phase of OKN (Dichgans & Jung, 1969; Dichgans, Körner, & Voigt, 1969; Körner & Dichgans, 1967). The slow phase of OKN is due to the "fixation reflex" counteracting the displacement of the retinal image of the outer world. The quick phase permits the eye to continue the fixation movement after a short interruption for an indefinite period of time (e.g., Ter Braak, 1970).

OKN, although it cannot be imitated or stimulated at will, may be strongly influenced by attention level and by conditioned reflex mechanisms. Jung (1953) reported diminution of OKN when attention decreased and its suppression when a stationary object was imagined behind a rotating striped drum. The influence of attention on the slow phase of OKN has been analyzed quite recently by Dichgans and Jung (1969). The appearance of OKN and also its blocking were used as a criterion of elaboration of conditioned oculomotor reflexes by several authors (e.g., Guensberger & Zikmund, 1956; Ruff, 1961; Ruttkay-Nedecký, 1959; Ruttkay-Nedecký & Zikmund, 1957; Visser, Kuhuwael-Tonneman, & Esch-Krijger, 1959; Visser, Kuhuwael-Tonneman, & Hueting, 1962). Guensberger and Zikmund (1956), for example, reported that OKN may appear in subjects with eyes open as a conditioned oculomotor response to an acoustic stimulus. The blocking of OKN as a conditioned reflex effect appearing in spite of a simultaneous perception of optokinetic stimuli, has been reported by Guensberger and Schmidt (1961). Thus, there may exist, under certain rather artificial conditions, a disjunction of the OKN from visual motion perception. In one case OKN is present without appropriate visual stimulation and in another it is blocked when a visual perception of movement takes place.

The question arises as to what physiological mechanisms are responsible for OKN during visual imagery of optokinetic stimuli. Two possible mechanisms might be presumed: (a) Vivid visual images or visual hallucinations involve a component of retinal stimulation which is mediated by hypothesized centrifugal impulses from the brain structures activated when a visual image arises. When the retinal elements are excited, retino-eye movement feedback mechanisms give rise to OKN in the same way as they do during visual perception. Some neurophysiological evidence supporting such a speculation was recently discussed by Brady (1970). (b) It might also be hypothesized, however, that the close integration of the visual and oculomotor mechanisms in visual motion perception is reflected in simultaneous reactivation of both these mechanisms during vivid visual imagery. The evocation of a visual image results in reactivation of an appropriate eye movement pattern. Thus, neurophysiological mechanisms engaged in visual imagery seem to be, to a certain extent, similar to those underlying visual perception.

There exist several other studies supporting the view that the pattern of oculomotor activity present when a particular visual stimulus is perceived might form an inherent component of an image or a memory trace of the stimulus stored in the brain. An inherent oculomotor component having an organising function in visual perception and in visual imagery was recently proposed in a more general fashion by Hebb (1968). Hebb believed that if the image is a reinstatement of the perceptual process it should include the eye movements; thus, the oculomotor accompaniments of imagery should not be adventitious but essential. Noton and Stark (1971) suggest on the basis of the study of the so-called scanpath during pattern perception and during pattern recognition that the oculomotor component involved in visual perception is an integral part of the memories on which recognition is based. These authors presume that the subject's internal representation or memory of the pattern is, at least under certain conditions, an alternating sequence of sensory and motor memory traces.

Sheehan (1966) hypothesizing a functional similarity between imagining and perceiving concludes, however, that there exist individual differences in vividness of imagery which are related to differences in correspondence between imaging and perceptual behavior. This aspect should be taken into account also when the relation between the occurrence of nystagmoid (or whatever other) eye movements and the reporting or signalization of vivid visual imagery is investigated. Results from our own work indicate that there exist even in OKN during motion perception intersubject differences which may also be reflected in eye movement activity during visual imagery. Close analysis of these relations obviously requires further study.

References

Adrian, E. D. The dominance of vision. *Ophthalmological Society of the United Kingdom,* 1943, **63,** 194–207.

Adrian, E. D., & Matthews, B. H. C. The Berger rhythm: Potential changes from the occipital lobes in man. *Brain,* 1934, **57,** 355–384.

Amadeo, M., & Shagass, C. Eye movements, attention and hypnosis. *Journal of Nervous and Mental Disease,* 1963, **136,** 139–145.

Antrobus, J. S., Antrobus, J. S., & Singer, J. L. Eye movements accompanying day dreaming, visual imagery and thought suppression. *Journal of Abnormal and Social Psychology,* 1964, **69,** 244–252.

Aserinsky, E. Physiological activity associated with segments of the rapid eye movement period. In S. S. Kety, E. V. Evarts, and H. L. Williams (Eds.), *Sleep and altered states of consciousness.* Baltimore, (Maryland: Williams & Wilkins, 1967. Pp. 338–350.

Aserinsky, E., & Kleitman, N. Regularly occurring periods of eye motility, and concomitant phenomena during sleep. *Science,* 1953, **118,** 273–274.

Aserinsky, E., & Kleitman, N. A motility cycle in sleeping infants as manifested by ocular and gross bodily activity. *Journal of Applied Physiology,* 1955, **8,** 11–18.

Asher, J., & Ort, J. S. Eye movement as a complex indicator. *Journal of General Psychology,* 1951, **45,** 209–217.

Barratt, P. E. Use of the EEG in the study of imagery. *British Journal of Psychology,* 1956, **47,** 101–114.

Bender, M. B., & Teuber, H. L. Spatial organization of visual perception following injury to the brain. *Archives of Neurology and Psychiatry,* 1947, **58,** 721–739.

Bennet-Clark, H. C., & Evans, C. R. Fragmentation of patterned targets when viewed as prolonged after-images. *Nature (London)*, 1963, **199**, 1215–1216.

Berger, H. Über das Elektrenkephalogramm des Menschen. Zweite Mitteilung. *Journal für Psychologie und Neurologie*, 1930, **40**, 160–179.

Berger, H. Über das Elektrenkephalogramm des Menschen. X. Mitteilung. *Archiv für Psychiatrie und Nervenkrankheiten*, 1935, **103**, 444–454.

Berger, R. J., & Oswald, I. Eye movements during active and passive dreams. *Science*, 1962, **137**, 601.

Brady, J. P. Physiological implications of hypnotic visual hallucinations. Paper presented at International Colloquium on Oculomotor System and Brian Functions, Bratislava-Smolenice, 1970.

Brady, J. P. & Levitt, E. E. Nystagmus as a criterion of hypnotically induced visual hallucinations. *Science*, 1964, **146**, 85–86.

Brady, J. P., & Levitt, E. E. Hypnotically induced visual hallucinations. *Psychosomatic Medicine*, 1966, **28**, 351–353.

Brady, J. P., & Rosner, B. S. Rapid eye movements in hypnotically induced dreams. *Journal of Nervous and Mental Disease*, 1966, **143**, 28–35.

Brindley, G. S. The discrimination of after-images. *Journal of Physiology*, 1959, **147**, 194–202.

Brindley, G. S. Two new properties of foveal after-images and a photochemical hypothesis to explain them. *Journal of Physiology*, 1962, **164**, 168–179.

Brown, B. B. Subjective and EEG responses to LSD in visualizer and non-visualizer subjects. *Electroencephalography and Clinical Neurophysiology*, 1968, **25**, 372–379. (a)

Brown, B. B. Visual recall ability and eye movements. *Psychophysiology*, 1968, **4**, 300–306. (b)

Brown, B. B. Recognition of aspects of consciousness through association with EEG alpha activity represented by a light signal. *Psychophysiology*, 1970, **6**, 442–453.

Chowdhury, K. R., & Vernon, P. E. An experimental study of imagery and its relation to abilities and interests. *British Journal of Psychology*, 1964, **55**, 355–364.

Cohen, D. B. Current research on the frequency of dream recall. *Psychological Bulletin*, 1970, **75**, 433–440.

Craik, K. J. W. Origin of visual after-images. *Nature (London)* 1940, **145**, 512.

Deckert, G. H. Pursuit eye movements in the absence of a moving visual stimulus. *Science*, 1964, **143**, 1192–1193.

Dement, W., & Kleitman, N. Cyclic variations in EEG during sleep and their relation to eye movements, body motility and dreaming. *Electroencephalography and Clinical Neurophysiology*, 1957, **9**, 673–690.

Dement, W., & Wolpert, E. The relation of eye movements, body motility and external stimuli to dream content. *Journal of Experimental Psychology*, 1958, **55**, 543–553.

De Morsier, G. Les hallucinations visuelles diencéphaliques. Premiére partie. *Psychiatria Clinica* 1969, **2**, 167–184. (a)

De Morsier, G. Les hallucinations visuelles diencéphaliques. Deuxiéme partie. *Psychiatria Clinica* 1969, **2**, 212–213. (b)

Dichgans, J., & Jung, R. Attention, eye movements and motion detection: Facilitation and selection in optokinetic nystagmus and railway nystagmus. In C. R. Evans and T. B. Mulholland (Eds.), *Attention in neurophysiology*. London: Butterworth, 1969. Pp. 348–376.

Dichgans, J., Körner, F., & Voigt, K. Vergleichende Skalierung des afferenten und efferenten Bewegungssehens beim Menschen: Lineare Funktionen mit verschiedener Anstiegssteilheit. *Psychologische Forschung,* 1969, **32,** 277–295.

Ditchburn, R. W. Eye-movements in relation to retinal action. *Optica Acta,* 1955, **1,** 171–176.

Ditchburn, R. W., & Fender, D. H. The stabilized retinal image. *Optica Acta,* 1955, **2,** 128–133.

Drever, J. Some observations on the occipital alpha rhythm. *Quarterly Journal of Experimental Psychology,* 1955, **7,** 91–97.

Drever, J. Further observations on the relation between EEG and visual imagery. *American Journal of Psychology,* 1958, **71,** 270–276.

Dunbar, E. *Emotions and bodily changes.* New York: Columbia Univ. Press, 1954.

Durup, G., & Fessard, A. L'électrencephalogramme de l'homme. Observations psychophysiologiques relatives à l'action des stimuli visuels et auditifs. *L'Année Psychologique,* 1935, **36,** 1–35.

Evans, C. R. Some studies of pattern perception using a stabilized retinal image. *British Journal of Psychology,* 1965, **56,** 121–133.

Evans, C. R. Further studies of pattern perception and a stabilized retinal image: The use of prolonged after-images to achieve perfect stabilization. *British Journal of Psychology,* 1967, **58,** 315–327.

Evans, C. R., & Piggins, D. J. A comparison of the behaviour of geometrical shapes when viewed under conditions of steady fixation and with apparatus for producing a stabilized retinal image. *British Journal of Physiological Optics,* 1963, **20,** 1–13.

Feldman, M., & Bender, M. B. Visual illusions and hallucinations in parieto-occipital lesions of the brain. In W. Keup (Ed.), *Origins and mechanisms of hallucinations.* New York: Plenum, 1970. Pp. 23–35.

Foulkes, D. Dream reports from different stages of sleep. *Journal of Abnormal and Social Psychology,* 1962, **65,** 14–25.

Gassel, M. M. Occipital lobe syndromes excluding hemianopia. In P. J. Vinken and G. W. Bruyn (Eds.), *Handbook of clinical neurology.* Vol. 2. Amsterdam: North-Holland Publ., 1969. Pp. 640–679.

Gellhorn, E., & Loofbourrow, G. N. *Emotions and emotional disorders.* New York: Harper, 1963.

Golla, F. L., & Antonovitch, S. The relation of muscular tonus and the patellar reflex to mental work. *Journal of Mental Science,* 1929, **75,** 234–241.

Golla, F. L., Hutton, E. L., & Walter, W. G. The objective study of mental imagery. I. Physiological concomitants. *Journal of Mental Science,* 1943, **89,** 216–223.

Goodenough, D. R., Shapiro, A., Holden, M., & Steinschreiber, L. A comparison of dreamers and non-dreamers: Eye movements, electroencephalograms and the recall of dreams. *Journal of Abnormal and Social Psychology,* 1959, **59,** 295–302.

Graschenkov, N. J., & Latash, L. P. About the active character of the orienting reflex. In A. A. Volkov, A. N. Kabanov, and R. M. Meschersky (Eds.), *Brain reflexes.* Moscow: USSR Scientific Academy Press, 1963.

Gross, J., Byrne, J., & Fischer, C. Eye movements during emergent stage 1 EEG in subjects with lifelong blindness. *Journal of Nervous and Mental Disease,* 965, **141,** 365–370.

Guensberger, E., & Schmidt, P. Some characteristics of conditioned reflexes with verbal reinforcement arresting optokinetic nystagmus in man. *Activitas Nervosa Superior,* 1961, **3,** 249–256.

Guensberger, E., & Zikmund, V. Conditioned optokinetic nystagmus (in Slovak). Československá fysiologie, 1956, 5, 381–387.

Hebb, D. O. Concerning imagery. Psychological Review, 1968, 75, 466–477.

Hermann, G., & Pötzl, O. Die optische Allaesthesie. Studien zw. Psychopathologie der Raumbildung. Abhandlungen aus der Neurologie, 1928, 47, 1–302.

Horowitz, M. J. The imagery of visual hallucinations. Journal of Nervous and Mental Disease, 1964, 138, 513–523.

Jacobson, E. Electrical measurements of neuromuscular states during mental activities. III. Visual imagination and recollection. American Journal of Physiology, 1930, 95, 694–702.

Jacobson, E. Electrophysiology of mental activities. American Journal of Psychology, 1932, 44, 677–694.

Jeannerod, M., & Mouret, J. Etude comparative des mouvements oculaires observés chez le chat au cours de la veille et du sommeil. Compte Rendu des Séances de la Société de Biologie, (Paris), 1963, 156, 1407–1410.

Jouvet, M., Pellin, B., & Mounier, R. D. Etude polygraphique des différentes phases du sommeil au cours des troubles de conscience chroniques (comas prolongés). Revue Neurologique (Paris), 1961, 105, 181–186.

Jung, R. Nystagmographie: Zur Physiologie und Pathologie des optisch-vestibulären Systems beim Menschen. In G. V. Bergmann (Ed.), Handbuch der inneren Medizin. Berlin-Göttingen-Heidelberg: Springer, 1953. Pp, 1325–1379.

Kamiya, J. Behavioral, subjective and physiological aspects of drowsiness and sleep. In D. W. Fische and S. R. Maddi (Eds.), Functions of varied experience. Homewood, Illinois: Dorsey, 1961. Pp. 145–174.

Kohlrausch, A. Der Verlauf der Netzhautströme und der Gesichtsempfindungen nach Momentbelichtung. Pflügers Archiv für die gesamte Physiologie des Menschen und der Tiere 1925, 209, 607–610.

Körner, F., & Dichgans, J. Bewegungswahrnehmung, optokinetischer Nystagmus und retinale Bildwanderung. Graefe's Archiv für Ophthalmologie, 1967, 174, 34–38.

Kreitman, N., & Shaw, J. C. Experimental enhancement of alpha activity. Electroencephalography and Clinical Neurophysiology, 1965, 18, 147–155.

Külpe, O. Outlines of psychology. London: Swan Sonnenschein, 1893 (3rd Ed., 1909).

Kurtz, J. Ophthalmo-neurological diagnostics (in Czech). Prague: SZN (State Publishing House of Public Health), 1957.

Ladd, G. Contributions to the psychology of visual dreams. Mind, 1892, 1, 299–304.

Legewie, H., Simonova, O., & Creutzfeldt, O. D. EEG changes during performance of various tasks under open-closed-eye conditions. Electroencephalography and Clinical Neurophysiology, 1969, 27, 470–479.

Lenox, J. R., Lange, A. F., & Graham, K. R. Eye movement amplitudes in imagined pursuit of a pendulum with eyes closed. Psychophysiology, 1970, 6, 773–777.

Leuba, C. Images as conditioned sensations. Journal of Experimental Psychology, 1940, 26, 345–351.

Lindsley, D. B. Emotion. In S. S. Stevens (Ed.), Handbook of experimental psychology. New York: Wiley, 1951. Pp. 473–516.

Lorens, S. A., Jr., & Darrow, C. W. Eye movements, EEG, GSR and EKG during mental multiplication. Electroencephalography and Clinical Neurophysiology, 1962, 14, 739–746.

Lynn, R. Attention, arousal and the orienting reaction. Oxford: Pergamon, 1966.

Meenes, M., & Morton, M. A. Characteristics of the Eidetic Phenomenon. Journal of General Psychology, 1936, 14, 370–391.

Molinari, S., & Foulkes, D. Tonic and phasic events during sleep: Psychological correlates and implications. *Perceptual and Motor Skills,* 1969, **29**, 343–368.

Moore, C. S. Control of the memory image. *Psychological Review,* 1903, **4** (Whole No. 17). Pp. 277–306.

Moskowitz, E., & Berger, R. J. Rapid eye movements and dream imagery—are they related? *Nature (London),* 1969, **224**, 613–614.

Mulholland, T. Feedback electroencephalography. *Activitas Nervosa Superior,* 1968, **10**, 410–438.

Mulholland, T. The concept of attention and the electroencephalographic alpha rhythm. In C. R. Evans and T. B. Mulholland (Eds.), *Attention in neurophysiology.* London: Butterworth, 1969. Pp. 100–127.

Mulholland, T., & Evans, C. R. Oculomotor function and the alpha activation. *Nature (London)* 1966, **211**, 1278–1279.

Mulholland, T., & Runnals, S. Increased occurrence of EEG alpha during increased attention. *Journal of Physiology,* 1962, **54**, 317–330.

Mundy-Castle, A. C. The electroencephalogram and mental activity. *Electroencephalography and Clinical Neurophysiology,* 1957, **9**, 643–655.

Noton, D., & Stark, L. Scanpath in eye movements during pattern perception. *Science,* 1971, **171**, 308–311.

Ohm, J. Die klinische Bedeutung des optischen Drehnystagmus. *Klinische Monatsblätter für Augenheilkunde,* 1922, **68**, 323.

Oswald, I. The EEG, visual imagery and attention. *Quarterly Journal of Experimental Psychology,* 1957, **9**, 113–118.

Oswald, I. *Sleeping and waking.* Amsterdam: Elsevier, 1962.

Parmelee, A. H., Jr., Wenner, W. H., Akiyama, Y., Schultz, M. A., & Stern, E. Sleep states in premature infants. *Developmental Medicine and Child Neurology,* 1967, **9**, 70.

Paterson, A. S. The respiratory rhythms in normal and psychotic subjects. *Journal of Neurology and Psychopathology,* 1935, **16**, 36–53.

Penfield, W., & Jasper, H. *Epilepsy and the functional anatomy of the human brain.* Boston, Massachusetts: Little, Brown, 1954.

Penfield, W., & Kristiansen, K. *Epileptic seizure patterns.* Springfield, Illinois: Thomas, 1951.

Penfield, W., & Pérot, P. The brain's record of auditory and visual experience. *Brain,* 1963, **86**, 595–696.

Penfield, W., & Rasmussen, T. *The cerebral cortex of man.* New York: Macmillan, 1950.

Perky, C. W. An experimental study of imagination. *American Journal of Psychology,* 1910, **21**, 422–452.

Piggins, D. J. Perception of a square viewed as a prolonged after-image. *Atti della Fondazione Giorgio Ronchi,* 1968, **23**, 149–172.

Popov, N. A., & Popov C. Contribution a l'étude des fonctions corticales chez l'homme, par la méthode des réflexes conditionnés electrocorticaux. I. Action de l'alcool sur les images consecutives et leur conditionnement. *Compte Rendu de l'Academie des Sciences,* 1953, **237**, 930–932.

Popov, N. A., & Popov, C. Contribution a l'étude des fonctions corticales chez l'homme par la méthode des réflexes conditionnés electrocorticaux. V. Deuxiéme système de signalisation. *Compte Rendu de L'Academie des Sciences* 1954, **238**, 2118–2120.

Ratliff, F. The role of physiological nystagmus in monocular acuity. *Journal of Experimental Psychology,* 1952, **43**, 163–172.

Richardson, A. *Mental imagery*. London: Routledge & Kegan Paul, 1969.

Roffwarg, H., Dement, W., Muzio, J., & Fisher, C. Dream imagery: Relationship to rapid eye movements of sleep. *Archives of General Psychiatry*, 1962, **7**, 235–258.

Roffwarg, H., Dement, W., & Fisher, C. Preliminary observations of sleep-dream pattern in neonates, infants, children, and adults. In E. Harms (Ed.), *Problems of sleep and dreams in children*. New York: Pergamon, 1964 (Monographs on Child Psychiatry No. 2). Pp. 60–72.

Ruff, P. W. Bedingter optokinetischer Nystagmus beim Menschen. *Psychiatrie, Neurologie und Medizinische Psychologie*, 1961, **13**, 294–298.

Ruttkay-Nedecký, I. A contribution to the physiology of eye movements. *Physiologia Bohemoslovaca*, 1959, **8**, 55–60.

Ruttkay-Nedecký, I., & Zikmund, V. *Psycho-biographical analysis of curricula vitae as a methodical element in the investigation of the functional ability of the CNS in men and its correlation towards experimental criteria*. (In Slovak.) Bratislava: SAV (Publishing House of the Slovak Academy of Sciences), 1957.

Sachsenweger, R. Clinical localization of oculomotor disturbances. In P. J. Vinken & G. W. Bruyn (Eds.), *Handbook of clinical neurology*. Vol. 2. Amsterdam: North-Holland Publ., 1969. Pp. 286–367.

Schiff, S. K., Bunney, W. E., Jr., & Freedman, D. X. A study of ocular movements in hypnotically induced dreams. *Journal of Nervous and Mental Disease*, 1961, **1**, 59–68.

Sem-Jacobsen, C. W., Petersen, M. C., Lazarte, J. A., Dodge, H. W., & Holman, C. B. Intracerebral electrographic recordings from psychotic patients during hallucinations and agitation. *American Journal of Psychiatry*, 1955, **112**, 278–288.

Sheehan, P. W. Functional similarity of imaging to perceiving: Individual differences in vividness of imagery. *Perceptual and Motor Skills*, 1966, **23** (6, pt.), 1011–1033.

Short, P. L. The objective study of mental imagery. *British Journal of Psychology*, 1953, **44**, 38–51.

Short, P. L., & Walter, W. G. The relationship between physiological variables and stereognosis. *Electroencephalography and Clinical Neurophysiology*, 1954, **6**, 29–44.

Simpson, H. M., Paivio, A., & Rogers, T. B. Occipital alpha activity of high and low visual imagers during problem solving. *Psychonomic Science*, 1967, **8**, 49–50.

Singer, J. L., & Antrobus, J. S. Eye movements during fantasies. *Archives of General Psychiatry*, 1965, **12**, 71–76.

Slatter, K. H. Alpha rhythm and mental imagery. *Electroencephalography and Clinical Neurophysiology*, 1960, **12**, 851–859.

Sokolov, Y. N. *Perception and the condition reflex*. New York: Pergamon, 1963.

Stewart, C. A., Smith, I., & MacFarlane, I. The alpha rhythm, imagery and spatial and verbal abilities. *Durham Research Review*, 1959, **2**, 272–286.

Tart, C. T. A comparison of suggested dreams occurring in hypnosis and sleep. *International Journal of Clinical and Experimental Hypnosis*, 1964, **12**, 263–289.

Ter Braak, J. W. G. Optokinetic nystagmus and attention. *International Journal of Neurology*, 1970, **8**, 34–42.

Totten, E. Eye movements during visual imagery. *Comparative Psychology*, 1935, **11**, No. 3.

Visser, P., Kuhuwael-Tonneman, M., & van der Esch-Krijger, C. Recherches psychophysiologiques du nystagme optocinétique chez l'homme. *Journal de Physiologie* (*Marseille*) 1959, **51**, 576–577.

Visser, P., Kuhuwael-Tonneman, M., & Hueting, J. E. Some remarks on conditional optokinetic nystagmus in man. In *Human problems of supersonic and hypersonic flight.* New York: Pergamon, 1962. Pp. 161–169.

Walsh, F. B., & Hoyt, W. E. The visual sensory system: Anatomy, physiology and topographic diagnosis. In P. J. Vinken and G. W. Bruyn (Eds.), *Handbook of clinical neurology.* Vol. 2. Amsterdam: North-Holland Publ., 1969. Pp. 506–639.

Weinberger, L. M., & Grant, F. C. Review of visual hallucinations and their neuro-optical correlates. *Archives of Ophthalmology,* 1940, **23**, 166–199.

Weitzenhoffer, A. M., & Brockmeier, J. D. Attention and eye movements. *Journal of Nervous and Mental Disease,* 1970, **151**, 130–142.

Williams, D. Temporal lobe syndromes. In P. J. Vinken & G. W. Bruyn (Eds.), *Handbook of clinical neurology.* Vol. 2. Amsterdam: North-Holland Publ., 1969. Pp. 700–724.

Wittkower, E. Further studies in the respiration of psychotic patients. *Journal of Mental Science,* 1934, **80**, 692–704.

Yarbus, A. L. Perception of the stationary retinal image. *Biofizika,* 1956, **1**, 435–437.

Yarbus, A. L. Perception of an image stationary relative to the retina. *Biofizika,* 1957, **2**, 702–712.

Zikmund, V. Objective manifestation of unconditioned stimulus imagination and its influence on forming conditioned optokinetic nystagmus. *Activitas Nervosa Superior,* 1964, **6**, 64. (a)

Zikmund, V. The effect of dexphenmetrazine on visual imagery. *Activitas Nervosa Superior,* 1964, **6**, 207–208. (b)

Zikmund, V. Relation between physiological and psychological indices of the visual imagery of a motion stimulus pattern. *Activitas Nervosa Superior,* 1965, **7**, 179. (a)

Zikmund, V. Some psychophysiological characteristics of the visual imagery of a moving stimulus pattern. *Proceedings of the 8th. International Congress of Neurology, Vienna, 1965.* Pp. 209–212. (b)

Zikmund, V. Oculomotor activity during visual imagery of a moving stimulus pattern. *Studia psychologica,* 1966, **8** (4), 254–274.

Zikmund, V. Eye movements during the orienting reaction and during certain kinds of mental activity. In I. Ruttkay-Nedecký, L. Cigánek, V. Zikmund, and E. Kellerová (Eds.), *Mechanisms of orienting reaction in man.* Bratislava: Publishing House of the Slovak Academy of Sciences, 1967. Pp. 93–99. (a)

Zikmund, V. The effect of methylphenidate on visual imaginative capacity. *Activitas Nervosa Superior,* 1967, **9**, 421–422. (b)

Zikmund, V. The time course of the oculomotor component of orienting reaction. In C. R. Evans and T. B. Mulholland (Eds.), *Attention in neurophysiology.* London: Butterworth, 1969. Pp. 247–257.

Zikmund, V., & Visser, P. Effect of evocation of a visual image of the unconditioned stimulus on elaboration of conditioned optokinetic nystagmus. *Physiologia Bohemoslovaca,* 1964, **13**, 202–206.

Zikmund, V., & Visser, P. Zum Einfluss psychologischer Faktoren auf die Ausarbeitung bedingter Reflexe bei Menschen. Kortiko-viszerale Physiol., Pathol. und Therapie. *Abhandlungen der Deutschen Akademie der Wissenschaften zu Berlin,* 1966, **2**, 435–439.

AUTHOR INDEX

Numbers in italics refer to the pages on which the complete references are listed.

A

Abramovitz, A., 5, *32,* 326, *329*
Adams, J., 284, 285, *308*
Adams, J. A., 170, *172*
Adams, P. A., 155, *173*
Adler, L. L., 316, *328*
Adrian, E. D., 364, *381*
Akiyama, Y., 369, *385*
Alexander, R. A., 256, 266, *277*
Allen, V. L., 347, *354*
Amadeo, M., 370, *381*
Ames, L. B., 327, *328*
Andersen, M. L., 335, *354*
Anderson, R. C., 262, 269, *275*
Anisfeld, M., 269, *279*
Antonovitch, S., 360, *383*
Antrobus, J. S., 99, 103, 104, 105, *106,*
    121, 123, *129,* 175, 176, 177, 178,
    183, 186, 189, 192, 200, *201, 202,*
    286, *307,* 317, *328,* 370, *381, 386*
Antrobus, J. S., 99, 103, 104, 105, *106,*
    370, *381*
Apoko, A., 315, *328*
Ardis, J. A., 51, *58*
Arieti, S., 57, *58,* 76, *79*
Arlow, J., 286, *307*

B

Arnheim, R., 3, *31,* 313, *328*
Arnold, M. B., 4, *31,* 116, *127*
As, A., 123, *127*
Asch, S. E., 132, *145*
Aserinsky, E., 36, *58,* 98, 104, *106,* 369,
    381
Asher, J., 370, *381*
Atwood, G. E., 246, *249,* 266, 267, *275*
Austin, J. L., 345, *353*
Aveling, F., 85, *106*

B

Bach, M., 104, *108*
Bachant, J., 104, *107*
Baddeley, A. D., 261, *275*
Bahrick, H. P., 171, *172,* 263, *275*
Bailey, D. E., 340, *354*
Barnett, B., 50, *58*
Barnhart, E. N., 133, *145*
Barnsley, R. H., 138, *147*
Barr, H. B., 14, *31*
Barratt, P. E., 359, 364, 378, *381*
Barron, B. F., 36, *60,* 96, 102, 104, *107*
Bartlett, F. C., 84, 85, 88, *106,* 122,
    127, 149, *172,* 222, *229*
Bartley, S. H., 140, *145*

389

SUBJECT INDEX

A

Absorption in Daydreaming Scale, *see* Imaginal Processes Inventory
Abstractness-concreteness of stimuli, 138, 143, 156, 158–159, 243, 253–254, 255–257, 265, 270–272, 274, 323–324
Accommodation
  Piagetian concept of, 204, 303
Acting, *see also* Hypothetical instantiation
  involvement in, 347
Aesthetics, 133
After imagery
  control of, 110, 326–327
  eye movement rate in, 104
  physiological bases of, 357
Aftersensations, 54–55
Alpha blocking
  factors leading to, 364–365
  signalization of imagery and, 365–366
  variations in, 366
Anticipation
  Piagetian concept of, 318
Anxiety-Hysteria syndrome
  fantasy as related to, 200

Art
  communication and, 67
  imagery and, 77–78
Artifact
  assimilation effects and role of, 209
  imagery effects and, 89–91, 101–104, 240
  introspection and, 238–240
  recognition effects as influenced by, 159
  within-subjects effects and role of, 91
Artists
  conflict of opinion among, 64–65
  image modality and, 68–70
As-if behavior, *see* Hypothetical instantiation
As-if skills
  development of, 341–342
  hierarchy of, 339–340
Assimilation, *see also* Stimulus assimilation in image construction
  Piagetian concept of, 11, 204, 303
Association value, 155–156
Associative overlap, 268, 269, 271
A-thinking
  R-thinking and, 56–58